Data Warehouse Design Solutions

CHRISTOPHER ADAMSON
MICHAEL VENERABLE

WILEY COMPUTER PUBLISHING

John Wiley & Sons, Inc.
New York • Chichester • Weinheim • Brisbane • Singapore • Toronto

D1378166

Publisher: Robert Ipsen
Editor: Robert M. Elliott
Managing Editor: Erin Singletary
Electronic Products, Associate Editor: Mike Sosa
Text Design & Composition: Benchmark Productions, Inc.

Designations used by companies to distinguish their products are often claimed as trademarks. In all instances where John Wiley & Sons, Inc., is aware of a claim, the product names appear in initial capital or ALL CAPITAL LETTERS. Readers, however, should contact the appropriate companies for more complete information regarding trademarks and registration.

This book is printed on acid-free paper. ∞

Published by John Wiley & Sons, Inc.
Published simultaneously in Canada.

This publication is designed to provide accurate and authoritative information in regard to the subject matter covered. It is sold with the understanding that the publisher is not engaged in professional services. If professional advice or other expert assistance is required, the services of a competent professional person should be sought.

Library of Congress Cataloging-in-Publication Data:

Adamson, Christopher, 1967–
     Data warehouse design solutions / Christopher Adamson, Michael Venerable.
        p.   cm.
     "Wiley Computer Publishing."
     Includes index.
     ISBN 0-471-25195-X (pbk. : alk. paper)
     1. Data warehousing.   I. Venerable, Michael, 1962–
II. Title.
QA76.9.D37V46   1998
658.4'038'0285574—dc21   98-17957
                                                                        CIP

Printed in the United States of America.

10 9 8 7 6 5 4

CONTENTS

FOREWORD

The timing of this book in mid-1998 coincides with some fundamental shifts in the data warehousing market. Data warehousing has recently entered a more mature phase where most larger organizations have already built their first data warehouse or they at least are completing their first data warehouse. Many thousands of IS professionals have more than a passing acquaintance with data warehousing and all these professionals know that the data warehouse is very different from the transaction processing system. We have come a long way...

At the same time, many of the original assumptions about data warehousing have fallen by the wayside. At the beginning of this decade we thought the data warehouse was a highly-summarized tool for senior management, something just slightly more flexible than the annual report. We thought we couldn't change anything once it entered the data warehouse, and frankly, we thought of the data warehouse as an expensive luxury for occasional analysis. At the beginning of the 1990s, we designed data warehouses like a big aircraft manufacturer designs an airplane. Or at least it felt that way. The data warehouse design task was a significant undertaking. We thought we had to understand and anticipate all the uses of the data warehouse and we couldn't release any data from it until the data warehouse was complete.

We added to the complexity of the design task by using entity-relation modeling all the way from data cleaning through to data presentation.

Well, it should be pointed out that the "we" mentioned in this description didn't include all of us. A number of us had suspicions that many of the things in the preceding paragraphs were wrong, and had been wrong from the very beginning. The most obvious symptom of these suspicions is the renegade "data mart" movement that threatens to challenge all of the previously cherished notions.

The data warehouse market is now waking up to a much more practical, much more useful definition of the data warehouse. This realization is marking the beginning of the mature phase of the industry, but it requires some adjustment in thinking.

The data warehouse is now revealed as a true operational system. It is just as required and just as serious as the online transaction processing system. It needs to be as reliable and as available as the online system. But it is driven by a very different set of requirements. Above all, the data warehouse must be driven from business analysis needs. The data warehouse must be a mirror of management's urgent priorities. The data warehouse must respond to "what keeps management awake at night."

From the end user's perspective, the data warehouse must be a presentation facility. It must be understandable and "obvious" to the end user. It must be easy to use. The best definition of ease of use is One Click. Anything else is a compromise.

The end user demands that the data warehouse be fast. The end user doesn't care how much data is processed. What matters is how much information is delivered. The best definition of "fast" is instantaneous. Anything else is a compromise.

The end user demands that the data warehouse be flexible. The surrounding business is in a constant state of flux. New business perspectives, new competitive pressures, new organizations, and new data sources impose an ever-changing set of requirements on the data warehouse. The data warehouse must be resilient, and able to change. At the same time, the data warehouse must accurately describe the past.

The data warehouse must contain both summarized data as well as extremely fine-grained data, all the way down to basic transactions. The end user wants to see individual customer behavior, and that requires detail.

Finally, the data warehouse administrator has his or her own set of requirements in addition to the end users'. The data warehouse needs to be based on a set of design principles that are well articulated and well understood. Real human beings need to be able to design and maintain data warehouses. The hardware and software supporting data warehouses needs to be as much of a commodity as possible. The implementation of a data warehouse should be incremental and should be able to start small and grow later. The owner of a data warehouse should not have to depend on a "guru" to make the system work.

With all of these requirements in mind, we see that the new definition of the data warehouse is very different from the old definition. Adapting to this new definition requires some changes in our thinking. Above all, we need a design methodology that lets us achieve all of these objectives.

In the past few years, we have learned that these new requirements can be addressed effectively with a kind of data warehouse that we call *dimensional*. A dimensional data warehouse can be flexible, adaptable, resilient to change, constantly in a state of flux, and at the same time be understandable and obvious.

As we have built dimensional data warehouses, we have learned that the design isn't about technology. It's about interpreting the business requirements in an effective (i.e., dimensional) way. To state it as plainly as possible, the answer to the data warehouse design challenge is "the right data in a dimensionally designed database." This book is about "the right data in a dimensionally designed database."

Mike Venerable and Chris Adamson have written this book with a very practical and down to earth perspective. Fundamentally, they describe a set of specific dimensional database designs aimed at the basic elements of the business world. What I find appealing about this book is that they take the business perspective very seriously. Reading each chapter, it is clear that they don't want to proceed with the technical design until they have laid out the business perspective completely. Once the business drivers are understood, their vision is that it is almost obvious why each database schema design is capable of addressing a range of relevant business questions.

The book itself is a flow, with a starting point and an ending point. Mike and Chris work forward all the way from describing each target business, to expressing those businesses with dimensional designs, to delivering the results in useful reports. The book is an interesting blend of practical, down-to-earth explanations and state-of-the-art data warehouse practice. In that sense the book mirrors the current mood of the industry.

This book sticks with a fundamental, smoke-stack view of business. Every business has products and customers (or their analogs). Every business markets and sells the products to those customers. If the product is tangible, it must be manufactured, and it must be placed into inventory. A good product must be surrounded by good quality management. Virtually every manager who works in a company has plans and budgets, and at the end of the year they report their financial results and look to see where they are profitable. If the management team has their business under control, they probably manage "by the numbers" or to put it another way, by key performance indicators. And finally, the thoughtful management team may come to realize that the true value in their organization comes more from what they know, not what they make.

Mike and Chris resonate with this fundamental description of businesses and there is a compelling sense that this book applies to any organization. Following the logic of the previous paragraph, it is no coincidence that the book's chapters are sales, marketing, fulfillment, production, inventory, quality, budgets, financial reporting, profitability, and intellectual capital.

Each design in the book is thoroughly dimensional. The logic of each dimensional model is clearly explained. After reading each business description, the reader can see why the dimensional model works. Each dimensional model reacts gracefully to the changes wrought by the surrounding environment. New facts can be added to the fact tables. New dimensional attributes can be added to any of the dimensions. Whole new dimensions can be attached to existing schemas. And throughout all of these changes, all old applications stay up and keep running. The dimensional model is meant to address the data warehouse designer's needs for resilience.

The overall book functions like a "value chain" within a business, with the chapters of the book and hence the functions of the business, laid out conceptually from left to right across the page. Many real business would have some, or all, of the data marts described by Mike and Chris. Hopefully, it should be clear that these data marts share many of the master "conformed" dimensions like Calendar, Customer, Product, and Location. These conformed dimensions are the secret of the incremental development of the overall data warehouse. As the successive data marts are developed, they hook onto a kind of Data Warehouse Bus architecture defined by the conformed dimensions, much like the components of your PC connected to its bus architecture.

As data marts are added to the overall data warehouse, more powerful applications become possible by "drilling across" the separate data marts. If several of the data marts describe product movement, then in some sense the curtain lifts on the overall flow of product across the organization as the successive data marts are developed. Mike and Chris show how to accompany the simpler ideas of product movement with more sophisticated measures of cost, profit, and key performance indicators.

Reading this book and writing this foreword was a real pleasure. Mike and Chris have captured the new direction for data warehousing very effectively, and in a way that should be of practical benefit to the reader. I, at least, found the book very readable because each chapter is a kind of war story for a particular part of a business. But best of all, each chapter is a paradigm, or a practice run, for the way we all ought to design our data marts, and hence our data warehouses. Find the right data to answer the right business questions, and bring that data up quickly and cost effectively in a dimensional framework.

Ralph Kimball

ACKNOWLEDGMENTS

This book would not have been possible without our customers, past and present, who gave us the opportunity to learn about their businesses. We'd also like to thank all of our colleagues at Talus, the most creative and dynamic group of professionals either of us has ever had the opportunity to work with and learn from. Thanks to Bob Elliot and the staff at John Wiley, for their help and advice in the creation of this book. And special thanks to Ralph and Julie Kimball, without whose encouragement, this book would never have been written.

Mike Venerable

Special thanks to my wife, Laura, and daughter, Arielle, who tolerated this project despite the time required and distractions created. I would also like to thank my mother, who occasionally allowed me to play with keypunch machines when I was a kid. In the end, I wrote this book to make her proud.

Chris Adamson

Special thanks to my wife, Gladys, and sons, Justin and Carter, who were forced to give up a lot of time with me during the writing of this book. It has been a more intense undertaking than I ever expected. Thanks to family and friends, all of whom helped in their own ways. My parents provided moral support. My in-laws gave me a place to work in peace. My sister, sisters-in-law, and friends feigned interest and provided encouragement whenever I was running out of steam.

A note for my father, the English teacher. We know that the plural form of *schema* is *schemata*, not *schemas*. We agree that the use of the word *this* as a noun should be avoided. And yes, we mean *measurement* when we write *measure*. All these errors are committed by choice. The conversational style of this book required a relaxation of grammatical standards. Please forgive our deviations.

INTRODUCTION

D ata warehouses are not easy to build. Their design requires a way of thinking at odds with the manner in which traditional computer systems are developed. Their construction requires radical restructuring of vast amounts of data, often of dubious or inconsistent quality, drawn from numerous heterogeneous sources. Their implementation strains the limits of today's information technology. Not surprisingly, a very large number of data warehouse projects *fail*.

We meet people in a wide variety of industries who want to build data warehouses. Given the challenges they will face, we start by making sure the effort is worth the trouble. One of the first questions we always ask is, "Why do you want to build a data warehouse?" Frequently, we get replies like the following:

"Because we need to clean up our customer data."

"To centralize enterprise data in a single repository."

"So that we can write queries that come back from the database quickly."

"To keep our historic data on line."

Each of these answers focuses on a technological component or process. While some of them may be among the valid technical objectives of a data warehouse, *none of these answers are reason enough to build one*. Unless there are better reasons that have gone unstated, each of these projects will likely fail. Technology for its own sake serves no one.

Successful data warehouses are built for one reason: to answer business questions. The nature of the questions to be addressed will vary, but the intention is always the same. Projects that deliver new and relevant information succeed. Projects that do not, fail.

The Successful Data Warehouse

To deliver answers to businesspeople, you must understand their questions. It stands to reason, then, that the successful data warehouse begins with a strong understanding of the business process. This understanding must run very deep, because many of the questions the data warehouse will answer won't be known until long after it has been built.

The data warehouse design fuses business knowledge and technological know-how. More than any other component data warehouse development, the design will mean the difference between success and failure. If it is to answer business questions, the data warehouse must be designed in a way that directly reflects the way business-people think about their business process. If it represents the way people look at the business, the data warehouse will be able to answer questions that haven't yet been asked. Without this critical link to the business, the data warehouse will not deliver relevant information, whether the question is known or unknown.

But even a well-designed data warehouse isn't the answer to business questions, nor is the data it contains. Answers come in the form of reports, which extract information from the data warehouse and format it for presentation. Effective reports answer business questions clearly and concisely. Like the data warehouse design, they will only be successful when authored by someone who fully under-stands how the businessperson is thinking.

The key role played by business knowledge in the success of the data warehouse is best illustrated by example. Imagine two businesses. Each has completed a five-month project developing the first subject area of an enterprise data warehouse. The two businesses made similar financial investments in their respective projects, selected similar technologies to store and retrieve data, and have trained the same number of users to use the new system. Yet, during the first months that their new data warehouses are in operation, the businesses have very different experiences.

The first business has implemented an inventory data mart. In a matter of days, the way in which purchasers manage their inventory changes radically. Daily reports give them insight into the cost and value of their inventory, as well as the velocity with which it moves out of the warehouse. Instead of reacting to sales trends, managers can now manage inventory proactively *and* have a positive impact on the bottom line of the business. Within a few months, they can point to decisions that have saved millions of dollars—decisions made possible by the data warehouse. The data ware-house team is now working on a design for the next subject area.

The second business has completed a sales data mart. Their managers are bewildered by reports being left on their desks. Using calculators and spreadsheets, regional directors resummarize the information relevant to their divisions. Accountants notice that the sales numbers coming from the data warehouse do not match the weekly summaries produced by the Finance department. Because of the way margin is computed, the pricing managers don't use the system at all. The data warehouse team is preparing to make some major changes to the design of the system, providing they can secure the needed funding.

The difference in these experiences can be explained by the degree to which the data warehouse team understood the needs of the business. The first organization has a design that reflects the way managers look at inventory. It contains useful information, and the reports provide the information managers need to make decisions about inventory.

The second organization's reports don't address the needs of managers, who must work hard to get answers out of them. But it may not be possible to fix the reports. The data warehouse's margin calculation is disputed, and the sales numbers don't correlate with accounting data. In other words, the second organization's design does not reflect the way the business process is viewed.

Clearly, the design of the data warehouse and development of reports require a deep understanding of the business. Yet these tasks are likely to be undertaken by information technology professionals, not business decision makers. Is it reasonable to expect the project to succeed? The answer is yes. The key is in learning to apply technology toward business objectives.

Designing Business Solutions

This book is meant to help you, the technical professional, establish the critical link between the business and the data warehouse. You may be involved with data warehousing in a number of ways, either directly or indirectly. Your role may be project leader, analyst, subject matter expert, dimensional modeler, data transformation specialist, application developer, report writer, trainer, or database administrator.

Whatever the level or degree of your involvement, this book will help sharpen your business focus as you prepare for and execute a data warehouse project. You will learn to understand how businesspeople think, translate business requirements into an effective design, and present information from the data warehouse to businesspeople in a meaningful format.

You will also take away a solid understanding of the principles of data warehouse design. The many solutions presented range from basic to very complex. No assumptions are made about previous knowledge; the finer points of the models and their alternatives are explained in great detail. We will also identify recurring modeling and reporting patterns. Understanding the diversity of situations in which a technique can be applied helps prepare you to apply the technique appropriately in new settings.

If your relationship to the data warehouse is as a user, you, too, will find value in these pages. By learning how technology can be used to address business requirements, you will be better prepared to help technologists understand your needs. You'll also be better equipped to understand the solutions with which you are provided.

Learning by Example

Every business is different. Our intention is not to teach you how a particular business works, nor is it to provide template designs to solve common problems. Instead, we want you to develop the ability to learn for yourself how a business runs, and translate your knowledge into a data warehouse design that addresses its needs. We'll do this through a series of detailed case studies.

We have organized the content of this book around business processes, not technical features. Most chapters focus on a particular business process—examples include Sales, Inventory, and Production. Each chapter is organized around two or more diverse business cases, drawn from different industries with unique needs. We begin each case with a description of the business problem, often through a series of quotations from managers (The quotations and interviews in this text are hypothetical). We translate the business requirements into a data warehouse design, presented in detail and linked back to business objectives. And, of course, we show how the design can be used to deliver reports—reports that answer business questions.

We've grouped chapters together into informal sections based on common business themes. The first several chapters deal with the organization's relationship to the customer. They address Sales, Marketing, and Fulfillment. Next, we look at the principles of product management through chapters on Production, Inventory Management, and Quality. We look at the financial side of business and areas of strategic concern in chapters on Budgeting, Financial Reporting, Profitability Analysis, Intellectual Capital, Key. In the last three chapters, we change our focus from the business process to the process of building the data warehouse. These chapters address reporting tools, planning the data warehouse, and how to conduct interviews.

Using This Book

You'll get the most out of this book if you read it in its entirety. The succession of diverse examples will help instill your ability to identify and understand a business process, translate it into a schema design, and present useful information to businesspeople.

However, it's not necessary to read the book in sequence. If you are interested in a particular subject area, by all means, read it first. Keep in mind that even within an industry, not all businesses have the same needs. The examples we provide may not template onto your situation, but will provide useful insights that can be adapted to unique situations.

The data warehouse solutions in this book are designed using a set of principles known as *dimensional modeling*. For those unfamiliar with the technique, we present the relevant principles in Chapter 1. We'll make use of these principles through the remainder of the book to produce data warehouse designs that answer business questions.

Read Chapter 1 before you skip ahead. After that, feel free to choose your own path. We do recommend that you read *all* of Chapters 2 through 12, whether or not you do so in succession. If you skip a chapter altogether, you may miss a valuable business insight or a discussion of one of the finer points of dimensional modeling. Designs drawn from entirely different industries—even different subject areas— may well exhibit characteristics that apply to your situation.

The last three chapters will be of particular interest to technical professionals. Chapter 13, "Presenting Information," identifies important features of business reports and analyzes them from a technical perspective. This chapter will be useful to anyone coding a report, selecting query or reporting software, or building a tool of his or her own.

Chapter 14 should be read by those responsible for managing a data warehouse, funding it, or leading its implementation. We discuss how to plan and deliver an enterprise data warehouse. Special attention is given to the follies of extremes and how to avoid them—the "galactic data warehouse" and the "stovepipe data mart."

Those who will be collecting requirements for the data warehouse by interviewing businesspeople will want to read Chapter 15. This chapter will help you maximize what you learn about the business during these short but important encounters.

Conventions

We present a wide variety of business cases in this book. When we introduce a commonly accepted business term that is likely to have wide applicability, we call it out under the heading "Key Business Term." The business term in shown in bold, followed by a brief definition and common synonyms. Subsequent sentences may be used to provide examples, further detail, or closely related terms. For example:

Key Business Terms

General ledger. A ledger in which the financial accounts of a business are fomally summarized. Often referred to as *G/L.*

The heart of double-entry accounting, the general ledger remains balanced through offsetting transactions to debit and credit accounts. The list of accounts is often referred to as *the chart of accounts.*

When we wish to call attention to technical points, they are called out under the heading "TIP." Tips identify design principles, warn you of common pitfalls, and point out particularly difficult reporting techniques. Here is an example:

TIP

Always verify that the source data supports your design. If you do not consider the source of your data mart, you may be in for a rude awakening when it is time to actually build the data mart. The inability to deliver on a proposed solution will not be appreciated by businesspeople funding the effort.

The database schema designs in this book are presented in figures. We have kept the notation very simple, and it is fully explained the first time a schema appears in Figure 1.2. The schemas are also provided, complete with sample data, on the CD-ROM that accompanies this book. Additional figures are included as appropriate to provide graphic illustrations of key concepts.

The end results of our efforts are reports. We will number reports within chapters so that they are easily referred to. We will sometimes number report columns when it makes discussion of their construction easier. The reports are also provided in HTML format on the compact disc. In our discussions, when it is necessary to present rows of raw, unformatted data from the database, we will do so in tables. Tables will be numbered separately from figures and reports.

Occasionally, we will show small examples of SQL code. Don't panic! SQL knowledge is not a requirement of this book. In the rare cases that we use it, it will be explained. Comments will follow dashes. Code will appear in a distinct typeface as shown here:

```
select product.brand,          — The "Select" clause
       sum(sales_dollars),
       sum(margin_dollars)
  from shipment_facts,         — The "From" clause
       product
 where                          — The "Where" clause
       shipment_facts.product_key = product.product_key
```

Getting Started

Before we can begin developing data warehouse solutions for business problems, we need to explain the techniques we will use to construct our models. Chapter 1 introduces the principles of dimensional modeling. Read it before you go anywhere else. Don't worry if some of it doesn't make sense; it will become clear when we start working through examples.

Remember: The data warehouse is built to deliver answers to business questions. Success depends on your ability to understand and model a business process.

THE BUSINESS-DRIVEN DATA WAREHOUSE

This book is all about answering business questions. One subject area at a time, we will demonstrate how business needs can be represented in a data warehouse design, and how that design can be used to answer business questions.

While most computer systems are designed to *capture* data, data warehouses are designed for *getting data out*. This fundamental difference suggests that the data warehouse will be designed according to a different set of principles. Before we begin presenting solutions for various businesses, we must outline these principles.

The solutions we build follow a set of design principles called *dimensional modeling*, often referred to as the *star schema approach*. Although not new, the star schema has recently been popularized by Ralph Kimball. In his book, *The Data Warehouse Toolkit* (John Wiley and Sons, 1998), Dr. Kimball outlines the principles of dimensional modeling, using terminology that we will follow. We highly recommend Dr. Kimball's book to anyone involved in the design and implementation of a data warehouse.

If you haven't read *The Data Warehouse Toolkit*, this chapter is meant for you. It is a quick primer on dimensional modeling. Although not a replacement for Dr. Kimball's book, it provides the fundamentals that will be required to understand the designs in this book. You may want to skip this chapter if you are familiar with dimensional modeling; however, we suggest you review the summary of terms at the end of this chapter before you go on.

The Data Warehouse

The data warehouse exists to answer questions people have about the business. This function contrasts sharply with the purpose of the transaction systems within the business, and requires that the design of the data warehouse follow different principles. Dimensional modeling techniques, applied carefully, ensure that the data warehouse design reflects the way managers think about the business and that the data warehouse can be used to answer their questions.

Events and the Transaction Model

For any organization, the process of doing business is a series of events. The smallest startup and the largest multinational corporation alike are characterized by their own sets of significant activities. The nature and frequency of these events vary by business, but they are always there. A product is manufactured, one account is credited while another is debited, a seat is reserved, an order is booked, a shipment is packed, an invoice is generated, a payment is posted. These events are the life's blood of the business, the activities that contribute to its success or failure.

For any business, it is critical that detailed information about these events is captured. A set of computer systems known as *transaction systems*, or *OLTP systems*, captures this important detail. Most organizations have a variety of OLTP systems, each tracking a different type of activity. These systems are carefully designed to record business transactions, following a set of rules that ensure their consistency and the effective storage of their detail. Design principles of normalization and transaction consistency are critical to the OLTP system.

The design of an OLTP system is a window into the world of the micro-level transactions that drive the business. If you scrutinize a customer billing system, you will learn how invoice lines are structured and how they tie into shipments and orders. But it does not show you how managers look at the processes of booking orders, picking shipments, or invoicing customers. What is important about these processes? Sales dollars? Volumes? Margins? How do managers evaluate these processes? By product? By division? Over time? The OLTP system reveals none of this information. Its focus is at the detailed level of the individual events.

This event focus serves a critical function. Without a detailed picture of individual orders, shipments, or invoices, the business could not run. The OLTP system can be used to pull up an order, show the pieces of a shipment, or generate invoices—all of these functions are important. The OLTP system's normalized design ensures transaction consistency, and optimizes the storage of this information. But its focus on the individual transaction renders the OLTP system ill suited to answer questions that are not focused at this level. "What were the best-selling products last week?" "How often did we fulfill an order in more than two shipments?" "What's the quarterly trend on orders by region?" These questions would require construction of complex reports that take into account all the intricacies supported by the transaction model, if it hasn't overwritten critical detail needed to produce the correct answer.

Business Processes and the Dimensional Model

The data warehouse is designed to bridge this gap. It is built to answer the questions being asked throughout the business every day, questions not focused on individual transactions but on the overall process. In order to meet this requirement, the design of the data warehouse must directly reflect the way managers look at the business. If it does not, it will not be easy to answer their questions. This characteristic lies at the heart of the data warehouse. It distinguishes the data warehouse from the OLTP systems, and requires a design based on an entirely different set of principles.

Dimensional modeling, popularly known as the *star schema approach*, is a technique used to identify and represent the information that is important to people with business questions. The dimensional model serves as an analytic tool in planning the data warehouse, and as a physical design for its implementation in a relational database. Throughout this book, dimensional models are constructed to reflect the business needs and are used to answer the important business questions. When designed well, a dimensional model can be an invaluable aid to a business. This success is possible because the dimensional model structures information the way business people think about it.

The Business Vocabulary

To understand how people think about a business process, you need only listen to their questions:

"Show me gross margin by product category"

"Show me average account balances by educational level"

"How does inventory level compare with sales by product by warehouse?"

"What are our outstanding 180-day receivables by general ledger account?"

"What's the return rate by supplier?"

These questions share several common elements. Each centers around a business process: orders, account management, inventory management, accounts receivable, returns. Each requires summarizing a lot of activity as opposed to scrutinizing individual events. And each reveals terms important to the business within a subject area: margin, product category, account balance, education level.

Most importantly, each question reveals how the business tracks, or *measures*, the process in question. Gross margin is a measurement of the sales process for distributors. Banks monitor balances as part of the account management process. Warehouse managers track inventory levels. Accountants quantify receivables. Retailers measure return rates. Metrics such as these are used in every organization to monitor business processes. For some processes, there may be a single metric, while others may have a host of relevant metrics.

Any of these measurements is likely to be studied in a number of ways. Margin, for example, is broken out by product category in the first question. Other questions may require margin at a finer grain, perhaps for an individual product. Still others may want to look at margin by salesperson, by customer, or by time period. For a given measurement, there are always numerous parameters by which it may be broken out or rolled up. These parameters are often found after the word *by*, as in the preceding questions.

A data warehouse, designed to answer questions like these, must reflect the way the business process is viewed. Specifically, it must capture the measurements of importance to the business, and the parameters by which these measurements are viewed. These elements are represented in a dimensional model. The principles of dimensional modeling serve the analytic focus of the data warehouse, just as the principles of normalization serve the transaction focus of the OLTP system.

The Dimensional Model

A *dimensional model* is a direct reflection of the manner in which a business process is viewed. It captures the measurements of importance to a business, and the parameters by which the measurements are broken out. The measurements are referred to as *facts* or *measures*. We prefer the term *measure*, because it is more descriptive, albeit grammatically incorrect. The parameters by which a measurement can be viewed are referred to as *dimensions*. Consider a company that manufactures kitchen appliances and sells them to retailers. Table 1.1 shows a partial list of the measures and dimensions of importance when studying its order entry process.

The measures and dimensions in this partial list can be combined in a number of ways to answer a wide array of business questions. In fact, any of the measures in the list might be combined with any of the dimensions. We might examine Gross Sales Dollars at the detailed customer level (Customer Name) or rolled up by zip code (Customer's Zip Code). We might look at Margin Dollars for an entire year (Year of Order), or on a daily basis (Date of Order). In addition, we might examine combinations of these; for example, Gross Sales Dollars and Margin Dollars by Product Category and Quarter.

Table 1.1 Measures and Dimensions for the Order Entry Process

Measures	Dimensions
Gross sales dollars	Customer name
Total cost	Customer's state
Margin dollars	Customer's zip code
Quantity sold	Date of order
	Month of order
	Quarter of order
	Year of order
	Salesperson
	Sales territory
	Corporate region
	Product name
	Product brand
	Product category

Notice that there seem to be natural clusters of related dimensions. There are several dimension attributes that describe a customer, several that describe the time of sale, several that describe the salesperson, and several that describe the product sold. In Figure 1.1, we show the same dimensions and measures. This time, the measures are shown in a box in the middle of the page. The groups of related dimensions are each shown in boxes surrounding the measures.

The diagram in Figure 1.1 is a dimensional model. It is an excellent tool for identifying and classifying the important business components in a subject area. The diagram is easily understood by a business person. "Things I measure" go in the middle; "the ways I look at them" go in the surrounding boxes, loosely grouped together or categorized.

The Star Schema

It turns out that these boxes translate nicely into database tables that can be used to store all the information. A dimensional model like the one in Figure 1.1 does

Figure 1.1 Dimensional model for order process.

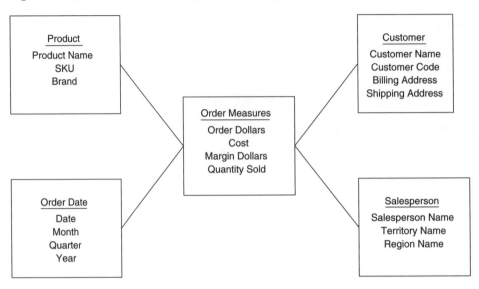

not change much when implemented in a relational database, where it becomes known as a *star schema*. Each box of dimension attributes becomes a table in the database, referred to as a *dimension table*, which is assigned a *primary key*. The primary key is never one of the attributes of the table or an ID from a source system—we'll explain why later. The center box becomes a very large table containing millions, or even billions, of rows. Popularly known as the *fact table*, it contains the measures, plus foreign keys that relate each measurement to the appropriate rows in each of the dimension tables. A star schema for the orders process is shown in Figure 1.2. We've added some extra detail, particularly to the time dimension.

Provided we are careful about how we define the measures and dimensions we will store, the database design is very effective in answering business questions quickly and accurately. Requests for information stored in these tables are expressed in a format called *Structured Query Language*, or *SQL*. We'll look at how SQL is used to query the data warehouse in Chapter 13, "Presenting Information." In broad terms, a query includes some constraints on dimensions, such as "1996 data only." It includes a series of requested dimensional attributes, such as Month and Product Category, and the sum of one or more measures found in the fact table, such as Sum of Sales Dollars. In SQL, the sum is referred to as an *aggregation operation*, that is *grouped by* the dimensional attributes of the request.

Figure 1.2 The orders schema.

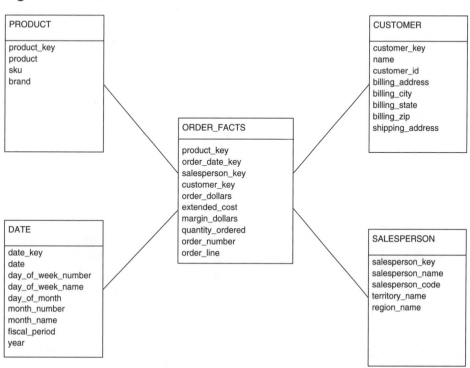

Multidimensional Databases

Dimensional models are not always implemented in relational databases. Several vendors offer *multidimensional databases*, or *MDBs*, which store information in a different format often referred to as a *cube*. The cube is constructed in such a way that each combination of dimensional attributes with a measure is either precalculated or easy to compute very quickly.

The advantage of the multidimensional database is that its speed allows users to change their perspective on the data interactively, adding or removing attributes to their view and receiving instantaneous feedback. This process is often referred to as *On-Line Analytical Processing*, or *OLAP*. Multidimensional databases are often referred to as *OLAP engines*.

Continues

Multidimensional Databases *(Continued)*

However, the nature of a multidimensional database also means that it cannot handle extremely large volumes of data. Large transaction volume can lead to cubes that consume vast amounts of storage, or do not perform. Similarly, the number of dimensional attributes stored in an MDB can impact size and performance of the cube. Some MDBs require that each dimension contain a single, predefined hierarchy that will be used to drill through the data. We have found that within an organization, there is a wide variety of ways people want to drill though the data—a single path can be frustrating.

Some of these problems can be solved by implementing a star schema in a relational database, and then using data from the star as the source for MDBs. This approach is frequently used when an organization wants to perform focused analysis on a small subset of a very large data set. When this approach is taken, the star schema is often referred to as the *data warehouse*, and the MDB is referred to as the *data mart*. Note that in this book, we will use these terms differently—see the end of this chapter for details.

Another solution involves placing the cube on a user's computer or application server. Many of the query tools on the market today take this approach. Using the tool, a user queries the star schema. The tool then takes the results of the query and formats them in a cube to permit quick analysis of the data. This approach is useful because it does not require administration of centralized cubes, but is subject to the processing limits of the PC or application server.

Our advice is to start by building a star schema in a relational database. The star schema will support a wide variety of reporting needs, and prove to be a significant asset to the business. The star schema can always serve as a source of clean, carefully organized data for multidimensional databases, should the need ever arise.

The dimensional model is powerful because it reflects the way business people think. It directly addresses their requirements, and relational database technology allows it to be used to answer questions quickly and accurately. Next, we'll take a closer look at the parts of the dimensional database design, and build a vocabulary that will be used throughout this book.

The Star Schema

Keep in mind that best practices suggest there are some important steps to take before you begin work within a particular subject area. Because there will be needs throughout the business that share common dimensions, it is important to map out an overall plan. By doing so, each star can be built so that it will work well in conjunction with the others. This planning does not require a massive, long-term project; it can usually be accomplished in several weeks. We will discuss this process in detail in Chapter 14, "Building an Enterprise Data Warehouse."

Before work can begin on a particular star schema, it must be decided what business process is being modeled. As this decision is one of scope, it is often made long before the design team is assembled. The next steps are to fix the grain of the fact table, identify the dimensions, and enumerate the measures.

The Grain

When designing a star schema, one of the first decisions to be made relates to the level of detail at which measures will be recorded. This level of detail is referred to as the *grain* of the fact table. It is crucial that every row in the fact table be recorded at exactly the same level of detail; not doing so would destroy the usability of the star schema. For our orders process, we will set the grain at the level of detail of the individual order line.

Failure to adhere to a grain can render the star schema difficult to use. Suppose that we were not careful about the grain of our orders fact table. We record most rows at the order line level, but we also record a few at the header level. Now, when we query the fact table, we have to be very careful. At the order line level, there is a relationship to customer, product, salesperson, and time. But at the header level, the relationship to a specific product disappears. We must carefully qualify each and every query we write to work around this distinction, being sure never to include rows at the order level when product is included in the query. Such restrictions are impractical. Instead, information relevant at a different grain should be stored in a second fact table, as we will discuss later.

In general, the strict adherence of a fact table to a chosen grain requires that the foreign keys relating a row in the fact table to dimension rows are never null. An optional relationship to a dimension is usually a sign of a grain problem, as are "fake" rows like a product called Not a Product. The rule against optionality can be relaxed when a dimension is not a part of the grain of the fact table. In Chapter 3, "Marketing," we will add a Promotion dimension to a sales schema without impacting its grain. It can be optional, but we prefer the technique of adding a Not on Promotion row to the table.

The Dimensions

Once the grain of the fact table is chosen, careful thought is given to the dimension tables. The goal should be to produce dimension tables with a large number of attributes, reflecting the rich set of details that surround any business process. For simplicity's sake, most of the dimension tables depicted in this book have fewer than 10 attributes. In the real world, it is not uncommon to have 100 or even 200 dimensions in a single dimension table. This is why dimension tables are often referred to as being *wide*.

The relationship between dimensions in a dimension table does not need to be strong. It is perfectly acceptable to include a set of attributes that are not directly related to one another in a single dimension table. For example, in the orders schema we have included the geographic region of the country in the salesperson table. This is possible because sales territories fall within regions. However, it would have been equally valid to include a geographic dimension table, separate from the salesperson dimension. It may also have been appropriate to include regional data, or even sales force data, inside the existing customer dimension table.

Resist any urge to apply the rules of normalization to dimension tables. The primary roles of the dimension table are to hold attributes that will be used to qualify queries, and to hold attributes whose values will be used to break out measures. Normalizing a dimension table does nothing to further these goals; in fact, a dimension table that has been normalized into a series of tables may detract from these goals. By spreading dimensional attributes out across several tables, queries become more complex, databases have a harder time fetching the data, and users wait longer for their answers. All this to save a few bytes in a dimension table that, in comparison to the fact table, is minuscule.

Keeping dimensions denormalized means that natural hierarchies within the data will be flattened out. In our orders schema, there are several examples. The time dimension table includes Year, Quarter, Month, and Date, along with several other attributes related to a specific date. These components have not been placed in a series of progressively more detailed tables; instead, the hierarchy is flattened out. While the year 1998 may appear in the table 365 times, this will be invisible to the end user; when measures are broken out by year, one occurrence of 1998 will appear on a report. Similarly, there is a flattened hierarchy in the Product dimension table, from category to brand to the specific product. It is not unusual to find several flattened hierarchies within a dimension table.

One of the hardest organizational realities to include in a dimension table is the recursive relationship. In our orders schema, we might have chosen to include the salesperson's department within the organization. Departments fall within departments, and at times we might want to roll sales up to a number of different levels. To meet this requirement, we would identify the top of the organizational hierarchy and the number of levels down from the top to which we want to report. Each of these levels receives its own attribute in the dimension table. Rows that correspond to salespeople at higher levels in the tree contain "N/A" values in the columns for lower-level attributes. An example of this technique can be found in Chapter 8, "Budgets and Spending," where a fixed number of categories and sub-categories are represented although the number of levels varies in the source system.

The dimensional characteristics of a significant entity can change over time. For example, a customer may have moved between this year and last. The customer's address and geographic profile, captured in a series of dimension attributes, have changed. We want the star schema to reflect where they were when last year's orders were placed, as well as where they are when this year's orders are placed. This phenomenon is referred to as a *slowly changing dimension*. There are three techniques used to handle these changes, which are addressed in the sidebar. In the case of the customer who moved, we simply add a new row to the dimension table with the new address, and relate it to any sales that took place after the move.

Most dimension tables are small in comparison to fact tables, but occasion-ally, dimension tables get quite large, particularly dimensions that are subject to many of the changes we discussed. In such cases, it is possible to reduce their size by separating some attributes into a separate dimension. We use this tech-nique in the banking schema in Chapter 3, "Marketing." The customer dimension, already large with several hundred thousand rows, requires a new row each time the demographics of a customer change. We control the growth of the customer dimension by separating out the demographic attributes that change over time into a separate Demographic dimension, sometimes referred to as a *minidimension*. We don't maintain a relationship from the customer to the demographic dimension; instead, we rely on the fact table to establish the link.

In addition to the dimension columns we have discussed, every dimension table has one additional attribute: its *key*. The primary key of a dimension table is always a single, system-defined attribute. In the name of performance, we stay away from multipart keys, or *concatenated* keys. We also don't rely on identifiers or keys that come from other systems, such as Customer_ID or the product's SKU. Such a dependency only leads to trouble. In the example where a customer moved from one state to another, we required a new row in the customer dimen-sion table. At the time of the move, it is unlikely the customer was assigned a new ID. Had we depended on the Customer_ID as our primary key, we would have been hard-pressed to add a new row to the customer table.

Slowly Changing Dimensions

When the attributes of a customer change, an OLTP system frequently overwrites the old values. When a customer moves from one state to another, the customer's address is simply updated in the customer table. This makes perfect sense in the world of transaction processing—it is still the same customer, only the details have changed. Regardless of where a business was when a transaction happened, all confirmations, shipments, and invoices should go to the new address. There is no need to keep track of the old address.

This approach is inappropriate in the data warehouse. It is very important to represent the correct location of the customer at the time of each transaction. Within the star schema, we need an alternative mechanism to handle changes. We refer to the phenomenon as a *slowly changing dimension*. There are three approaches taken, depending on the nature of the change.

The first approach for dealing with a change is to simply update the row in the dimension table. We might do this if a supplier's phone number changes, or a customer's gender is corrected. Dimensional attributes are updated when the change is a correction to an error, or the previous value is not significant in analyzing transactions. We refer to this as a Type 1 change.

In the case of a move, we need to be able to see where the customer was located at the time of each transaction, so that queries breaking out Sales by State are accurate. In this case, we need a Type 2 change. A new row is added to the customer dimension table, containing the same customer information but incorporating the new address. From the point of view of the star schema, the Type 2 change is not a change at all, but rather an entirely new row.

When a Type 2 change occurs, rows already present in the fact table remain linked to the original row. In our example, old orders remain linked to the row in the customer dimension table that contains the old address. New fact table rows are linked to the dimension row with the new address. A query breaking sales out by state over time correctly handles the change in location for the customer. If we are not concerned about the location of a customer, we simply omit address information from a query. All other attributes remaining the same, we receive a single row for that customer in our report.

The occurrence of Type 2 changes reveals why we must never use an external key as the primary key of a dimension table. What is viewed as a change in the star schema is likely to be different than what is viewed as a change in the source system. The change of address, for example, is likely to have been implemented as an update in the source system, while it is a new row in our star schema. The customer ID remains unchanged, so if we had used it as our primary key, we would now be forced to modify it or concatenate a sequence number. Developers charged with loading the star schema need to be very clear on what constitutes a row in each system, and how they differ.

A change in the same attribute may deserve a Type 1 change in some cases, but a Type 2 change in other cases. For example, we may correct an address if it was originally wrong (Type 1), or insert a new row if it is a true change (Type 2.) Unfortunately, we rarely receive the reason for a change from source systems. It is therefore important to determine how changes will be handled at design time. Each attribute can usually be assigned a Type 1 or Type 2 status.

A third approach is used less frequently, but is very powerful. It involves making a minor change to the design of the dimension table when the change occurs. Suppose that we redesignate the territories to which salespeople are assigned. Management wants to be able to do all reporting using both organizational structures, old and new. This allows them to study the impact of the realignment on the salespeople and their compensation, comparing commissions paid under the new plan to those that would have been paid under the old plan. To meet these requirements, we rename the Territory dimension attribute to Old_Territory, and leave the old values in it. We add a new Territory column, and populate it with the new assignment data. This approach is known as a Type 3 change, and is characterized by the required design change in the schema. Unlike Type 1 and 2 changes, which are usually isolated to a single row in the dimension table, Type 3 changes impact the entire table.

The Fact Table

After identifying the grain and dimensions, attention turns back to the fact table. We'll begin by focusing on the measures. As it turns out, there are three types of measures, one of which we need to avoid. After looking at these measures, we'll look at the other elements of a fact table.

Three Kinds of Measures

The most common measures are *fully additive*. We say a measure is fully additive when it is meaningful to summarize it by adding values together across any dimensions. In our orders schema, sales_dollars, extended_cost, margin_dollars, and quantity_sold are all fully additive measures. Although we record these measures in the fact table for a product, a customer, a salesperson, and a date, we can easily summarize them in any way we please. To look at sales for a month, we can add sales_dollars values together across all dates in a particular month. To look at margin for a product category, we add together the margin_dollars values for all products in the category.

A fully additive measure is very powerful because there are no limitations on how we use it. It can easily be summarized for any combination of dimension values, simply by rolling it up across any dimensions not requested. We've already mentioned that SQL lends itself to this type of aggregation quite easily. Fully additive measures can and should be included in the fact table.

In stark contrast to the fully additive measure is the *nonadditive* measure. Nonadditive measures cannot be added together across dimensions. Consider margin expressed as a percentage of sales, which we will refer to as *margin rate*. It represents the margin as a percentage, rather than a dollar amount. It would be easy to add margin_rate to our fact table, but this measure would be of little use, because we would not be able to summarize it according to the dimensions of interest for a given report. For example, on a particular day, a salesperson sells a customer four different products, each at a 25-percent margin rate. We can record the four transactions with 25-percent margin rates in the fact table, but we cannot roll it up to other levels of detail. An overall margin rate for the customer is not the sum of the four 25-percent values—this would produce a wildly inaccurate 100-percent margin rate. Is the power of the star schema lost for key indicators like margin that are nonadditive?

Luckily, there is a solution to this problem. Like our margin_rate, most non-additive measures are actually ratios of other measures. As we've already hinted, margin_rate is the ratio of margin_dollars to sales_dollars, and both of these measures are fully additive. The solution, then, is to break a nonadditive measure down into its fully additive components, and store those components in the fact table. Computation of the ratio can be accomplished within the application. We are now able to express margin_rate for any combination of dimensional attributes we please. Margin_rate for the customer in question, for example, is computed by retrieving margin_dollars and sales_dollars for the customer, then performing the division operation. Of course, computation of the margin_rate will require special care, particularly in reports that require summary rows. We'll take a look at this topic in Chapter 13, "Presenting Information."

A third type of measure is *semi-additive*. A semi-additive measure can be summarized across some dimensions, but not all. Consider a bank tracking account balances. The bank records balances at the end of each banking day for customers, by account, over time. This allows the bank to study deposits, as well as the individual customers. In some cases, the account balance measure is additive. If one customer holds both checking and savings accounts, we can add together the balances of each account at the end of the day, and get a meaningful combined balance. We can also add balances together across accounts at the same branch for a picture of the total deposits at each location.

However, we will be committing a grave error if we add together account balances for a single customer over multiple days. We would love it if the balance in our bank accounts at month's end was the sum of each daily balance, but this is just wishful thinking. The account balance measure is semi-additive. We can summarize it in any way we want, as long as we do not add together values for different days.

Semi-additivity is encountered when measures represent levels—examples include head counts, inventory quantities, or account balances. Semi-additive measures can be stored in the fact table, but we must take special care in how we use them. It is important that developers of queries or reports be aware of the dimension over which a semi-additive measure is not additive. For example, the account balance is additive across all dimensions but time. This does not mean that we cannot summarize the measure over time; it simply means we are limited as to how we can do so. We may not be able to meaningfully sum account balances over days, but we can certainly average them; in fact, this is how most banks determine the dollar amount on which to pay interest at the end of the month. We will encounter semi-additive facts in Chapters 3, 6 and 8, and discuss how to keep out of trouble with them.

Filling Out the Fact Table

Although not required, in practice, most fact tables are extremely large, ranging from tens of millions of rows to billions of rows. A particular row in the fact table contains only a handful of attributes: the numeric measures, and foreign keys to each dimension table. Whereas we characterized dimension tables as *wide*, we characterize fact tables as *deep*.

Another important characteristic of the fact table is its sparsity. We do not record rows in the fact table that represent no activity. This means that the fact table does not contain a row for every possible combination of dimension table rows. If a customer does not order a particular product on a particular day, there is no need to record a row in the table representing a quantity ordered of zero. This sparsity of the fact table is important in controlling its size. In Chapter 6, "Inventory and Capacity," we will look at what happens when zero rows are added to the fact table, destroying its sparsity.

Often, the fact table will include one or two dimensions. This is the case in our orders schema, where the fact table contains an order_number and order_line_number. These attributes are known as *degenerate dimensions*. They are not placed in a dimension table, simply because any attribute that might accompany them in an Order dimension table has already been placed elsewhere. Were we to construct an orders dimension anyway, it would be extremely large. If it included the order line, it would actually be the same size as the fact table. As such, construction of a separate dimension does little to help performance of the star schema. Occasionally, there may be value in moving degenerate dimensions out into a dimension table, if the values within them will be used to drill across stars. We'll talk about drilling across stars shortly.

Notice that the fact table does not require a system-generated key; instead, the primary key of a particular row in the fact table is identified according to the dimensions that make up its grain. This usually means that the primary key of the fact table is a concatenated key involving some subset of the foreign keys to dimension tables. In the case of our orders schema, the primary key of the fact table must also include our degenerate dimensions, because it is possible that the same customer twice ordered the same product from the same salesperson on the same day.

Occasionally, it is not necessary to store any measurement in a fact table. Sometimes, simply recording the relationship between dimensions at a point in time is all that a business needs to measure. This type of fact table is referred to as a *factless fact table*. Factless fact tables often record events like an employee reporting for work, or a student enrolling in a class. They are also used to record coverage, such as territory assignments of the sales team over time. Usually, we are interested in counting rows in a factless fact table. In order to make SQL more readable, a measure is added that contains the value 1. This allows the measure to be easily summed, rather than requiring a SQL Count Distinct construct.

We also like this approach because it lends itself nicely to the construction of aggregates.

Fact tables may contain multiple foreign keys to the same dimension. For example, the same fact may have multiple dates associated with it. The shipment_facts table in Figure 1.3 contains two relationships to the date table: one represents the date of the shipment, while the other represents the date of the original order. It is not necessary to construct two versions of the date table; instead, views, synonyms, or SQL aliasing can be used to reference two virtual copies of the date dimension table in a single SQL statement.

More than One Fact Table

The fact table and its associated dimensions are referred to as a *star schema*. It is never the case that all the measures and dimensions of importance to a business can be captured in a single star schema. To the contrary, the existence of multiple fact tables is the norm. When there are multiple fact tables, we often say there are multiple stars. Each star is a single fact table and its associated dimensions. We now look at several forces that drive us to design multiple stars.

Different Process, Different Star

The primary factor that drives the separation of measures into different fact tables is the business process. There are two reasons that different business processes lend themselves to individual stars: First, individual business processes tend to involve varying sets of relevant dimensions, and second, the measures relevant to each business process are usually collected at different intervals.

Variations in Grain

We've already looked at the order process for a manufacturer of kitchen appliances. Now let's look at the process of shipping orders. As with orders, shipments will be measured by quantities and dollar amounts. For example, we can study quantity shipped much the same way that we study quantity ordered. At the time of shipment, the business considers the sale completed and registers a receivable. Hence, a shipment has a set of dollar values associated with it that mirror those accompanying an order: the total sales dollars of a shipment, the total cost of goods shipped, and the margin. These shipment metrics are viewed along many of the same dimensions as our orders metrics: by customer, by salesperson, and by product.

There are some fundamental differences, however, in the way the processes are viewed, and how these measurements are collected. First, we observe that although there is some overlap with orders, shipments involve some additional dimension values. For a given shipment, we keep track of the shipper that was used to deliver the goods. We also need to keep track of two dates, rather than one: In addition to the date of the original order, we need to keep track of the shipment date.

So shipments and orders have different sets of attendant dimensions, with some overlap. Technically speaking, we say that the processes are measured at different grains. Earlier, we stressed the importance of adhering to a single grain within a fact table. Failure to do so renders the fact table very difficult to use, so it is clear that the two business processes, orders and shipments, will require separate fact tables.

In Figure 1.3, we have supplemented our orders schema with a second star used to measure the shipment process. Notice that order_facts is no longer in the center of the page; in order to represent both stars in a single diagram, it has been moved to the far left. The same dimensions shown in Figure 1.2 remain linked to order_facts; they appear to its right. The additional shipment_facts contains its own measures. Shipment_facts is linked to the same dimensions as order_facts; however, unlike order_facts, it includes two relationships to the time dimension table, plus a relationship to a new shipper dimension table.

Variations in Measurement Interval

On occasion, two business processes involve exactly the same set of dimensions. Other times, we may choose to omit the dimensions that distinguish one process from another. For example, we might choose to ignore the shipper and shipment date information surrounding shipments. Although the measurements are now recorded at the same grain as order_facts, it remains important to record them in separate fact tables. This is because the measurements of different business processes are taken at different times.

All the measures surrounding an order, such as quantity_ordered and order_dollars, are taken simultaneously at the point in time at which the order is recorded. Similarly, sales_dollars and quantity_shipped are measured simultaneously when a shipment is recorded. By contrast, measurements surrounding orders and shipments, such as the quantity_ordered and quantity_shipped, are measured at different times. The first is recorded when the order is placed, the second when the shipment is released. These measurements are rarely taken simultaneously.

We must continue to record these measures in separate fact tables. On the particular date that an order is placed by a customer for a product, there may be no shipment activity for that product and customer. On a particular date that a product is shipped to a customer, there may be no orders placed. Were we to

Figure 1.3 Orders and shipments.

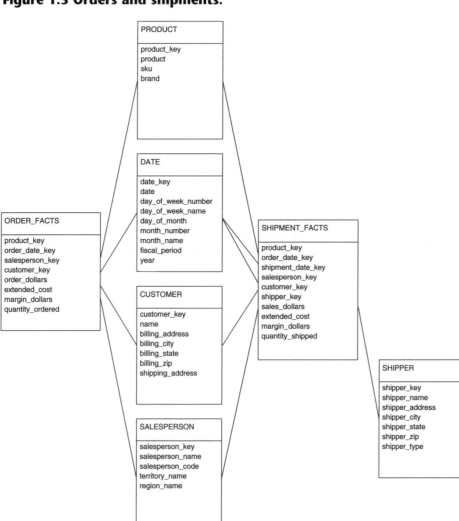

record quantity_ordered and quantity_shipped in the same table, we would be forced to load a zero for one each time the other is recorded. When we log an order, we also record a shipment quantity of zero, and vice versa. These extra zeros mean there will be a lot more data to search through when focusing on one process. Further, report developers will be forced to take measures to exclude the unwanted zeros from reports. We will explore these problems in more depth in Chapter 8, "Budgets and Spending."

Identifying Discrete Processes

It is often difficult to identify discrete business processes. To complicate matters, a single process can often be broken down into subprocesses. Shipments and orders, for example, might be referred to as Sales. How, then, can we be sure when multiple fact tables are required? When there is uncertainty, look for the characteristics we have observed: differing dimensional detail or grain, and differing collection intervals. Either is a clear sign that measures should be placed in separate fact tables.

First, look at the dimensional detail surrounding each measure. If the detail differs, the measures reflect differing processes, and therefore belong in multiple fact tables. Such a difference in grain was enough to tip us off to the fact that metrics like quantity_ordered and shipment_quantity belong in different fact tables. There are also times when only the timing indicator is present. In Chapter 8, "Budgets and Spending," we will observe that business processes may be measured at the same grain, but be measured at different times. When this happens, it is still important to make use of multiple fact tables; otherwise, reports are cluttered with a large number of extraneous zeros.

Even a single business process frequently requires multiple fact tables. We now focus our attention on the four situations in which this requirement emerges.

Core and Custom Fact Tables

The value in a dimension often determines what measures will be taken. Different types of products or customers, for example, may be measured in different ways. Consider the bank we discussed earlier, offering a wide variety of products, from deposit accounts to insurance. The bank snapshots account status at the end of each day, taking a number of measurements. At least one measurement, often referred to as the *primary* balance, or simply *balance*, is taken for every account; however, each account type may also feature its own unique measurements. For checking accounts, the bank may track the number of transactions, and fees collected. For interest-bearing accounts, the bank wants to track interest paid. Other product categories have their own unique measurements as well.

In cases where the measurements taken depend on a dimension value, account type in this case, it is appropriate to design a series of fact tables. One, known as the *core fact table*, contains measures common for all dimension values. In the case of the bank, the core fact table contains the primary balance measure. This fact table can be used to perform cross-product analysis. Additional fact tables are built for each specific product. In addition to the common measures, these *custom fact tables* include measures specific to the particular product. Although containing more attributes that the core fact table, each custom fact table only contains rows for a particular product type, rendering it much smaller. We will encounter core and custom fact tables in Chapter 3, "Marketing," in which a telephone company uses different metrics for residential customers and commercial customers.

Custom fact tables are often accompanied by custom dimension tables. Continuing our banking example, we observe that the account dimension for all products includes an account type and number. We include these in an account dimension with our core schema. However, some attributes are specific to particular account types. A savings account includes an interest rate, and a certificate of deposit includes a term. These attributes are placed in custom account dimensions to accompany the custom fact tables.

In other cases, heterogeneous products may require custom dimensions, but not custom fact tables. In Chapter 2, "Sales," we will see that a department store tracks a different set of product attributes within each department. A core dimension is used when querying across product categories, while custom dimensions can be used when limiting queries to a single category. There is no need for multiple fact tables, because the measurements are always the same.

Snapshot and Transaction

It is often necessary to construct multiple fact tables to monitor a single process because of the nature of the questions asked. Financial data warehouses often exhibit such requirements. In these cases, there is likely to be two kinds of questions. The first set of questions centers around the transactions that affect a given account or liability during a certain period of time. For example, "What were the total new billings for commercial customers this month?" or, "How much was spent under the office supplies budget line?" In each case, the question requires summarizing transactions that took place during a given month. These questions are answered by a fact table that represents monthly activity as a series of transactions.

A second set of questions calls for the status of individual accounts. For example, "How much remains in our office supply budget line?" or, "What are the outstanding receivables for commercial customers?" These questions require the net balance of all transactions leading up to a particular point in time. While this information can often be calculated from a transaction model, a status model serves more readily.

In this book, we will observe several business processes subject to this dual view. One set of questions deals with the individual transactions that impact the status, the other with the status as impacted by transactions. In these cases, two fact tables are built for the same business process. Transaction models are typically clean and powerful, and usually built first. Status models are subject to the dangers of semi-additivity, and must violate the sparsity guideline in the name of completeness. These nuances will be outlined in Chapter 8, "Budgets and Spending."

Coverage

Usually built to facilitate measurement of business processes, fact tables often fail to record important information when events do not trigger creation of a row. Consider our Orders schema: The fact table represents the intersection of each dimension, including customer, salesperson, and time, but rows are only included in the fact table when there is an order. This means that if a salesperson fails to take an order from a customer in his or her territory, there is no representation of the assignment of that salesperson to that customer.

What is needed here is a way to record the relationship of the sales force to customers over time. Because it represents the intersection of various dimensions, we construct a table that contains foreign keys to customer, date, and salesperson. While there is no measure in it, this table bears other hallmarks of a fact table: It contains foreign keys to various dimensions, and its own key is a concatenation of these foreign keys. We refer to this table as a *coverage table*.

Although part of the same business process as order_facts, the coverage table is best represented separately. It involves a different set of dimensions—product is not included. It is also measured at different times, sampled daily rather than each time an order occurs. As we've already seen, there are good reasons why these characteristics signal the need for separate fact tables. The coverage table is a form of factless fact table, because it contains no measures. Note that not all factless fact tables are coverage tables; some record actual events, such as an employee reporting for work, or a student attending a class.

Aggregation

The final situation in which multiple fact tables are built for a single business process involves precalculated summaries. As a fact table gets very large, query performance will begin to degrade. This situation is often addressed through hardware upgrades and database tuning; however, tremendous benefits can be reaped simply by summarizing existing fact tables. Enter the *aggregate table*.

Analysis of the queries against our orders schema might reveal that a large percentage of queries do not require particular dates or sales representatives. The performance of these queries can be significantly boosted by precalculating our measures summarized at a monthly and regional level. The resultant aggregate table will be much smaller, and therefore able to answer many of the same questions much faster than the original *base fact table*. Figure 1.4 shows the aggregate fact table order_facts_agg_by_month.

The aggregate table contains the same measures as the base fact table, but they are recorded at a different grain. Order_facts_agg_by_month table represents orders by customer, product, month, and region, as opposed to orders at the order_line level of detail. As a result, the degenerate dimensions order_number and order_line_number are no longer present. The foreign key to date has been replaced by a foreign key to month table, and the foreign key for salesperson has been replaced by a foreign key to sales_region. We refer to these new dimension tables as *dimensional rollups*.

Because it involves partially summarizing all measures across two dimensions, date and salesperson, this aggregate table is referred to as a *two-way* aggregate. Aggregates may summarize across any number of dimensions, either partially or completely. For a base fact table, there may be a wide variety of useful aggregates.

The key to successful deployment of aggregate tables is their invisibility. Because there are likely to be many of them, and because the inventory of aggregates is likely to change over time, applications should not be written to query aggregates directly; otherwise, each change to the list of available aggregates will require a rewrite of the application. Instead, applications are set up to query the base fact table. An aggregate navigator is deployed, armed with information about the various aggregates that

Figure 1.4 An aggregate table.

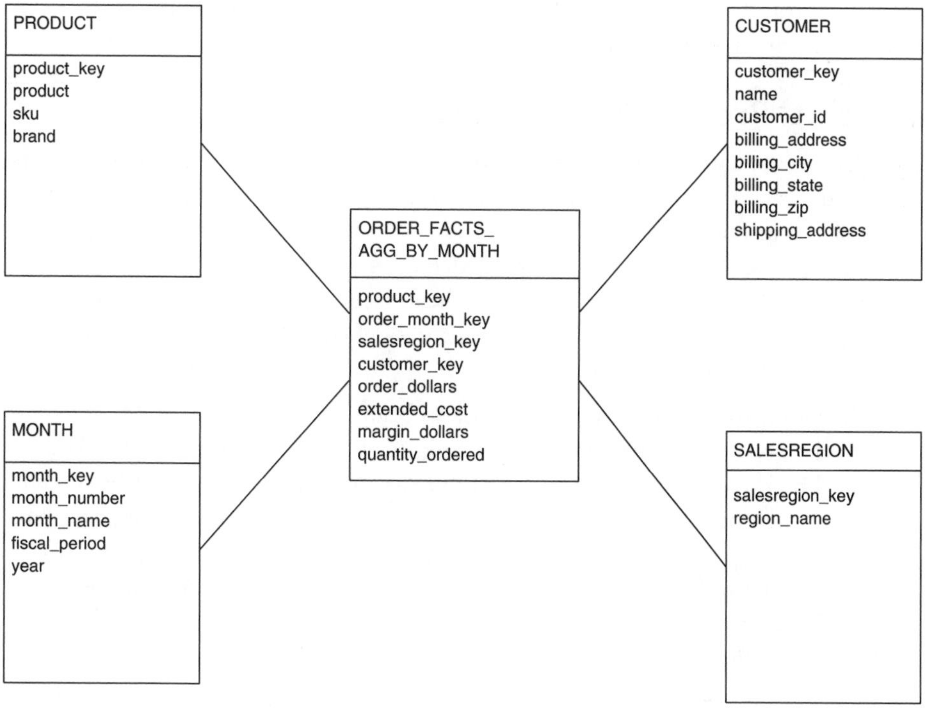

summarize fact tables. The aggregate navigator intercepts all SQL generated by an application, and adjusts it when an aggregate table can be used.

Aggregate navigators are deployed in a number of ways. Deployed as an intermediate tier between an application and a database, the aggregate navigator can deliver benefit to multiple applications simultaneously. Some database vendors have begun to incorporate the aggregate navigator directly into the RDBMS, which also benefits any application, with the added advantage that native database drivers can be used. Finally, some query and reporting tool vendors have added aggregate navigation functionality to their products. While useful, this form of aggregate navigation only serves the tool in question, and not any other applications that are used to query the data warehouse.

The Enterprise Data Warehouse

We have looked at a variety of factors that lead to the construction of multiple star schemas. If well designed, each schema does an excellent job in answering business questions focused on a particular process, but there are many business questions that cross process boundaries. In order to answer these questions, each star schema must be designed to work well with the others. This does not require a massive project to build the entire data warehouse at one time, but it does necessitate some initial planning.

Crossing Process Boundaries

Consider our appliance manufacturer, who has implemented the orders and shipments schemas depicted in Figure 1.3. A manager asks, "By product, what percentage of orders placed in January have shipped?" To figure out the percentage of orders shipped, we need to compare quantity_ordered with quantity_shipped. These measures are stored in order_facts and shipment_facts, respectively. Because it crosses process boundaries, we refer to the process of combining information from multiple fact tables as *drilling across*.

When a business question crosses process boundaries, there must be a linkage between the processes. This relationship can always be found in the dimensions referenced by the question. In the case of our manufacturer's question, the dimensions that touch both subject areas are product and date_ordered. Because we can capture quantity_ordered by product for a date_ordered, as well as capture quantity_shipped by product for the same date_ordered, we can link the two measures together. In Chapter 13, "Presenting Information," we will explore the mechanics involved in drilling across.

When there is no compatibility of dimensions across subject areas, we say that the dimensions are not *conformed*. Lack of conformed dimensions prevents us from answering questions that span subject areas. Suppose that we capture inventory levels on a weekly basis, and sales on a monthly basis. We can easily answer questions about sales, or questions about inventory; however, weeks do not roll up evenly into months, so we cannot answer questions that compare sales with inventory. Similarly, our appliance manufacturer might face problems if Product or Customer was defined differently within each schema.

Plan a Data Warehouse, Build a Data Mart

Organizations are often tempted to take their first steps into the world of data warehousing by designing and building a star schema focused on a particular process. This approach may be successful in the short term, but can lead to future problems. In the absence of an overall plan, it is likely that subsequent schemas will be introduced that do not conform with the first. Each useful in its own right, the schemas fail to answer questions that cross process boundaries. At the same time, there are likely to be redundant data load processes, incompatible technologies, and inefficient use of resources. Many industry analysts have wrongly attributed these problems to the data mart concept; in fact, they are failures in approach.

Long-term problems can be avoided through initial planning. Before the construction of the first star schema, it is important to consider all the business processes that will ultimately be addressed by the data warehouse. Each business process is identified, the grain is set for each fact table, and dimensions are carefully planned so that they conform across subject areas. This planning does not require a massive, long-term project. It can usually be accomplished in several weeks. We will discuss the process in detail in Chapter 14, "Building an Enterprise Data Warehouse."

Once the overall structure of the data warehouse is planned, it can be implemented incrementally, one subject area at a time. We refer to each subject area as a *data mart*; we refer to the set of interlocking data marts as the *data warehouse*. A data mart usually consists of a single fact table and its associated dimensions. Examples include the Orders and Shipments subject areas discussed in this chapter. Sometimes, a subject area requires multiple fact tables, as we will encounter in Chapters 8 and 10.

The benefits of planning the data warehouse are not evident until multiple data marts have been implemented. As each new data mart is brought on line, the business can answer questions about the new subject area. At the same time, additional questions can be answered that cross process boundaries. Because the data warehouse has been planned, its value is greater than the sum of the individual data marts.

Summing Up Dimensional Modeling Principles

Throughout this book, we will develop data warehouse design solutions for a series of businesses. The principles of dimensional modeling allow us to develop designs that address the business needs and can be used to produce reports answering business questions. Here is a quick summary of all the terms we have introduced in this chapter.

Online transaction systems, or OLTP systems, capture individual events and the detail that surrounds them. OLTP systems are usually designed following principles of normalization. They excel at answering questions about individual events, but are difficult to use to answer questions about business processes. These questions require aggregating transactions.

Data warehouses are designed to answer questions about business processes—questions that require aggregation of a large number of events. Dimensional modeling principles are used to ensure that the data warehouse reflects the way people think about the business.

Dimensional modeling is a means of representing the indicators of importance to a business, and the attributes by which these indicators are viewed. The indicators are referred to as *facts* or *measures*, and the parameters by which these measures are viewed are referred to as *dimensions*. The dimensional model can also be used as a database design, for implementation using relational technology.

Measures, sometimes referred to as *facts*, are indicators used by the business to evaluate a process.

Dimensions are descriptive values by which measures are "broken out," or "filtered." Because the same word is often used to describe a table that holds dimensions, we will sometimes refer to a dimension more specifically as a dimension *attribute*. In a report, dimension detail is usually placed in the columns farthest to the left, earning them the nickname "row headers." Dimensions are also the source of constraints on a business question.

Star schema. When representing a database design, the dimensional model is referred to as a *star schema*. Measures are stored in a fact table, and dimensions are stored in dimension tables. In conjunction with SQL, the star schema format allows any measure to be viewed in combination with any dimension.

Dimension tables are wide. They are not normalized. Their attributes may be only loosely related, and any hierarchies are flattened out. Each dimension table has a single, system-generated primary key. Keys from source systems are never used as keys in dimension tables, though they may appear as dimension attributes.

Slowly changing dimensions. The things described by rows in dimension tables change over time. There are three techniques that can be used to deal with these slowly changing dimensions. An example is the change of address of a customer. Most of the time, the data warehouse must preserve the description of a dimension at the time a measurement is taken, as well as capturing the new description when a new measurement is taken.

The **fact table** records measures at the intersection of a set of dimension values. In addition to measures, each fact table row contains foreign keys referring to particular rows in each of the dimension tables, and degenerate dimensions. Fact tables are usually sparse and very large. The primary key of a fact table is a multipart key including some subset of the dimension keys and degenerate dimensions.

Grain is the level of detail at which each row in a fact table is recorded. A grain statement may refer to an artifact of the business process, such as "orders at the order line level," or the grain may be defined as a relationship to key dimensions, as in "orders by product, date, customer, and time." Note that there may be dimensions that do not determine the grain of the fact table.

Additivity. The ability to roll up a measure across dimensions is referred to as *additivity*. Fully additive measures can easily be rolled up by summing them. Some measures, notably ratios, are nonadditive, meaning that they cannot be rolled up by summing them. These measures can usually be broken down into components that are fully additive. The additive components are stored in the fact table. A third type of measure can be summed across some dimensions, but not others. These semi-additive measures can be stored in the fact table, but special care must be taken when using them.

Degenerate dimension. A dimension that is stored in the fact table rather than a dimension table is referred to as a *degenerate* dimension. Degenerate dimensions commonly contain identification numbers of documents or transactions, such as an invoice number, an order number, or a transaction ID.

Measures are divided among **multiple fact tables** for a variety of reasons:

> Multiple fact tables are required when measures describe **different business processes**—collected at a different grain and at different intervals.

> Measures are divided among **core and custom fact tables** when a dimension value determines the measurement to be taken.

> Some measures, especially dollar values, are recorded in **snapshot and transaction tables** when the business requires looking at changes over time, as well as a level at a point in time.

> **Coverage tables** record inactivity that is not otherwise measured by a fact table.

> **Aggregate tables** are fact tables that summarize other fact tables. They are used to improve performance of the data warehouse.

Drilling Across. The answers to some business questions require combining information from multiple fact tables. The process of answering these questions is referred to as *drilling across*. To drill across, there must be equivalent dimensions that can be used to relate the measures from the fact tables. Called *conformed dimensions*, they must be equivalent, or one must be a subset of the other.

Planning. The data warehouse is an interlocking set of star schemas. It is not necessary to build the entire data warehouse at one time, but it must be carefully planned before work can begin within the first subject area. Among the major components of the plan are identification of the business processes, grains of the fact tables, and conformed dimensions.

Implementation. After it has been planned, the data warehouse can be implemented one subject area at a time. Each subject area is referred to as a *data mart*, and consists of one or more of the star schemas that have been planned. Data marts that are not implemented as part of a larger plan can be successful in the short term, but exhibit limitations in the long term.

Now that we have gotten the terminology of dimensional modeling out of the way, we will use it to develop solutions in a number of business areas.

SALES

2

S ales drive business. The clearest barometer of business growth is product or
service revenue. While profit is important, there is no profit unless there is a
sale. Sales results affect pricing decisions, marketing plans, and the stock
price of public companies.

Because this section is all about managing customers, the sales process is the
natural starting point. A sales transaction is the event that transforms a prospect
into a customer. It is the fundamental transaction in the business. Today, businesses manage the sales process in many ways. Building a data warehouse to support the sales subject area requires an understanding of the type of business, the
sales cycle, and how the sales process relates to marketing and pricing decisions.

In this chapter, we will examine three businesses with different needs in a
sales data warehouse. We will look at the sales organization, identify analytical
requirements, and propose data warehouse designs to meet those requirements.

Direct versus Indirect Sales?

The first step in understanding sales is recognizing how a business sells its products. Imagine a product, a company, and a customer. A customer looking for a
product must find someone who sells it. Likewise, a producer must find effective
sales channels for the product. As consumers, we make hundreds of retail purchases each year, but rarely do we purchase goods directly from the producer. The
seller is often a merchant acting as a sales agent for the producer. Some merchants
purchase goods at wholesale prices and then mark up the price for retail sale.
Other merchants act purely as agents, holding no merchandise inventory. Service
sales agents often act in this manner. Insurance agents do not purchase wholesale
life insurance to then resell; they instead represent many different companies and
their respective products.

The relationship between merchants and producers must be considered in designing the sales data warehouse. For example, purchasing clothing at a department store is usually a customer/merchant relationship. Ignoring store brands, department stores usually sell goods manufactured by other companies. We purchase cars in a similar manner. The car dealer acts as a sales agent for the manufacturer, often representing more than one manufacturer at a single location. But like a department store, the dealer must prepurchase inventory from the manufacturer. From the perspective of the producer of the clothing or the car, the relationship with the consumer is *indirect*.

The opposite approach is to sell a product directly to the end consumer, known as *direct sales*. A large database vendor will employ a large direct sales force to penetrate a vast customer base. Banks sell lines of credit, commercial loans, and mortgages directly to businesses and consumers. Direct sales organizations are interested in managing the performance of their internal sales assets.

Key Business Terms

Indirect sales. Transactions that are, from the perspective of the producer of the goods, sold through a channel other than the producer's internal staff.

For example, manufacturers often use independent sales representatives to sell products. Movie production companies sell their products through theaters, video stores, and pay-per-view systems.

Direct sales. Transactions that are, from the perspective of the producer of the goods, sold directly to the end consumer. For example, health club memberships are normally sold directly to a consumer by health club representatives. Household services, such as plumbing or electrical repairs, are normally sold directly by the company providing the service.

The seller/customer relationship varies by industry. Some industries use both indirect and direct sales to move products. In this chapter, we will examine two companies that use different sales techniques, and one that acts only as a merchant. The companies, their customers, and the sales methods are presented in Table 2.1.

Table 2.1 Various Sales Methods

Company	Customers	Sales Method
Automobile manufacturer	Consumers	Indirect sales through dealerships
Database software company	Corporations, government, consumers	Mix of internal direct sales force and indirect sales through resellers
Retail department store	Consumer	Direct seller of other companies' merchandise

In each case, the design of the sales data warehouse changes to adapt to the sales method. The automobile manufacturer monitors product sales and dealer performance, while the database software company balances direct and indirect efforts. The department store, as merchant, is concerned with overall sales and the optimal use of limited floor space and time.

Indirect Sales

The decision to use an indirect sales method is strategic. Indirect selling creates a partnership between a producer of goods or services and the agent who does the selling. The company that produces the product places an important business responsibility in the hands of an entity that it does not directly control. While the tradition has been in place for decades in some industries, companies must continually monitor and assess the benefits and costs of using an indirect sales strategy.

What is traditionally thought of as retail consumer sales is largely an indirect selling activity. Few of the goods sold in department and grocery stores are actually produced by the retailer. Even store brands are produced by secondary sources that also produce similar products under other brand names. For a food processing company, each retailer and store brand is a different channel for its products. For a large consumer goods company like Procter & Gamble or Frito-Lay, each retail chain is a channel for sales. The balance of power in the retail world is constantly shifting. Hot brands generate sales, while popular stores attract customers. Most retailers have incredible clout with producers and charge for shelf space. Some producers have brands that are powerful enough to demand free shelf space and preferential placement. The amount of money made by the retailer on a specific product is dynamically determined by its ability to negotiate the lowest wholesale price from the producer, while selling at the highest price tolerated by the public.

Other channel arrangements are more structured, with predefined pricing and commission structures, quotas, and other terms. Automobile dealers, software resellers, travel agents, and insurance agents all operate within a more restrictive environment than normal retailers. The channel has a more structured relationship with the producer, and both sides make investments in the relationship. These investments may include franchise fees, employee training, shared advertising costs, or investments in technology. The role of the sales channel in these cases is different than in a retail relationship. The channel partner is more of an advocate for the product and, in some instances, is totally dependent on a single producer for success.

Today, companies are carefully examining their indirect channels. While often a good way to reduce costs and introduce new products, technology has enabled some companies to discard or reduce their dependence on channels. Many insurance companies have moved away from agent channels, preferring to sell over the phone or Internet directly to the consumer. Travel agents face continuing commission cuts and efforts by airlines to divert travelers to Internet-based reservation systems. In this environment, the cost and effectiveness of indirect sales channels are critical business issues.

Car Sales Are Up!

The sales subject area for an automobile manufacturer may seem simple at first. News reports describing the latest uptick or downturn in sales at the Big Three are familiar. What kind of analytical needs would an automobile manufacturer have beyond these simple reports? Obviously, the automaker is first concerned with how each model is selling, and what flavors of that model sell best. Time and product dimensions are standard components of any sales data warehouse design. The content of the time dimension includes the time key, month, day, date, year, day of week, and quarter. A rich time dimension gives flexibility in reporting.

The product dimension includes a product key, the model, color, make, and year for each car. But what other characteristics of an automotive product might be important? When designing the product dimension, include the discriminators used to differentiate the product in the marketplace.

Key Business Term

Discriminators. Descriptive characteristics of a product that further describe it and are relevant to purchasing decisions.

Discriminators for a men's suit would include cloth, color, style/cut, weight, and size. They can be used in business analysis to better understand what moves merchandise. Automobiles have a different set of discriminators than clothing. Tracking discriminators allows the business analyst to monitor performance of various product styles, influencing production and marketing plans.

Discriminators in service industries are equally important. A bank offering a variety of checking account plans should track the characteristics of each plan in the product dimension. An insurer will carry attributes describing variations of coverage within specific lines of business. In fact, service industries are adept at creating and altering product lines in response to markets. Without the constraints of a typical manufacturer, the service business can assess the marketplace and fill gaps with new product lines. The availability of rich, descriptive, product performance data is crucial.

These attributes should relate to factors in the consumer's buying decision. Identifying industry-specific product attributes creates an effective sales data warehouse. Read the following quotation from a sales analyst for a large automaker. Identify the additional attributes for the product dimension. Are other dimensions and attributes suggested by the quotation?

> *We have been watching our category sales drop significantly for trucks. We are at the end of the model life for both light- and medium-duty pickups. Minivans continue to drive our sales, and they are our most profitable product line. We are considering a dealer credit for last quarter based on minivan sales volume, but I need to cost it out first.*
>
> *Also, our finance division is complaining that the lease terms we introduced in September are unprofitable. I need to know if dealers are simply shifting customers to leases to simplify their sales efforts. These leases were unadvertised and dealers were only supposed to use them as a last resort to close a customer.*

Several additional attributes are apparent. First, there are categories for products, two of which are minivans and trucks. Also note the reference to light- and medium-duty pickup trucks. It is important to understand the nuances of a particular customer's product dimension before finalizing the design. In this case, there is an intermediate grouping between category and model, referred to as *line*. Sample rows from the first-cut product dimension might look something like Table 2.2.

The sales analyst is interested in more than just how many pickup trucks are sold each month. Demographic data about customers is also mentioned. This information is tracked in a customer demographic dimension, grouping customers by different combinations of age, gender, income, and geography. This dimension does not require a row for each customer; rather, each sales transaction is related to a demographic row that describes the purchaser. The degree of demographic segmentation, and the resulting customer demographic dimension, varies by industry.

The dealer dimension is included to manage the primary sales channel. A long time institution in the U.S. auto market, the auto dealer is a key part of the automakers' business model. Some automakers are trying to reengineer dealer networks, removing poor performers and thinning out geographic territories. This strategy is often complicated by the original franchise agreements that created the dealer/manufacturer relationship. Automakers clearly need data on dealer performance to optimize sales and make decisions on which dealers should be eased out of business.

Table 2.2 The Product Dimension

Product Key	Model Name	Model Styling Package	Line	Category	Exterior Color	Model Year	Interior Color
1	Laredo	Silverado	Light duty	Truck	Red	1997	Tan
2	Laredo	Standard	Light duty	Truck	Red	1997	Tan
3	Laredo	Terra Luna	Light duty	Truck	Red	1997	Tan

Another important requirement is the method of payment. An automobile is a large purchase for most consumers, and loans and leases are commonly used to reduce the initial cash outlay when buying a new vehicle. The availability of favorable financing and lease terms is a popular way to generate sales. In our example, the company offered leases only as a last-ditch customer incentive to close the wavering buyer. The analyst suspects that some dealers are using the leases before trying standard, more profitable financing options.

Our first-cut, simple star schema design would look something like Figure 2.1.

The grain of our fact table is the sale of an individual vehicle to a customer. The fact table contains only the dimension foreign keys and facts about the sale of each vehicle. The actual sales price, MSRP base price, options price, dealer add-ons, full price, dealer credits, dealer invoice, and down payment amount are all recorded.

Our sales fact table contents are summarized in Table 2.3.

Table 2.3 Measures for the Sales Fact Table

Fact	Meaning	Source
Actual sales price	The amount of money paid by the customer to the dealer for the vehicle. This includes any amount received via a finance agency.	Dealer sales reporting system.
MSRP base price	The base price for the model, style, and line sold.	Manufacturer's internal price listings.
Options price	The price of manufacturer options that are added to the MSRP base price to determine full manufacturer price.	Manufacturer's option price listing.
Dealer add-ons	The price of dealer add-ons, such as undercoating, aftermarket stereos, floor mats, and other trinkets.	Dealer sales reporting system. Dealers may be reluctant to provide this information to the manufacturer.

Continues

Table 2.3 Measures for the Sales Fact Table *Continued*

Fact	Meaning	Source
MSRP full price	The sum of the MSRP base price and the options price. Represents the best price the manufacturer could expect.	Derived at loading from other data.
Dealer credits	The sum of various credits provided to the dealer for various reasons.	Various, including marketing department information and accounting system data.
Dealer invoice	The amount paid at invoice by the dealer, before applying credits. Includes the cost of options.	Dealer invoicing system.
Down payment	The cash provided by the customer to the dealer at the time of purchase.	Dealer sales reporting system.
Manufacturer proceeds	The amount of money the manufacturer received as a result of the sale. In our design, the dealer invoice less dealer credits.	The actual manner of deriving this fact is dependent on the manufacturer/dealer relationship.
Dealer proceeds	The amount of money the dealer receives from the sale. In our design, the sales price less dealer invoice plus dealer credits.	As in manufacturer proceeds, the dealer proceeds will depend on the relationship.

Note that many measures are related. Dealer and manufacturer proceeds are derived from other attributes. These relationships are best understood by examining the steps in the process of selling the vehicle.

1. The dealer takes delivery of a vehicle and is invoiced by the manufacturer. This step establishes the dealer invoice, the MSRP base price, and the options price.

2. Either prior to or concurrent with a sale, the dealer adds on other revenue-generating items. The traditional items, like floor mats and cell phones, are obvious. Extended service contracts not sponsored by the

Figure 2.1 The automaker sales schema.

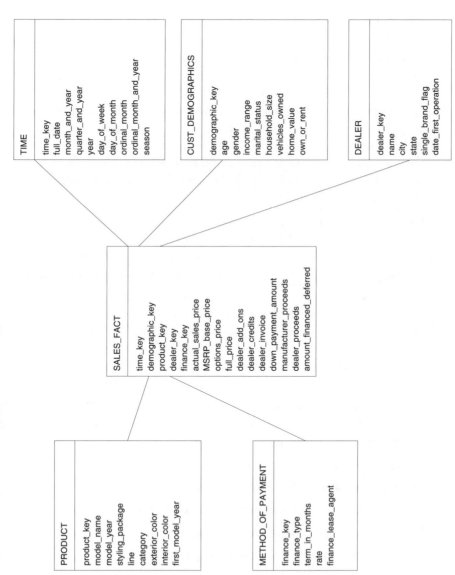

manufacturer are another possibility. These dealer add-ons differ from options because the revenue goes directly to the dealer.

3. The sale is completed. The customer either pays cash, finances the vehicle, or leases the vehicle. The actual sales price is determined from this transaction, as is the down payment. The down payment can apply to a lease or finance transaction. For a cash transaction, it equals the actual sales price.

4. Finally, the dealer receives incentive payments from the manufacturer at various times. It is common for factory incentives to be paid to the dealer for meeting sales goals, moving stagnant models, or underselling a competitor's model. These amounts are represented as dealer credits in our design. The source for dealer credits is likely to be different from the dealer sales system. These credits may be applied or awarded after a given period of time and recorded in the auto manufacturer's financial system. The complexity of loading this data may preclude its population in the periodic load stream used for the rest of the fact table.

With all these facts in place we can calculate our two additional and important facts, dealer proceeds and manufacturer proceeds. Alternately, we could store just the component attributes for each fact. The savings in storage, assuming each would require 2 bytes for storage and a 10,000,000 row fact table, would be around 39 megabytes.

But there is a price to pay for not storing a commonly used, derived fact. Dealer and manufacture proceeds must now be calculated in reports and queries as required. We must remember how to calculate it correctly each time we develop a report. The calculation itself requires a good understanding of the business, and we must teach ad hoc query formulators how to do it.

It is safe to assume that these are key measures, since they represent the split of transaction spoils between merchant and producer. Cutting the redundant measures from our design results in the following:

• Makes development of reports more complex

• Increases the potential for errors in reports

• Increases what we must document and teach to business users

• Limits the capabilities of ad hoc access to the database

• Saves a hundred dollars' worth of disk space

The costs clearly outweigh the benefits. This issue is a hard one for developers accustomed to designing transaction systems. In the name of simplicity and ease of use, we must overcome the urge to eliminate redundancy.

In addition to noting how some measures relate, we must provided explicit definitions for each. Producing a table like this one is an important task during the design of a data mart. The information is significant, both for the business users who will ultimately use the system, and for the developers who will be charged with loading the data into it.

TIP

There should never be any doubt about the precise meaning of any measure in the fact table. Each should be explicitly defined, in terms of what it means, how it is calculated, and how it relates to other measures.

Ambiguity can lead to trouble. Margin, for example, is often calculated in many different ways within a single organization. In a sales system, it may incorporate only the cost of the items sold, while financial planners may produce complex activity-based costs. If it is not clear which calculation is used within the data mart, assumptions of business users and data loaders may differ.

Also remember that if a measure is not what the business person expects, it is wrong. The failure is *never* in the business person's interpretation of the data mart, but in the team's presentation of the data and education practices. The onus is on the developers to prevent misunderstandings.

The method of payment dimension includes the type of payment used by the customer: cash, finance, or lease. Cash transactions are straightforward, but finance and lease sales require that we record additional attributes. We include the attributes term, rate, and finance/lease agent to further describe these types of transactions.

There are some obvious challenges in loading our data warehouse. Examining the dealer sales reporting system would identify how much of the data is collected and reported electronically. Combining information from the dealer reporting system with internal production systems would probably give us the needed product information. The Vehicle Identification Number (VIN) should be common among our transaction systems.

Demographic data will be more difficult. Our first line of defense in gathering this data is the dealer. We must discover if the dealer collects the demographic data we are seeking at the time of transaction. If not, we are left with historical transactions for which no information is available, regardless of any future collection demands we make on the dealers.

We do have some options for historical data. The most obvious is to canvas, via mail or telephone, past buyers. This will cost money, and compliance from customers is not assured. An alternative is to provide customer lists to a householding agency that can associate the names with various demographic attributes. We can then correlate these indicators with the customers and their past transactions to create our demographic dimension.

Answering the Sales Analyst's Questions

From our completed design, we can answer many questions. The first two questions are derived from the sales analyst's comments gathered in our earlier interview:

1. What is the cost of a post facto dealer incentive of $200 per minivan sale over the last three months? The incentive is only offered to dealers whose minivan sales are over 80 units for the quarter, or whose minivan sales have increased at least 25 percent over the previous quarter?

2. Since September, what dealers have the highest percentage of lease transactions?

The first question is answered by the data presented in Report 2.1. Using the parameters "sales greater than 80 units," or "quarterly minivan sales increase >= 25%," we retrieve the eligible dealers, units sold, and a derived column equal to units sold × $200.

Report 2.1 Planning for incentives.

Dealer Credit Analysis for Minivan Sales
(80 units sold or 25% quarterly increase)
Q3 1997

Dealer	Units Sold Q3	Sales Increase (Q2 to Q3)	Projected Incentive
Allenville	128	12%	$25,600
Buena Loco	67	35%	$13,400
Costa Mesa	120	17%	$24,000
Dillard Duncan	45	28%	$9,000
Franklin City	89	22%	$17,800
Hendersonville	91	11%	$18,200
Mishockton	77	48%	$15,400
San Leandro	81	19%	$16,200
Titusville	56	31%	$11,200
Total Incentive Cost			$150,800

This report is simple to produce and provides a framework for analyzing the incentive. The user may change the parameters of the query or adjust the incentive amount to adjust the cost. It is not, however, the end of the exercise for the business analyst. The cost of the incentive should be weighed against the overall budget for incentives. The impact on vehicle profitability must be assessed as well. Will the incentive effectively increase future sales? Is the incentive amount enough to motivate dealers? A single subject area data mart can provide a great deal of additional information for the business user. This new-found wealth of information does not obviate the need for creative, critical business analysis. It may even trigger additional information needs, increasing the demands on it.

Report 2.2 is an attempt to answer the second question. It calculates the distribution of sales by financing/deal type: cash, finance, or lease. Ordering by the percentage of lease deals highlights those dealers that may be overly reliant on the incentive program.

However, this first analytical step is incomplete. Remember that the sales analyst is interested in unprofitable lease terms introduced since September. This report simply shows that some dealers have a higher percentage of leases than others. A better analytical question is, "What dealers have shown an increased proportion of lease transactions since September?" This question and the data shown in Report 2.3 are more valuable in finding out which dealers may be shifting deals to leases.

It is possible to chart or otherwise obfuscate this data. Other than a simple line chart, it is difficult to present a clearer picture of what is happening. Column and bar charts representing the same data are unappealing. Any visual lift is lost in the "busy-ness" of the chart. This simple matrix allows the analyst to easily

Report 2.2 Abusing the lease incentive.

Distribution of Sales by Financing/Deal Type for All Dealers
July–December 1997

Dealer	Lease	Finance	Cash
San Leandro	49%	45%	6%
Villa Hills	39%	51%	10%
Mountain View	38%	56%	6%
Bayside	31%	68%	1%
Millers	28%	60%	12%
Miejo Robbins	26%	53%	21%
Cheviot	20%	76%	4%

Report 2.3 Fine-tuning the lease incentive analysis.

Leases as a Percentage of All Transactions by Dealer
August–December 1997

Dealer	Aug	Sept	Oct	Nov	Dec
San Leandro	22%	27%	35%	51%	55%
Cheviot	20%	21%	19%	16%	19%
Millers	21%	33%	28%	31%	29%
Bayside	12%	33%	31%	27%	40%
Mountain View	31%	27%	31%	28%	33%
Villa Hills	21%	24%	34%	46%	61%
Miejo Robbins	24%	41%	36%	24%	28%

track the performance of each dealer in the months since the leases were introduced. It may be time for phone calls to San Leandro, Bayside, and Villa Hills.

Understanding Direct Sales

The previous discussion introduced the use of an indirect channel, automobile dealers, to sell a high-cost product. The solution we designed allowed analysis of both dealer and product performance in the sales process. Automobile manufacturers push the bulk of their product through this channel. The dealer engages in active, direct selling with individuals who visit the dealership. The automaker is challenged with managing the dealer relationship.

There is a subtlety in dividing direct, active selling from passive, demand-driven selling. The automobile industry uses advertising and brand loyalty to create demand; however, once the prospect enters a dealership, the dealer's direct sales process takes over. This last stage of active selling makes car buying stressful for most people. By removing themselves from the negotiating process, automakers are insulated from any associated ill will. Owners who love their new cars but hate the dealer are quite common.

Other businesses cannot avoid one-on-one customer selling. Some do so to reduce risk. Banks sell commercial lines of credit and business loans directly to ensure the customer is worthy of the credit being offered. The interaction between the loan officer and management gives the bank a better feeling for the company, its operations, and the legitimacy of its business plan.

Other businesses use a direct sales force to ensure maximum revenue from large accounts. This applies when the actual use of the product in an organization is difficult to quantify. Consultative sales techniques are used to size up the account and sell in as much product or service as possible. The knowledge gained by a loyal, commissioned direct sales representative is a key tool in maximizing revenue.

This is a primary reason why your database software vendor probably relies on direct sales. The prospective value of large customer accounts demands a direct sales approach. A single large corporate account can lead to millions of dollars in revenue. The dynamics of such large transactions require an intimate understanding of businesses needs, decision-maker motivations, budgets, and purchasing cycles. However, database vendors normally supplement their direct sales effort with indirect sales via resellers. Resellers provide a low-cost alternative channel for products. They are used to cover less lucrative accounts that do not attract the organization's best account managers. This hybrid of direct selling and reselling complicates the sales data mart for any large software organization.

Software Sales

Imagine an organization that sells complex database software, competing against Oracle, Sybase, Informix, Microsoft, and IBM for database dollars. A sophisticated direct sales effort is supplemented by resellers. Measuring performance against quarterly plans is increasingly complex. Software product lines are constantly in flux. New versions are marketed ahead of availability, often slowing sales of existing lines while customers await the latest innovation. This lucrative, high-stress business attracts some very demanding sales professionals.

Once assigned to the Sales data warehouse project, the most intimidating task is meeting the sales end users. Salespeople have a reputation, deserved or not, for being somewhat aggressive. The best ones are disciplined, hard working, persistent, and always in a hurry. Getting time with a sales manager can be a challenge. Once there, knowing something about sales will make the meeting much more enjoyable. And rest assured, they will have plenty to say in the interview.

The most important difference between salespeople and the rest of us is compensation. Most direct sales people are paid a small base salary. This base salary is not enough to live on, since most salespeople are paying off fancy cars and big mortgages. They must sell to avoid impending financial collapse. When they sell, they earn commission on the amount of the sale. This environment requires constant, accurate, timely sales reports. Compensation is almost always driven by making a quarterly quota.

A large database software company, with a large sales force, alternate sales channels, and an evolving product line, can benefit from a straightforward data warehouse design. The vice president of Sales might express the following concerns:

> *The biggest grief I face each quarter is a lack of consistent, timely information. The federal sales reps still submit sales reports to the old orders system. The commercial reps use the new automated sales order system integrated with our receivables package.*
>
> *Also, my channels market is a mess. Channel sales are recorded in the receivables module also, but that doesn't mean we can realize the revenue. That's because the reseller pre-buys the software at discount from us, then sells it. But how much they project to sell and how much we eventually ship is a different number. The reseller transaction is entered in the old orders system, but can't be counted as a sale until I know the end customer. In the end, I have three different views of sales, with lots of quality spreadsheet time for my regional managers.*

The current solution clearly fails to meet the sales executive's need for timeliness and completeness.

Different Sources, Inadequate Systems

The vice president of Sales has been victimized by the evolving sales environment. Within his own organization, two different reporting mechanisms are in place. Ideally, everyone would use the same internal sales system, but even powerful executives can be thwarted by entrenched habits and systems. The reseller issue is even more complex. Channel sales are recorded first as a sale in the old orders system. These transactions cannot be counted as revenue until an end customer is identified, probably when a shipping order is received from the reseller.

With sales transactions collected in different systems, the integration of information from the operational environment is an arduous task. It is easy to imagine an administrative assistant to the Sales VP running reports on the sales tracking system and the accounting system, cutting and pasting the data into a spreadsheet, and then formatting a report. Quarterly, the assistant would then merge the spreadsheets together, but adjustments and returns against previous months would not be included.

This process would be repeated throughout the sales organization. Regional managers, district managers, vertical industry managers, and channel managers all require periodic, unified sales data. Other people outside the sales organization would also be looking for this data. The executive team, product managers, product marketing managers, and finance are all chasing this unified sales data. Everyone wants to be able to slice it and dice it. It is easy to underestimate the market for a good data warehouse.

Designing the Direct Sales Data Warehouse

Reviewing the input of the vice president of Sales, and using our understanding of software sales, the following dimensions are identified:

Product. Including the product key, product name, version, operating system, date first offered, category (database, connectivity, utility, application development tools), supported/not supported. The license type and threshold are also included in our product definition. This supports recording server- and user-based licensing. Table 2.4 displays the representation of the basic information in this dimension for the RDBMS product.

This design allows some flexibility in mixing server- and user-based licenses for the various products, versions, and operating systems.

Customer. Including the customer key, name, market segment (Federal, Commercial, Higher Education, State/Local), vertical industry (Oil, Insurance, Banking, etc.), billing location, and shipping location.

Discount. A dimension to document discounts offered for direct sales. The type of discount is used to differentiate between list price deals and discount transactions. Examples might be end of year, end of quarter, vertical industry specific, market segment specific, or a combination of these elements.

Table 2.4 A Few Rows from the Product Dimension

Product Key	Name	Version Number	Operating System	License Type	Threshold
1	InterBase	3.7	NT	Server	1
2	InterBase	3.7	HP UX	Server	1
3	InterBase	3.7	Solaris	Server	1
4	InterBase	3.7	AIX	User	12
5	InterBase	3.7	AIX	User	24
6	InterBase	4.1	NT	Server	1

Channel. Including the channel key, channel type (Direct, Reseller, Value-Added Reseller, Hardware Preinstallation Reseller), vendor name, level (identifying classes of vendors, like Bronze, Silver, Gold), channel manager, region, address.

A **standard time dimension** containing any commonly used time attributes for this business.

The grain of the fact table is the sale of a product to a customer, essentially an order line item. We will include the list price, discount amount, actual sales price, and net proceeds for each product sale. A typical deal might include a relational database license, connectivity software, and a load utility. Each of these product sales transactions would be a separate row in our fact table. We will also include the degenerate order dimension, represented by order number, in the fact table.

The net proceeds attribute serves the same purpose as in our automaker example. Because the reseller buys the software from the company at a discount, the actual sales price is not always equal to net proceeds. Only direct sales, sold by the internal sales force, generate this amount. For reseller sales, the company only realizes the discounted price the reseller is obligated to pay on a sale to an end customer. For example, we may sell InterBase 4.5 for Solaris at a list price of $10,000 per server. We discount this price by 30 percent for resellers, allowing them to purchase the software for $7,000 and sell it to an end customer at whatever price they negotiate. If the reseller discounts 10 percent to the customer, selling the software for $9,000, the reseller pocket the $2,000 difference. This is the fundamental business transaction recorded by the fact table.

The issue of when to realize the revenue for a reseller's order of software is worth reviewing. Aggressive software companies often book revenue based on advance orders from resellers. The reseller is usually not required to pay for the software until it is sold to an end customer. Leftover inventory is carried forward for sale in the next quarter, or simply canceled. The entire process is conducted on paper, with no software shipped to the reseller. If the company producing the software records the total amount ordered to the reseller, it may be misstating results. This is not uncommon, and frequently results in a restatement of revenue. In our business, we will be conservative and only record a sale to a reseller when the reseller identifies the customer it was sold to and the price at which it was sold. Collecting this data may require some changes in what information we require of a reseller before physically shipping the product. Hopefully, they will oblige our needs in exchange for timely software delivery to their customers.

Our preliminary star schema is presented in Figure 2.2.

Figure 2.2 The software vendor's sales schema.

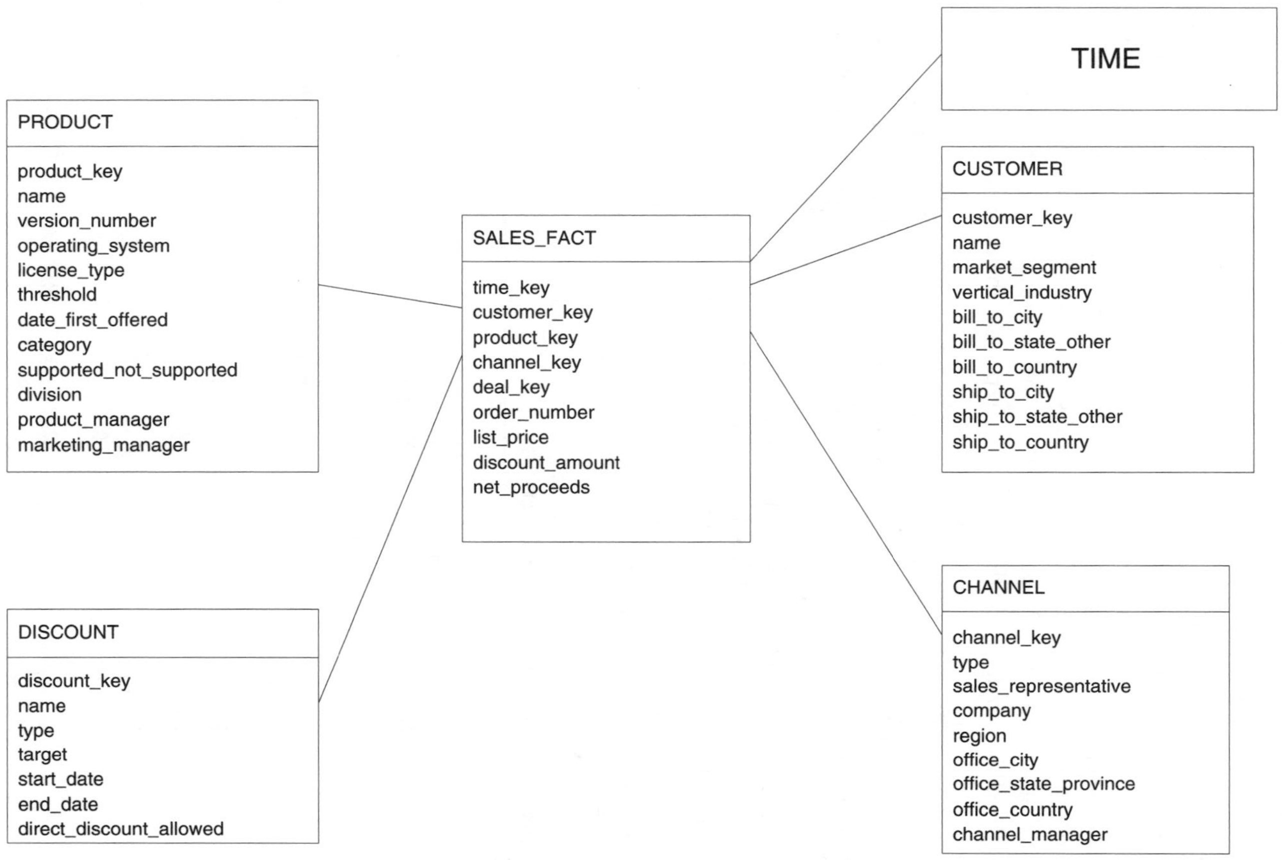

TIME

CUSTOMER
customer_key
name
market_segment
vertical_industry
bill_to_city
bill_to_state_other
bill_to_country
ship_to_city
ship_to_state_other
ship_to_country

CHANNEL
channel_key
type
sales_representative
company
region
office_city
office_state_province
office_country
channel_manager

SALES_FACT
time_key
customer_key
product_key
channel_key
deal_key
order_number
list_price
discount_amount
net_proceeds

PRODUCT
product_key
name
version_number
operating_system
license_type
threshold
date_first_offered
category
supported_not_supported
division
product_manager
marketing_manager

DISCOUNT
discount_key
name
type
target
start_date
end_date
direct_discount_allowed

How flexible is this design? The set of rows from the discount dimension depicted in Table 2.5 gives an idea of how this design supports the business.

The direct discount allowed column is not used to calculate the discount amount on each sales fact; it is the maximum discount allowed for a given promotion. For example, a sales representative could use the Aerospace discount to cut up to 25 percent off a sale, but may only need to give 18 percent to get the deal. Comparing the maximum discount to the actual discount given will identify strong negotiators and overly generous discount strategies. The 0-percent value in the first row and the 100-percent value in the last row are placeholders. Finally, the from and to dates for these two rows represent the earliest and latest transaction date from the sales fact table.

Essentially, the table records different discounts offered over the course of time. Although it is somewhat flexible, it attempts to provide structure to sales discounting. This structure may be arrived at by reviewing past discounting strategies and confirming that similar strategies are planned for the future. The first row is associated to sales where no promotion is applied. We can also use the sixth row to identify oddball sales in which an undefined discount was negotiated by the sales representative outside the scope of existing rules.

This is a simple discount design that could certainly be expanded. Discount dimensions and their cousins, the deal and promotion dimensions, are difficult to

Table 2.5 The Discount Dimension

Discount Key	Name	Type	Target	Start Date	Direct End Date	Discount Allowed
1	No discount	List	None	1/1/90	4/30/97	0%
2	Aerospace: end CY	Vertical	Aerospace	12/1/96	12/31/96	25%
3	Federal FY close	Segment	Federal	6/14/96	9/30/96	40%
4	End of quarter	Segment	Commercial	9/15/96	9/30/96	35%
5	SE region boost	Regional	Southeast	8/1/96	12/31/96	18%
6	Sales rep	Sales Rep	None	1/1/90	4/30/97	100%

generalize, varying widely among businesses. Promotion dimensions are discussed further in Chapter 3, "Marketing." The types of discounts offered and deals given vary by company, industry, and year. Also notice that the discount dimension does not include the product associated with the deal. That association occurs in the fact table.

Our channel dimension, depicted in Table 2.6, handles both the direct and reseller channels. This is accomplished by associating direct sales facts with an appropriate record in the channel dimension.

The Type column separates our direct internal sales force ("Direct") from the resellers. In this example, the first row represents a reseller in Atlanta managed by Roberts, a channel manager. The second row shows that Roberts also manages the SE region for direct sales, and the database company's name is shown in the company column. The third row represents an international reseller in the United Kingdom. Some readers may find their skin crawling with this loose handling of data, especially the mixed meaning of the Manager column. In this case, it works and is easily understood by the end user. While it may represent the merging of two columns properly normalized in the transaction world, in the data warehouse world it simplifies the design. The distinction between channel and internal sales manager can be made using the type dimension. We can look at Roberts's performance as a channel manager, regional manager, or both.

Answering the Sales VP's Questions

With the new design and an ad hoc query tool we can begin to answer some of the sales organization's concerns. First, time series reporting across many dimensions is possible. Reports at the corporate, regional, country, and state levels are easily generated. Product sales levels are obvious, as is channel performance data.

More specific concerns of the VP of sales can also be addressed. The first report, shown in Report 2.4, delivers the current and prior year-to-date sales for a specific product by market segment. The warehouse loading process creates a unified view of channels and direct data, which simplifies this type of report. Most of today's ad hoc tools support the ability to drill into this data interactively.

This report paints a clear picture of sales activity. A new version of the company's database product was released at some point in the prior year. The current year is the first full year of release and the response in most segments is strong. Only the federal market has been slow to adopt the new product. In fact, sales in that market are down across all versions. This drop-off would likely trigger additional action by the company.

Table 2.6 The Channel Dimension

Key	Type	Sales Rep.	Company	Rgn.	City	State	Ctry.	Channel or Sales Manager
1	Reseller	Franklin	USOFT	SE	Atlanta	GA	US	Roberts
2	Direct	Alpaugh	Interdata	SE	Atlanta	GA	US	Roberts
3	Reseller	Scallion	UKSOFT	UK	London	None	UK	Stevenson

Report 2.4 Market segment sales for InterBase.

InterBase Product Sales Report by Segment
as of 3/27/98

Segment	Version	YTD	Prior YTD	Change (%)
Commercial	3.7	312,991	540,628	–42%
	4.1	1,007,201	1,232,550	–18%
	4.5	2,121,609	219,899	865%
Federal	3.7	159,078	897,440	–82%
	4.1	412,873	528,962	–22%
	4.5	89,467	128,931	–31%
Higher education	3.7	41,784	7,120	487%
	4.1	48,813	65,774	–26%
	4.5	81,929	12,376	562%
State/local	3.7	127,892	88,574	44%
	4.1	78,603	218,730	–64%
	4.5	89,508	41,657	115%

Viewing direct sales versus channel sales is easily accomplished. Report 2.5 is one product of this integrated view. The report depicts the percentage increase in overall sales and the percentage of revenue generated by resellers. The report shows regions where sales growth is helped by resellers. It also shows where resellers may only be cannibalizing sales from the direct sales force.

The Merchant's Data Warehouse

Our first two sales examples were designed for producers. Their primary concerns are product performance in the marketplace and the effectiveness of sales channels. A merchant looks at the world differently. They are concerned with effective utilization of the resources, normally space, labor, and marketing dollars, used to move products. Some merchants, like an auto dealership, handle only a few products and deal with only a few producers. Others, like a grocery store or independent insurance agent, handle a larger variety of goods.

These merchants have a stronger position relative to producers than an auto dealer selling only one or two lines. A grocery store can charge vendors for coveted shelf space at eye level in addition to selling goods at markup. They are in business to maximize sales volume, moving bags of chips or cartons of soda in the

Report 2.5 Reseller impact on sales growth.

Reseller Sales Impact
Change in Year over Year Monthly Sales
versus % Revenue from Resellers

Region	Channel	Oct	Nov	Dec	Jan
Southeast	% change in sales	21%	19%	17%	8%
	% of revenue from resellers	11%	12%	9%	14%
Northeast	% change in sales	–9%	–4%	3%	7%
	% of revenue from resellers	5%	17%	14%	8%
Mid-Atlantic	% change in sales	3%	–2%	4%	2%
	% of revenue from resellers	12%	27%	34%	31%
Midwest	% change in sales	17%	31%	24%	15%
	% of revenue from resellers	13%	15%	16%	14%
Southwest	% change in sales	21%	22%	21%	31%
	% of revenue from resellers	5%	21%	18%	17%
Northwest	% change in sales	11%	9%	31%	26%
	% of revenue from resellers	11%	21%	17%	13%

back door and out the front door. By capturing extensive, detailed sales data, merchants can stock the best-selling products, gain an upper hand in dealings with producers, and optimize promotional efforts.

The Department Store

A large department store handles thousands of products in a single year. Their offerings have higher turnover than an automaker or software company. A department store chain must know what sells, where it sells, when it sells, and how much of it will sell. The department store is the ultimate channel for an ever-changing array of producers.

A buyer for a large department store chain is not unlike a commodities speculator. The buyer works with suppliers to select products that will be hot sellers in coming months. Apparel buyers at large department store chains try to influence trends with their purchases. One bad season can be disastrous for a buyer's career.

The department store allocates floor space to the buyer's choices. Floor space is expensive for a department store, with higher lease and operating expenses than a discount retailer; therefore, they demand a higher margin from every product. The first time a product is put on display, the price reflects the best margin the retailer expects. With a limited window to sell a product such as apparel, the retailer must use time well. If the product does not move quickly, it will likely not move at all.

As an example, imagine two clothing racks at a local department store. On one rack, a popular dress flies off at the rate of two sales per hour for a one-week period. On the second rack, a sale occurs every two hours. Each rack occupies the same amount of floor space. The difference in bottom-line impact to the store can be significant, as shown in Figure 2.3.

With little difference in cost to the retailer, except extra labor generated to ring up more sales of rack 1 items, the difference is significant. The sales data warehouse for the merchant is the foundation for profitability analysis, and is discussed further in Chapter 10, "Profitability."

Winter Coats

To better understand this process, we will examine the seemingly simple case of children's winter coats. Each spring, buyers interview manufacturer representatives, analyze style trends, and place their bets. They commit to buying various styles of winter coats. The manufacturers then buy fabric and begin production. The coats are delivered to stores in late summer, well before school starts. This single event is critical to department stores. Families spend more on children's clothing during the back-to-school event than at any other time, and stores want to take advantage of this willingness to buy. Even though a winter coat might hang in the closet until December, the sales opportunity happens well in advance.

A large marketing effort is launched to generate interest. The back-to-school event has a three- to four-week window. By the second week, the retailer must know what coats are selling or not selling; otherwise, the event passes, inventory piles up, and floor space is poorly utilized. The earlier the retailer has accurate sales data, the better. Examine the scenarios in Table 2.7, and the reactions by the retailer. None of these actions would be feasible without timely, rich sales data.

Reacting quickly to each scenario allows a retailer to maximize revenue per square foot, optimize pricing strategies, and alter marketing plans. There is no

Figure 2.3 Moving merchandise.

	Rack 1	Rack 2
Operating Hours	84	84
Sales per Hour	x 2	x 0.5
Units Sold	168	42
Unit Price	x 32.99	x 32.99
Revenue	$5,542.32	$1,385.58

Table 2.7 Retailer's Response to Indicators

Scenario	Indication	Retailer Response
Indian summer in New England softens demand.	Overall traffic is down due to good weather. Coats are selling at 40% of forecast.	Advertising campaign with warm weather theme. Deep discounting to spur demand.
Winter weather comes early to Midwest.	Traffic is stable, but demand for coats is 150% of forecast.	Move inventory in from other regions (New England?). Avoid discounting. Look for additional inventory from manufacturers.
Underpriced the hottest styles.	Lowest entry price line of coats is selling out.	Raise prices on this line. Look for similar lines from other suppliers. Ensure style trend is national. If regional, move inventory.

time to wait for the end-of-month report. Questions must be asked, answers given, and actions taken in real time. The pace of competition drives large retailers to create sophisticated data warehouses to track sales.

It is a bit intimidating to think of the winter coat scenario replicated hundreds of times each season for a retailer. Every product line creates similar challenges. Holidays offer the opportunity to increase sales or miss the boat. Large chains must forecast and execute the sales process in an increasingly volatile environment. Fickle consumers demand quality, low price, and service all at once. A chain that spans climates and regions must recognize the peculiarities of each market. Many retailers are adept at tailoring product offerings at stores based on the demographics of nearby customers. This process is impossible without a rich, frequently updated data warehouse.

Answering the Retailer's Questions

Our example leads to a data warehouse design for a large department store chain, operating scores of stores across many states. Each store is divided into departments familiar to any consumer, including housewares, clothing, accessories, furniture, toys, and home entertainment. Departments are further subdivided into categories. Clothing is divided into men's, women's, and children's categories. Categories are divided into product lines, like coats, casual shoes, dress shoes, and swimwear. Brands and supplier information are also tracked in the product dimension. A buyer is associated with each product, and other characteristics are noted if deemed discriminators.

The product dimension for a large retailer, if goods are intermixed, could end up with an abundance of columns. It is not easy to design a product dimension that records differentiating characteristics for both home electronics and clothing. The color of clothing is important, while the color of a television is not. Our design is intended for basic analysis across all categories, not for detailed analysis of category attributes. If detailed analysis of clothing or any other category is desired, it is appropriate to consider a core star, product star design. This design technique is discussed in Chapter 3, "Marketing," and also described in Dr. Ralph Kimball's book, *The Data Warehouse Toolkit* (John Wiley and Sons, 1996).

Our initial design is presented in Figure 2.4.

We have included a store dimension to analyze performance in various geographies. The location, size in square feet, cost per square foot, manager, and date opened are recorded for each store location.

For our fact table, we have chosen a granularity of daily product sales at a given price for each store. This is an important distinction from a grain that does not include sales price. Few large retailers sell an item at the same price across different regions. By storing the information at the sales-price level, we can comprehend all the different prices at which the product was offered throughout the chain. We can also record discounted prices at a single location. This is accomplished by tracking the original price of the item at each location. When an item is sold at full price, the sales price equals the original price. Collecting original prices at each location should not rely on an original price transaction occurring at a store, since that transaction may never occur. The load process should gather this information directly from the system that is used to determine original prices for each item.

The design could include these two nonadditive facts in the product dimension. The product dimension would grow in size, with extra rows for products at each price. It is simpler to leave these attributes in the fact table. A discount dimension could also be used to track discounts. This dimension is of value when the motivations for discounts are usually known and worth analyzing, as in our software vendor example. In the case of our retailer, the discounts are assumed to be store-specific actions to move stagnant inventory.

Our facts are simply the units sold and total sales.

Figure 2.4 The retail sales schema.

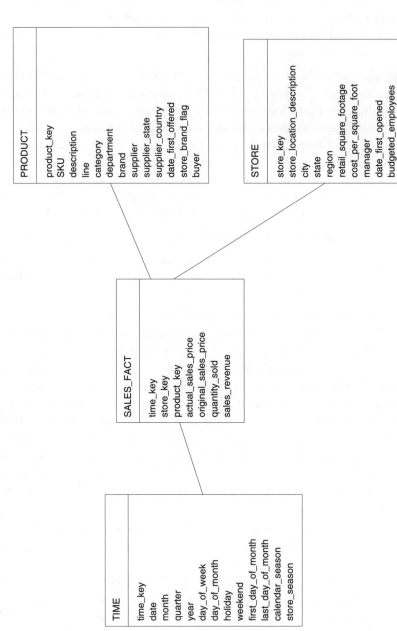

Coat Sales by Product—Stagnant Inventory

With this simple design, we can generate reports that track how coats are selling in the early weeks of the back-to-school season. Report 2.6 simply lists brand sales by region for a four-week period.

The results show that the Northeast region has seen significantly lower results than the Mid-Atlantic and Midwest. These figures can now be compared to forecasts, weather, marketing, and promotions. Our design easily identifies fast- and slow-selling items in any category. Report 2.7 lists the 10 slowest-selling products. We can see that one supplier's items are clearly out of fashion with today's buyers.

Report 2.6 Sales by region and brand.

Brand Sales by Region
Line: Winter Coats   Dept: Children
From: 8/4/97 To: 9/1/97

Store	Brand	Quantity	Sales Revenue
Northeast	Chimney Rock	249	$22,383
	Wee Kids	218	$10,730
	Templeton	154	$7,919
	Duck South	109	$6,750
	NHL Logo	34	$2,531
Northeast Total		**764**	**$50,313**
Mid-Atlantic	Chimney Rock	561	$51,797
	Wee Kids	420	$23,419
	Templeton	321	$15,048
	Duck South	118	$8,378
	USFL Logo	67	$5,433
Mid-Atlantic Total		**1487**	**$104,076**
Midwest	Chimney Rock	520	$41,018
	Wee Kids	433	$17,030
	Templeton	219	$10,223
	Duck South	108	$6,192
	USFL Logo	63	$5,105
Midwest Total		**1343**	**$79,567**

Report 2.7 Slow sellers.

10 Slow Movers—by Sales Revenue
8/97

SKU Number	Description	Line	Brand	Supplier	Sales Revenue
817444-432	10-lb test line	Fishing supplies	Monostar	Monostar	$12.04
773134-910	Spatula, metal	Kitchen equipment	Chef Ronaldo	Chef Industries	$32.02
893134-911	Egg separator	Kitchen equipment	Chef Ronaldo	Chef Industries	$34.91
994134-908	Salad bowl set	Kitchen equipment	Chef Ronaldo	Chef Industries	$56.04
433003-054	Sentovfluer	Men's cologne	Ronaldo	Chef Industries	$87.94
817402-449	DEET Fresh	Camping supplies	Monostar	Monostar	$91.41
718201-594	Photocube	Photography	Peking Plastic	Peking Plastic	$103.55
773831-901	111 Recipes of Love	Kitchen equipment	Chef Ronaldo	Chef Industries	$140.04
582031-943	70s Moments	Music media	Epoch Records	Epoch Records	$187.45
482000-003	Tefla Sock	Men's clothing	Sock Works	Tasmanian	$194.59

Notice that Chef Ronaldo branded items are dominating the list. Perhaps the company's buyer in housewares overestimated the value of the brand name.

Summing Up Sales

In examining the sales process for three different businesses, we have identified some important factors that affect the design of an effective sales data warehouse. These include:

Type of business. Determine whether the business is a merchant or producer of goods. The merchant needs information to maximize utilization of resources and is looking for the best-selling products. The producer must optimize sales channels in addition to producing best-selling products.

How goods are sold. Understand who makes the sale, especially for producers. They are keenly interested in optimizing the cost of sales. Ensure the data warehouse design comprehends all the sales channels used by the business.

The basic transaction. For each business, it is important to model and understand the fundamental transaction. Make sure that the facts included in the design are clearly defined and accurately calculated. Verify the relationship of facts and the formula for each derived attribute both in interviews and by reviewing actual data.

Really understand the business. The data warehouse designer must clearly comprehend the business, its concept of operations, product discriminators, and even its market position. This understanding can only improve the relevance and value of the design.

This chapter has introduced the customer to the business by way of a sales transaction. In the next chapter, we examine the subtle, complex courtship that first raises the interest of that elusive customer.

MARKETING

In Chapter 2, we said that sales drives the business. Marketing, in turn, drives sales. Marketing activities can have broad impact within a company; increasing sales is one obvious impact. But marketing techniques can also be used to focus the *way* a company sells, and often have profound effects on the products themselves.

The more information available to marketers, the more effective their efforts are. Because of the powerful bottom-line impact marketers can have, their need for information is often the driving force behind a company's initial foray into the world of data warehousing. In this chapter, we will study a diverse set of marketing needs drawn from three industries. We will see how each unique set of requirements can be addressed with the right design.

What Is Known about the Customer?

At the center of all marketing activities is the customer. It is the customer who ultimately buys a product. Marketers work to find potential customers, make their products known to them, stimulate demand, retain existing customers, and sell them additional products.

The activities of a marketing group vary greatly by industry, and even within an industry. One factor that accounts for the difference in approach is the level of knowledge about the customer. If you know a great deal about individual customers, you can learn how to effectively sell your product, and to whom you should be trying to sell it. If you have a large number of unknown customers, you may focus on broader efforts to make segments of the population aware of your product, or bring them to your store.

Sophistication of customer view varies by industry. Table 3.1 illustrates the differing customer views in the three industries we will study in this chapter: a grocery store, a telephone company, and a bank.

Table 3.1 The Customer View in Three Industries

Industry	Product	Customer View
Grocery store chain	Reseller of produce and packaged goods to retail customers.	Relatively anonymous customer. Marketing campaigns are designed to bring customers into the store and evaluated based on sales data.
Telephone company	Standard telephone service, add-ons such as call waiting and voice mail, ISDN, Internet access, high-speed communications such as 56KB/T1/T3, cellular service.	Customer information is available, but not centralized. Deregulation is causing increased competition. A clear view of the customer is required to maintain a competitive advantage.
Banking	Deposit accounts, credit cards, installment loans, mortgages.	Sophisticated view of the customer is required to effectively sell the product and maintain profitability.

On one end of the scale are relatively anonymous retail transactions. At day's end, your local grocery store does not have the names and addresses of everyone who bought golden delicious apples that day. But the grocery store can use marketing techniques designed to bring more people into the store. With a well-designed data mart, the effectiveness of these campaigns can be studied.

In some industries, the customer is not as anonymous. Your telephone company, for example, knows exactly who you are and where you live. This information is required both to provide you service and to bill you for it. But because the industry has historically been a regulated monopoly, the phone company's view of the customer is not very well developed. For example, it may be difficult to identify numerous telephone lines, high-speed data lines, and other services with a single corporate customer. Data warehousing is helping to change this.

Nowhere is the view of a customer more sophisticated than in banking. Your bank knows who you are, where you live, and what your social security number is. It also knows how much money you have, how much your home is worth, whether you tend to carry a balance on your credit cards, and what your investment style is.

Marketers for the bank employ sophisticated analysis techniques to attract, retrain, and cross-sell to customers. They can also analyze the profitability of customers. Their data marts are valuable tools.

In this chapter, we will study a company in each of these industries. Each company's unique needs will be studied and translated into effective data mart designs, with the marketing group in mind.

The Grocery Store

We will focus on the primary activity of a grocery store: sales. We already looked at sales in Chapter 2, "Sales." This time, we will pay special attention to the marketing activities associated with the sales process.

The grocery store operates on volume. Margin on each item that passes the register is relatively low, so the key to profitability is to maximize the number of items sold. For a successful grocer, sales at a single store for a single day can be comprised of millions of individual items. For a chain of stores, the number becomes many times higher. In this volume business, everyone is a potential customer, and the marketing objective is to bring as many of these potential customers into the store as possible.

Today's grocery stores are able to measure sales at a very fine level. Detailed information is gathered at the point of sale. As each item is dragged across the bar-code reader, a record of the transaction is stored. But for the chain in our case study, almost nothing is known about the customer. This anonymity is not always the case; see the sidebar for examples of techniques used to eliminate it.

Learning More about the Retail Customer

The grocery store studied in this chapter possesses little knowledge about the customer, but there is plenty it can do to change this situation. Usually driven by marketing needs, a wide variety of techniques have been developed to learn more about the people who pass the checkout counter.

Grocery stores often issue "preferred customer" cards. These cards offer privileges like check cashing, or special discounts on selected items. A shopper obtains one of these cards by filling out his or her name, address, and phone number on a short form. A bar code or ID is imprinted on the card, so that it can be scanned at the checkout

Continues

Learning More about the Retail Customer *(Continued)*

register. Each time the shopper uses the card, the store can correlate the purchase with the shopper.

Other retail outlets have adopted the simple practice of asking customers at the checkout counter for their area code or zip code. This information is associated with the purchase at the time of sale. While it does not allow a retailer to understand the individual customer, it does provide geographic information that can be used to profile customers or assess effectiveness of local marketing activities.

When you use a store coupon, you are often required to fill in your address, zip code, or phone number. The information is associated with your purchase, and the retailer is now able to profile you, as well as directly correlate the marketing campaign that produced the coupon with your purchase.

A grocery store is much like the retail department store in Chapter 2, "Sales." The grocery store sales process can be summarized as the *resale* of packaged goods, produced and marketed by other organizations, to retail customers. The nuances of this definition give us important clues about our marketing activities. The grocery store is *reselling* goods. Our marketers are not directly concerned with demand creation for a specific product or brand; this is already covered by someone else who produces the product. The "someone else" is probably an external company, but can also be an internal organization responsible for store brands. Whatever the case, the individual products are being minded by another party. Marketing's responsibility is to ensure that people are walking in the door to buy things.

Of course, a grocery store is not always reselling in the technical sense. Some goods are sold on consignment, and others are produced in house. But the basic sales model effectively captures these transactions. Each item that passes the register is sold to the customer for a specific price, and in some way has an associated cost. Note also that there are other revenue-generating processes of interest at the grocery store. A grocery store chain manufactures and markets its own "store brand" products. Another revenue-generating activity is the sale of shelf space to manufacturers and distributors. No less important than sales, each of these processes can be studied in a separate data mart.

Grocery Store Sales Schema

The grocery store we are going to study already has a sales schema, and is interested in enhancing it to address marketing needs. The fact table, shown in Figure 3.1, captures item sales by store and day. A daily grain was chosen because the volume of sales is so high that capturing the individual lines on register receipts would quickly become too large. This level is no problem for analyzing sales, and we soon find that it satisfies marketing objectives as well.

The three dimensions are day, item, and store. The fact table contains several measures, shown in Table 3.2. Remember that each of these measures represents the total for a product, day, and store, and not an individual purchase.

Table 3.2 Definition of Grocery Store Measures

Measure	Definition	Equivalences/Notes
quantity_sold	Total quantity sold	
gross_sales	Total dollars rung up for the product before coupons	
manufacturer_ coupon_dollars	Total value of manufacturer coupons used by consumers	Item coupons only.
store_coupon_dollars	Total value of all store coupons used	Item coupons only.
net_sales	Total dollars rung up after coupons are deducted	Equivalent to gross_sales minus manufacturer _coupon_dollars minus store_coupon_dollars.
cost	Total cost to the grocery store	Calculated using unit cost for the day. Activity-based costing not included.
margin_dollars	Total margin	Equivalent to net_sales minus cost.
basket_count	Number of register receipts on which the item appears	This fact is not additive across products.

Figure 3.1 The grocery store star, before incorporation of marketing needs.

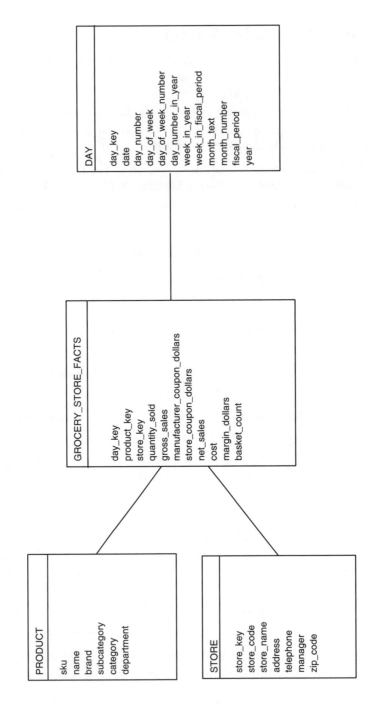

The measures selected allow analysis of *gross* or *net* sales. Gross sales are the total dollar sales prior to the deduction of coupons. Net sales are the total dollar sales after coupons have been deducted. Coupon deductions are recorded in two separate measures, one for manufacturer coupons and one for store coupons. The distinction is important, because each category impacts the bottom line of the store differently.

This design requires store and manufacturer coupons to be associated with specific items. If our point-of-sale system does not associate coupons with an item, we will not be able to deliver the system as designed. We will be much better off if we find this out now. If we discover the problem at load time, we will have a lot of explaining to do.

TIP

Always verify that the source data supports your design through careful review of the available data. If you do not consider the source of your data mart, you may be in for a rude awakening when it is time to actually build the data mart. The inability to deliver on a proposed solution will not be appreciated by business people funding the effort.

Since the grain of our fact table is at the item level, we must exclude any coupons that apply to an entire sale. This has been noted in our definitions table. For example, a coupon that offers $10 off a purchase of $100 or more does not apply to an individual item, so there is no place for it in this schema. Were it important to include this type of discount, we would add an other_discounts column, into which we can allocate the overall discount to line items.

There are two measures that are derivable from other measures: net_sales and margin_dollars. Because they are important to the business, they have been included in their own columns. As we learned in Chapter 2, "Sales," there is no need to be stingy with disk space—it will only cost more in terms of effort to build reports later.

The last measure in Table 3.2 is basket_count. This measure represents the number of register receipts on which the item appeared at that location on that day. We have noted that this measure is semi-additive; while it is acceptable to sum basket_count across stores or days, it is not acceptable to do so across items. To do so would potentially count the same basket more than once. We will need to be very careful when using basket_count in reports, and we must think twice before providing it to end users in an ad hoc query tool. We'll look at how tools deal (or don't deal) with semi-additive facts in Chapter 13, "Presenting Information."

The fact table does *not* include unit price. The business has not expressed an interest in conducting price-point analysis, so this level of detail is not required. If needed in the future, it can be calculated from existing measures as gross_sales divided by quantity_sold. Note that unit price is not additive; had it been placed in the fact table, we would have considered it a degenerate dimension.

Key Business Terms

Unit price. The price of a single item.

Extended price. The total price for a group of items.

When items are bought, sold, ordered, or shipped, they are often done so in quantity. For example, each line on an order shows an item, how much it costs, how many are being purchased, and what the total charge is. The total charge is referred to as the *extended* price, while the single item price shown is referred to as the *unit* price.

The unit and extended descriptors are also applied to various other elements of an order. *Unit cost* represents the cost of a single item to the vendor, while *extended cost* multiplies this by the total number of items purchased. Similarly, a business might deal with *extended margin*, *extended discounts*, and so on.

Most of the time, the extended amounts will be recorded in fact tables. They are fully additive, and therefore easier to work with. We can freely aggregate them over a number of dimensions, for useful analysis. Unit amounts are provided as dimensions, when useful for price-point analysis.

The sales schema has been in production for a year at the grocery store, and has proven very helpful. The grocery store is interested in modifying the model based on the needs of marketers. We are sent to talk with the person whose job is to make sales happen. We'll use her input to add the marketing perspective to the design.

Grocery Store Marketer

Because information is key to her success, the vice president of Marketing for the grocery store chain is readily able to tell us what information she needs and how she uses it. We start out by asking what her primary objectives are, given that each product the store sells already has a manufacturer who markets it.

My primary mission is to bring people into the store. But people don't shop here because of the name of our store, so we can't just promote ourselves. The two main reasons people come here instead of going to a competitor's store are price and convenience. Since price is the primary motivator, we often use it to attract shoppers. That requires us to focus on products.

During any given week, we place numerous products on promotion. Actually, what is on promotion may vary by region or store. We try to choose popular products, or to promote items in a category that is popular, so that the promotion will have wide appeal. Sales data helps us make these decisions. Sometimes we also time promotions for periods that might otherwise be slow.

We promote these items in many ways: on television, radio, in the paper, in circulars, and via mailbox stuffers. For the newspaper, we may include our circular with the Sunday paper, or take out smaller advertisements in weekday papers. Also, we sometimes have in-store demos, where free samples are given away or special displays are set up. These are often set up by the distributors of the products, who coordinate with the store managers.

The point of the promotion is to get people into the store, so there is usually some type of price reduction involved. It might be a coupon, a discount to Savings Club Cardholders, or a temporary price reduction. There are usually a couple of items that are on promotion without a price reduction. This can happen when there is a special display set up, or when a "regular low price" is highlighted in a circular.

A successful promotion is one that increases sales. That can be hard to measure, since there are always lots of items on promotion. We can't attribute a bump in overall sales to a particular promotion. Occasionally, we try, by controlling as many factors as possible. We use a control region with no promotion, and compare the percent increase in sales before and after a set of promotions.

The main way we judge success is by looking at sales of the promoted item. We compare them to sales when the item was not on promotion, or to sales in a different region where the promotion did not run. If sales are stimulated, we can assume we are meeting our objective: bringing people into the store.

We would also like to be able to look at what combinations of promotions are most effective for various product types. We have a sense for this right now, but lack the hard data to back it up.

Several important things can be gleaned from this discussion. We have learned that the primary objective of marketing efforts is to increase sales. The main mechanism for doing so is the promotion. Promotions are used to bring people into the store, where they will presumably buy more than just the promoted item. Numerous details about promotions have been disclosed:

- A promotion is the combined set of efforts targeted at a particular item.
- There are several ways in which an item might be promoted. Examples include print, radio, television, advertising, and price reductions. Some of these types have subcategories.
- Promotions do not always include cost savings for the consumer.
- At any given time, more than one type of promotion may be in effect for a single item.
- Some promotions may be in effect only in certain regions.

We have also learned how marketing uses, or would like to use, information about sales:

- Raw sales information can be helpful. Popular items are often targeted for promotions. Campaigns are sometimes planned for time periods when sales are slow.
- Although the marketing objective is to increase overall sales, promotions are evaluated by studying sales of the promoted item. Ideally, they compare sales where a promotion is in effect with sales where the promotion is not in effect. This may be done by comparing time periods or different regions.
- Comparing different combinations of promotion types is useful.

The Promotion Dimension

To accommodate marketing's needs, we add a promotion dimension to our star schema. The promotion dimension will be used to capture the combination of promotion techniques in effect at the time of sale. Since we're capturing sales on a daily basis, and all promotions run one week, we can add the promotion dimension to the existing schema without impacting its grain. Examples of what may be found in the promotion dimension are shown in Table 3.3.

Note that the promotion dimension has not been normalized. Each fact in the fact table will include a key to only one row in the promotion table; each promotion technique is represented by its own flag column in the dimension. In addition to the flags, we have included description columns for some of the promotion types. Newspaper promotions, for example, may be of type "Sunday Supplement" or "Weekday."

The design of our promotion dimension does not attempt to model the relationship between a promotion and an item; instead, we rely on the fact table to take care of this detail for us. We can analyze sales of items on promotion, because each fact is an intersect between an item and a promotion. But we are missing one important capability: We cannot look at items that were on promotion that did not sell. No rows are generated in the fact table for these items; hence they are never linked to the promotion dimension. If this shortcoming is a significant concern to our marketers, we can build a coverage table between our dimensions to address it.

For this grocery store, detailed costs of promotions are not tracked, and they are not given names. But were this information available, we would simply add a few columns to the dimension to record it. These extra columns would result in many more rows in the promotion dimension; each combination of promotion techniques would be represented multiple times. Discounts associated with the promotion could also be recorded in the fact table, enabling detailed analysis of campaign costs.

We have included a row for situations in which no promotion is in effect. This approach eliminates the additional complexities that would otherwise be necessitated by an optional relationship. When searching for rows with no promotion, we will not be required to use an alternate SQL syntax that employs outer joins or tests for null keys. We will also be allowed to combine facts where no promotion is in effect with those involving a single specific promotion without complex union queries.

Table 3.3 A Wide Promotion Dimension for the Grocery Store

Promotion	Paper	Paper Type	Price Reduction	Reduction Type	Demo	Demo Type	Radio	Mail	Television	Media
U	U	Unknown	U	Unknown	U	Unknown	U	U	U	Unknown
N	N	n/a	N	n/a	N	n/a	N	N	N	None
Y	N	n/a	Y	Coupon	N	n/a	N	Y	N	None
Y	N	n/a	Y	Reduction	N	n/a	Y	N	Y	Television, Radio
Y	Y	Sunday Supplement	Y	Savings Club Cardholders	N	n/a	Y	N	N	Radio, Paper
Y	Y	Weekday	Y	Coupon	N	n/a	N	N	N	Paper
Y	N	n/a	N	n/a	N	n/a	Y	N	Y	Television, Radio
Y	N	n/a	N	n/a	Y	Taste Test	N	N	N	None
Y	N	n/a	Y	Reduction	Y	Video Display	N	N	N	None
Y	Y	Sunday Supplement	Y	Reduction	N	n/a	Y	N	Y	Television, Radio, Paper
Y	N	n/a	Y	Reduction	N	n/a	Y	N	N	Radio
Y	Y	Sunday Supplement	Y	Reduction	N	n/a	N	N	Y	Television, Paper

TIP

The relationship of the fact table to each of the dimension tables should always be mandatory. Include a not applicable row in the dimension if required. Reporting will be greatly simplified in numerous situations.

We can also extend this "NULL avoidance" principle beyond the foreign keys in the fact table to *every attribute* in the data mart. Placing NULLs in columns that do not apply only makes life more difficult when querying the data mart because NULLs require a different set of comparison operators from other values. Unfortunately, "Not Applicable" cannot be placed in fields that do not hold textual data. Where these values are not available, NULLs may be necessary.

Known to the Business, but Not to a System

To accurately load sales data into the grocery store data mart, complete information on all promotions in effect must be known at load time. Sometimes this requirement can be challenging. While computer systems are used to carefully record sales transactions, promotion information is not necessarily captured in a system.

It is usually necessary for store managers to record promotion information in point-of-sale systems. The primary reason this is done is that promotions involve price reductions. But a store manager may not have complete information on the promotion. Were radio and television used, or just radio? The point-of-sale system may not capture this data anyway, and as we have seen, some promotions don't involve a price reduction at all. In these cases, there is no guarantee the information will be recorded.

Each promotion has been orchestrated by someone in the business. In the case of an extensive media campaign, it will be someone in corporate marketing. In the case of a special display erected in a store by a distributor, it may be the store manager. Somewhere there is always someone who knows about each promotion, yet there is not necessarily one person who knows about all the promotions. This situation represents a serious challenge to the data mart developers.

Continues

> **Known to the Business, but Not to a System *Continued***
>
> Each element of data in the data warehouse must have an explicit source. Those responsible for loading the data mart cannot create something from nothing. A requirement for information without a standardized source is problematic.
>
> The solution may be orchestrated by the developers, but it must be implemented by the business. It is not practical for the data warehouse development team to become living agents who scour the business weekly for promotion information. Instead, it must be left to the business to compile that information for the data warehouse. If the data warehouse team is effective in communicating the need for a concerted effort, and if the business perceives a significant analysis benefit, the information will be found. Because this new business process to gather promotion information is likely to be informal, the team must monitor it on a regular basis and not permit it to slip.

Resiliency of the Dimensional Model

The intention is to begin capturing the promotion information when the new dimension table is added to the schema. A foreign key will be added to the fact table referencing the new dimension. The promotion dimension therefore includes an "unknown" row that will be used for the year's worth of data that has already been collected, for which promotion data is unavailable. Should it prove useful, the data warehouse team may attempt to reconstruct the promotion status for the previous year.

The sales schema's ability to absorb this new dimension illustrates the resiliency of the dimensional model. Quite easily, we have enriched the set of detail surrounding sales metrics, benefiting an entirely new group within the organization. Changes like this are commonplace. Star schemas in production are frequently enhanced with new measures, new dimensions, or entirely new dimension tables as in this example. These modifications reflect the changing way the business processes are viewed.

Why Not Normalize the Promotion Dimension?

Developers new to data warehousing may cringe at the sight of our promotion dimension. Each type of promotion has its own column, as well as a description in some cases. Basic rules of normalization familiar to designers of OLTP databases require elimination of repeating attributes and groups like these. They would say this table is in violation of first normal form. In a normalized model, we might replace all our promotion flags and descriptions with a simple pair of promotion and description columns. An example is shown in Table 3.4.

Because each promotion type has its own row in this dimension table, it places the fact table in a many-to-many relationship with the promotion. If a particular item were purchased while radio, television, and direct mail promotions were in effect, we would need to link its one row in the fact table to the three appropriate promotion rows. And, of course, any single promotion type may relate to many rows in the fact table. A many-to-many relationship like this must be resolved by an "intersect table," as shown in Figure 3.2. The shaded fact_promo table is used to track relationships between each fact table row with each relevant promotion row.

Designers of OLTP systems will be quick to point out that a normalized relationship will make it easy to add additional promotion types in the future. However, the cost is steep when it comes to analysis. Remember that each fact now has many potential promotion rows associated with it. A SQL Select statement that joins a fact to the promotion dimension will cause facts to be repeated

Table 3.4 A Normalized Version of the Promotion Dimension

Promotion	Description
Paper	Sunday Supplement
Paper	Circular
Reduction	Reduction
Reduction	Coupon
Reduction	Savings Club Cardholders
Radio	n/a
Demo	Taste Test
Demo	Video Display
Radio	n/a
Television	n/a
Mail	n/a

Figure 3.2 A fact table in a many-to-many relationship with a dimension—Don't do this!

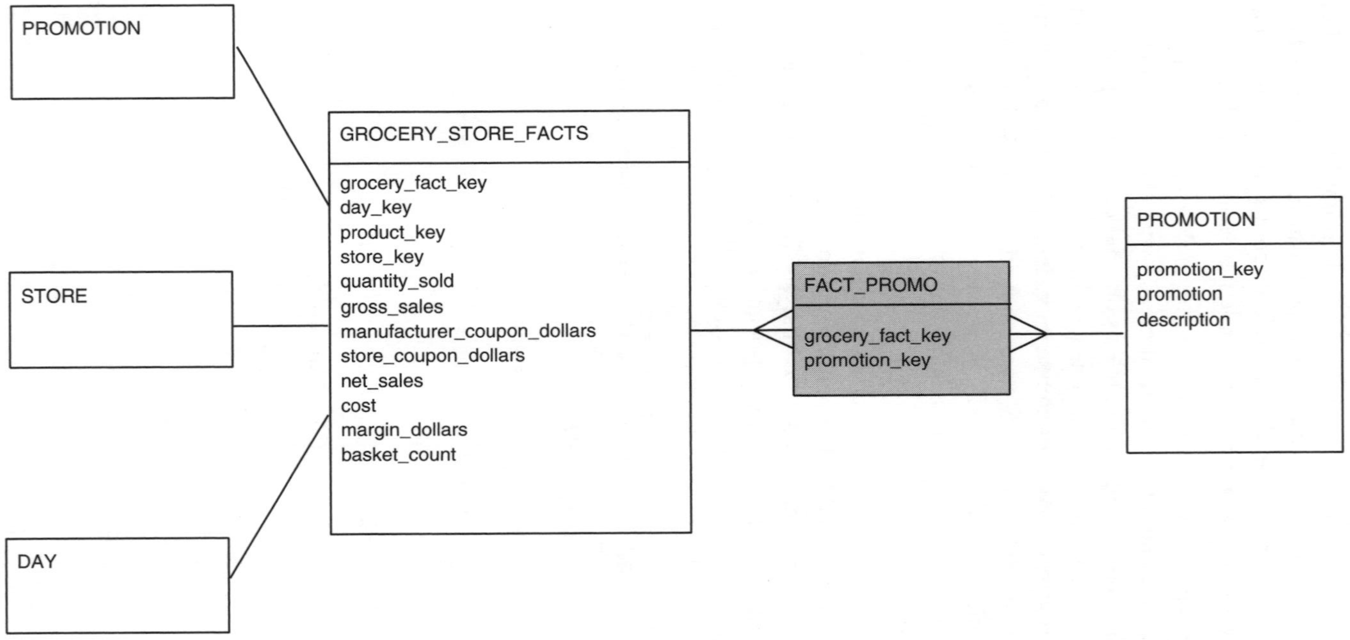

when there are multiple promotions in effect. For example, suppose the fact table contains a single row for January 1st purchases of Captain Cola at the Springfield store location. On that day, 75 bottles were sold. Captain Cola was being promoted by television, radio, and newspaper on that day. The 75 bottles will be repeated three times in a query that links the fact table with the promotion structure. Here is the SQL; database results are shown in bold.

```
rem Many-to-many between fact table and promotion dimension
rem leads to wrong results
 Select sum(grocery_facts.quantity),
      promotions.promotion
  from grocery_facts,
      fact_promo,
      promotion,
      day,
      product,
      store
  where product.name = 'Captain Cola'
   and store.store_name = 'Springfield'
   and day.day_number_in_year = 1
   and grocery_facts.grocery_fact_key =
      fact_promo.grocery_fact_key
   and promotions.promotion_key = fact_promo.promotion_key
   and day.day_key = grocery_store_facts.day_key
   and product.product_key = grocery_store_facts.product_key
   and store.store_key = grocery_store_facts.store_key
group by promotions.promotion
/
```

Sum(Quantity)   Promotion
-------   -----
75   Radio
75   Television
75   Newspaper

To avoid errors like this when using this normalized promotion dimension, we must take care *not* to retrieve any measures! Otherwise, we will get incorrect results when more than one promotion is in effect. And the situation gets worse. Looking for rows where a particular combination of promotions was in effect will now require multiple correlated subqueries. To find sales where radio and television promotions were in effect, we must issue a query like this one:

```
Select item.item_name,
     sum(grocery_facts.quantity_sold)
  from grocery_facts,
```

```
    item
where grocery_facts.item_key = item.item_key
  and exists(
    select *
    from grocery_promo,
      promotion
  where grocery_promo.grocery_fact_key =
      grocery_facts.fact_key
    and grocery_promo.promotion_key =
      promotions.promotion_key
    and promotions.promotion = 'Newspaper')
  and exists (
    select *
    from grocery_promo,
      promotion
    where grocery_promo.grocery_fact_key =
      grocery_facts.fact_key
    and grocery_promo.promotion_key =
      promotions.promotion_key
    and promotions.promotion = 'Radio')
  group by item.item_name
```

TIP

Remember that the data warehouse is a database designed explicitly for reporting and analysis. Resist all urges to normalize dimensions. To do so will render your reporting tasks more difficult in many ways, and substantially degrade performance.

By contrast, the original design of the promotion dimension makes it easy to look up the combination of promotion techniques in effect. Specific combinations can be searched by placing simple conditions on the individual flags. If we are particularly concerned about ease of use, we might replace the Y or N values with more descriptive text, such as "Radio" and "No Radio."

```
Select item.item_name,
    sum(grocery_facts.quantity_sold)
  from grocery_facts,
    items,
    promotions
  where grocery_facts.item_key = item.item_key
  and grocery_facts.prmotion_key = promotion.promotion_key
  and promotion.television = 'Y'
```

```
and promotions.radio = 'Y'
group by item.item_name
```

Clearly, we will have a much easier time developing our reports using the original denormalized design. In the future, if a new promotion type is added, we can always add an additional column to this table. For the existing rows, it can be populated with N or n/a.

Let's take a look at how our "marketing-aware" Sales data mart can help the vice president of Marketing.

Grocery Store Reports

We've designed a schema that should help marketing decide what to promote, evaluate how well the promotions did, and compare the effectiveness of different type of promotions. Let's look at some reports that illustrate each of these capabilities.

Targeting a Promotion

The senior vice president of Marketing told us that items are put on promotion to bring people into the store. It is important, then, to choose popular items to promote. Even before the promotion dimension was added to the fact table, the schema was able to support this function. Because the schema includes a basket_count measure, marketing can use it to determine popular items.

Recall that the basket_count measure is an indication of how many different shoppers bought the product that day. Because a shopper can return to the store more than once in a day, we called it "basket count" instead of "shopper count." By looking at the basket count for particular products, we can judge which ones appeal to the largest number of shoppers. But we must be very careful.

Remember that our basket_count is not additive across products. Suppose that I go shopping and purchase a gallon of whole milk for my infant son, and a half-gallon of skim milk for myself. Each of these products has a row in the fact table for the day I bought them and the store where I purchased them. In each of these rows, my purchase will be included in the basket count. Both products are part of the milk subcategory of dairy foods. If we produce a report that shows basket_count by subcategory, my basket would be counted twice—once for the skim milk, and once for the whole milk. But it is only *one* basket. The report violates additivity rules; our basket_count is not additive across products.

There are two ways to deal with this problem. We can look at basket count at the item level. This gets around the additivity problem by simply avoiding it. But it also means the focus of the report is on specific items, like a particular brand of milk, rather than on the category "dairy products" or the subcategory "milk."

If our marketers would prefer to assess popularity of individual subcategories, we can provide them with item averages of basket count by category. But this approach could potentially obscure any "blockbuster items" within a particular category, and may place categories with a large number of items that do not move at a disadvantage. While this second option seems to have more disadvantages, we should not rule it out. Instead, we take the options, along with the pros and cons, and let the marketers decide what they want to see.

Assuming the marketers prefer the first option, product-level basket counts that include category and subcategory, we might produce a report like the one shown in Report 3.1.

Report 3.1 Top five sellers help target promotions.

Basket Count:
Top Five Items by Week for 20 Stores

Week and Year	Ranking	Item	Subcategory	Category	Basket Count
10/1996	1	Fizzy Cola 2-liter	Bottled soda	Carbonated beverages	21,296
	2	Farmhouse Dairy— gallon whole	Milk	Dairy	18,107
	3	DinnerTime Chicken Combo	Frozen dinners	Frozen	18,013
	4	Sun Juice 8oz	Concentrated orange juice	Frozen	17,500
	5	Delitos 16oz	Potato chips	Snack foods	18,495
11/1996	1	Farmhouse Dairy—gallon whole	Milk	Dairy	22,593
	2	Fizzy Cola 2-liter	Bottled soda	Carbonated beverages	19,293

Continues

Report 3.1 shows that carbonated beverages are consistently among the most popular products over a period of three weeks. Two different carbonated beverage products have made it into the top five during the period, and in two of the three weeks shown, they were both present. A product from the carbonated beverages category should meet the popularity requirement for a good promotion.

TIP

Rankings like the ones in Report 3.1 are commonly requested by business people. Unfortunately, it is quite difficult to get standard SQL to construct rankings for fetched data. As a result, we usually do rankings *after* fetching data from the database. Many of the query and reporting tools on the market today still do not feature this capability. We'll look at these issues in detail in Chapter 13, "Presenting Information."

Report 3.1 Continued

Week and Year	Ranking	Item	Subcategory	Category	Basket Count
	3	Happy Cloud 4-pack	Bathroom tissue	Paper goods	17,641
	4	Bowl of Os condensed	Canned soup	Soups	17,291
	5	Arnold's Chicken Cuts	Chicken	Meats	16,950
12/1996	1	Dinner Time Pasta Platter	Frozen dinners	Frozen	24,223
	2	Captain Cola 2-liter	Bottled soda	Carbonated beverages	23,184
	3	SuperDippin' Chips 16oz	Potato chips	Snack foods	21,294
	4	WipeAways 4-pack	Paper towels	Paper goods	19,292
	5	Fizzy Cola 2-liter	Bottled soda	Carbonated beverages	18,873

Remember that this report is not an indication of the volume of business. If we had wanted overall sales, we would have used the quantity_sold fact in place of basket_count. Because it simply measures sales volume, quantity_sold does not tell us if the item was popular, or how many people bought it.

Before deciding to target a bottled soda product for a promotion, our marketers might want to look at a few more reports. They may break the figures out by region to verify that high sales in one region are now skewing the overall figures. This is easily done by adding region_name from the store dimension to our report. Marketing may also want to check if promotions were already in effect for any of these products, possibly pushing them into the top five. We can do this by including the promotion flag. Since promotions may be in effect for one region and not another, we should break this report out by region.

In addition to supporting the decision of *what* to promote, the Sales data mart can help the marketers decide *when* to run promotions. Time periods with particularly slow sales might be targeted by a series of promotions in order to increase business. To look for slow periods, we use the net_sales measure to produce the chart in Report 3.2.

Evaluating the Promotion

Let's assume that based on the basket_count report, the marketing department has decided to promote a particular bottled soda in two regions. The marketers combine radio, television, and price reduction to promote Captain Cola in one

Report 3.2 Charting sales by week reveals slow periods.

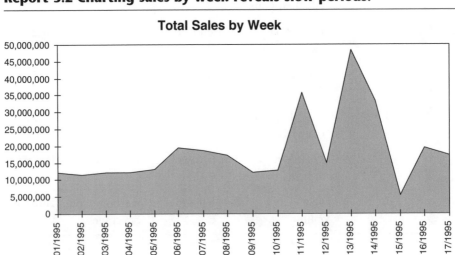

region, and simply use radio and price reduction in another. In the remaining four regions, there is no promotion.

First we can compare sales where the item was on promotion with sales where the item was not on promotion. Our basket_count and generic promotion flag will be used for this comparison, and we will break the information out by week. Captain Cola is only on promotion in two out of six regions. Even if the promotion is effective, overall sales numbers will be much higher where it is not being promoted. We do not want to skew the results, so we will compare the store average where it is on promotion with those where it is not. The result is shown in Report 3.3.

Marketing also wanted to be able to look at the impact of differing combinations of promotions. Looking at regions where Captain Cola is on promotion, we can easily examine the impact of adding television to the mix. The report in Report 3.4 was produced by limiting the query results to rows in the fact table for Captain Cola, during the weeks the promotion was in effect, and for sales where a promotion was in effect. The promotion flag was used for this last condition. The result set is thereby limited to stores in regions where some sort of promotion was offered. We know there are only two such regions. For one, the combination will include television, and for the other, it will not. Based on what we already know about the promotions, we know there will be no other differences, so we simply add the television flag to the select clause of our query to break out average store basket counts.

This approach is possible because we know that after placing the condition on the query, the television flag is the only attribute in the promotion dimension that will vary. When more complex comparisons of combinations of promotion

Report 3.3 Assessing impact of promotion.

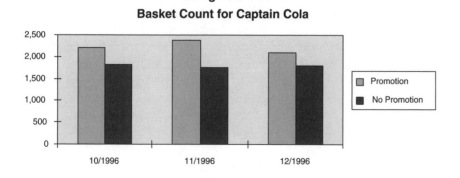

Report 3.4 Assessing impact of promotion techniques.

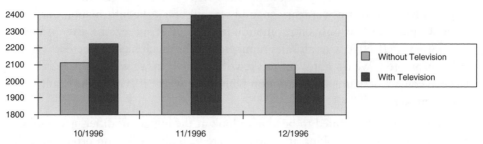

types are required, we might use our media column instead. The variance in this single column can then be easily plotted and compared.

Marketing also expressed an interest in checking if the promotion of an item gives an overall boost in sales to other items in the subcategory bottled sodas. Let's turn to our quantity_sold measure, which is fully additive across categories, to answer this question. We will exclude Captain Cola from the query, so that we can see the true effects on the remainder of the items in the bottled sodas subcategory.

Reports 3.5 and 3.6 plot exactly the same data, yet imply very different results. In Report 3.5, we see a slight gain at best, though sales in the middle of the promotion seem to drop. Perhaps many customers chose to purchase Captain Cola instead. Whatever the case, the change appears not to be significant. But in Report 3.6, the sales seem to surge. Now there appears to be a significant trend. These two charts look so dramatically different because they use different scales

Report 3.5 Were sales flat...

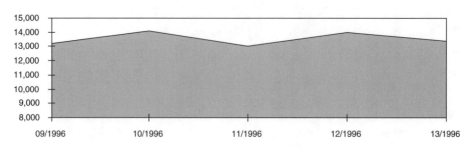

Report 3.6 ...or did they fluctuate?

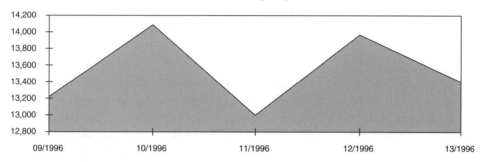

Sales by Week:

Bottled sodas excluding Captain Cola

on their Y axes. Whether intentionally or not, it is easy to place a spin on data when charting it. For this reason, we tend to avoid charting. This data can be presented in a simple table, allowing the reader to determine significance.

The Telephone Company

With a large pool of anonymous customers, the grocery store marketers focused on items to promote, and measured success based on sales. Now we'll look at a business that has some basic information about it customers, and see how this information is used by marketers.

The phone company knows more about its customers. After all, it must have a name and address to which to send a monthly bill. Despite the fact that this information is available, it is often difficult for the phone company to know just who its customers are, or what services they buy. The reasons stem from the history of the industry.

Until the 1980s, the phone company was a regulated monopoly. With little direct competition, the phone company worried less about individual customers and more about delivery of various services. Entire organizations within the phone company worked almost independently of one another to provide different types of services. This independence meant that systems designed to support these services were also isolated from one another. Standards were not in place to ensure that similar information was entered the same way in various systems. And because there was little competition, there was little need to carefully identify an individual customer.

Consider a midsized business customer. They would likely receive several different bills from the phone company for POTS alone. (POTS stands for "Plain Old Telephone Service," i.e., standard phone lines.) Individual lines were to be billed to the person within the organization who ordered them. Though a company name was recorded, no effort was made to standardize how it was entered. Little if any effort was made to relate all the lines billed to a single company. Even the same person might not have been identifiable. The record for each line billed to an individual might have had his or her name spelled in different ways.

Other services, such as 56KB or T1 lines, were managed by separate organizations, resulting in more individual bills to the business. Ads in the telephone directory were placed with another organization within the phone company. This group only recorded enough information to send an invoice; the billing name was not associated to a particular business. Calling for service required interfacing with yet another organization. The support groups logged enough information to get to the caller and solve the problem. The effort to correlate trouble calls with a given telephone line or business was weak at best.

With all these groups working in relative isolation, using their own systems, and taking no steps to ensure a consistent picture of the customer, the phone company was unable to answer several basic questions: Who are our biggest customers? Which customers use more than one of our products? What is the average number of service calls per year for a business with less than 25 telephone lines?

Deregulation and diversification are forcing changes in the way the telecommunications industry looks at customers. Despite recent legislation, the phone company remains largely unchallenged for your local telephone service; however, they have branched out into other services for which there is competition. With more to sell, and the possibility of other companies selling the same thing, the importance of understanding the customer has increased. A new emphasis on marketing has emerged; customer information can provide a competitive edge.

This new view presents serious challenges for the telephone company. Information from numerous systems must be combined. Each system may have different standards for entry of data, different requirements for the population of important fields, and varying levels of data quality. As the data warehouse team works to merge data from these systems, the systems themselves are being modified to support a future customer view that is more coordinated.

Deregulation also allows the phone company to get involved in new lines of business, such as cellular service. These businesses add to the number of systems that may contain important information on their customers. To make matters more complicated, local telephone companies are now merging with one another. Each merger doubles the number of systems to contend with, and increases the complexity of the problem.

The Telco Marketer

We will now speak with the recently hired vice president of Residential Marketing for a regional telephone company. A new position created as part of a corporate restructuring effort, he is charged with bringing together and coordinating marketing efforts from various product groups, and we are charged with developing a data warehouse to help him. Here's what he has to say:

> We are in the midst of a major change in focus. Our sales and marketing forces are being reorganized to reflect a shift from product focus to customer focus. It is a big change that will probably take us several years, because our systems are organized around products and regions. It is still very hard for us to get a good picture of who a customer is. The information is out there, but it's scattered across a bunch of different systems and entered in many different ways.
>
> We really have two major customer categories: consumers and businesses. We need to know a lot of the same information for these groups, but each has some unique requirements as well. I am in charge of our Residential Marketing efforts. Sometimes we call this consumer marketing.
>
> For consumers, we need a good composite picture of all the services provided to a given home. We can get a lot of the information pretty easily, because most homes already receive a single invoice; however, we still have two invoice systems for different regions.
>
> Also, we go elsewhere for a lot of additional information. Some services, such as ISDN and Internet access, are still billed separately. Our parent company provides information on the use of cellular phones.
>
> It would be useful to have all this information available monthly. We would like to look at a composite picture of a residential customer. What combination of services does he or she have, how much time is spent on the phone; what is the total billing

amount? We try to pull this information together so that we can identify likely candidates for selling additional products. We call this cross-selling.

In the future, as our marketing efforts become more sophisticated, we will also want to be able to look at the changes in service on a monthly basis—what was added, what was dropped, and so forth. Drops can help us identify services that may be in need of retention efforts, and additions will be useful in reviewing the success of our campaigns. One other thing we are gearing up to try is making special offers to customers who are moving within our coverage area. This is an ideal time to sell them new services, because they contact us, rather than vice versa.

This executive is facing some major challenges, but he has given us a solid idea of what he needs in the short term. He has also hinted at some things that will be needed in the future, and has given us an idea of how the information he needs overlaps with needs in another subject area.

We have been told by the vice president that a key requirement is the ability to analyze the combination of services sold to each customer. He wants to use this to target likely prospects for the sale of additional services.

In the future, he will want to use the data mart to look at changes in service over time, presumably to gauge the effectiveness of marketing efforts. He also pointed out that looking at services being dropped will allow him to identify at-risk customer profiles. Contacting others who fit the profile can possibly prevent them from dropping the service.

Key Business Terms

Cross-selling. The technique of selling additional services to existing customers.

Retention effort. A marketing activity aimed at preventing loss of existing customers.

We have also learned something extremely important to our effort: The needs of the Residential Marketing team have significant overlap with the Commercial marketers. Although we are not building the data mart for the commercial side of the business, it is important for us to consider it. If we do not, future expansion may be difficult. We have been told that much of the information in each subject area is the same, which implies that there may be some analysis that can be done across all customer types. If an effort is under way to build a data mart on the commercial side, both teams will benefit from coordination. If there is not a current effort, we can ensure that our design will mesh well with anything that is built in the future.

The executive has revealed that the commercial and residential marketers have some identical requirements, and that there is some additional unique information in each area. In the long run, the most flexible solution may include not two, but three stars. One, called the *core* star, would contain all information common to both types of customers. Separate *custom* stars for Commercial and Residential Marketing contain the same information that is in the core star, as well as any additional facts and dimension attributes specific to their respective subject areas.

In this scheme, our Residential Marketing data mart would be one of the custom stars. We will be building it before there is a data mart for the commercial customers, but we have been told that there are equally important needs in that area. We need to be sure that we choose our grain and set up our dimensions to maximize the amount of overlap we will eventually have with the commercial side. This effort will allow future construction of a core star for cross-functional analysis of all customer types.

The Residential Billing Data Mart

We're ready to put together a design for the telco's Residential Billing data mart. As we design the data mart, keep in mind our primary objectives:

- Provide a composite picture of services provided to each customer
- Facilitate cross-sell analysis
- Follow individual customers when they move
- Monitor changes in service

Data for our schema will come from five different source systems: our two call-billing systems, ISP billing, the parent company's cellular billing, and the ISDN system. There are a large number of sources, so this will be a significant project. Each of these systems operate on monthly billing cycles, so the grain of our time dimension will be month.

Our schema will represent a monthly snapshot of services by customer. There will be an obvious need for a customer dimension, and we must pay close attention to it. We have been told that the company wishes to track customers as they move within the service area, so an address or phone number will not be sufficient to identify the customer. If there is no solid source attribute that will allow us to track a customer, we will be unable to accommodate this need. Luckily, the billing system

Building Core and Custom Stars

Sometimes, what should go into a dimension "depends." The attributes of a customer, for example, depend on what kind of customer it is. For a residential customer, attributes include name, address, social security number, and telephone number. For a business, attributes include name, address, number of employees, and business type. Some of these attributes are recorded for each type of customer, like a name and address. But each type also has some unique attributes, such as the social security number of the residential customer and the number of employees in a business. The same can be said for measures: sometimes, they "depend." The telco doesn't want to record the number of service calls for residential customers, but they do for commercial customers. For all customers, total billing amount is relevant.

We have heterogeneous subsets of data within the subject area, but there is significant overlap. In many cases, a data mart can focus simply on the overlap and deliver value to the business. In other cases, it may be necessary to delve into the details of one subset—residential customers only. A third option is to do both: One schema is designed to focus on all common elements, while additional schemas focus on the various details—residential and commercial.

In Chapter 1, "The Business-Driven Data Warehouse," we said that the schema encompassing common elements is referred to as the *core* schema. Each schema that provides additional detail for a part of the subject area is referred to as a *custom* schema. What is the best way to develop a family of schemas like this? One might expect the core schema to be built first, with the more detailed custom schemas to follow. This expectation is brought about by the relative simplicity of the assigns a customer identification number that is separate from the telephone account number. We also have a social security number we can use to verify accuracy.

To make it easy to find rows in the fact table for customers who moved that month, we will include status dimension with a new_residence flag. During a customer's first month at a residence, the customer's row in the fact table will include a key to a row in the status dimension in which a new_residence flag is set to Y.

core schema's design. It has fewer attributes, so it must be easier to build. Plus, it will be of interest to a wider group of users.

But these assumptions often prove wrong. The number of attributes in the schema is not a good gauge of the complexities that will be involved in loading it with data.

The complexity and duration of the loading task are functions of the number of source systems. When deciding how to phase development of core and custom schemas, look at the number of source systems that will be required for each. Consider a subject area that will require a core schema and two custom schemas. One data source is shared by the custom schemas, but each also has an additional data source. This means that while each custom schema has two sources, the core schema has three. In this case, the business will see more immediate benefit if one of the custom schemas is built first, since it only involves two sources. Next, the second custom schema is built. Again, only two sources are required, and one of them is now familiar to the developers. Once both custom schemas are on line, the core schema can be built by merging the homogeneous data from each of the custom stars.

In other cases, the scope of a data mart project makes a *de facto* determination about which star will be built first. Our telco study is an example; the team is working to build a schema for Residential Marketing. The checks are being written by the vice president of Residential Marketing, who is not about to wait for the team to build two other star schemas before getting around to doing the Residential Billing star. However, the team should take the time to consider the grain and dimensions of the other schemas, to ensure that its design will fit into the big picture.

> ### The Enterprise-Wide Data Warehouse and the Data Mart
>
> In the past, an *enterprise-wide data warehouse* or a unified *operational data store* would be built prior to making any data available to business users via a data mart. With a track record of multimillion-dollar budgets and multiyear development projects before benefits are delivered to the business, this approach is giving way to an incremental approach, where stars are brought on line one at a time. When designed so that they will conform with future data marts in related subject areas, these data marts reap immediate business benefits and stand ready to integrate with a larger enterprise landscape. This topic is discussed in Chapter 14, "Building an Enterprise Data Warehouse."
>
> Some businesses are willing to develop a "throwaway" data mart, to be replaced or extensively modified when the next subject area is brought on line. This practice can be useful in high-impact subject areas, but for our telco, it is out of the question, because the data mart will be very expensive. Why? Loading data into the mart is the most difficult and time-consuming part of its development. With each additional source system, the complexity increases. We identified at least five separate sources of data for the consumer billing subject area. Imagine having to throw away all that work two years later, when it is discovered that the customer view in the data mart doesn't integrate well with other parts of the data warehouse. Our telco will be well advised to consider the overall landscape of the future data warehouse before building the Consumer Billing data mart.

For all subsequent months, the customer's row will include a key for a status row in which the flag is set to N.

Choosing the Right Grain for Cross-Sell Analysis

To facilitate the cross-sell analysis, we must capture the combination of services a customer has each month. We can do so in two ways, each distinguished by a different grain for the fact table. Our first option, shown in Figure 3.3, is to place a row in the fact table for each service billed to a customer in a given month. The second option, shown in Figure 3.4, is to have one row in the fact table per customer per month, enumerating the specific services through a series of flags. This second option looks very similar to the "wide" promotion dimension we built for the grocery store, while the first option attempts to normalize the relationship

Figure 3.3 Grain by service, month, and customer.

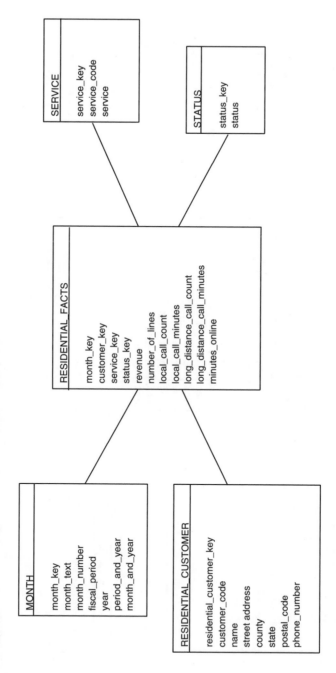

Figure 3.4 Grain by customer and month.

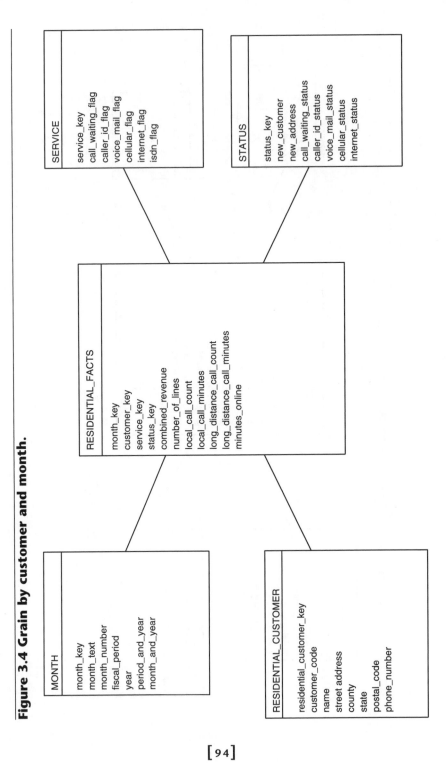

through a change in grain to the fact table. We'll look at each option carefully before making a decision.

In option one, each individual service receives a separate row in the fact table. The dimension we are left with will be well normalized. A sample of the data that might be found in the service dimension is shown in Table 3.5. This breakout requires our fact table grain to be monthly sales by customer and service. All our measures, such as number of calls, call minutes, and billed amount, must be captured at this level.

We have identified cross-sell analysis as a basic requirement for our data mart. Consider how this proposed design would facilitate the question, "Which customers have ISDN but not Internet access?" For each row in our fact table, we must determine if the customer has ISDN, and does not have Internet access, before deciding to include that row in our total. But each service a customer has is recorded in a separate row. We will not be able to make our determination on a row-by-row basis.

Instead, we will be forced to choose between using a subquery or correlated subquery approach to answer the question. Using a subquery that identifies customers' Internet access, we can qualify a main query that looks for ISDN customers. The SQL would look like this:

```
Select residential_customer.name
from residential_customer,
    residential_facts,
    service
where residential_facts.customer_key =
residential_customer.customer_key
```

Table 3.5 Including Service in the Grain Forces a Narrow Dimension

Code	Service
Cell	Cellular
POTS	POTS
CW	Call waiting
VM	Voice mail
IS	Internet access
DT	ISDN

```
and residential_facts.service_key = service.service_key
and service.service_type = 'ISDN'
and residential_facts.customer_key not in (
    select distinct customer_key
    from residential_facts,
        service
    where residential_facts.service_key= service.service_key
    and services.service_type = 'Internet'
```

This SQL has been simplified; it would also be necessary to isolate the particular month in both the main query and subquery. Similar results could be achieved through a correlated subquery, but we will spare you the code. Suffice it to say, it will be equally complex. In situations where more cross-sell analysis of more than two products is required, we might be forced into *multiple* subqueries. Whatever we do, it looks like it will be an awful lot of work to perform the cross-sell analysis using this schema.

There are some other problems with this design as well. Because each service gets a single row in the fact table, we must record the same measures for each service. We have at least one measure, number_of_lines, that is not applicable to some of the service types, such as Internet access. Another potential complication could result if services are sold in packages. Because our grain is monthly sales by customer *and service*, we are forced to break out, or "unbundle," billing charges to the service level. This exercise holds no analysis value for the business.

TIP

Always be careful when going to the business community for information that is not in a system. If you encounter resistance, there may be a good reason for it. Interpret this as a sign that your design needs work.

You may be in search of something known to the business but not a system, such as the promotion information at the grocery store. This information will provide valuable analytic functionality. Business people will recognize this fact, and be willing to provide the needed information.

However, when you encounter resistance, your requirement may hold little or no business value. For example, the telco does not maintain the prices of individual components of a package, and sales are not summarized that way. When we ask for a formula to break these prices out, we are greeted with quizzical stares and confusion.

The first approach seems to have numerous drawbacks. We have different measures for each service type, some of the cost information is not normally broken down the way that we would need it to be, and cross-sell analysis will require some heavy-duty SQL. Let's look at the second option, shown in Figure 3.4.

In this design, we have reduced the grain of the fact table: Each customer gets only one row per month. To track the different services, we have extended the service dimension with a series of flags. This approach is not unlike the promotion dimension for the grocery store. Although it does not follow the rules of normalization sought after for OLTP systems, it makes our cross-sell analysis much easier.

Much as we looked at combinations of promotions for the grocery store, we can use this table of flags to compare combinations of services. For example, our question about ISDN users is now asked with a very simple SQL statement:

```
Select residential_customer.name
from residential_customer,
     residential_facts,
     service,
     month
where month.month_text = 'January'
  and month.year = 1997
  and service.isdn_flag = 'Y'
  and service.internet_flag = 'N'
  and month.month_key = residential_facts.month_key
  and service.service_key = residential_facts.service_key
  and residential_customer.customer_key =
residential_facts.customer_key
```

Cross-sell analysis will be much easier with this design, and for good measure, we have even added a number_of_services attribute to the dimension. This column will aid marketing in assessing its overall success at selling additional services over time. This design also resolves the problems surrounding our measures. The number_of_lines measure can lie alongside the billing_amount measure; no longer must it be directly associated with services for which it is meaningless. The business will not be required to break out costs in ways that are irrelevant.

Because this second option makes the cross-sell analysis easier while resolving problems the first design had with measures, it is clearly the way to go. Let's take a look at the rest of the design.

Turning Dimensions into Measures: The Status Dimension

In addition to cross-sell analysis, we were told that analysis of service changes would be necessary. To facilitate this, a series of columns corresponding to each service is added to the status dimension. These columns will take on one of three values: Dropped, Added, or Unchanged. Table 3.6 shows some examples.

Like the service table, this dimension table is wide and denormalized. The grain we have chosen for the fact table necessitates this approach. Analysis of service changes will be easy: We simply examine the appropriate status flags. If we are interested in finding accounts that added a particular service, we use the appropriate flag in the where clause of the query.

In addition to being useful in filtering queries, the status information can provide useful metrics as well. For example, adds and deletes for each service type can be summed up and grouped by month. This requires a bit of SQL wizardry, but can be done on many databases. This SQL statement, for example, totals the adds and deletes of the voice mail service by month:

```
Select month.month,
       sum( decode ( status.voice_mail_status, 'Deleted', 1, 0 ))
voice_mail_deletes,
       sum( decode ( status.voice_mail_status, 'Added', 1, 0 ))
voice_mail_adds
from month, status, residential_facts
 where month.month_key = residential_facts.month_key
and    status_status_key = residential_facts.status_key
group by month.month
```

This piece of SQL transforms a single dimension attribute into two measures. If this form of status change totaling will be required frequently, we may choose to formalize these measures. For each service, two columns are added to the fact table: one for adds and one for deletes. We will populate the columns with 0s and 1s. The SQL to total adds and deletes is now simplified on two fronts. Adds and deletes are now each recorded in their own columns, and the columns contain numeric data that is easily summed.

```
Select month.month,
     sum(voice_mail_deletes ),
     sum( voice_mail_adds)
 from month, status, residential_facts
 where month.month_key = residential_facts.month_key
 group by month.month
```

Because the adds and deletes contain only 0 or 1, they look like flags. As such, one might be tempted to leave them in the status table. Truly numeric and additive, however, the fact table is the logical place for them. At the cost of a bit more storage space, we gain a more comprehensible design, and eliminate the

Table 3.6 Status Dimension Table

new_customer	new_address	call_waiting_status	caller_id_status	voice_mail_status	cellular_status	internet_status	isdn_status
N	N	Added	Unchanged	Unchanged	Unchanged	Unchanged	Unchanged
N	N	Unchanged	Unchanged	Unchanged	Unchanged	Unchanged	Unchanged
N	N	Unchanged	Unchanged	Dropped	Unchanged	Unchanged	Unchanged
N	N	Unchanged	Unchanged	Unchanged	Dropped	Added	Unchanged

need to join to the status table when totaling service additions or deletions. When aggregate tables are built, we will store values higher than 1 in these columns, and they will no longer resemble flags.

The status table does reveal one drawback of the decision to use a wide service dimension: Since it is wide, it will not be easy to get the total number of adds and deletes across all services. We will need to retrieve the number of adds and deletes for each service, as in the SQL, and then add the service totals together. To avoid this eventuality, we can add number_of_adds and number_of_deletes into the fact table.

Telecom Reports

Let's take a look at some examples of reports supported by this design. First, we will build a report that can be used on a monthly basis to gauge the success of cross-sell activities. A first cut at this report is shown in Report 3.7.

While it holds useful information, this report overlooks *how* marketing uses it. They're looking at trends. Is the number of four or five service customers going up or down? To see if there is an increase in the number of four service customers in February, we must check the January number, scan down to the February number, and perform the computation in our head.

Report 3.7 The trend is difficult to read in this cross-sell report.

Cross-Sell Analysis

Month	Number of Services	Number of Customers
January 1996	5	75,000
	4	121,100
	3	740,294
	2	1,374,238
	1	2,347,953
	Total:	4,658,585
February 1996	5	75,000
	4	122,394
	3	750,192
	2	1,400,999
	1	2,200,999
	Total:	4,549,584

The report can be adjusted to make the trend easier to see. In Report 3.8, February counts are placed directly next to January counts, and a column is added to show the percent of change. Now, marketing can instantly see the change in this key indicator.

This report can be adjusted to include more than two months, so that the trend can be observed over a longer period of time. Or, marketing may prefer to compare the totals of the first month of each quarter, rather than consecutive months.

TIP

When building reports, don't forget that not all measures are in plain sight. For example, the Number of Customers columns in these reports don't come from a column in the fact table. The customer count is gathered simply by counting rows, because each one represents a single customer. Because it does not have a column in the fact table, the customer count is called a *factless fact*.

Number of Customers is retrieved by using the SQL Count(*) function. All dimension attributes involved (month and number_of_services in these reports) are placed in the group by clause of the query.

A word of caution: This factless fact is semi-additive. We cannot aggregate the number of customers over time.

Marketing can use the data mart to look at the correlation of specific services. Correlations can be useful in several ways. Highly correlated services might

Report 3.8 Placing two time periods side by side gives visibility to trend.

	Cross-Sell Analysis		
Number of Services	Number Customers January 1996	Number of Customers February 1996	Change
5	75,000	75,000	0
4	121,100	122,394	+1%
3	740,294	750,192	+1%
2	1,374,238	1,400,999	+2%
1	2,347,953	2,200,999	–6%
Total:	4,658,585	4,549,584	

help pinpoint likely customers. For example, if most voice mail users also have call waiting, it might be worthwhile to market call waiting to voice mail users who don't have it.

High correlation is not always what the marketers are looking for. Where services are interdependent, low correlation may indicate a likely prospect pool as well. For example, the telephone company provides Internet access as well as ISDN service. Most of the ISDN users are probably Internet users, because the primary use of ISDN is to connect to an Internet access provider.

Report 3.9 breaks out ISDN users based on whether they also use the phone company for Internet access. Based on this chart, it is clear that most of our ISDN customers have turned elsewhere for Internet access. A marketing campaign targeted at ISDN users without Internet service may well be in order.

The time series in Report 3.9 prompts new questions. While the total number of ISDN users is increasing, the number who rely on the phone company for Internet access is relatively constant. Are new ISDN customers going elsewhere for Internet access? Are existing Internet customers jumping ship? A quick report filtering on the ISDN status flag would help answer these questions. If existing Internet customers are dropping their service, a retention campaign is in order. If the new ISDN users are not using Internet service, a cross-sell effort is required. Since they're already on the phone ordering ISDN, it is a perfect opportunity to suggest Internet access as well.

Report 3.9 Do users of ISDN also have Internet service?

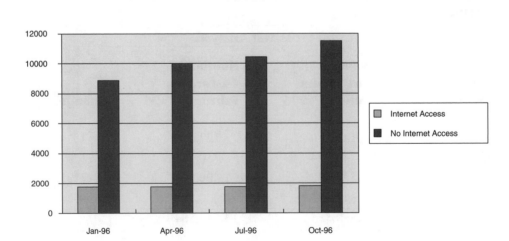

ISDN Users

The VP of Residential Marketing mentioned another time when the customer is already on the phone: at the time of a move. He mentioned that there is a concerted effort to get people to add services when they move within the telco's service area. The new_residence flag in our status dimension helps assess these efforts.

Clearly, Report 3.10 shows the efforts to sell services to customers who are moving are working well. A total of 970 services were added by existing customers who moved in January, while only 14 were dropped. Most of the success has been with call waiting; other services show only marginal gains.

Retail Banking

The grocery store had relatively anonymous customers, and the telephone company was in the process of developing a picture of its customers. Now we turn to banking, where marketers possess very detailed profiles of their customers. For banks, the data warehouse can support sophisticated marketing campaigns.

Banks offer many products. In addition to the traditional checking and savings accounts, there are CDs, IRAs, mortgages, auto loans, home equity loans, credit cards, and even insurance or investment services. While each of these products can be profitable to the bank, many of them carry a high level of risk.

Because of the nature of their products, banks are well motivated to gather lots of information about their customers. Even if your mortgage is not with the bank, they will still find out how much principal you owe, and whether you make

---

Report 3.10 Are we selling more services to customers who are relocating?

Service Changes
Existing Customers at New Address
Number of Relocated Customers: 2200

Service	Adds	Drops
Call waiting	766	12
Voice mail	28	0
Caller ID	96	2
Call forwarding	72	0
Call return	8	0
Total:	970	14

your payments on time. This information will influence decisions about whether you should be offered a home equity loan or yet another credit card. It can also be used to improve the effectiveness of marketing efforts.

External Data

Banks and other financial service organizations possess a lot of detailed demographic data about their customers, and their prospects. Even if your mortgage is with a different organization, your bank is likely to know all about it. Banks get all this information about you from other organizations.

We refer to information that comes from outside an organization as *external data*. In the case of banks, most of this external data is purchased; however, they don't buy it from other banks. Instead, they turn to organizations that are in the business of gathering this information and selling it.

Anyone who has applied for a mortgage is likely to have seen a report on his or her finances from one of the major credit bureaus. Information is also for sale that doesn't identify individuals, but instead, identifies likely characteristics of a larger group. Your income level, home value, and even the type of car you are likely to drive are routinely "estimated" based on averages taken from samples in your neighborhood.

External data is not always purchased. Census data can easily be obtained from the government, and organizations that work together often find that sharing data can benefit both parties. Retailers often share inventory data with their suppliers. This allows the retailers to keep their shelves stocked, so they don't miss a sale. The supplier benefits from the relationship, too; because the product is always on the shelf, consumers are never forced to sample a competitor's product.

External data about competitors is often valuable. A company comparing its own product's sales with a competitor's can track its *market share*. This is common in manufacturing and television broadcasting. External data about competitors can also drive pricing decisions. We'll look at these concepts in Chapter 9, "Financial Reporting," and in Chapter 12, "Key Measures and Ratios."

We have come to the office of the Marketing director for a regional bank with about 45 branches across three states. The bank employs some sophisticated marketing techniques, but is interested in streamlining its process by building a data warehouse.

What we're really doing is selling the bank's products: accounts. We've got several major categories of accounts, with several types of account in each category. For example, one category of accounts is deposit accounts. Within that category, there are several types, such as checking and savings. Then there are the specific products. We've got about 15 checking products, including Budget Checking, Basic Checking, and Interest Checking.

We market our products to internal and external customers. Most marketing activities involve direct mail. We've got 500,000 accounts, and over 100 products, so we can't just mail promotions to everyone. Instead, we need to be cost effective. We do this by studying the characteristics of current customers for a particular product. By understanding current customers, we can identify prospects likely to respond to a mailing. Right now we do this by grabbing month's end information on accounts. We look at all the characteristics of the customer, including the combination of accounts he or she has and the balances. Unfortunately, it is not easy for us to look at the history of accounts over time.

When I refer to a "customer," I'm not talking about an account holder. What is important to us when looking for potential responders, or risky prospects, is the collective profile of the household. A household might be composed of several people holding many different accounts. Of course, there are some things, like branch location, which are relevant at both the account level and the household level, but a lot of what we look at in making decisions is recorded only at the household level. I'm talking about things like income level, education level, number of children, and so on.

These demographic characteristics of households may change over time. Also, individuals may move in or out of the household, the income band may change, and so on. We'd like to have the history of the demographic characteristics of the household over time if we're going to look at account history.

Today, when we do a mailing that promotes a product, we have a lot of trouble analyzing the results. We have a lot of different systems to contend with, and there are a couple of things we get on paper only. What we would really like to be able to do is look at all the accounts that were opened by people who received the mailing. The data is probably in our systems, but right now, the main way we gather it is via questionnaires distributed with account applications. Ideally, we would look at how many recipients responded to the mailing, and compare this rate to the rate of account openings by nonrecipients. This would let us evaluate the success of our marketing activity. By understanding our responders, we might also be able to market more effectively the next time. Ultimately, we would even like to be able to look at these accounts and see if they are actually profitable for the bank.

This interview has given us a lot of information about what is important to the bank's marketers. We've been given an overview of the products and customers, and how marketing activities are used to sell more products to internal and external customers. The design of our data mart will need to meet the following requirements:

- Maintain history on each individual account
- Associate each account with a household customer
- Provide detailed profiles of customers that reflect changes over time
- Track the status of accounts over time

The Banking Schema

At first glance, the needs of the bank seem quite similar to those of the telco. There will be customers, services, and status. There are two key differences, though, and they will force a different design approach.

The bank and the telco both sell a number of products to their customers. For the telco, we referred to them as *services*, while the bank's products are *accounts*. The bank has a very large number of products. The Marketing director told us that there are 15 kinds of checking accounts, and over 100 accounts overall. The telco's relatively small number of products allowed a wide service table, but for the bank, this table would be too wide.

Like the telco, the bank wants a composite picture of all the services sold to a customer. The bank's "customer" is not an individual, but rather one or more individuals in a family who reside together. This customer is referred to as a *household*. Consider the Jones family. Mr. Jones holds checking and savings accounts with the bank, Mrs. Jones has a credit card from the bank, and the couple also holds a mortgage. All four of these products were sold to the Jones household. It is this household that the marketers think of as the customer.

We also learned from the Marketing director that there is information at the individual account level that is often required. Branch locations, for example, are specific to each account, and not the household. Mr. Jones may have set up his deposit accounts with an officer at one branch, while two separate officers at another branch approved Mrs. Jones's credit card and the mortgage. The bank may want to compare the success of different branches, so the grain of the fact table cannot remain at the household customer level. The account information requires a grain that goes deeper than the household customer level.

Because the bank has a wider array of products, and because it requires tracking detail at a level lower than the customer, we cannot use the same design strategy employed by the telco. Instead, we opt for a design very similar to the one we ruled out at the telco. Our grain will not be at the customer level, but at the account level. The design is shown in Figure 3.5.

The household dimension is used to relate multiple accounts. Note that this is not done via a relationship from account to household; instead, the fact table maintains the link. Each account is related to the household it is a part of via the fact table. This method allows accounts to move in and out of households over time, so we can capture the changes to a household.

Associated with each household is a much richer set of attributes than the telco had for its customers. Dimensions like income band, home value, and number of children will serve the marketers well. Much of this *demographic* information will be periodically updated by the bank, and we have been told that capturing its history is important. In the interest of making the schema easier to load and use, we have opted to split these demographics out into a separate dimension, though logically it may be considered household information.

The account dimension contains the attributes relating to an individual product held by a customer. There are about half a million accounts, so this will be a fairly large dimension. Product information has therefore been split out into its own dimensions. This separation seems redundant, but it will improve performance of queries that do not require access to the full account dimension, and reduce the amount of indexing overhead.

Figure 3.5 The banking schema.

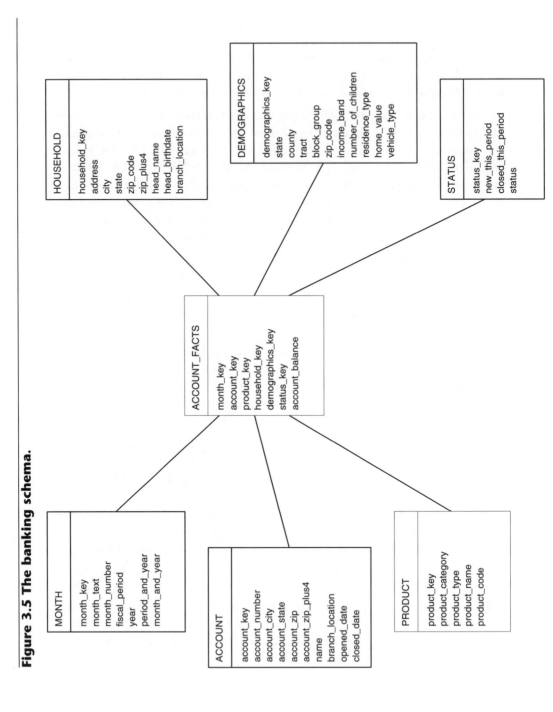

HOUSEHOLD

household_key
address
city
state
zip_code
zip_plus4
head_name
head_birthdate
branch_location

DEMOGRAPHICS

demographics_key
state
county
tract
block_group
zip_code
income_band
number_of_children
residence_type
home_value
vehicle_type

STATUS

status_key
new_this_period
closed_this_period
status

ACCOUNT_FACTS

month_key
account_key
product_key
household_key
demographics_key
status_key
account_balance

MONTH

month_key
month_text
month_number
fiscal_period
year
period_and_year
month_and_year

ACCOUNT

account_key
account_number
account_city
account_state
account_zip
account_zip_plus4
name
branch_location
opened_date
closed_date

PRODUCT

product_key
product_category
product_type
product_name
product_code

TIP

The household dimension can be one of the most challenging to load. The bank is likely to already be using software to "household" customers by applying an algorithm used to correlate names, addresses, phone numbers, social security numbers, and so forth.

If we rely on the householding that is already being done, we may have to source our data downstream from the systems that actually collect the account transactions. This decision may make our data mart vulnerable to changes in intermediate systems, and may shield it from advantageous changes in the source. It also may mean that our data mart never replaces the systems the Marketing director complained about.

If we attempt to do householding ourselves, we will require a significant additional investment, software, and time to establish our data mart.

As in the telco design, there is a status table. This status table is much smaller, but equally powerful. It captures new accounts and closed accounts. Open and closed dates appear on the account itself, but the separate status attribute will free us from tedious SQL date comparison semantics in some situations, making queries easier to write.

Because we are storing a single row for each account, we must store the same facts for each account. While we record finance charges on credit cards, there is no such fee on a checking account. We have the same problem with the dimensional attributes. Some types of accounts have maturity dates, others do not. Should we need to capture this heterogeneous data, we might build core and custom schemas. As discussed earlier, the custom star includes any attributes specific to the particular account type. We will build custom schemas for the bank in Chapter 10, "Profitability."

Unlike the telco's service dimension, the bank's schema cannot accommodate a wide product dimension including flags for all the various products. There are a couple of reasons we cannot use this technique. First, we need to track accounts individually. This necessitates a fact table grain that is too fine to incorporate a composite view of the products in use by the household.

Second, the dimension would be very large. There are over 100 products. Assuming every possible combination of products existed, it would contain somewhere on the order of 2^{100} rows—an astronomical number. Realistically, it would be much smaller, limited by the number of accounts, though a bit larger to allow for changes over time. While not an issue for a series of flags, the bank's product dimension would require more descriptive data—product categories, types, and names—that might be queried on its own, or *browsed*. This requires us to take measures to reduce the number of rows in the dimension. Somewhere around 100,000 rows, it becomes difficult to browse a dimension table. This was not a concern for the telco. With 20 products, its dimension might grow to 1,000,000 rows, but no one would bother to browse a series of flags.

For the bank, cross-sell analysis will require hard work. Instead of exploiting a simple series of flags in our SQL, we will have to employ subqueries for some of our analysis. While not a disaster, we can eliminate this requirement by building a household-level fact table. This table will not include keys to account, product, branch, or status—the grain of these dimensions is too fine. Instead, we only include keys to household, month, and a very wide version of the product dimension.

Beyond Reports: Using the Banking Data Mart

We have delivered a richly detailed schema for our bank marketers to use. Unlike the other schemas we have seen in this chapter, many of the uses of this data mart will not involve reports; instead, it will serve as a source for analysis activities.

The schema will be used to identify prospects based on demographic correlations, generate mailing lists, and cross-reference recipients with new account openers to measure the effectiveness of a mailing. The bank can also look beyond the response rate to study the respondents themselves. A profile of the respondents may help narrow the focus of future marketing activities, so that the next prospect pool is more likely to respond.

Identifying Likely Prospects

The banking data mart can be used to identify very focused correlations between demographic attributes or measures and the use of a product. As with the telco, correlations may be used to target customers for cross-selling, or identify at-risk customers for retention efforts.

The bank can look for correlations in a number of ways. Sets of data may be selected out of the data mart and fed into data-mining tools or statistical analysis packages. These tools automate much of the work involved in identifying relationships between various data elements. Marketers will also be free to ask questions directly of the schema, and interpret the results themselves.

Report 3.11 illustrates that owners of luxury vehicles are more likely to have an investment account than those who drive other vehicle types. Luxury

---

Report 3.11 Owners of luxury cars are more likely to hold investment accounts.

Investment Accounts
Average Number of Investment Accounts per Household
by Automobile Type

Category	Average Quantity Investment Accounts
Luxury	.333
Family	.292
Sport	.103
Basic	.021
Unknown	.155

---

vehicle owners without an investment account might be likely prospects for direct marketing campaigns. The schema records a wide array of demographic data in addition to vehicle type. Observations like this one may be combined together to produce more effective marketing campaigns.

Generating Mail Lists

Based on data like these, marketers can make decisions on how to sell a particular product. In this case, we decide to market to owners of luxury vehicles. How is this accomplished? Two common marketing activities are direct mailings and tele-sales. In both cases, a particular product is promoted to a particular group, usually with some sort of offer.

For example, a mailing might offer reduced fees on an investment account for the first six months. This mailing can be targeted to customers who don't have an investment account but possess attributes of those who do. The mail list can be pulled directly from our schema via SQL. This example pulls the names and addresses of customers who own luxury vehicles with over $50,000 in less than three accounts, one of which is a SaversPlus account, as of January 1997. We've omitted some of the joins to make it easier to read.

```
Select customer.name,
    customer.address,
    customer.city,
    customer.state,
    customer.zip_code
```

```
from customer,
    account_facts,
    time,
    demographics
where time.month = 'January'
  and time.year = 1997
  and demographics.vehicle_type = 'Luxury'
  and exists ( select *
    from account_facts af2,
        products
    where af2.customer_key = account_facts.customer_key
      and aft.time_key = account_facts.time_key
      and aft.product_key = products.product_key
      and products.product = 'SaversPlus' )
group by customer.name,
    customer.address,
    customer.city,
    customer.state,
    customer.zip_code
having count(*) < 4 and sum( balance) > 50000
```

Marketing might also look for prospects who are not current customers. Names and addresses can be purchased from third parties such as credit bureaus. The same set of qualifications used to select likely prospects out of the pool of existing customers are supplied to the third party. The party may return a list of names, or may actually execute the mailing for marketing.

Evaluating the Mailing's Impact

After a particular marketing activity has taken place, the schema can be used to look at its results. The grocery store did this by scrutinizing overall sales of the promoted item. The bank's marketers can get more specific, because they know their customers well, and also know exactly who got the mailing.

Either the account-opened date in the account dimension, or the account_status column in the status dimension will allow us to detect new accounts that have been opened. We need to qualify this list so that it only includes recipients of the mailing. This can be done by maintaining a table that contains the keys of the households in question. In Chapter 13, "Presenting Information," such a table of keys is referred to as a *study group*. The table can be created by changing the first few lines of the SQL statement that was used to formulate the mail list.

```
create table investment_offer as
Select distinct customer_key
from...
```

If we've built this table, we can find the respondents who opened the account being promoted with a simple query. The critical conditions on this query are shown in bold.

```
Select count(*)
 from account_facts,
    time,
    product,
    investment_offer
 where account_facts.customer_key = investment_offer.customer_key
  and product.product = 'SuperInvestor Fund'
  and account.date_opened < to_date( '31-JAN-1997' )
  and time.month = 'May'
  and time.year = 1997
  and time.time_key = account_facts.time_key
  and product.product_key = account_facts.product_key
  and account.account_key = account_facts.account_key
```

Instead of joining to the customer table, we have joined to a table that contains only the keys of the recipients of the mailing. This operation eliminates any customers who did not receive the mailing. The next condition ensures that we are only looking for accounts of the type promoted in the mailing. The account-open date is checked to see if the account was opened after the mailing was sent out. Because a count of customers is not additive over time, we have filtered for a single month and year to avoid double-counting. We chose a date well after the mailing.

This SQL statement returns a single number: the number of accounts opened by receivers. We can divide this number by the number in the mail group to get a response rate.

We cannot assume that every person who received our investment account offer and opened an account did so because of the mailing. Some may have been planning to open an account anyway; the mailings may have been thrown away. To account for this possibility, a control group may be set up. Every 25th prospect is removed from the mail list. We track their customer keys separately from the recipients of the mailing. We can subtract the response rate of the nonrecipients from the response rate of the recipients to calculate the lift generated by the marketing effort.

Key Business Terms

Lift. The difference between the response rate of a marketing effort and the overall sales rate. The lift percentage represents the direct impact of the marketing activity. The overall sales rate may be replaced by the rate for a control group, to refine the calculation.

Response rate. The percentage of individuals contacted by a marketing effort who accepted the offer.

Marketing is now able to pinpoint the effectiveness of its campaigns, but the power of this data mart does not end here. Because we know exactly who the respondents were, we can study them closely. By comparing them to nonrespondents, marketing can look for characteristics of the respondents that may have made them more likely to buy. A data-mining tool may reveal that the biggest discriminator between respondents and nonrespondents is a home value over $250,000. Future marketing efforts can include this discriminator in the selection criteria for the mail list, leading to an increased response rate.

It may not be possible to perform this analysis on the entire pool of recipients of our marketing campaign. Many marketing efforts are directed not only at current customers, but also at noncustomers, whose names were bought from an outside source. These external prospects will not have keys in the data mart. Our study group will not be sufficient to identify respondents. Even if names and addresses of all recipients are available, changes in spelling or punctuation will make correlation of new account holders with the mailing recipients quite difficult.

Profitability and Contact Management

Already in possession of one of the most sophisticated customer data sets to be found in any industry, banks are now looking for new ways to be more effective. One way this is done is by looking at the profitability of new and existing customers, based on a complex, product-specific group of formulas. We will look at how a bank studies customer profitability in Chapter 10, "Profitability."

Marketers also recognize that by contacting customers too often, they can actually have a negative impact on sales. By tracking the history of

Summing Up Marketing

Looking at three industries, we have learned a lot about the business of marketing and how data marts can be designed to support it.

It is often easy to enhance an existing schema for marketing purposes. At the grocery store, where nothing is known about the customer, Marketing uses promotions to stimulate sales. We saw how a wide promotion dimension could be added to an existing sales schema. This simple enhancement allowed marketing to review the success of promotions and compare different promotion techniques.

Don't normalize dimensions. As we saw with the grocery store's promotion dimension, such efforts ultimately lead to reporting difficulties.

Exercise care when using semi-additive measures. A semi-additive measure like the grocery store's basket_count can easily be summarized across an incompatible dimension. The results are inaccurate, and the business consequences can be disastrous.

Build a composite picture of the customer when possible. At the telco, information about customers was available but spread across systems. By bringing it together in a data warehouse, we brought the customer into focus. A wide product table allowed cross-sell efforts. The status dimension allowed retention analysis.

Core and custom schemas can be useful. When dimensional detail determines what measures are taken and how they are viewed, a family of schemas may be in order. The telco required custom schemas for commercial and residential customers. In Chapter 10, "Profitability," we will see that the bank requires custom schemas for each type of product.

contact with each customer, marketing can avoid this situation. In Chapter 10, we develop a Contact schema, in which a contact_facts table is used to track communication with customers. Combined with the account_facts schema, contact_facts can be used to screen out those who have already been contacted more than three times last year. The logic may get even more sophisticated; if a customer has responded to a recent mailing, we may want to place his or her household back in the pool of prospects, even if we have exceeded the three-contact threshold.

Enrich the model with demographic detail. For the bank, we allowed account as well as household-level analysis. We exploited the detailed set of customer demographics to identify attributes of prospective customers, build mailing lists and control groups, analyze response rates, and profile the respondents.

All three schemas deliver more than the simple capability to report on sales. By facilitating detailed analysis, they help marketing to *increase* sales, and because they help the business *sell smarter*, each of these schemas can offer a competitive advantage to the business.

FULFILLMENT

4

Chapters 2 and 3 introduced the first two stages of the customer relationship, sales and marketing. Marketing creates the demand in the prospective customer's mind to purchase a product. The sale marks the exchange of money for product between customer and vendor. The final stage of the relationship is *fulfillment*. This step is increasingly seen as critical to long-term business success. Customers do business with companies that continually meet the expectations created by the marketing process. This is true of service and product industries, retailers and manufacturers, and in consumer or business-to-business transactions. The secret of great brand loyalty is carefully managing the balance of expectations and fulfillment.

The concept of fulfillment is easily imagined. An order placed with a catalogue retailer results in a shipment of goods. A trip to a fast-food restaurant results in a quick, fresh meal. The fulfillment process can be as simple as cooking a burger, or as complex as taking a phone order, custom building a personal computer, and then express shipping it to the consumer's home or business. It can end with the transaction and exchange of goods, or continue beyond the initial sale. For example, mail order computer companies typically provide free telephone support for some period after the sale to ensure the customer successfully sets up the device. The consumer's initial experience with the product for a short period after the sale is considered part of the vendor's fulfillment commitment.

Service fulfillment is less concrete. A corporation's monthly insurance premium provides health care service for an employee. The fulfillment process includes the continuing set of interactions between the employee and one or more health care providers. Many consumers go years without an automobile or homeowner's insurance claim, only to find their initial fulfillment experience—a claim against a long-standing policy—less than satisfying. In these cases, fulfillment is an open-ended experience with unpredictable costs for the vendor.

Similarly, a manufacturer often bears a fulfillment burden for a product long after the sale. An auto manufacturer must offer a postsale warranty to be competitive in today's market. Appliance vendors, home builders, and electronics companies offer repair and service warranties that carry on long after the sale. The impact of such obligations on the profitability of the manufacturer is clearly important.

Finally, a single transaction can involve fulfillment obligations by more than one party. For example, attending a movie involves the consumer with both the theater and the film company. A noisy, dirty theater with poor sound and over-priced popcorn can ruin a fine movie. Conversely, a bad movie cannot be saved by comfortable seating and bargain snacks. Can the consumer always separate the components of the value proposition in such a transaction? This is a common issue for retailers offering a myriad of products. The retailer is responsible primarily for a competitive price and a comfortable shopping experience; the manufacturer of each product is responsible for its quality.

 Key Business Term

Fulfillment. Goods provided and actions taken by the vendor to satisfy the value proposition underlying the sale of a product or service.

Fulfillment actions vary by industry. Catalogue retailers fulfill orders by shipping product. The grocery store fulfills the value proposition of a sale by providing the item to the consumer. Both extend the proposition to include the acceptance of returns in the event the product is of poor quality.

When an item is sold at retail, a portion of the fulfillment responsibility lies with the manufacturer. The item is assumed to have a standard degree of quality and serviceability. The terms of the sale may include a warranty or guarantee. Fulfilling the terms of such promises is a part of fulfillment for the manufacturer.

Fulfillment and the Value Proposition

It would be naïve to think that all companies are explicitly concerned about fulfillment being an abundantly positive experience for the consumer. Fulfillment is a process, not a feeling, and is not always manifested by extraordinary service or a great product. It must be seen in the context of the value proposition offered.

There is no better illustration of the value proposition's importance in the fulfillment process than commercial airline travel. Anyone who has flown both first class and coach class can vouch for the chasm that exists between life in front of and behind the curtain. Airlines offer coach and first-class passengers a distinctly different fulfillment experience. In front of the curtain are fine china, free drinks, and wide leather seats. Behind the curtain in coach are marginal food, bar prices, and bucket seats from a Vega. But everyone knows and understands the value proposition offered. Coach class promises on-time service with safety. First class offers a pampered experience on top of the baseline of safety and timeliness.

Understanding the value proposition is useful in constructing a data warehouse that includes key fulfillment data. When the fulfillment process breaks down, it is important to capture what elements of the value proposition are at risk. This is an area of the business where transaction systems may not yield the truth without some coaxing. But in today's environment of high expectations, choice, and competition, measuring fulfillment is imperative.

In our discussion, we will examine three elements of fulfillment that are commonly measured. These are:

Time. The time it takes to fill an order relative to the expected time is critical in an age of tightened value chains, just-in-time inventory, and logistics outsourcing. Businesses like Federal Express and Domino's Pizza built themselves on timely fulfillment and, in turn, created new industries.

Cost. The cost of fulfillment is crucial if it fluctuates by transaction. Service or product transactions that include indeterminate commitments on the part of the vendor are common. These include medical insurance orders, warranties, and service contracts that must be carefully managed.

Dissatisfaction. Understanding the cost of a dissatisfied customer, a returned product, or an unfilled order can be difficult to measure. Unfulfilled customers are rarely repeat customers. Moreover, returns often generate additional costs beyond lost revenue.

Our discussion begins with an innovative marketing concept for a business with a compelling reason to measure fulfillment.

Flowers and Time

Flowers are a time-honored way of sending a message. Whether in celebration or sympathy, people love to send flowers. Clever entrepreneurs have recently devised a new way to market and sell flower arrangements. They orchestrated a marketing campaign around a single toll-free number that allowed consumers to order from a long list of representative products. Next they contracted with nurseries and florists around the country to fulfill these orders. The vendor simply takes the order and then outsources fulfillment—no delivery trucks, greenhouses, or green thumbs are needed. This ingenious business model offers the consumer several advantages, including:

Reliability. The company reliably manages the delivery of an appropriate flower arrangement to the intended recipient when and where it is expected.

Convenience. It is no longer necessary to visit or call a florist. Sending flowers over long distances is simplified. In fact, with a single phone call, the customer can send flowers anywhere in the country.

Selection. Selecting an appropriate arrangement is completely outsourced. The customer relies on the company to make that decision from a long list of predefined product categories. Simply provide the occasion and price range and the customer service representative will offer up several appropriate options.

Value. Coupled with improved selection and convenience, these vendors offer an equivalent product at a reasonable premium over traditional florists. Ironically, the order may be filled by the same florist the customer would have traditionally used.

However, by outsourcing fulfillment, the company is vulnerable to problems in that process. The need to proactively monitor and manage fulfillment is critical to long-term success. Problems in the fulfillment process are a constant threat to brand identity and perceived value. Arrangements must arrive on time, in good condition, and be equal in quality to competing products offered by traditional florists.

Flowers over the Phone

Imagine establishing such a company, TeleBloomers, to sell flowers directly to consumers via a toll-free phone line. We can quickly envision and design a sales data mart for our enterprise with our lessons from Chapter 2, "Sales." The schema is presented in Figure 4.1.

Figure 4.1 The TeleBloomers sales data mart—step 1.

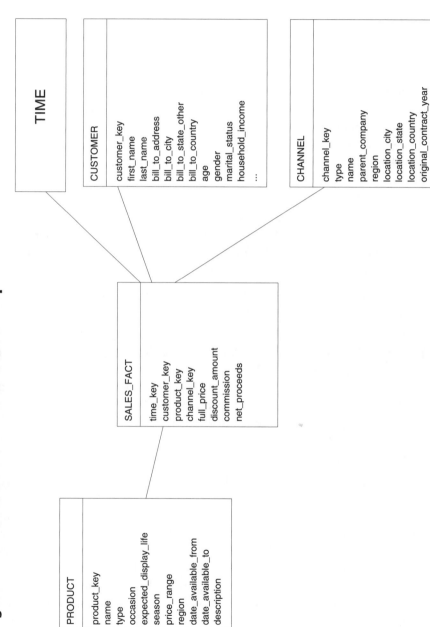

TIME

CUSTOMER

customer_key
first_name
last_name
bill_to_address
bill_to_city
bill_to_state_other
bill_to_country
age
gender
marital_status
household_income
...

CHANNEL

channel_key
type
name
parent_company
region
location_city
location_state
location_country
original_contract_year

SALES_FACT

time_key
customer_key
product_key
channel_key
full_price
discount_amount
commission
net_proceeds

PRODUCT

product_key
name
type
occasion
expected_display_life
season
price_range
region
date_available_from
date_available_to
description

To support basic sales subject area requirements, we include the following dimensions:

Customer. A dimension to track individual customers. A fast-growing dimension that will eventually enable analysis of buying trends, and support tactical marketing campaigns.

Product. A comprehensive list of all products. Product attributes important to the flower industry, including expected display life, occasion/holiday (birth of son, birth of daughter, marriage, secular funeral), type (living plant, cut flowers, etc.), season, price range, region, and dates available are included.

Time. The standard time dimension, with special emphasis on seasons and holidays.

Channel. A listing of all distribution channels used throughout the system to deliver orders. These are divided by type (nursery, grower, florist), geographic information, and original contract year.

The grain of our fact table is a product ordered by a customer delivered through a channel tracked to the hour and date the order is taken, or essentially a transaction-grained sales fact table.

The fact table for orders includes all the dimensional foreign keys and appropriate measures for each transaction. These are full price, discount amount, commission, and net proceeds. Commissions vary by channel, and discounts vary by season. We could add deal and promotion dimensions, but they are omitted here for simplicity. We now have a good foundation to work on as we add fulfillment data.

On-Time Delivery

We can use elements of our value proposition to generate fulfillment requirements. The timeliness of a delivery is most important. The late arrival of a funeral or wedding arrangement negates its value. Each order must be processed, prepared, and delivered on time. We will add two measures to our fact table to account for on-time performance. First we will include the expected delivery date and hour to establish the expectations of the customer. The actual delivery date and hour are added to measure performance against expectations. Again, we must insure that this information is tracked by our operational systems. The company call center's order entry software will obviously capture the expected delivery date. The point-of-sale system will capture the actual delivery date and time reported by the fulfillment vendor.

We can track additional steps in the order life cycle, assuming our transaction system monitors each step. The values might be "order taken," "channel notified," "channel confirmed," "delivery complete," and "delivery confirmed." Assuming each step is tracked in a status history table in the order entry system, this data can be converted into a set of date and hour measures that give even more detail on the fulfillment process—we simply transpose the rows in the status history table to each order fact row. We will round to the hour in this example. The precision of date and time measures will vary by industry. The last status value, "delivery confirmed," is not used until the order remains in "delivery complete" status for 30 days with no negative feedback from the customer. Other than the "order taken" column, the date- and hour-based measures are implemented as optional foreign keys related to clones of our standard time dimension. Our time key is a reference to the "order taken" date and hour, and is a mandatory foreign key column. The remaining time measures are optional foreign keys.

Consider the impact of these changing status values on the design of our data warehouse load process. The average time to process an order through the "delivery complete" step is 3 days. On average, 27 days pass before the final "delivery confirmed" status is conferred. When should an order be loaded, assuming a daily load process? Our first thought might be to load orders when they reach the "delivery complete" status prior to the start of the load process. Unfortunately, this creates an unintended 3-day time lag in order volume analysis. A Friday load will miss all orders since Wednesday. The business may need to notify suppliers to replenish stock for popular items. A 3-day delay in accurate order reporting and analysis may be unacceptable. Instead, we should load all orders daily and continually monitor each order for changes in its status history. This is a complex, yet common, load problem.

The history of a single order in three load steps is shown in Figure 4.2.

Disposition of an Order

The other aspect of reliability the company must track is the disposition of each order. What do we do about orders that receive negative feedback? The delivery process may break down, the flowers could be left at the wrong house, office, or hospital. An unscrupulous fulfillment vendor may attempt to cover up its own mistakes. Our transaction system should allow some form of postdelivery feedback from the customer. If a customer calls or writes with a complaint about the accuracy or timeliness of a delivery, a refund is probably in order. Failure to fulfill an order is a serious event, as any hint of unreliable service from a national, seemingly anonymous vendor is the most obvious reason to use a local florist. We refer to the outcome of the fulfillment process as its *disposition*.

Figure 4.2 The evolving order.

Load 1: Initial order loaded after COB on July 9, 1997.

Order ID	Order Taken	Channel Notified	Channel Receipt Confirmed	Delivery Complete	Delivery Confirmed	Expected Delivery NLT
000011348	12:00 07/09/1997	12:00 07/09/1997	15:00 07/09/1997			18:00 07/10/1997

Load 2: Order updated after COB on July 10, 1997, reflecting a completed delivery.

Order ID	Order Taken	Channel Notified	Channel Receipt Confirmed	Delivery Complete	Delivery Confirmed	Expected Delivery NLT
000011348	12:00 07/09/1997	12:00 07/09/1997	15:00 07/09/1997	17:00 07/10/1997		18:00 07/10/1997

Load 3: After 30 days, order updated with delivery confirmed on August 8, 1997.

Order ID	Order Taken	Channel Notified	Channel Receipt Confirmed	Delivery Complete	Delivery Confirmed	Expected Delivery NLT
000011348	12:00 07/09/1997	12:00 07/09/1997	15:00 07/09/1997	17:00 07/10/1997	12:00 08/08/1997	18:00 07/10/1997

In this example, we use a disposition dimension to capture the outcome of every order. Recall the business rule that an order must age 30 days with no negative customer feedback before it receives "delivery confirmed" status. For each order loaded in the data warehouse, the disposition is initially "unknown." If negative feedback is received during the 30-day aging process, the order is assigned "unsatisfactory" as a disposition; otherwise, it is upgraded to "satisfactory" 30 days after it was filled. The disposition foreign key in the sales fact table can be updated in this case.

Dispositions often must be stitched together from a web of transaction data. Unsatisfactory order information may be found in a reversal transaction that grants a refund for a given order. A refund justification column might be used to record the reason the customer was dissatisfied with the order. In our case, this column includes the values late delivery, no delivery, product quality—appearance, product quality—size/value, product quality—inappropriate, and product quality—other. We use these values to add a descriptive attribute, reason, for an unsatisfactory order fulfillment disposition. The disposition dimension is shown in Table 4.1.

We have added a substantial amount of information to our overall design to support fulfillment monitoring. The disposition dimension allows the company to focus on specific quality problems. Date and hour facts record the critical time elements of each order, allowing channel performance to be closely monitored. The company now has a mechanism to track the reliability and convenience elements of its value proposition. Of course, the basic functionality of the sales data warehouse design carried over from Chapter 2, "Sales," is also retained. The design is presented in Figure 4.3.

Table 4.1 The Order Disposition Dimension

Disposition Key	Disposition	Reason
1	Unknown	Pending
2	Satisfactory	None
3	Unsatisfactory	Late delivery
4	Unsatisfactory	No delivery
5	Unsatisfactory	Product appearance
6	Unsatisfactory	Product size/value
7	Unsatisfactory	Product inappropriate
8	Unsatisfactory	Product other

Figure 4.3 Sales and fulfillment schema.

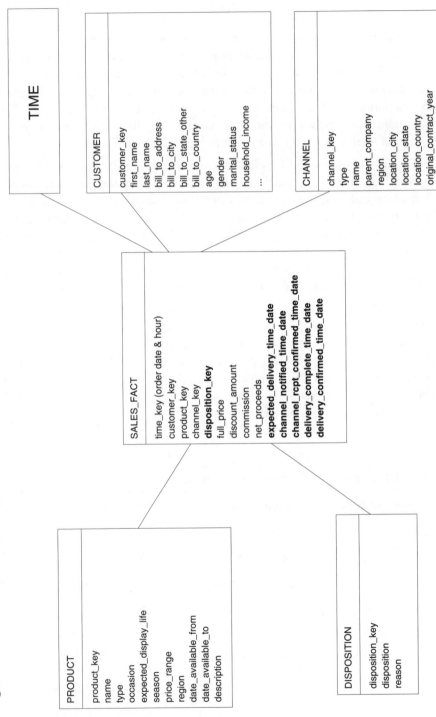

TIME

CUSTOMER

customer_key
first_name
last_name
bill_to_address
bill_to_city
bill_to_state_other
bill_to_country
age
gender
marital_status
household_income
...

CHANNEL

channel_key
type
name
parent_company
region
location_city
location_state
location_country
original_contract_year

SALES_FACT

time_key (order date & hour)
customer_key
product_key
channel_key
disposition_key
full_price
discount_amount
commission
net_proceeds
expected_delivery_time_date
channel_notified_time_date
channel_rcpt_confirmed_time_date
delivery_complete_time_date
delivery_confirmed_time_date

PRODUCT

product_key
name
type
occasion
expected_display_life
season
price_range
region
date_available_from
date_available_to
description

DISPOSITION

disposition_key
disposition
reason

A few additional notes: We have not included a returns fact table in the design. In this business, there is no return transaction; flowers are neither returned nor exchanged. We simply track the unfulfilled orders. In businesses where merchandise may be returned, a returns fact table, conformed to the product dimension, should be considered.

Also, how do we account for refunds offered to customers with unsatisfactory experiences? We must track the event and the financial impact. If we offer unconditional refunds, we can simply change the "unsatisfactory" value in our disposition dimension to "refund." If refunds are not always offered, we can add "refund" and the appropriate reasons to the disposition dimension. The added rows are illustrated in Table 4.2.

The financial impact of the refund is accounted for by a refund amount fact. When a refund occurs, the load process must now comprehend the event and update the data warehouse with appropriate information. Assuming again a daily load process, it will be common to receive refund information at a later load cycle after the order is created. Initially, the order will have an unknown disposition and zero for the refund amount. When a refund occurs, a later load cycle must associate the appropriate disposition dimension row to the order and update the refund amount as appropriate. The result is the ability to allow for the refunds short of adding a separate refund fact table.

Reporting on Fulfillment

Our design supports many reporting and analytical requirements critical to the business. Channel performance is an obvious area of concern. The company relies on contract florists, nurseries, and growers to arrange and deliver products. Poorly performing channel partners must either improve or be replaced.

Table 4.2 Refund Rows for the Disposition Dimension

Disposition Key	Disposition	Reason
9	Refund	Late delivery
10	Refund	No delivery
11	Refund	Product appearance
12	Refund	Product size/value
13	Refund	Product inappropriate
14	Refund	Product other

Report 4.1 Where are refunds a problem?

TeleBloomers Inc.
Refund Percentages by Region
2/97–7/97

Region	Qty. Refunds	% of Total Sales
Northeast	3,215	2.2%
Southeast	1,132	0.3%
Midwest	899	0.9%
Central	546	1.1%
Southwest	2,178	2.1%
Northwest	769	0.4%
Canada	43	0.1%
Hawaii	112	2.1%
Total	8,894	

Report 4.1 provides a regional breakdown of the number and percentage of unsatisfactory delivery outcomes resulting in a refund during a six-month period.

Report 4.2 is the result of further analysis of the Northeast region to identify vendors with a high percentage of orders that result in refunds.

Report 4.3 identifies the number of vendor-reported late deliveries and the number of customer-reported late delivery refunds for the same set of vendors. If

Report 4.2 What percentage of orders result in refunds?

TeleBloomers Inc.
NE Region Refund Percentages by Vendor
2/97–7/97

Vendor	City	Orders	Refunds	Refund Rate
Smallwood Flowers	NY	24,930	1,249	5.0%
Templeton Nursery Inc.	RI	11,204	742	6.6%
Calijersey Nursery Group	NJ	22,490	409	1.8%
Hudson River Florists	NY	3,092	449	14.5%
Ernesto Bros. Greenway	NJ	23,901	197	0.8%
Flowering Meadows	CT	3,244	169	5.2%

Report 4.3 Which Northeast vendors have the highest incidence of late deliveries and late-delivery refunds?

Late Delivery Report
NE Region

Vendor	Orders	Vendor Reported	Customer Reported
Smallwood Flowers	24,930	650	427
Templeton Nursery Inc.	11,204	312	118
Calijersey Nursery Group	22,490	201	70
Hudson River Florists	3,092	62	156
Ernesto Bros. Greenway	23,901	121	82
Flowering Meadows	3,244	82	46

vendors are accurately and honestly reporting this information to TeleBloomers, the number of customer refunds should be less than the number of vendor-reported deliveries, since some customers will not request a refund. Using this hypothesis, we can begin to look more closely at Hudson River Florists.

Returns: A Second Fact Table

The flower delivery business does not need to track returns, only refunds. A few simple additions to the sales schema supported the fulfillment analysis needs. Another advantage for TeleBloomers is that each customer is known; there are no anonymous transactions. Each order is taken over the phone and a credit/debit card is required for purchase. The company easily accumulates customer information over time, which is useful for marketing. For fulfillment purposes, a dissatisfied customer must contact the business to get a refund. We exploit this opportunity by gathering additional information about the fulfillment problem, including what channel and product are involved.

But not all businesses can easily capture the who of a sales transaction, or the why of a refund or return. Anonymous transactions are common in retail. Although it is impossible to track every return back to a known customer sale, we can track returns by product, store, and time. We can use our department store from Chapter 2, "Sales," to examine how returns might be tracked. First, review the schema design for the department store. Note the fact table grain is product by day by store by price.

Key Business Term

Anonymous transaction. A sale that cannot be associated with an individual, named customer.

Despite the efforts of many businesses to improve the collection of customer information, a majority of retail transactions are still anonymous.

The anonymous transaction has important implications in any business attempting to measure customer activity. For example, a grocery store may be able to identify buying habits for customers using credit/debit cards. Should the store make decisions about marketing, pricing, or promotions based on this information? What if these customers only represent 20 percent of register tickets and 25 percent of total sales?

For fulfillment purposes, what does a retailer need to understand about a returned item? After all, the retailer is not directly responsible for the quality of the goods sold. If a consumer purchases an expensive coat and decides the style or fit is inappropriate, the retailer simply returns it to the rack for someone else to purchase. If the goods are of poor quality, the retailer can simply return it to the manufacturer. Is the return merely an inconvenience to the retailer, or is it something more?

Consider a retailer with a value proposition based on superior products and service. Bad merchandise damages the company's image in the consumer's eye. A disproportionate number of returns attributable to one manufacturer may cause the retailer to reconsider buying from that source in the future. This is especially true if the returns are driven by product quality issues. The return itself is an inconvenience for the customer and the retailer, taking up time and eroding goodwill. Tracking returns may be a necessary enhancement to our sales data warehouse.

Identifying which products are being returned and why is critical to the quality product and superior service elements of such a retailer's value proposition. To monitor these items we will create a separate fact table. The original sales fact table included both price and day in the grain statement. Since the loading process for both sales and returns is likely to access the same source systems, we will also track returns on a daily basis, and include the store and product foreign keys. The primary difference in the grain of our returns fact table is the omission of price information. The final design tracks the quantity and dollar amount of returns by store, product, and day, and is presented in Figure 4.4.

Figure 4.4 The returns fact table and original sales schema.

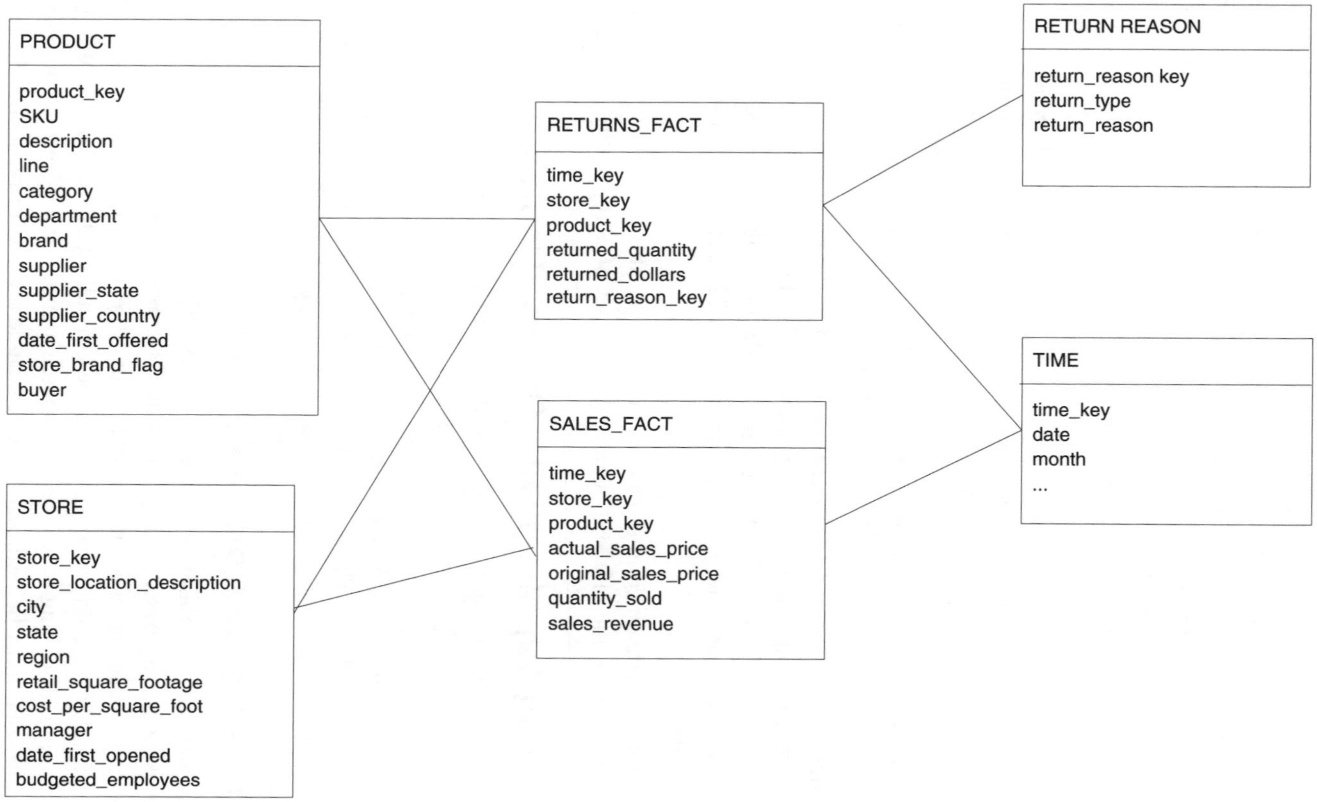

RETURN REASON

return_reason key
return_type
return_reason

TIME

time_key
date
month
...

RETURNS_FACT

time_key
store_key
product_key
returned_quantity
returned_dollars
return_reason_key

SALES_FACT

time_key
store_key
product_key
actual_sales_price
original_sales_price
quantity_sold
sales_revenue

PRODUCT

product_key
SKU
description
line
category
department
brand
supplier
supplier_state
supplier_country
date_first_offered
store_brand_flag
buyer

STORE

store_key
store_location_description
city
state
region
retail_square_footage
cost_per_square_foot
manager
date_first_opened
budgeted_employees

This design tracks the quantity and value of returns, and is useful for identifying stores, products, and suppliers with potential problems. However, it does not identify the *why* of the return. As in the flower business, the reason for the return is important information. Hopefully, our retailer has implemented a process that embeds collecting the reason in the exchange transaction.

Returns can be grouped by their financial impact on the retailer. A consumer may wish only to exchange an item; therefore, the financial impact of an exchange is zero, assuming it is for an identical product. Exchanges due to defective merchandise resulting in a refund reduce sales. Returns for store credit do not affect cash flow, but do result in a liability that the store must eventually fulfill. It must also reduce the sales quantity and revenue attributable to the returned product accordingly. Because each type of return has a different impact on the business financially, the company should track each type.

Provided all this data is consistently collected in the point-of-sale system, we can add a return dimension and use it to define the three types of returns: exchange, store credit, or refund. We will include an attribute to describe the various reasons why a customer might return an item. The return dimension is presented in Table 4.3.

Note that the reason column has important implications for the product supplier because it helps identify and quantify the impact of poor-quality merchandise.

Identifying Suppliers with Quality Problems

With our new schema populated, we can quickly identify problem suppliers. Report 4.4 lists suppliers with a percentage of return dollars to sales dollars greater than 5 percent, a forgiving threshold. The report uses the conformed product dimension attribute, Supplier, constrained on the months April, May, and June, and the year 1997. This report uses the value of the return, and excludes exchanges for reasons of size, gift, change of heart, and none given.

Quantifying the Cost of Returns

Another interesting capability of our new schema is the ability to examine the cost of a return using activity-based costing methods. Assume that we commission a study by some high-dollar management consultants to estimate the cost of labor associated with a return. This would include the time spent handling the return, accounting for the return, and restocking of shelves with merchandise. For damaged or unusable merchandise that must be returned, we will include the cost of repacking the items

Table 4.3 The Return Dimension

Key	Return Type	Reason
1	Exchange	Size
2	Exchange	Merchandise damaged
3	Exchange	Merchandise inoperative
4	Store credit	Merchandise damaged
5	Store credit	Merchandise unusable
6	Store credit	Merchandise quality
7	Store credit	Gift received
8	Store credit	Change of heart/opinion
9	Store credit	None given
10	Refund	Merchandise damaged
11	Refund	Merchandise unusable
12	Refund	Merchandise quality
13	Refund	Change of heart/opinion
14	Refund	None given

Report 4.4 Suppliers with quality problems.

Suppliers with 5 Percent in Returns
Q2 1997

Suppliers	Sales	Returns	Returns
Branswide	$189,009	$13,609	7.2%
Naturalize	$204,219	$12,457	6.1%
Templeware	$342,830	$18,513	5.4%
Lazy Dayz	$23,092	$1,201	5.2%
Freed Still	$320,238	$16,332	5.1%

Table 4.4 The Cost of a Return

Reason	Cost per Return
Change of heart/opinion	$1.29
Gift received	$1.29
Merchandise damaged	$3.11
Merchandise quality	$3.11
Merchandise unusable	$3.11
None given	$1.29

for return. The consultants' study assigns costs to each individual return, as shown in Table 4.4.

Now, looking across all products and locations, we can calculate the labor cost of returns. This information provides additional insight into the return situation presented in the first report. By including the quantity of returns, we can calculate the costs incurred by the retailer as a result of the supplier's poor merchandise. Report 4.5 depicts the costs incurred because of the previously identified suppliers.

Open-Ended Fulfillment

When fulfillment involves only providing a product for a given amount of cash, an expanded sales schema can usually handle the requirement; however, not all fulfillment models are this simple. Some companies sell products that have a long

Report 4.5 Cost of returns for suppliers with over 5-percent returns.

Suppliers	Number of Returns	Extended Cost
Branswide	1,237	$13,609
Naturalize	890	$12,457
Templeware	475	$18,513
Lazy Dayz	400	$1,201
Freed Still	2,042	$16,332

Cost of Returns
Q2 1997

fulfillment cycle with an indeterminate amount of cost associated with the order. This is an extension of basic transaction-level fulfillment.

The best examples of this are industries that commit to a level of service or quality in exchange for an advanced or continuing payment. Examples are presented in Table 4.5.

In each case, the cost of fulfillment should not exceed the future value of the advance payment. Despite the differences among these businesses, fulfillment costs have a direct impact on the bottom line. The level of advance payment is set by a predicted amount of fulfillment costs over the life of the agreement. Each business must determine a break-even point that considers the advance payment's current and future value, the number of agreements needed to pool risk, and the average cost of each agreement.

A medical insurer, for example, sets a monthly premium price of $450. A portion of this premium is used to operate the business, leaving only a portion to pay for medical care of the insured. Assume that $350 per member is left for reimbursements. In this case, the average cost per member must remain below $350 per month to ensure profit for the insurer. Tracking the cost of fulfillment, with dimensions like provider, procedure, region, and plan, provides the insurer with information on the continuing health of its business.

Notice also that the insurer's commitment is direct and the value proposition is a premium payment for health care. The home appliance manufacturer has a different commitment, implied in the warranty associated with a purchased product. The basic transaction is for an appliance, but the warranty attaches an implied serviceable life to the value proposition. The manufacturer must carefully monitor

Table 4.5 Open-Ended Fulfillment Examples

Business	Advance Payment	Fulfillment Costs
Medical insurance	Monthly premium	Cost of medical services rendered to the insured over the course of the relationship
Home appliances	Warranty agreement	Cost of service calls and parts during the warranty period
Software	Support and maintenance fees	Telephone support and bug fixes for the period covered in the license agreement

warranty costs by product. Consumers have come to expect generous warranties when purchasing durable goods, automobiles, and other big-ticket items.

Software companies are less sure of product quality and the ability to predict maintenance costs. Rather than embed these fulfillment costs in the license transaction, an annual maintenance and support contract is provided for a percentage of the original license cost. If a customer buys $400,000 worth of database software, an additional 20 percent, or $80,000, may be paid for maintenance. The customer then receives updates, bug fixes, and some level of telephone support; of course the number of bug fixes and the quality of telephone support is often less than expected by the customer. Today, software companies rarely compete on the quality of either the basic product or support. As the industry matures and product quality improves—perhaps wishful thinking—the cost of fulfillment will become as important as it is to an appliance manufacturer.

Fulfilling Warranty Commitments

Purchasing a home appliance is an occasional event for the average consumer. Refrigerators, washers, dryers, and dishwashers are *durable goods*, not *consumables*. We expect a major appliance to perform reliably for several years. Manufacturers compete as much on reliability as any other element of value.

Key Business Terms

Durable goods. Products that are intended to last more than a few months and provide continuing service to the consumer. Examples include appliances, vehicles, furniture, and furnishings. Clothing is often considered a durable good.

Consumables. Products that are destroyed or consumed by use. Examples include paper products, food, beverages, and office supplies.

Over the last 10 years, the reliability of many home appliances has improved dramatically. As quality improves, each manufacturer creates more ambitious warranty plans. The manufacturer that seizes the high ground of quality and offers a superior warranty should be able to charge a premium price. Consider two companies building a line of appliances, one with low prices and the other with higher prices but a better warranty. The premium that the high-reliability company receives must be enough to cover warranty service. This is essentially a gamble based on the ability of the company to execute a high-quality manufacturing process.

To correctly analyze warranty costs relative to sales, we will need two fact tables: sales and warranty costs. The dimensions for sales include time, channel, and product. The channel and time dimensions are familiar from Chapter 2, "Sales." The product dimension is the most important in this example, and must be conformed between the sales and warranty costs fact tables to enable drill-across querying. We will use the model number and nomenclature to identify the product. Model numbers roll up into product lines, like washer, dryer, or gas range. The basic product dimension is partially depicted in Table 4.6.

Our sales fact table is a monthly snapshot of sales by product and channel. Our warranty costs fact table also tracks costs by product and month of purchase. The grain also includes the month the warranty cost was incurred. This subtle addition is important to supporting warranty cost analysis. By storing the cost of warranty repairs for a product based on the month it was originally placed in service, the business can include the age of the appliance when analyzing warranty costs. This is in addition to basic calculations of warranty costs by model or line. The design is presented in Figure 4.5.

To illustrate the requirement, consider a request to track warranty costs by month of service for a specific model. This is a different requirement than simply tracking costs over time. We must move all models to a starting point of zero months of service and then allocate costs by service month after that time. This is the reason for including service month in the warranty_facts table. Using this fact as a dimension, we can group cost for a single product by service month rather than by when the cost is incurred. This gives us a better picture of the warranty

Table 4.6 A Few Rows from the Product Dimension

Product Key	Model Number	Nomenclature	Line
1	45-WSH-9910	Dynamo 2000	Washers
2	46-WSH-0903	Dynamo 2100	Washers
3	46-WSH-0990	Dynamo Jumbo 2000	Washers
4	42-DRY-9429	Dynamo Gas 1800	Dryers
5	34-RNG-2319	KitchenPro Gas 2900	Gas ranges

Figure 4.5 The sales and warranty costs schema.

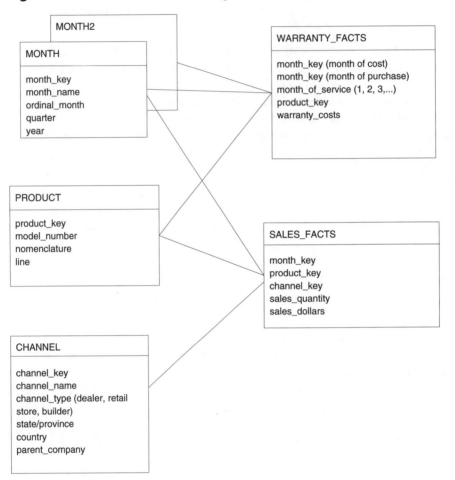

cost profile of each product. Report 4.6 presents warranty costs per month for model 45-WSH-9910.

The company probably has a predictive cost model that is used in pricing each product, with an anticipated warranty cost profile on a per-unit basis. If the actual costs profiled here exceed the predicted costs, the company must consider several actions that require additional data gathering and analysis. These actions would likely include:

Altering the predictive model to account for increased costs and project the impact on profitability.

Report 4.6 Warranty costs by service month, model 45-WSH-9910.

Model Number	Service Month	Warranty Costs
45-WSH-9910	1	$7,890
	2	$4,716
	3	$2,150
	4	$1,490
	5	$8,923
	6	$1,094
	7	$7,921

Collecting manufacturing quality data to determine the warranty cost drivers in the production cycle.

Correlating date of manufacture, date of sale, and date of first production across manufacturing sites to determine if early production runs are responsible for an inordinate amount of warranty costs. This requires an integrated view of the product throughout the value chain. See Chapters 5 and 10 for a detailed description of this concept.

Raising prices to cover increasing warranty costs. This is a difficult option to justify, as the company would likely price itself out of the market. It also would cover up the underlying quality issues driving these costs.

To provide additional information on this product, we can calculate the quantity in service from the sales fact table and compare the average cost per unit by service month to the predictive model. This information is presented in Report 4.7 and shows that even though the longest any individual unit has been in service is seven months, per-unit costs are already more than 40 percent of the predicted costs.

While this information gives some indication of trouble with this product, it does not compare the cost amount with the amount of warranty risk the company faces. To do so, we must first calculate the number of total warranty months the company is responsible for by multiplying the quantity sold by the standard warranty months for the product. If the standard warranty for model 45-WSH-9910 is 24 months, the company has 3211 × 24 total warranty months outstanding, or $77,064.

Some of these months have already passed and some costs incurred. We can calculate an actual cost per warranty month measure by determining how many

Report 4.7 Actual and predicted per-unit warranty costs.

Model Number	Service Month	Warranty Costs
45-WSH-9910	1	$7,890
	2	$4,716
	3	$2,150
	4	$1,490
	5	$8,923
	6	$1,094
	7	$7,921
	Total Cost to Date	$34,184
	Units in Service	3,211
	Cost per Unit to Date	$10.65
	Predicted Cost per Unit	$24.31

service months have passed for all units in service. We can use the current month to calculate the number of service months for all units. For example, units purchased in January 1997 have been in service three months at the end of April, four months at the end of May, and five months at the end of June. Report 4.8 calculates the number of months in service for the 3211 units sold to date with sales beginning in January and the calculation done at the end of July.

From this table we can see that 11,661 of the 77,604 months outstanding have passed, which is only 15 percent of the company's total exposure for this

Report 4.8 Months in service.

Purchase Month	Units	Months in Warranty Service	Total Months in Service
January	341	7	2,387
February	212	6	1,272
March	460	5	2,300
April	612	4	2,448
May	588	3	1,764
June	492	2	984
July	506	1	506
Total	3,211		11,661

product. We can also develop a more granular measure of warranty costs that can be tracked over time: average cost per warranty month. This measure is presented for three models in Report 4.9.

This report gives us the best picture of warranty costs for each model. We can now use these figures to project warranty costs and refine predictive models used to calculate prices. We may also want to work closely with manufacturing to identify quality problems for models with high warranty costs. Also, a review of warranty cost histograms for each model should be used to further validate our assumptions. The company now has a better view of warranty costs for all products. The schema is continually updated, and the results of analysis are used to improve the predictive models that drive pricing decisions. We have created a rather complex model of warranty costs out of a simple data warehouse design that is a natural, easily conformed extension of our basic sales star schema.

Summing Up Fulfillment

As we were writing this chapter of the book, American business faced a fulfillment crisis. A strike against UPS disrupted the order fulfillment process of thousands of businesses. In the face of the crisis, the company's competitors were reluctant to sign up disgruntled UPS customers. These competitors were already operating at near capacity and were unwilling to increase costs to service new accounts that might soon defect back to UPS.

The strike brought a small piece of fulfillment to the nightly news, but interest faded quickly after the strike was settled. Other than UPS management and the strikers, the only people who will never forget the strike are the businesses who suffered economic losses as a result. Their inability to fulfill customer orders had a material impact. Are other businesses unsuspectingly vulnerable to disruption of their fulfillment processes? In an environment of cutthroat competition,

Report 4.9 Creating a meaningful measure of warranty costs.

Model Number	Cumulative Warranty Costs	Months in Warranty Service	Average Cost Per Warranty Month
45-WSH-9910	$101,548	36,557	$2.93
46-WSH-0903	$24,716	21,940	$1.13
46-WSH-0990	$28,158	8,874	$3.17

de facto quality expectations, and fickle customers, measuring fulfillment is becoming increasingly important. A failed fulfillment process can erode brand loyalty, sending today's customer into the waiting arms of a competitor.

To construct an effective fulfillment solution, remember to:

Understand the value proposition. Each company has a specific value proposition, offering a balance of quality, features, and cost. This value proposition sets customer expectations for the product.

Identify elements of the value proposition in the fulfillment process. There are usually two or three key elements of the value proposition that are crucial to satisfying the customer's expectations. The time to fill an order and the occurrence of refunds are elements tracked in operational systems that could be related directly to TeleBloomers' value proposition.

Using these guidelines, we can identify crucial measures of corporate performance not usually found on the balance sheet or income statement. The measures that flow from fulfillment analysis are near the gears of the business, identifying problems long before they are reflected in periodic financial reports. Fulfillment analysis is often the first line of defense for a company's value proposition.

PRODUCTION

5

In Chapters 1 through 4, we looked at the interaction between customers and companies. In the three chapters that make up this section, we begin to look more closely at the products that companies sell. This chapter examines the production of finished goods. The term *production* has a specific meaning in the information systems community when used in conjunction with words like *system* or *application*. A production system or production application is one that has been implemented and is operational. In this chapter, the term *production* refers to producing a product. In that context, the term *production data warehouse* does not mean a generic data warehouse that is operational. Rather, it means a data warehouse specifically designed to support a production process, like manufacturing. It covers the production of items for sale to customers, whether they are individual consumers, companies, or governments. In this chapter, we will examine examples of discrete, continuous process, and hybrid manufacturing.

Improved production has been the catalyst for much of humankind's economic advance over the centuries. The first major improvements in production occurred in agriculture, where better methods of growing liberated our ancestors from subsistence activities. The Industrial Revolution, born of improved production, transformed the western world in the nineteenth century and continues to transform economies in the twentieth century. As the Industrial Age begins to peak, the Information Age has emerged in the late twentieth century to again revitalize the global economy. In this economy, production of knowledge products is increasingly important.

For our discussion, we will define *production* as the transformation of existing materials or assets into a product of greater value. This definition applies to agriculture, discrete manufacturing, process manufacturing, and software development. Even a product as seemingly nonindustrial as a newspaper is the result of a production process. Figure 5.1 provides examples in each of these production categories.

Figure 5.1 Types of production.

Production Family	Inputs	Product
Agriculture		
	Soil, minerals, sunlight, seeds	Crop
Discrete manufacturing		
	Cloth, thread, rivets, zippers	Denim jeans
Process manufacturing		
	Crude oil, heat, additives	Gasoline, motor oil
Discrete/process hybrid		
	Barley, hops, water, sugar	Beer
Knowledge		
	Intellect, programming language	Application software

In each case, there is a consistent underlying economic model that describes production. This model balances the costs of inputs to the production process and the cost to execute the process with the value of the goods produced by the process. We can use this model to describe oil refining, personal computer manufacturing, newspaper publishing, or any other nonservice business. Optimizing the value added to the inputs by the production process. Management activities focus on controlling the cost and quality of inputs and optimizing production process execution to produce the most valuable goods at a predictable pace and quality. Figure 5.2 presents this model in a generic form.

This model can be used to frame requirements for almost any production example. Questions asked about the production process can usually be related to production inputs, the production process, or production output. Typically, a production data warehouse tracks the following information:

Cost and quantity of inputs. The production data warehouse should include information about the material, components, or other assets consumed or transformed in the production process. In an assembly operation, this includes the parts and components of the finished product. In process or basic manufacturing, it includes the raw materials, like iron ore or crude oil, that are transformed into the product. In the production of knowledge products, the inputs are more abstract.

Figure 5.2 A simplified model of production.

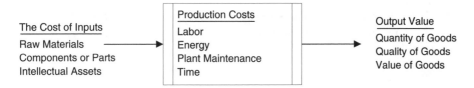

Cost of the process. There are costs associated with executing a production process. Quantifying those costs and relating them to output is a primary requirement of the production data warehouse. Categories of process costs include labor, production equipment depreciation, energy, and plant maintenance. Activity-based costing is one technique commonly used to improve overhead allocations that require a significant amount of process data.

Output and utilization. The production data warehouse tracks the output of finished goods or products at an agreed level of detail. Measuring production is obviously important. Production data is used track production cycles, identify production problems, and compare production results among facilities. Production output data is also used to calculate factory overhead costs.

In each of our examples, we will attempt to address all of these areas of concern for the manufacturer. The designs presented in this chapter are general examples of solutions. Readers familiar with manufacturing will forgive us for watering down the designs for a broader audience. Our objective is simply to present a few workable designs that introduce the reader to dimensional modeling and design techniques in a manufacturing environment.

Manufacturing

Our examples of production come from the manufacturing industry. In this chapter, we divide manufacturing into three types: *discrete, continuous process,* and *hybrid*. The requirements for managing each type vary to some degree, and the automation of these production processes is advancing rapidly. With this automation, the data specific to each type is increasingly available. Each type of manufacturing is distinct and requires minor variations in the design of a production data warehouse. This is in contrast to the financial reporting subject area, where one design can satisfy most manufacturing needs.

Key Business Terms

Discrete manufacturing. A manufacturing process that produces discrete end item products from various components. Discrete manufacturing examples include automobiles, computers, televisions, and compact discs.

Continuous process manufacturing. A manufacturing process that combines constituents into a bulk quantity product through a continuous process. Process manufacturing includes the production of gasoline, motor oil, and other by-products from crude oil. Other examples include chemical manufacturing, paint manufacturing, and food additive production.

Hybrid process manufacturing. A manufacturing process that includes elements of continuous and discrete manufacturing. One example of hybrid processes is tire manufacturing, where a discrete item is produced from by-products of continuing processes. Another example is beer or spirits production, which includes mixing, brewing, aging, and discrete packaging in a single facility.

There are some common elements of manufacturing that we can count on, regardless of the type. The common building block of production is the *production unit*. Not a Hollywood term, the production unit is an agreed standard unit for measuring output from a production process. Defining the production unit is important because it forms the basis of the product dimension and is the unit of measure for production quantity.

The most obvious production unit is an individual item. Some manufacturers refer to these units as *eaches*, counting each item as it rolls off the production

Key Business Term

Production unit. The unit of measure by which production outputs are measured.

For a discrete manufacturer, it is normally *each*, while for process manufacturers, it may be liters, gallons, barrels, grams, or some other standard unit.

line. For an automaker, a production unit at an assembly plant is a car of a certain make, year, and model. The automaker is likely to further divide the make-model-year combination into specific variants, with different engines or option packages. Regardless of the grain of the product dimension, the automaker counts production in eaches.

A component manufacturer who supplies the automaker would also use each as a production unit. The seat manufacturer, the tire supplier, and battery supplier all track production output in individual production units; the paint manufacturer, however, does not. A paint manufacturer measures production in a bulk standard measure, either gallons or liters. A refinery typically measures output in barrels or gallons, while an aggregate company measures dry asphalt production in tons. These bulk standard units are used in process manufacturing and hybrid manufacturing.

Another important type of production unit is the *package*, which is a combination of the individual unit and the bulk standard unit. A brewery, for example, may produce cans, bottles, and kegs of beer for distribution. In this case, the production unit varies by production line. For a brewery, it is important to measure both package and bulk production. Each package should share a standard, or at least convertible, unit of measure. A six-pack of beer is a roll-up of eaches, the cans of beer, with each can containing a predefined quantity of product measured in bulk standard units. Tracking both the quantity of packages produced and the amount of bulk standard units produced is a common requirement.

Another common element of any manufacturing data warehouse, closely related to production, is the *basic product*. The term *product* is tossed around in many companies as if everyone understands the precise meaning. Unfortunately, our experience has found more than one perspective commonly exists on how to define a product. In the production data warehouse, the challenge is to define product at a level that provides the maximum amount of analytical flexibility. It is ideal, although rare, that the basic product idea is shared among marketing, sales, and production.

Returning to the example of an automaker, the lowest level of product definition is more than make-model-year. The production process likely tracks the color, options, body style, interior package, and other characteristics. Each unique combination represents a variant of the make-model-year that may be analytically significant. The basic product definition should be explored in production first, because the amount of product detail captured in the factory is rarely exceeded in any other subject area. This basic product definition can then be validated by other groups—marketing and sales, for example—to create a common understanding of how the company as a whole views the basic product.

Key Business Term

Basic product. The lowest commonly shared instance of a product offered by a company, with an agreed identifier and a common set of attributes.

For a book publisher, the basic product is a book by an author in a specific form, like hardcover, paperback, tape, or CD-ROM. This is a different concept than the combination of author and title. For the editorial department, author and title may serve to identify the product adequately, but for sales and production, the form of the work is equally important. The basic product is lowest-level definition.

Production in Discrete Manufacturing

Discrete manufacturing of end item products is a form of manufacturing familiar to most people. We drive to work in cars, watch televisions, and use personal computers. All of these are examples of discrete manufacturing, where the consumer product represents an assemblage of parts and subassemblies. The assembly of parts into an individual unit of production is a good place to start our examination of production.

Our example is a manufacturer of personal computers, both desktop and laptop devices. The company manufactures none of its own components, instead assembling components from suppliers into a final product. Assembly manufacturing is common in electronics and computers, where component innovation is continuous. The computer manufacturer acts as a bridge between the marketplace and innovation. Improved monitors, bigger disk drives, and faster chips are developed by suppliers. The manufacturer determines what combination of these innovations is marketable, and at what price.

Producing Computers

Our manufacturer, Zeon Technologies, produces a variety of products at four production facilities located worldwide. Two facilities produce only desktop machines, while two others produce both desktop and laptop computers. At each facility, more than one production line is in place and capable of producing more than one model. The characteristics of the production facilities are:

Phoenix, Arizona. The original Zeon production facility, Phoenix has two production lines that produce only desktop machines. The lines contain aging equipment and can produce only one configuration of computer at a time. Retooling results in some downtime when switching between configurations or models.

Elk Grove, California. The newest of Zeon's facilities, purchased from a failing competitor, Elk Grove has two modern, flexible production lines. One production line can produce several variants of four desktop models, while the other has similar capability for the notebook line.

Taegu, South Korea. A joint venture with a South Korean conglomerate, Taegu produces laptops on one flexible production line and desktops on two older production lines.

Madrid, Spain. The Madrid plant is a modern desktop production facility, with two production lines capable of producing variants of three models.

The diverse production capabilities create a problem for Zeon, as it must continually balance global demand with diverse manufacturing capabilities. Strategically, the company intends to retire all old production lines and increase flexible capacity. Correctly timing this capital investment requires an improved understanding of worldwide production. Currently, production reporting is done against unique computing environments at each facility and painfully aggregated for an enterprise view. An integrated production data warehouse is needed to better understand global production trends and improve planning.

Production Dimensions for Discrete Manufacturing

Interviews with the plant managers and production planners at each facility would help identify the dimensions required for an integrated view of production. Prior to our tour, we sketch out a draft dimensional model, Figure 5.3, that supports production analysis.

This sketch gives a basic conceptual understanding of the subject area, but it does not provide details on the grain of the fact table or the attributes of the dimension. These are determined in the interview process. Our interviews, conducted at each facility, yield the following requirements:

Production reporting. Each facility must be able to report on the output of product by production line. Daily production is the desired grain for measuring output. There is also a need to measure production activity on a monthly basis. Retooling, maintenance, scheduled and unscheduled production stoppages, and production are recorded in each plant's manufacturing control system.

Product definition. The basic product was identified by consensus among the facilities, and each product has a specific model number and description. There are two important attributes of the basic product identifier, hard disk capacity in GB and CPU/Clock Speed, which are consistently available. Other characteristics, such as RAM, CD-ROM drive speed, and power supply information are not captured consistently across production lines and should be excluded from the initial design.

Component usage. An additional requirement that increases our original scope is the need to track component use during production runs. Each factory has a sophisticated component-tracking capability, and components are allocated from inventory by production run. This includes both serial components and bulk items. Tracking component use against standard bill-of-materials use would be valuable in identifying variances in standard versus actual input costs. It could also improve the accuracy of finished goods inventory value calculations.

These requirements can be applied to our draft design to refine our notion of facility and product. We would first change the facility dimension to a production line dimension. It is common for a factory to maintain more than one production

Figure 5.3 Sketch of production warehouse design.

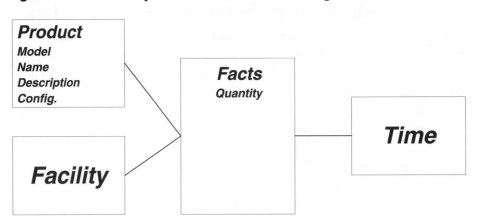

line. Facility_name becomes an attribute of that dimension, with sample rows presented in Table 5.1.

Product definition has been clarified in the interviews resulting in a product dimension with a grain of model number. A sample of rows from the product dimension is shown in Table 5.2.

This is a thin product dimension, but the basic product consensus was determined by the interview process. Other characteristics would be helpful, increasing the specificity of our basic product. Unfortunately, the manufacturing control systems used in the different facilities did not provide the information consistently. A later iteration of the design, perhaps after installation of a common ERP system, might support a more detailed basic product definition. The design team should always plan to take on additional dimensional attributes in future iterations. The implementation of a data warehouse usually triggers a number of operational system changes to make additional attributes available for analysis. Appending additional dimensional attributes and facts is a major part of managing the implemented data warehouse.

Our production output design for Zeon is depicted in Figure 5.4.

Two other analytical requirements will change our design more substantially. The first is the desire to track production activity at each plant. To satisfy this

Table 5.1 The Production Line Dimension

PL_key	Line_name	Facility	Country	Line	Type
1	Madrid Z Flex	Madrid	Spain	Desktop	Flexible
2	Madrid Y Flex	Madrid	Spain	Desktop	Flexible
3	Old Timer	Phoenix	U.S.	Desktop	Standard
4	Down Time	Phoenix	U.S.	Desktop	Standard
5	ROK Flex	Taegu	South Korea	Notebook	Flexible
6	ROK One	Taegu	South Korea	Desktop	Standard
7	ROK Two	Taegu	South Korea	Desktop	Standard
8	Elk One	Elk Grove	U.S.	Desktop	Flexible
9	Elk Two	Elk Grove	U.S.	Notebook	Flexible

Table 5.2 The Product Dimension

Prod_key	Model Number	Family	Line	CPU	HD_size
1	Z2000-996-X	Z2000	Notebook	L6/155	1.5 GB
2	Z2000-211-X	Z2000	Notebook	L6/120	1.2 GB
3	Z2000-201-X	Z2000	Notebook	L6/90	1.2 GB
4	D4000-901-D	D4000	Desktop	L6/155	2.2 GB
5	D4000-902-D	D4000	Desktop	L6/190	2.2 GB
6	D4000-909-D	D4000	Desktop	L6/225	2.2 GB
7	D1000-101-R	D1000	Desktop	R6/90	0.8 GB
8	D1000-111-R	D1000	Desktop	R6/90	1.2 GB
9	D1000-211-R	D1000	Desktop	R6/120	1.2 GB

requirement, we will create a second fact table at the grain of production line by month by activity. The activity dimension identifies various categories of line activity. A sample of entries is provided in Table 5.3.

This simple extension of our design provides important information on what is happening on production lines across all facilities. Our design forces all time to be accounted for in a month, which can be validated during the load process. This design extension provides a foundation for cross-facility planning. Specifically, the ability to separate idle production capacity from other normal activities should improve global capacity planning. This schema, using the conformed production facility dimension from the original use schema, is presented in Figure 5.5.

The other requirement discovered in our interviews was the need to measure component use across all production facilities. This again requires the addition of a fact table to our design in order to measure component use by production line, product, component, and day. The ability to map components to products is simple in the older production facilities—each line can only produce one model at a time. In a flexible manufacturing environment, mapping components to products is more complex. The component use must be determined at the unit level. Most modern flexible manufacturing lines and ERP systems support some level of component use tracking during the production process.

Figure 5.4 Production output design for Zeon PCs.

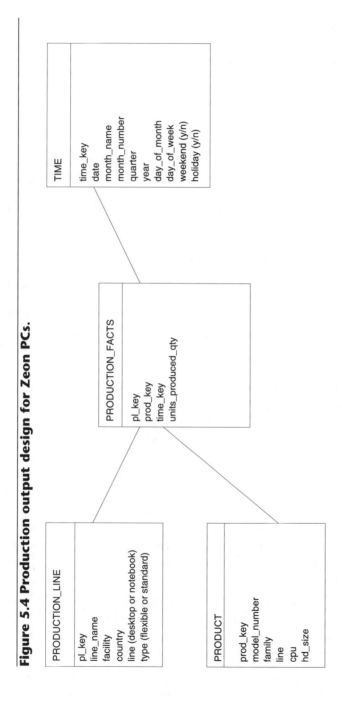

TIME

time_key
date
month_name
month_number
quarter
year
day_of_month
day_of_week
weekend (y/n)
holiday (y/n)

PRODUCTION_FACTS

pl_key
prod_key
time_key
units_produced_qty

PRODUCTION_LINE

pl_key
line_name
facility
country
line (desktop or notebook)
type (flexible or standard)

PRODUCT

prod_key
model_number
family
line
cpu
hd_size

Table 5.3 The Activity Dimension

Activity_key	Activity	Category
1	Standard production	Production
2	Shakedown production	Production
3	Holiday shutdown	Scheduled shutdown
4	Weekend shutdown	Scheduled shutdown
5	Off-hours shutdown	Scheduled shutdown
6	Idle shutdown	Unused capacity
7	Maintenance shutdown	Scheduled shutdown
8	Repair shutdown	Unscheduled shutdown
9	Retooling	Scheduled shutdown
10	Equipment installation	Scheduled shutdown
11	Other activity	Other

To meet this requirement, we must introduce a component dimension. The component dimension is similar to the product dimension, because a basic component definition must also be determined. This basic component definition can be used to link production use to facts in the inventory and purchasing subject areas. By conforming the component dimension with other parts of the enterprise data warehouse design, we gain additional operational benefits. Chapter 6, "Inventory and Capacity," discusses inventory in depth, while Chapter 14, "Building an Enterprise Data Warehouse," describes the benefits of conformed dimensions when constructing an enterprise-wide data warehouse. The design extension uses the conformed production line, product, and time dimensions from the basic production schema. The completed production design, including component use, production measurement, and activity, is depicted in Figure 5.6.

The fully integrated design addresses requirements related to output, use, and the quantity of inputs used to produce finished products.

Reports for Discrete Manufacturing

With our new design populated, we can begin to address reporting needs from production facilities around the world. Again, we do not mean to minimize the

Figure 5.5 Measuring activity and use.

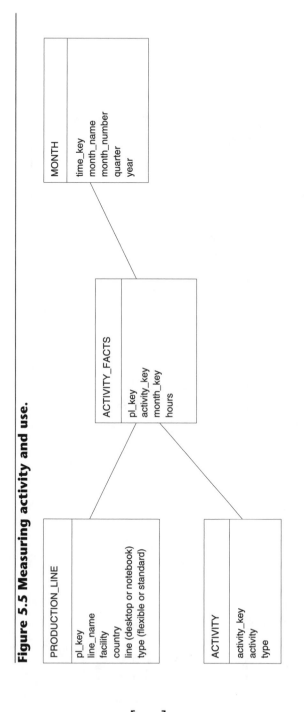

Figure 5.6 The completed production design.

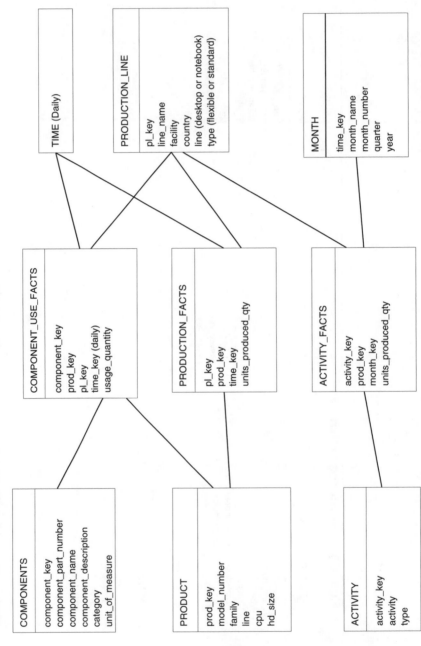

complexity of loading these designs. We consider the loading of the data warehouse to be the most difficult and time-consuming task in a data warehouse project. This scenario in particular would involve many loading challenges: Each plant has a unique set of production systems, and the plants are located around the world and operate in different time zones. Managing the initial and incremental data loads is nontrivial. Fortunately, new extract, transformation, and load software (ETL) is emerging to at least structure and automate some parts of the problem.

Our first report covers global production output for a three-month period beginning in May 1997. The report, only one page of which is shown in Report 5.1, provides a snapshot of monthly production levels at each plant and for each product. The page of the report shown provides information on notebook computer production for 1997, compares that production with the previous three-month period, and compares its forecasts. The forecasts are not included in our design, so we can assume that this report included a second data source.

Remember that we added a component use fact table. In the next report, we examine the use of a single component worldwide. The component, a coated screw used in almost all products, has a use curve consistent with unit production. The graph in Report 5.2 plots screw use together with monthly production in units. Comparing production to use of components, or consumption of raw

Report 5.1 Global production output.

Zeon Computer Corp.
Global Production Report

Page 12

Period: May–July 1997
Family: Z2000

Production Summary

Elk Grove	Product	This Period	Prev. Period
	Z2000-996-X	8,261	3,218
	Z2000-211-X	7,718	8,270
	Z2000-201-X	6,296	3,880
Taegu	Product	This Period	Prev. Period
	Z2000-996-X	14,309	8,813
	Z2000-211-X	12,901	6,181
	Z2000-201-X	16,902	5,085
Worldwide	Product	This Period	Prev. Period
	Z2000-996-X	22,570	12,031
	Z2000-211-X	20,619	14,451
	Z2000-201-X	23,198	8,965

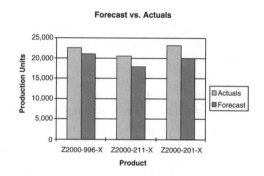

Report 5.2 Component use and production levels.

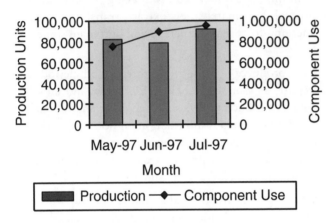

Component Use vs. Production
Coated 12mm std thread alum. screws

materials, is in itself valuable. However, with the current design we are unable to identify component utilization levels that are inconsistent with expected use as defined by the bill-of-materials for each product. Later, we will add this capability in a hybrid manufacturing environment.

We also augmented our design to track production activity at each plant. This extension supports the analysis of activity within a single plant, or across all production facilities. With this information, we can create a report that determines an average activity distribution across all plants, and compare each plant to the average. Report 5.3 compares Madrid activity to the global average. It also presents a comparison of production activity to corporate production standards used to determine production incentives for factory employees and managers. The report first presents the total hours available for the month, 744, and subtracts the expected weekend and off-hour shutdowns. The Madrid plant is currently working two production shifts five days a week. The activity details and percentages are calculated against only the planned production hours. By calculating production activity against planned production, the report eliminates variances in holidays, scheduled off hours (one shift versus two plant production), and work weeks (five-day versus six-day).

These reports demonstrate the flexibility of our design and address each portion of the production economic model. The first report measures production output, the second measures production inputs, while the third report examines the

Report 5.3 Madrid activity versus average activity.

May 1997 Production Activity Report—Madrid, ESP

Activity Summary

Days	31
Production days	22
Total hours	744
Weekend hours	216
Holiday hours	0
Scheduled off hours	176
Planned production hours	352

Activity Details

Category	Activity	Hours	Percentage of Production Hours	Standard Average	Global Average
Other	Other activity	1.6	0.5%	0%	1.2%
Production	Shakedown production	0		0%	1.7%
Production	Standard production	319.6	90.8%	96%	91.3%
Scheduled shutdown	Equipment installation	0		0%	0.5%
Scheduled shutdown	Maintenance shutdown	13.1	3.7%	2%	2.2%
Scheduled shutdown	Retooling	0		0%	0.0%
Unused capacity	Idle shutdown	0		0%	0.6%
Unscheduled shutdown	Quality shutdown	17.2	4.9%	1%	2.3%
Unscheduled shutdown	Repair shutdown	0.5	0.1%	1%	1.8%

process itself. The design can be used for a large number of additional analytical needs and augmented with additional dimensional attributes in the future.

Production in Continuous Process Manufacturing

Continuous process manufacturing refers to production that transforms inputs, usually constituents of a formula or recipe, into a finished product. Continuous process manufacturing results in bulk output of product at a standard unit of measure. Many processes of this type result not only in a final product, but various by-products that may or may not be valuable. Some by-products require special handling and reprocessing; for example, many chemical production processes create hazardous by-products requiring special handling monitored by federal and state environmental agencies. Our example of continuous process manufacturing is a large soft drink company. The company's production facilities are continuous process manufacturing plants that produce syrup products that are sold in bulk to bottling companies. The bottling companies mix the syrup with carbonated water and other ingredients to produce a final product that is then bottled or canned and packaged for sale.

Producing Syrup

As you would expect, a large soft drink producer will have several production facilities. Some large companies in this industry actually outsource all manufacturing, not just bottling and packaging, maintaining only the role of product formulator and brand manager. For our example, we will assume our soft drink company, Fizzy Cola, retains ownership and operational control of all production facilities.

Our design is similar to that of the PC manufacturer in that it will include product, facility/production line, and time dimensions. The product dimension includes a production unit of measure, gallon, much as discrete manufacturing uses *each*. The basic product is a type of soft drink syrup identified by formula name and product name. Because the production process may change over time to reformulate a product, we include the formula in the product dimension's grain. This allows the company to track different variants in a product's evolution. We also incorporate the concept of production runs to separate executions of the manufacturing process. A production run is essentially one cycle of loading the production equipment with ingredients, applying labor and energy, and producing a batch of syrup. Because of the differences in product formulae, a production run produces only one product. Each facility may execute several runs per day, perhaps changing products in between. Each facility may also have more than one production line, and each production line may have different daily capacities.

Our fact table simply contains the quantity produced by each product's standard unit of measure. In our bulk production facility, we measure only in gallons. The completed design is depicted in Figure 5.7.

Using this simple design, the soft drink manufacturer can integrate production reporting across all facilities.

Now that we can measure production output, we can shift our focus to tracking ingredient and factory overhead costs that are related to production. The cost of producing any product is determined by adding the cost of ingredients or components to the cost of operating the production facility. While the definition is simple, gathering this information and applying it correctly is a challenge. One complication of tracking product costs is traceability. In the past, it was considered impractical to attempt to track the cost of ingredients, raw materials, or components on a production-unit or production-batch basis. In continuous process manufacturing, it is often impossible to trace ingredient costs. If we fill a storage tank with fructose from two or three different shipments, how do we know which shipment's fructose is used in which batch of syrup? To overcome this problem, accountants devised inventory costing methods that are applicable to both raw material and finished goods inventory. The two traditional methods—accounting class flashback warning—are FIFO and LIFO.

LIFO and FIFO: Determining Ingredient Costs

There are two traditional inventory costing methods that provide us with the ability to arrive at a cost for production ingredients. Assume that the company had fructose inventory transactions as presented in Table 5.4. Now assume that total production in January of cola was one batch of 25,000 gallons. Assume that each gallon of cola syrup requires 0.25 gallons of fructose. What was the cost of the fructose used in producing January's 25,000 gallons?

First we must determine how much fructose would normally be required, in this case, 0.25 multiplied by 25,000, or 6250 gallons. Using the *FIFO* (first in, first out) method, the manufacturer uses the 3000 gallons in inventory first, then 3250 gallons from the January 3 purchase. No fructose is used from the January 15 purchase, at least from an accounting standpoint. Since it's all stored in a holding tank, no one could know which fructose was used. The cost of fructose for the batch is calculated as shown in Table 5.5.

The *LIFO* (last in, first out) method uses the last-received fructose first. LIFO is generally frowned on in the accounting community, although it is helpful in

Figure 5.7 Soft drink production output schema.

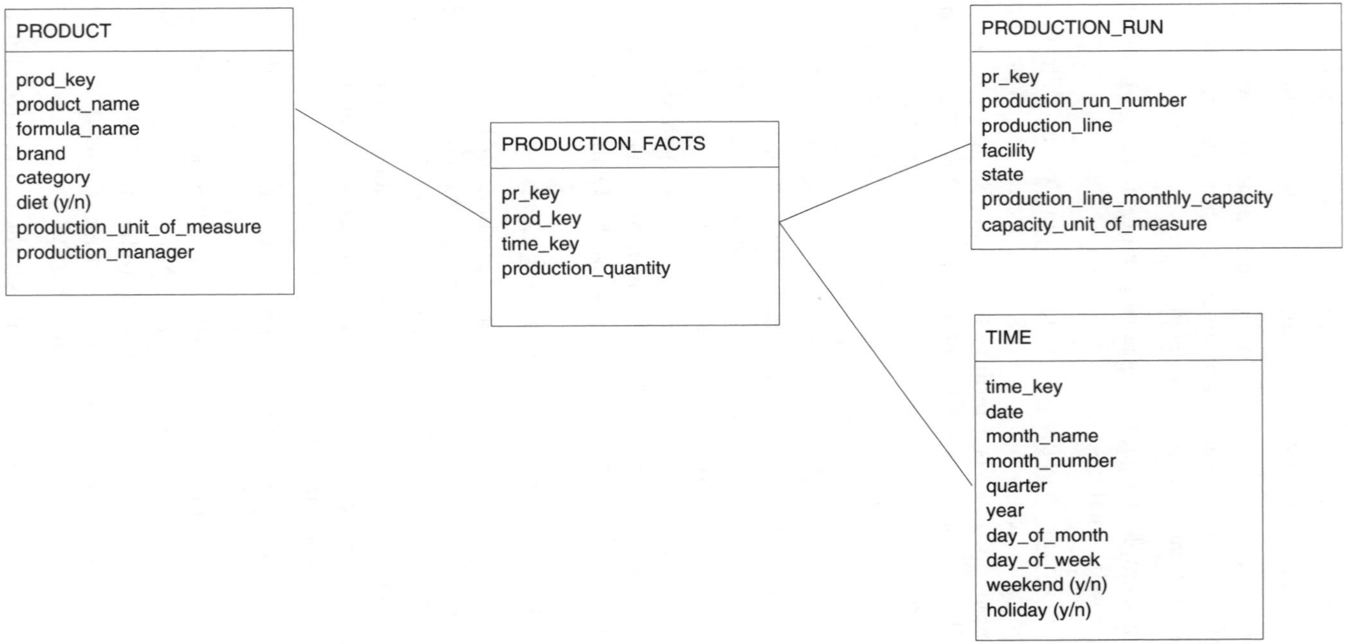

PRODUCTION_RUN

pr_key
production_run_number
production_line
facility
state
production_line_monthly_capacity
capacity_unit_of_measure

TIME

time_key
date
month_name
month_number
quarter
year
day_of_month
day_of_week
weekend (y/n)
holiday (y/n)

PRODUCTION_FACTS

pr_key
prod_key
time_key
production_quantity

PRODUCT

prod_key
product_name
formula_name
brand
category
diet (y/n)
production_unit_of_measure
production_manager

Table 5.4 Fructose Syrup Inventory

Purchase Date	Gallons	Total Cost	Unit Cost
Balance on 1/1	3,000	$4,500	$1.50
Purchase on 1/3	5,000	$8,000	$1.60
Purchase on 1/15	18,000	$25,200	$1.40

reducing taxes during inflationary times. Although this practice is rarely used, Table 5.6 shows the calculations to illustrate the difference.

Notice that all of the fructose comes from the last shipment. In this case, LIFO increased the cost of goods sold for the product produced in January, thus decreasing the gross income for the batch. For discrete manufacturer tracking, the cost of components is often more precise. Components are often barcoded or grouped by lot, and as these lots are used in production, the cost associated with each item is tracked. It is more likely than not that the manufacturer knows the direct material and direct labor cost of an individual car, computer, or television within a 10-percent margin of error. Our soda manufacturer is faced with a more difficult task: So many of its ingredients are received and stored in bulk that separating them out is impossible. So how do we allocate ingredient costs to a production run?

For the purposes of a production data warehouse, we can use a standard ingredient cost to approximate the cost of production. The standard cost is determined periodically and used to plan pricing strategies and cost finished goods inventory. If the projected costs are off significantly, the accountants will eventually raise or lower the cost of goods sold in the accounting system. The data warehouse team can use these standard unit costs to calculate an ingredient cost

Table 5.5 FIFO Cost of January's Fructose

Source	Gallons Used	Unit Cost	Extended Cost
Beginning inventory balance	3,000	$1.50	$4,500
Purchase on 1/3	3,250	$1.60	$5,200
Total	6,250	NA	$9,700

Table 5.6 LIFO Cost of January's Fructose

Source	Gallons Used	Unit Cost	Extended Cost
Purchase on 1/15	6,250	$1.40	$8,750

during the load process by multiplying the standard unit cost by the actual quantity of ingredients used. Our soft drink company measures production output and ingredient use by batch. In other industries, the process may run continuously, or ingredients may not be as carefully measured out. In these companies, output and ingredient use may be tracked on a daily, weekly, or monthly basis.

The ingredients use fact table and the new ingredient dimension are shown in Figure 5.8. Note that this fact table tracks the *actual* quantity used in production and calculates the cost based on a standard per-unit cost. The ingredient use quantity is not derived from the product-to-ingredient ratio, which is used only in calculating standard uses.

Direct Labor and Factory Overhead

Two other costs that are of interest in production are *direct labor* and *factory overhead*. Direct labor is that labor which can be directly attributed to a product. For Fizzy Cola, this means tracking direct labor attributed to a production run. We can construct a fact table at the grain of production run by facility, day, labor category, and by product. The labor category dimension includes an attribute to distinguish standard from overtime labor hours and costs. We can calculate the cost of direct labor by multiplying the number of hours by a standard labor rate, which is calculated periodically by the accounting department.

Ingredient and direct labor costs can be attributed directly to a product, factory overhead costs cannot. These costs, of which there are scores of types, are tracked at the production facility level. In the production data warehouse, we will simply track factory overhead categories by month, type, and facility. Allocating these costs to specific products is accomplished using cost allocation strategies discussed in Chapter 9, "Financial Reporting." A sample of rows from the fact table, with descriptors replacing foreign keys, is presented in Table 5.7.

These dimensions and the production_costs fact table provide detailed monthly reporting on production costs for each facility. The final design, including production, ingredient, direct labor, and factory overhead fact tables is presented in Figure 5.8.

Figure 5.8 Production schema with ingredient, direct labor, and factory overhead costs included.

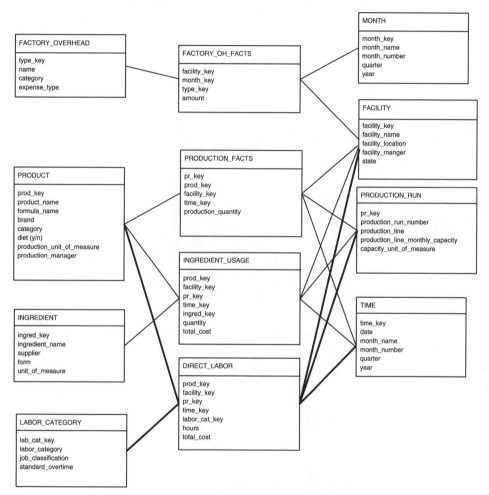

Note that we have created a separate facility dimension in this design since factory overhead is not tracked at the production-line level. We also created a separate month dimension because of the grain of the factory overhead fact table. Despite this difference in grain, the overlapping dimensions of time and month, and the common dimension of facility, support some important facility-level reporting capabilities.

Table 5.7 Factory Overhead Fact Table Rows (with Descriptors)

Facility	Month/Year	Cost Code	Cost Name	Category	Amount
Lima	March/1997	A295-997-199	Electrical	Utility	$23,984
Lima	March/1997	A295-997-300	Contract labor	Indirect labor	$412,961
Lima	March/1997	A241-997-009	Water use fees	Govt. fee	$12,909
Lima	March/1997	A221-997-103	Plant security	Indirect labor	$88,963
Lima	March/1997	A789-997-812	Plant maintenance	Indirect labor	$89,702
Lima	March/1997	A881-997-005	Plant maintenance OT	Indirect labor	$12,902
Lima	March/1997	A743-997-020	Production equipment depreciation	Depreciation	$117,855

Reporting on Continuous Process Manufacturing

With the design in Figure 5.8 populated, our continuous process manufacturer can address most analytical needs in the product subject area. Reports based on data from individual fact tables answer questions about production output, materials use, labor costs, and overhead costs. We are also able to successfully drill across and compare facts from all four fact tables as long as we aggregate by month and facility. Of course, we must also include only these common dimensions in our report. An example of such a report is presented in Report 5.4.

This ability to correlate overlapping dimensions across fact tables is a common remnant of an evolving data warehouse. Even though the dimensions are not conformed at the primary-key level, the equivalent domain of values shared for month in both the daily and monthly time dimensions allow us to correlate facts among different fact tables. Overlapping attributes evolve in many ways, the most common being completion and implementation of a design without a view of the entire enterprise.

Report 5.4 Correlating production with costs.

Fizzy Beverage Corporation
Gross production and costs by facility
Month: June   Year: 1997
Note: Costs are presented in thousands of $

	Anaheim	Gardenia	Northridge	Sutterville
Production (1000s of GL)	112.9	121.4	212.4	143.7
Ingredients	162.7	181.9	310.5	212.8
Direct labor	368.7	412.9	681.6	356.7
Utility costs	12.1	11.2	28.7	18.6
Depreciation	26.7	35.2	22.8	41.7
Government fees	11.6	11.2	7.9	6.2
Other factory overhead	112.9	128.5	213.2	161.4
Taxes	48.6	49.4	51.7	28.9
Total Costs	743.3	830.3	1316.4	826.3
Cost per 1000 gallons of production	6.584	6.839	6.198	5.750

In the end, we have created a series of production fact tables that provide a comprehensive view of the process, including the cost of inputs, the cost of the process, and the output of the process. We can also apply the direct labor and factory overhead fact tables to the discrete manufacturing design created for Zeon. The major difference between the discrete and continuous process design is the unit of production.

Production in Hybrid Manufacturing

The syrup product produced by Fizzy Cola is sold to bottling companies around the country. Some bottlers have only one production facility and produce only a few packaging variants. Others serve large metropolitan areas and have more than one facility and several packaging options. We will examine a large bottler in southern California, Pacific Bottling, serving an area from Los Angeles to San Diego. Pacific has four large bottling facilities that take base syrup from Fizzy, mix it with other bulk ingredients, and produce bottles and cans for retail distribution. They also produce pressurized mix containers for restaurants.

Pacific is a hybrid manufacturing company, first mixing the base Fizzy syrup with carbonated water and other ingredients to produce bulk soda. The company then packages the bulk soda products in various end-item configurations, like 12-ounce can, 2-liter plastic bottle, or 24-ounce plastic bottle. These end items are then configured into predefined packages, such as 24-pack of 12-ounce cans, 6-pack of plastic bottles, 2-pack of 2-liter bottles, or individual end items. The typical hybrid manufacturer produces a bulk product and then converts it to a standard set of end items for sale and distribution. The requirement to track production at each major conversion step is clear: The continuous process step of bulk production, the bottling/canning operation step of end-item production, and the packaging step all must be managed.

In this case, understanding the base product in production is the first step in cross-process measurement. Pacific produces eight finished products in bulk for packaging, all carrying the Fizzy brand. These products are Fizzy Cola, Fizzy Diet Cola, Fizzy Root Beer, Fizzy Diet Root Beer, Fizzy Fresh, Fizzy Diet Fresh, and two flavors of noncarbonated iced tea, Lemon and Cherry. Production of these items is measured at the bulk production step of the process. Each product requires a specific recipe for a production run, with standard ingredients. Fizzy requirements for production measurement include measuring bulk production, ingredient use, and variances from standard usage plans.

To illustrate the use of recipes, similar to a formula in chemical production, we will examine the recipe for Fizzy Cola. The recipe, shown in Figure 5.9, identifies

Figure 5.9 Fizzy Cola recipe.

```
Fizzy Industries Proprietary

Fizzy Cola Recipe, Version 01/1998

Max. Batch:  40,000 Gallons
Min. Batch:  10,000 Gallons

Ingredients (Amt. per Gallon of output)

Fizzy Bulk Syrup - Cola 1/98,    12 oz.
Fizzy Bulk Sweetner, 22.5 oz.
Carbonated Additive, 40 oz.
Fizzy Carmel Color Additive, 1 oz.
...
```

the minimum and maximum batch size, process time, and ingredient amounts to produce one gallon of Fizzy Cola.

Pacific and other bottlers use this recipe to produce Fizzy in differing batch sizes. Each product has a recipe identifying standard ingredients and amounts. Recall that Fizzy allows for changes in the formula for the syrup product. It is also likely that Fizzy changes the recipe coincident with a formula change; however, the recipe may change independent of the formula. For the bottler, formula changes in the syrup may or may not be important, but recipe changes can affect ingredient costs. Pacific has determined that it does not need to track changes in formulae, only changes in recipes. Therefore, the basic product for Pacific is defined as product name and recipe.

Our design to track production, ingredient use, direct labor, and factory overhead is similar to the design used by Fizzy. We will omit the direct labor and factory overhead fact tables to avoid overcrowding the remaining figures. There are two fact tables, one for bulk production and another for ingredient use. The product, time, standard unit of measure, and production line dimensions are conformed between the two fact tables. Fizzy did not require a standard unit of measure dimension since it only measured the production of one thing, syrup, using one standard unit of measure, gallons. The first stage of our design, dealing only with bulk production of soda, is depicted in Figure 5.10.

Reports for Hybrid Manufacturing

This design satisfies the requirement to measure bulk production and ingredient use across bulk products, production lines, and plants. An example of such a report is presented in Report 5.5.

Figure 5.10 Production and ingredients use schema.

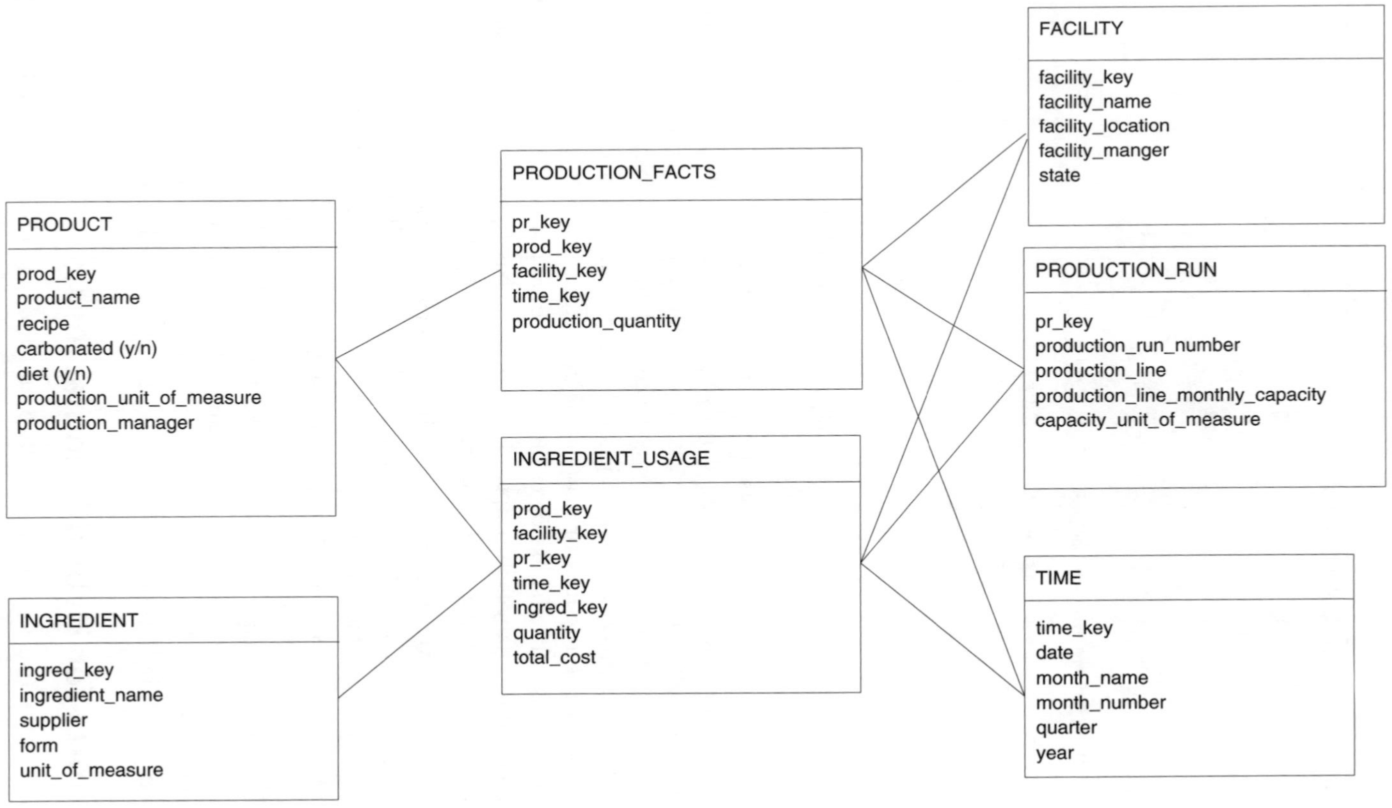

FACILITY

facility_key
facility_name
facility_location
facility_manger
state

PRODUCTION_RUN

pr_key
production_run_number
production_line
production_line_monthly_capacity
capacity_unit_of_measure

TIME

time_key
date
month_name
month_number
quarter
year

PRODUCTION_FACTS

pr_key
prod_key
facility_key
time_key
production_quantity

INGREDIENT_USAGE

prod_key
facility_key
pr_key
time_key
ingred_key
quantity
total_cost

PRODUCT

prod_key
product_name
recipe
carbonated (y/n)
diet (y/n)
production_unit_of_measure
production_manager

INGREDIENT

ingred_key
ingredient_name
supplier
form
unit_of_measure

Report 5.5 Production report for Pacific Bottling.

Pacific Bottling Ingredient Usage Report

Period	Q1 1998

Product	Fizzy Diet Cola

		San Diego	
Total Production	Gallons	428,831	
Ingredients		Usage	Ratio per GL
Syrup Base	Fluid Ounces	37,892	0.09
Carbonated Water	Gallons	398,232	0.93
Flavor L11	Fluid Ounces	12,907	0.03
Flavoring L12	Fluid Ounces	18,744	0.04
Purified Water	Gallons	23,909	0.06

		Glendale	
Total Production	Gallons	511,230	
Ingredients		Usage	Ratio per GL
Syrup Base	Fluid Ounces	41,210	0.10
Carbonated Water	Gallons	406,771	0.95
Flavor L11	Fluid Ounces	18,772	0.04
Flavoring L12	Fluid Ounces	27,409	0.06
Water	Gallons	19,088	0.04

The report displays gross production and ingredient use for two Pacific production facilities for the first quarter of 1998. Gross ingredient use is displayed, along with the ratio of ingredient use to gallons produced. This column allows the company to compare use ratios among plants to detect excessive waste or spillage.

A simple design extension to our schema will add additional value. The starting point is the recipe we reviewed earlier. Each recipe identifies the standard ingredient amount and unit of measure for a predetermined unit of production. In our example, a gallon of Fizzy Cola required 12 ounces of Fizzy Cola syrup.

Remember that we are tracking actual ingredient use in the ingredient use fact table. If we construct a similar fact table with the measure of standard quantity per unit of production, using the conformed dimensions of ingredient and product, we can calculate standard use for any level of production and compare it to actual use. Figure 5.11 presents the design changes to support ingredient use variance analysis.

With this design in place, Report 5.5 can be extended. Report 5.6 uses the same production data as Report 5.5, comparing actual and standard ingredient use for the first quarter. The cost of the excess use is calculated using the standard ingredient cost originally used to calculate total_cost in the ingredients use fact table.

Bottling and Canning the Product

The first-stage design is used to manage production in the continuous process step for Pacific. Once production of the bulk product is complete, bottling and canning operations commence. The bulk product, gallons of completed beverages, is now injected into bottles and cans. We can treat each bottle and can as a separate output from a discrete manufacturing process. Even though this process may be concurrent with creating the completed bulk beverage, there is still a need to separate the data for each process step. We refer to these bottle and can variants as either a *least-salable item* (LSI) or *base unit*. Either term refers to the end items produced in the bottling stage of production that will be sold at retail individually or grouped in packages.

To build an LSI production fact table, we will reuse our product, facility, and time dimensions from the bulk production schema. To differentiate between continuous process, bottling, and canning production lines, we divide bulk production runs from LSI production runs. This is accomplished by creating a bulk production run dimension and an LSI production run dimension. Ideally, we will be able to trace the source bulk production run from which the LSI production run is filled. Traceability of production run costs will improve inventory valuations and help trace any quality problems discovered in the marketplace. It also allows the company to trace how much of a bulk production run is actually transformed into product.

Linking Production Steps

To link production steps, we convert LSE production to gallons. The LSE fact table should contain both the quantity of LSE units produced and the equivalent

Figure 5.11 Ingredients use and standard recipe design.

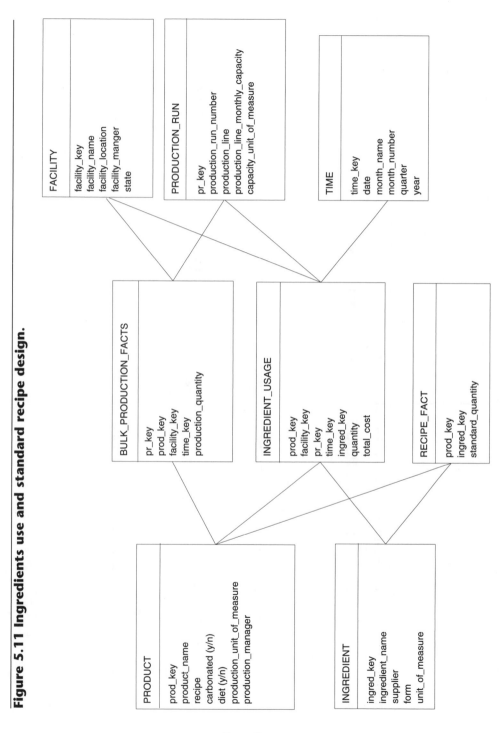

Report 5.6 Adding ingredient costs and waste costs.

Pacific Bottling Excess Ingredient Usage

Period   Q1 1998

Product   Fizzy Diet Cola

Total Production	San Diego 428,831					
Ingredients			Actual Usage	Standard Usage	Excess Usage	Excess Cost
Syrup Base	Fluid Ounces		37,892	34,306	3,586	896
Carbonated Water	Gallons		398,232	394,525	3,707	260
Flavor L11	Fluid Ounces		12,907	12,865	42	53
Flavoring L12	Fluid Ounces		18,744	12,865	5,879	11,111
Purified Water	Gallons		23,909	21,442	2,467	543
					Total Cost	12,863

[174]

production in gallons. To illustrate the conversion of product through the production process, consider a 37,000 gallon batch of Fizzy Cola produced by Pacific. Fizzy Cola is produced in the following standard units: 12-ounce can; 24-ounce plastic bottle, 16-ounce plastic bottle, and 2-liter bottle. Each of these standard units is then packaged. The quantity of standard units produced from this batch is presented in Table 5.8, with a calculation of equivalent gallons for comparison to batch size.

Notice that the total equivalent gallons are 35,245.5, less than the total batch input of 37,000 gallons. The difference may be a normal amount of loss for the bottling and canning processes, or may represent excessive spillage or other production problems.

From the standard production units of cans and bottles, packages are produced. Pacific also would like to track the number of packages produced and the equivalent number of gallons. This is accomplished by adding a third production fact table and a package dimension. This fact table includes the number of packages produced, the number of LSEs in those packages, and the equivalent production in gallons. The standard units from our example batch are packaged as shown in Table 5.9.

The total equivalent gallons from packaging is 35,058, again slightly less than the bulk production run quantity. Losses may be due to product sampling or damage in the packaging process. The company can now trace the disposition of a bulk production run through LSI and package production steps.

The final design to track each production step includes three fact tables and is presented in Figure 5.12. The dimensions of time, bulk_production_run, and product are conformed among these three tables. Coupled with the ingredients_usage, direct_labor, and factory_overhead fact tables described earlier, this design covers a broad range of production management needs.

Table 5.8 Standard Units Produced from a Batch

Standard Unit	Standard Units Produced	Equivalent Gallons
12-ounce can	138,800	13,012.5
24-ounce plastic bottle	66,000	12,375.0
16-ounce plastic bottle	32,400	4,050.0
2-liter bottle	11,000	5,808.0

Table 5.9 Packages Produced from a Batch

Standard Unit	Packaging Option	Packages Produced	Equivalent Gallons
12-ounce can	6-pack web	5,000	2,812.5
	12-pack carton	500	562.5
	24-pack case	200	450.0
	48-can vending flat	2,000	9,000.0
24-ounce plastic bottle	6-pack web	10,000	11,250.0
	12-pack carton	500	1,125.0
	24-bottle vending flat	—	—
16-ounce plastic bottle	6-pack web	5,000	3,750.0
	12-pack carton	200	300.0
2-liter bottle	single	7,000	3,696.0
	2-bottle shrinkwrap	2,000	2,112.0

Some readers may want to combine the LSI and package production fact tables. Whether this is feasible or advantageous depends on whether additional dimensions for either fact table exist, how production data is collected, and the amount of variance between gallons produced in LSI production and the gallons eventually packaged. Other readers may recognize the potential to add packaging costs to the package production fact table. While there is some commonality of requirements within an industry, the specific requirements of each company's production environment will undoubtedly differ.

Summing Up Production

Touring a factory is an interesting field trip for the IT professional. The production of tangible products is in many ways familiar to those who construct intangible knowledge products. In some ways, the production of physical products may seem more satisfying. Production is always the most complicated operational process for a manufacturer. Remember that the type of manufacturing has an influence on the data warehouse design. The design team should also have a clear understanding of the cost allocation model used by the manufacturer.

Figure 5.12 The completed design for hybrid production.

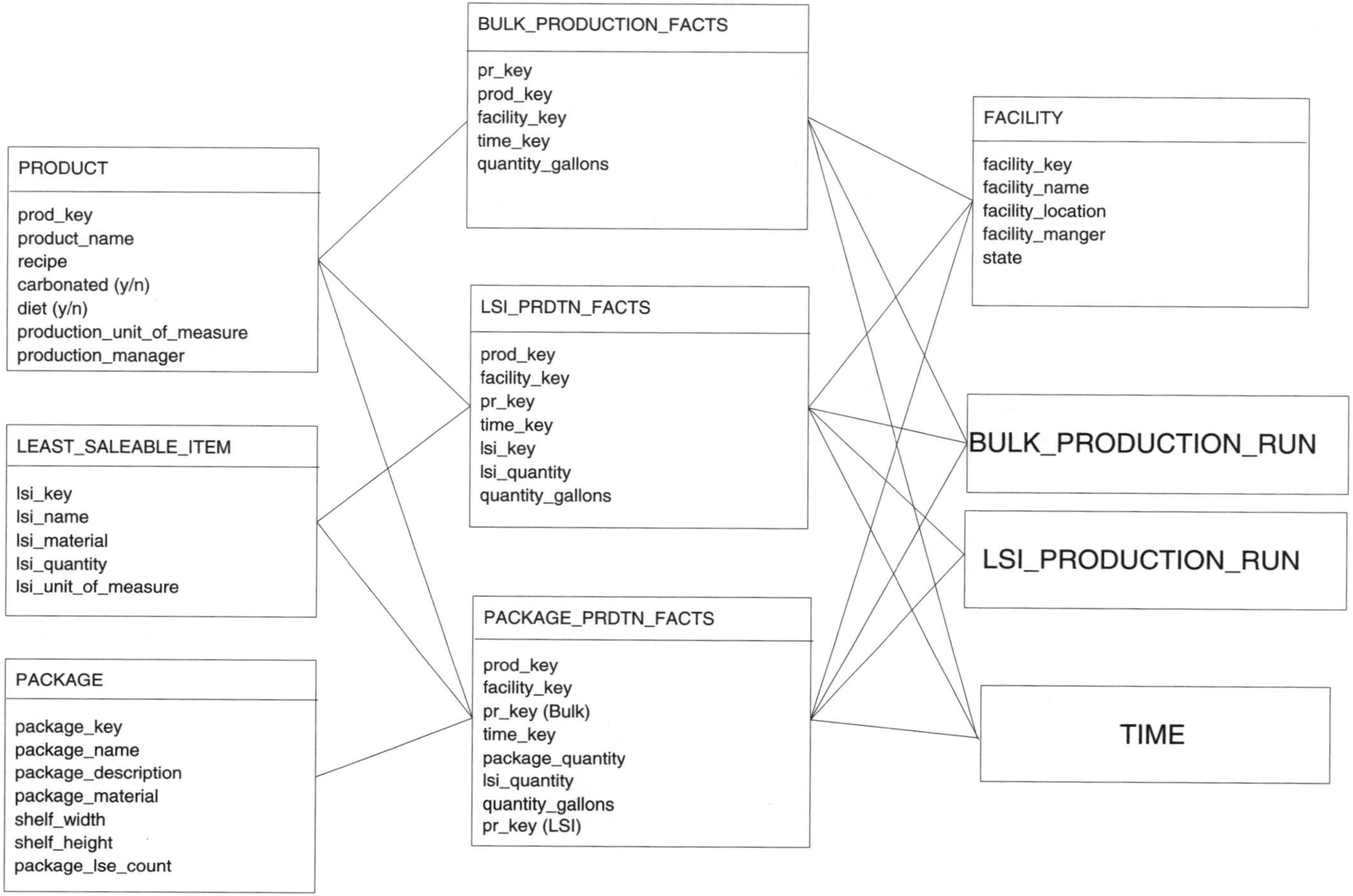

PRODUCT

prod_key
product_name
recipe
carbonated (y/n)
diet (y/n)
production_unit_of_measure
production_manager

LEAST_SALEABLE_ITEM

lsi_key
lsi_name
lsi_material
lsi_quantity
lsi_unit_of_measure

PACKAGE

package_key
package_name
package_description
package_material
shelf_width
shelf_height
package_lse_count

BULK_PRODUCTION_FACTS

pr_key
prod_key
facility_key
time_key
quantity_gallons

LSI_PRDTN_FACTS

prod_key
facility_key
pr_key
time_key
lsi_key
lsi_quantity
quantity_gallons

PACKAGE_PRDTN_FACTS

prod_key
facility_key
pr_key (Bulk)
time_key
package_quantity
lsi_quantity
quantity_gallons
pr_key (LSI)

FACILITY

facility_key
facility_name
facility_location
facility_manger
state

BULK_PRODUCTION_RUN

LSI_PRODUCTION_RUN

TIME

Remember also that the production data warehouse should track the following information:

- The cost and quantity of inputs to the manufacturing process, including parts and components, or raw materials, used in producing the product.

- The costs associated with executing a production process, including labor, production equipment depreciation, energy, and plant maintenance.

- The output of finished goods or products by plant, production line, product, and time.

Production today is highly automated, with computerized production equipment, process control software, and integrated ERP systems providing unheard-of amounts of information. Many of the future improvements in production will come directly from the better use and application of this information. In this chapter, we have provided a simplified framework for analyzing production and building an appropriate data warehouse. This framework should help the data warehouse team find the proper dimensions, attributes, and facts to address the problems unique to each manufacturing environment.

INVENTORY AND CAPACITY

6

Inventory plays a key role in many business decisions, and its management has direct impact on the bottom line. The amount of product on hand is a factor in purchasing, manufacturing, and pricing. The product levels must be carefully managed by manipulating quantity and pricing. Ineffective inventory control can lead to runaway costs or dissatisfied customers, while effective inventory management maximizes the profitability of the business.

People who look at inventory ask a wide variety of questions. The most basic inventory issue is "How much is on hand?" Other questions require more complex analysis, such as "How much should it cost?" and "How much should we have?" These questions come from all parts of the business, highlighting the critical role inventory plays. Clearly, the inventory data warehouse can be a valuable tool. Because the business questions can be profound, designing the inventory data warehouse is a challenge.

Closely linked to inventory is the concept of *capacity*. Common in service industries, businesses with a fixed capacity to service customers must pay close attention to its utilization. The rate at which capacity is used is referred to as *utilization*. Prices must be carefully managed to achieve desired utilization levels. Questions include "What is our capacity?" and "How did the price change impact use?"

In this chapter, we will prepare schema designs for two businesses. A supplier of medical products strives to maintain sufficient inventory to meet 100 percent of customer demand, without unprofitable overstocking. A hotel has a fixed inventory capacity, and monitors its use to set pricing and develop marketing plans. We'll provide examples of how particular business needs lead to specific design elements, and explore the unique complexities of inventory and capacity reporting.

What Kind of Inventory?

Loosely defined, *inventory* is the quantity of goods or materials on hand. Several classes of items may be kept in inventory, including raw materials, capital equipment, and even investments. Sometimes, inventoried items are not tangible. For example, a cable network's programming inventory consists of the right to show programs. Programming bought from suppliers can only be run a set number of times or within a specific time window, while internally produced programming may be used indefinitely.

Key Business Term

Inventory. The quantity of goods or materials on hand or available for use.

Product Inventory

There are many forms of inventory. A manufacturing organization like those studied in Chapter 5, "Production," maintains an inventory of finished goods, as well as an inventory of the materials that are used to produce those goods. As the end item moves through the production process, its identity changes and so does its disposition in inventory. At the end of the process, the finished end item is now part of the business's *product inventory*, ready for sale to customers. Product inventory is the focus of this chapter.

For many businesses, product inventory is *acquired* rather than *produced*. Inventory of this type may undergo similar transformations brought about by a value-added process. For example, a reseller of computer products may package products together, and subject equipment to a quality assurance process prior to making it available for sale. Each transformation impacts the status of inventory, and there may be different details of interest to the business at each point along the way. At the end of the process, the item becomes a part of the product inventory.

Once ready for sale, an item may be involved in several inventory transactions before it finally disappears from inventory. An item may be moved between locations or warehouses. It may endure a status change, going from Available to Reserved for a particular customer or sales team. If quality problems are identified with a particular product or supplier, inventory items might be placed on hold and subjected to additional quality assurance tests. The disposition of inventory items is important to the business.

Businesses maintain differing levels of focus on their product inventories. An automobile manufacturer tracks specific cars down to the vehicle identification number. Each car is built to individual specifications, including trim line, options, and color. By contrast, a bicycle manufacturer mass-produces a large number of identical products each day. There is no way to identify individual bicycles, nor is there a need to do so; inventory is tracked at the model level instead.

In some cases, inventory management can extend beyond the confines of the business. Some companies assume responsibility for maintaining a customer's inventory. For example, suppliers of baked goods to grocery stores often assume responsibility for stocking shelves directly. The bakery must monitor the inventory level at the grocery store. Many retailers provide inventory data to their suppliers, enabling them to set up contracts that offload inventory management to the supplier.

Capacity to Serve

Now think about your doctor's practice. What is the doctor's product inventory? Start by identifying the product. She is paid to consult patients, diagnose maladies, and prescribe treatments. The doctor's product is her service; her product inventory is her ability to treat patients. If she divides a 10-hour day into 20-minute consultations and works five days a week, her weekly inventory would be 150 appointments. She refers to this as her *capacity*.

Capacity-based inventory has two distinguishing characteristics: It is usually intangible, and it is very expensive to produce more. The doctor's appointments, for example, cannot be found in a bin at a warehouse. She also can't increase her appointment inventory beyond a definite limit. She may be able to squeeze a few ill patients into her schedule each day, but these are made possible because she leaves two to four appointments unscheduled. She can stay a little late each night and see one or two extra patients, but that's her limit. She can't manufacture or order additional appointments. She can only produce more inventory by making a significant capital investment—increasing her office space and taking on a partner.

Like a product on a shelf, capacity represents something of value that can be sold to a customer, so it is not much of a stretch to refer to the amount of capacity as *product inventory*. Not surprisingly, businesses with limited capacity to service customers often refer to their capacity as *inventory*. Other businesses refer to capacity as *fixed inventory*. As we will see in this chapter, capacity can be measured in much the same way as an inventory of physical products.

Capacity-based inventory is usually found in service industries. Doctors, lawyers, and consultants all sell services. You can't feel their product, though you may notice its impact on your wallet. There is an effective upper limit to what they can sell without a significant capital investment.

Key Business Terms

Capacity. The amount of customer demand that can be serviced at a given point in time. Capacity has a maximum limit, beyond which significant capital investment would be required.

Service industry. A business whose primary product is not tangible. Some service industries bill based on time, like doctors, lawyers, plumbers, and electricians. Others charge for the specific service rendered. For example, an Internet access provider sells access to the Internet, a travel agent receives a commission to arrange your travel itinerary.

Your long distance company sells you telephone connections to distant relatives. You can't see or touch one of these connections, nor can you look somewhere and count how many are taking place at a point in time. There is an upper ceiling to the number of calls the company can connect at any point in time. Additional customers cannot be serviced beyond this limit without a major capital investment in fiber, copper, equipment, and personnel. For the long distance company, *circuit inventory* represents capacity.

Many businesses have a significant investment in physical assets, but their *product* is still intangible. Consider an airline. You can count the number of airplanes operated, or even the number of seats. These things are tangible, but they are not what the airline sells. An airplane is merely a *capital asset* that enables the airline to provide a service. The airline sells you the right to sit in a particular seat during a particular flight on a particular day. As with other service industries, the product is intangible, or difficult to count. The airline has a definite upper limit to the number of flights it can schedule, unless it invests in more airplanes, pilots, flight attendants, and hangars.

These businesses work hard to make sure that they are making the most of their capacity. For example, the doctor tries to manage her practice so that she is always operating at or near her capacity. If many appointments go unscheduled, she begins to take on more patients. If she is booked solid, she stops taking on new patients. Likewise, lawyers won't be able to stay in business if their schedules are empty; a long distance company cannot recover the cost of its infrastructure if no one places calls; an airline will not make money flying empty airplanes.

Define Your Focus

When building an inventory data warehouse, it is important to understand what kind of inventory is to be studied. A single business may maintain many types or stages of inventory, each requiring its own model. It is crucial to begin with a shared understanding of scope. Will you be studying materials for production, or product inventory? If product moves from unallocated to allocated states, where will you be focusing your attention? Are we looking at physical inventory or capacity? All these questions will impact the design of the data warehouse.

It is equally important to gain a firm understanding of the business questions to be addressed, as they will influence the nature of your models. If the questions center around things that happen to inventory, such as packing, shipping, receiving, and returns, your model will likely be transactional. If the questions center around the quantities in inventory, the speed at which inventory moves, or its value, you will require an inventory status model.

In this chapter, we will study the inventory needs of two businesses. The first, a medical supplier, maintains inventory on a huge number of products it sells to hospitals. Inventory must be sufficient to meet customer demands, without excessive overstocking. Inventory information is a critical component of the purchasing process. We'll develop an inventory model that helps the supplier maintain appropriate inventory levels. Next we will look at a hotel chain, whose capacity to accommodate customers is limited by the number of rooms. The hotel must maintain a delicate balance between price and utilization. We'll put together a model that helps the hotel manage its capacity. Along the way, we will link features of the models to business objectives, and show the kinds of reports they can produce.

Supplier Inventory

Imagine what it would be like to order office supplies for your company if you had to deal directly with the manufacturer of every item. Filling the supply cabinets would require dozens or even hundreds of phone calls each week. Your Rolodex would overflow with the names and numbers of sources for everything from copier toner and paper to file folders and sticky notes. You would need backup manufacturers as well. When your usual ballpoint pen manufacturer is out of red ones, you need to get them from someone else. The office staff would be busy receiving hundreds of small deliveries each month, and the accountants would have hundreds of bills to pay and reconcile.

Like most businesses, yours probably turns to an office supply company. The office supply company stocks a wide variety of office products from a large number of manufacturers. This makes it easier for you to order everything with a single call. If they are out of your preferred red pens, you don't have to call around to locate an alternate. You get a single shipment, and a single bill. The office supply company saves you lots of time, effort, and money. You don't have to maintain hundreds of relationships; they take care of that. Because they have lots of other customers like you, they can do so more effectively.

A distributor of medical supplies is much like your supplier of office products. The ultimate "middlemen," they buy all kinds of items from manufacturers, and resell them to hospitals, laboratories, and doctors' offices. They stock everything from tongue depressors and bandages to rubber gloves and surgical gowns. Success for medical product suppliers is measured by their ability to meet customer needs without overstocking.

Inventory is both an asset and a liability for medical suppliers. Their value proposition is the availability of a wide variety of products, delivered in a timely manner, from a single source. Inventory enables this value proposition. The more products that are in the warehouse, ready to be delivered, the better the supplier will be able to meet customer needs. But running a warehouse costs money, as do the products stored there. Maintaining too much inventory can cut into the supplier's profits.

Success of the business depends on effective management of inventory. A delicate balance must be struck between customer needs and costs. With too little inventory, customers will look to someone else for their medical supplies. With too much inventory, the business will fall into the red. We've been assigned to work with a medical supplier who recognizes the potential value of inventory information. We begin by talking to the vice president of Logistics, who reports to the chief operations officer. She's in charge of the day-to-day operations of the warehouses, including the buyers who purchase items that go into inventory.

> *Effective inventory management is critical to our business. In each region of the country, we've got a warehouse dedicated to serving our customers. At any point in time, we might need to know how much of an item we have at a particular warehouse. Sometimes, we look at the combined inventory of a group of products, like a type of bandage that might come from several suppliers. Or we*

may assess inventory by product category or subcategory. Some folks are less concerned about particular locations; they'd be looking at combined inventory for a product, across all locations.

All the information about what is on hand is available today, though it's not that easy to pull it together the way we want it. What we can't do is study what was on hand a month ago, or look at inventory trends. We'd like to look at average inventory levels over time. This ability would help us to evaluate the effectiveness of our inventory and plan better for the future.

When we plan inventory for an item, we compare the amount currently on hand to the amount sold during the past 30 days. For each type of product, we try to maintain a particular percentage of monthly sales quantities. We've also got a sophisticated demand forecast system that helps us plan inventory. It produces demand estimates for the upcoming 30 days, and sometimes we will use that metric in place of the prior 30-day sales.

Of secondary importance is the ability to look at the velocity of inventory. To do this, we need to have access to the quantity shipped during the month. Some people like to use this comparison to forecast the amount of money required to maintain inventory, but we discourage that viewpoint. The reason is simple: It builds in the assumption that we will not improve our inventory management. We may have been able to move more inventory had it been available. One of our primary customer service objectives is to have 100 percent of the products our customers need in stock, so we want our forecasters and buyers to be looking at sales quantities rather than shipment quantities.

For similar reasons, we don't concern ourselves with the value of inventory. Our primary objective is to be able to meet customer demands, so that they never have a reason to turn elsewhere. Selling high-margin, high-velocity products is nice, but we have to stock the products our customers need.

Supplier Inventory Design

The primary objectives of the medical supplier's inventory data mart are:

- For any given month, allow inventory to be analyzed across products or locations.

- Over time, allow analysis of average inventory for a product or group of products.

- Facilitate comparison of inventory levels with 30-day demand, as represented by sales during the prior period or the demand forecast for the upcoming period.

The fact table will record inventory levels on the last day of each month. After the prototype is in production, the business may choose to move to daily snapshots. The change will impact our time dimension, but we'll have all the hard loading issues worked out. The grain of the fact table is month, item, and location. Four measures will be recorded (see Table 6.1).

Quantity_on_hand is inventory, as sampled at month's end. It can be summed for multiple products or locations to provide a combined inventory level for a given month. However, it is not appropriate to sum quantity_on_hand over more than one month. It should be obvious that doing so would potentially double-count individual physical items. For example, if a particular box of SaniShield 2" Bandages remained on a shelf from January through March, it would be captured in the quantity_on_hand measure for each of the three months. Summing inventory for the SaniShield 2" Bandages for the first quarter would triple-count it.

Table 6.1 Inventory Measures

Measure	Definition	Equivalencies/Notes
quantity_on_hand	Inventory level of an item in a region at the end of a month	Not additive over time
quantity_sold	Sales of an item in a region during the month	Rough representation of actual demand
demand_estimate	Estimated demand for the item in a region for the next month	Computed externally
quantity_shipped	Amount of a product that was removed from inventory and shipped to a customer during a month	Used to calculate velocity

As with the semi-additive basket_count measure from Chapter 3, "Marketing," quantity_on_hand can be aggregated over the problem dimension if averaged rather than summed. For example, it would be reasonable to request the average monthly inventory level of SaniShield 2" Bandages during the first quarter. The vice president of Logistics mentioned that this type of question is common. The model supports this form of analysis, but we will soon discover that the average we want is not always going to be easy to get using SQL.

We've also included quantity_shipped in the fact table. Combined with the inventory level, it can be used to calculate the *velocity* of inventory. The vice president of Logistics told us that the she does not like to use this information to plan inventory because it does not account for the business's failure to meet demand. Quantity_shipped does not include product that would have been shipped had it been available For example, shipments of tongue depressors may have totaled 200 cases during a month, while there were orders for 300. Additionally, the quantity shipped during a given month may include items that were destined for customers in other regions. In an optimal situation, all orders are shipped from the warehouse closest to the customer. High velocity does not imply efficiency. However, the vice president of Logistics has admitted that quantity_shipped is still used within the business to compute this metric.

Key Business Term

Velocity. A measure of the rate at which inventory moves in and out of the warehouse.

Velocity is measured differently from business to business. Often referred to as *turns*, it is usually computed as the ratio of quantity *shipped* during a *period* of time to the quantity *on hand* at a *point* in time.

Rather than look at the actual speed at which inventory moves off the shelves, the vice president of Logistics would like to look at the inventory level in comparison to the demand during the period. To allow this comparison, we have included two additional measures. The first is quantity_sold, which represents the total sales of the product in the region during the month. The ratio of quantity_on_hand to quantity_sold can be used to assess how close to a month's supply current inventory comes. We can also multiply this number by 30 to indicate the day's supply on hand.

Quantity_sold is preferable to quantity_shipped for this assessment because it factors in the effectiveness of inventory. Unlike shipments, which may be bound to a different region, the sales numbers can be recorded in the region to which the order will be delivered. Use of a sales level also allows planners to estimate what could have moved, rather than what did move. Inclusion of quantity_sold does have one possible drawback: It is likely to come from a different source system than the inventory data.

TIP

Quantity_sold is best retrieved from the order entry system. Be careful when an inventory system provides sales quantities. If the inventory system is not integrated with sales, the numbers should be distrusted. They may result from an imperfect interface, rely on data that has been rekeyed, or be skewed by adjustments. Instead, trace the sales quantity upstream to its source.

If an orders or sales data mart has been built that conforms with the Inventory data mart, quantity_sold can be sourced from the other mart. In the latter case, quantity_sold can even be omitted from the inventory design, since it can be combined with quantity_on_hand in a drill-across query. See Chapter 1, "The Business-Driven Data Warehouse," for more information on drilling across.

Though more useful to the distributor than quantity_shipped, quantity_sold is not a perfect picture of demand. The sales force has access to inventory, and can tell customers what is in stock when taking an order. A customer may be interested in five cases of bandages, but orders only three cases upon learning that five are not available. Another product may be substituted for the balance, or it may be purchased from a competitor.

The vice president of Logistics indicated that the business has an alternate way to look at demand: A demand forecast system that crunches historic data produces monthly forecasts. Rather than duplicate the sophisticated efforts of the demand forecasting software, we will take the estimates it produces, since they are available at the right grain. We have called it demand_estimate. Because we are letting another system compute this figure, we have built a weakness into the inventory design. Should the formula for computing forecast change at a point in time, all data previously loaded into the data mart will contain a demand forecast based on one formula, while data loaded subsequently will incorporate a forecast based on a different formula. It behooves us to be sure the business is willing to live with this decision.

The vice president of Logistics indicated that the value of goods in inventory is not taken into account by the medical supplier. They do not want customers to have to turn elsewhere to place orders, and are therefore willing to carry items in inventory that are expensive or do not move. Retailers and manufacturers are likely to look at inventory differently. The retailer has limited shelf space. Carrying product that does not move or has minimal margin does not make as much sense. By including the cost and value of goods in inventory, they can compute the marginal return of their inventory based on its velocity by multiplying velocity by margin.

The dimensions for the inventory schema are straightforward. As previously mentioned, the grain of the fact table is defined by the month, item, and region dimensions. The model, as shown in Figure 6.1, does not require any additional dimensions. The item dimension includes several interesting attributes, including the category and subcategory characteristics mentioned in the quotation. Each row in the region dimension corresponds to an individual warehouse, and includes the name of the larger sales territory within which it falls. When sales territories are shuffled, new rows will be written to the region table that reflect the changes. Past history will remain linked to the previous rows.

With a relatively small number of dimensions and facts, the inventory model looks quite simple. But the quantity_on_hand is semi-additive, and will be required in every report needed by the vice president of Logistics and her staff. As we prepare to develop inventory reports, we must remain on guard against the hazards of semi-additivity. One wrong move, and an incorrect report might prompt a manager to make some changes in inventory that could hurt the business.

Inventory Reports

The inventory data mart can answer a wide range of questions, and addresses all the concerns of the vice president of Logistics. We will explore its range by looking at five reports. Along the way, we'll learn a few new things about semi-additive facts and averages.

Point-In-Time Inventory Reports

Let's begin with the most basic of inventory questions: How much of a particular product is on hand? For the first example, we want to know how much of each product in the bandage category was on hand in each region during the month of January 1997. There are two constraints that will be placed on the query we build. The category attribute in the item dimension must be equal to "bandage,"

Figure 6.1 Inventory.

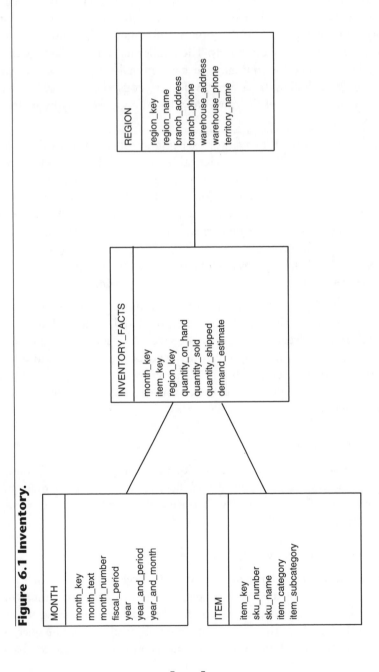

and the year_and_month attribute of the month dimension must be equal to "1997 January." We will bring back the SKU_name, SKU_number, Region, and the sum of quantity_on_hand.

In Chapter 1, "The Business-Driven Data Warehouse," we warned that careful thought must be given to any query that includes a semi-additive measure. In this report, the quantity_on_hand measure is used, which has been documented as not additive across time. A review of the query should indicate whether its use is appropriate. The query will be constrained to return data for only a single month, January 1997. The grain of the time dimension is monthly, so there will be no danger of summing quantity_on_hand over time. Had the grain of the fact table been daily, there would have been an issue. The query for this report makes proper use of the semi-additive fact, so we can go ahead and develop it. The result is shown in Report 6.1.

Report 6.1 A basic inventory report.

<table>
<tr><td colspan="4" align="center">**January 1997 Inventory**
Bandage Category</td></tr>
<tr><td>**SKU Number**</td><td>**SKU Name**</td><td>**Region**</td><td>**Sum of Quantity on Hand**</td></tr>
<tr><td>928474</td><td>SaniShield 2"</td><td>North</td><td>201</td></tr>
<tr><td></td><td></td><td>South</td><td>172</td></tr>
<tr><td></td><td></td><td>East</td><td>32</td></tr>
<tr><td></td><td></td><td>West</td><td>153</td></tr>
<tr><td>928247</td><td>SaniShield 3"</td><td>North</td><td>478</td></tr>
<tr><td></td><td></td><td>South</td><td>56</td></tr>
<tr><td></td><td></td><td>East</td><td>18</td></tr>
<tr><td>8593023</td><td>MediMax 2"</td><td>North</td><td>489</td></tr>
<tr><td></td><td></td><td>South</td><td>108</td></tr>
<tr><td></td><td></td><td>East</td><td>55</td></tr>
<tr><td></td><td></td><td>West</td><td>47</td></tr>
<tr><td>8593083</td><td>MediMax 3"</td><td>North</td><td>304</td></tr>
<tr><td></td><td></td><td>South</td><td>382</td></tr>
<tr><td></td><td></td><td>East</td><td>101</td></tr>
<tr><td></td><td></td><td>West</td><td>94</td></tr>
</table>

Note that there is no row in our report for SaniShield 3" bandages in the Western region. This omission is not a mistake; rather, it reflects the *sparsity* of our fact table. If there is no inventory of a product at a location for a given period, there is no need to load a row into the fact table. Loading a zero row for a product that was not in inventory would make the fact table very large, especially when we consider how many products are discontinued, or changed enough to receive a new row in the item dimension. We'll see later that sparsity causes problems when we try to use SQL's average function.

Some people in the business may not want to see this level of detail; instead, one manager asks us to show inventory for 2" bandages and inventory for 3" bandages. Particular SKUs are not of concern, as the different brands are easily substituted for one another. He also wants to see the total inventory for all regions. To produce this report, we simple sum the quantity_on_hand measures for 2" products and 3" products. We'll add summary rows showing subtotals for each region. We're using a semi-additive fact, so a quick check is once again in order. Quantity_on_hand will now be summed across products, adding quantities for each of the 2" and 3" bandages. In our report calculations, we'll also be summing quantity_on_hand across regions. The measure is fully additive across products and regions, so the report passes the additivity check. The result is shown in Report 6.2.

Report 6.2 Inventory summed across products and regions.

January 1997 Inventory
Bandages

Bandage Type	Region	Sum of Quantity on Hand
2"	North	690
	South	280
	East	87
	West	200
	All regions	**997**
3"	North	782
	South	438
	East	119
	West	94
	All regions	**1,433**

TIP

Report 6.2 requires grouping SKUs together into groupings for "2-Inch" and "3-Inch." A review of Item dimension reveals that there are no attributes that contain such groupings. The category attribute takes on the value Bandages for all these products, and the subcategory attribute takes on values like Pads and Rolled. Since the data mart does not have an attribute that returns data like "2-Inch Bandages" and "3-Inch Bandages," we will have to construct these groups ourselves, within the reporting application. To do this, the full list of bandage products and how they are broken into groups must be known at the time the report is built. We will most likely perform this grouping within the application, rather than in a database query.

Another executive looks at this report and notices that the inventory levels are much higher for 3" bandages. She is curious if this is normal, or if January was an unusual case. She requests that the report be modified to show 2" and 3" bandage inventories across all regions for each of three months. We consult our rules of additivity, and this time notice that the report is no longer constrained to a single month. The condition on our query will now allow three months of data through. A red flag goes up, because we know that quantity_on_hand is not additive across time. But the requested report will break out the totals by month, so our additivity rules still check out. A time series is acceptable, as long as we don't sum over multiple periods. We deliver the report shown in Report 6.3.

Report 6.3 Inventory time series.

	97Q1 Inventory 2" and 3" Bandages	
Bandage Type	**Region**	**Sum of Quantity on Hand**
2"	January	997
	February	329
	March	657
3"	January	1433
	February	405
	March	702

It is very easy to take this report one step further and commit a serious mistake. The previous report had useful subtotals, so why not this one? Contemplating adding a total of quantity on hand across all months for each bandage type, we once again check our additivity rules, and this time or check fails! A subtotal for each type would require summing our quantities over time, which is forbidden. Most end-user query tools dutifully construct totals when users request them. We'll have to be careful with this data. Many business users would spot the error in this simple report, but in a larger, more complex report, such a mistake might be less obvious.

TIP

When summing a semi-additive measure, the dimension across which it is not additive must be used to constrain the query, as in Reports 6.1 and 6.2, or the semi-additive measure must be grouped by the dimension in question, as in Report 6.3.

In the latter case, special care must be taken not to further total or subtotal the semi-additive measure within the reporting application—doing so could spell disaster. If totals are added to Report 6.3, a buyer who glances at them may mistake them for an average, and assume that inventory levels are high, when in fact they are quite low.

So far, we've been very careful not to aggregate quantity_on_hand over time, because the result is meaningless. This fact is obvious to a business person, but easily overlooked by a developer. Adding together the month-end quantities for January, February, and March produces a number that has no meaning. It does not represent the quantity on hand at the end of the period; the March value alone tells us that. As the sum of inventory on three different days, it is clearly not an indication of what inventory was like at any point during the period. It does not even show the total number of physical items that were in inventory over the three-month period, because products that did not move are double-counted, and comings and goings between samplings are not visible.

So what about the questions the vice president of Logistics mentioned that required looking at inventory over time? Don't panic—the model can answer these questions. That's because they won't require presenting *sum* of inventory levels; instead, they require presenting metrics that aggregate inventory in *other* ways.

Inventory over Multiple Periods

While the sum of inventory levels over time is not meaningful, the sum can be used as part of a calculation that *is* meaningful. For example, we can use the sum of inventory over time in the computation of an average inventory level.

Consider the business question "What was the average month-end inventory level for each product in the Bandage category?" The report will require SKU_name, SKU_number, region, and an average of quantity_on_hand. The query will be constrained to only retrieve data for the first quarter of 1997. Our additivity rules forbid presenting a sum of quantity_on_hand over time, but we're going to show an average. Things check out, so we deliver Report 6.4.

Look easy? Not so fast! While removing the additivity barrier, the use of averages ushers in a new set of problems. This report could easily fall victim to a

Report 6.4 Averaging month-end inventory.

97Q1 Inventory
Bandage Category

SKU Number	SKU Name	Region	Average Monthly Quantity on Hand
928474	SaniShield 2"	North	201
		South	172
		East	32
		West	153
928247	SaniShield 3"	North	478
		South	56
		East	18
		West	200
8593023	MediMax 2"	North	489
		South	108
		East	55
		West	47
8593083	MediMax 3"	North	304
		South	382
		East	101
		West	94

sparsity problem. Recall that the Report 6.1 showed no row for SaniShield 3" Bandages in the Western region during January. Because inventory of the product was zero, no row was recorded. The absence of zero rows means our fact table will have at least a minimal degree of sparsity. In and of itself, this sparsity is not an issue; however, it will make the process of computing an average a bit difficult.

The average of a set of values is defined as the sum of the values divided by the number of values. Let's calculate the average month-end quantity of SaniShield 3" bandages in the Western region for the first quarter. We know there were none on hand at the end of January. Suppose that there were 300 on hand at the end of February, and 300 at the end of March. The average is computed by summing the month-end totals and dividing by the number of months. The result is (0+300+300) / 3, or 200.

Unfortunately, standard SQL will not perform this calculation correctly. The SQL average function takes an argument, such as quantity_on_hand, sums it over a range of rows, then divides by the *number of rows* that were summed. This plan sounds about right, but recall that our fact table is sparse. For SaniShield 3" bandages in the Western region, the fact table only contains two rows for the first quarter. There is no "zero row" for January. SQL will incorrectly compute the Western region's average month-end inventory of SaniShield 3" Bandages as (300+300) / 2, or 300. This problem is easily avoided by staying away from the SQL average function and computing averages manually.

TIP

Sparsity in the fact table will throw off SQL-computed averages. A developer coding a report must use SQL's Sum function instead, and divide by the correct number. But what if end users are building reports with an ad hoc query application? Chances are, they never even look at the SQL their tool generates. In Chapter 13, "Presenting Information," we'll take a look at how the sparsity issue impacts the selection of query and reporting tools.

The astute reader might notice that this problem can easily be avoided by loading the zero rows—that is, rows containing the number zero—into the fact table. This approach proves undesirable, because it leads to very large fact tables. It would also force the data mart to carry a lot of excess baggage. Over the course of a year, a large number of products are discontinued, or changed enough to be considered a new product. We'd be forced to load rows containing zero for all products no longer stocked; otherwise, a report that included both time periods when the product was stocked and time periods when it was no longer stocked would return incorrect results. At the initial load of the data mart, the number of zero rows will not seem significant, but over time, the quantity will grow to become a tremendous burden. We could make the arbitrary decision to stop loading zeros when a new year begins, but this would require us to refrain from building queries that aggregate across year's end.

TIP

Loading zero rows allows us to use the SQL average function by eliminating the sparsity problem. But the decision requires severe compromises in terms of fact table size, data loading efforts, and the type of questions that can be asked. These compromises are not worth the benefits. There's another good reason not to bother with zero rows: As the next report reveals, sparsity is not the only problem with SQL averages.

As before, let's modify this report for the corporate planners. They are less concerned with the inventory levels in each region, and more interested in companywide totals. Report 6.5 removes the regional breakouts. There is only one row for each product. The Average Monthly Quantity on Hand column now shows the average monthly number on hand *throughout the company* during the quarter.

Though it looks simple, this report is actually more challenging than the previous one. For this report, the SQL average function won't get us the answer we need, *even if zero rows have been loaded*. The correct way to compute the average for each product is to take the sum of quantity_on_hand for all regions over the course of the first quarter, then divide by the number of months—three. Remember that SQL takes the sum and divides by the number of rows. In our

---

Report 6.5 Average month-end inventory across regions.

97Q1 Inventory
Bandage Category

SKU Number	SKU Name	Average Monthly Quantity on Hand
928474	SaniShield 2"	171
928247	SaniShield 3"	218
8593023	MediMax 2"	202
8593083	MediMax 3"	210

fact table, each product may have up to twelve rows for first quarter—one for each of the four regions (North, South, East, West) for each of the three months. Even if we have loaded zero rows, the SQL average will divide the sum by the wrong number. SQL has failed us again, and now loading zero rows doesn't help.

This time, we are facing the *grain* problem. We need to divide by the number of periods covered by the query, not the number of rows in the fact table. This problem wasn't visible when working on the previous report, because we were grouping our average by product and region. At that level, the number of rows would have been equal to the number of months—but only if there had there been zero rows. The grain of our average happened to coincide with the grain of the fact table. But for Report 6.5, we are aggregating over the region dimension as well as time. In this situation, the number of rows will not equal the number of months, even if there are zero rows.

Unfortunately, SQL does not let us specify the dimension over which we want to average. To cope with the grain problem, we must calculate the average ourselves. We use SQL to retrieve the sum, and divide by the number of periods. The number of periods can be determined by looking carefully at the query. Conditions in the where clause will reveal any constraints made on time; the Select and Group By clauses will reveal the level to which aggregation is being performed.

TIP

It is almost never appropriate to use the SQL average function. If sparsity is not an issue, you'll probably face the grain problem.

When the dimension over which we want to average is time, as in this example, we say that we want to take a *period average*. The grain problem often centers around time, and tool vendors may boast about "period average capabilities." There are often situations, however, in which we want to average over a dimension other than time. See the sidebar for details.

More about Averages

The grain issue is often referred to as the *period average problem*, because the dimension over which we want to average represents time periods. However, grain issues are encountered in other situations as well.

Suppose that a group of planners is preparing to open a new regional division for the company. They need to stock the new region with

Continues

inventory. They would like the initial inventory level of each item to be sufficient to meet demand for the first three months. The planners estimate that sales in the new region will be about 25 percent below the corporate average. They would like to use the sales data mart to figure out the average regional sales for each product.

The grain of the sales data mart is item sales by customer by day. In addition to the item and day dimensions, there is a salesperson dimension, which contains the region name. The planners would like to get average sales by product and region for a particular quarter. For each product, they need to get the quarter's quantity sold and divide by the number of regions. Since the grain of the fact table is at the customer and salesperson level, SQL will not do the job—there are too many rows. The planners need to take a regional average. They face the same problem we faced in computing a period average; SQL does not allow specification of the grain of the average. Developers of the report must sum quantity sold, and divide the result by the number of regions.

Because of all the problems with the SQL average function, developers must calculate averages themselves, but sometimes it is hard to choose a number to use as the divisor of an average computation. In retail, for example, fiscal periods have varying numbers of weeks. Computing average weekly inventory levels by quarter becomes problematic; some quarters have more weeks than other quarters.

Some developers attempt to solve this problem by using the SQL "count distinct operator." By counting distinct time keys in the query, as in "count (distinct time_key)," the developer effectively places a measure into SQL that correctly represents the number of periods, regardless of what attributes appear in the group by clause of the query. Unfortunately, this solution falls victim to the sparsity issue: Zero rows are not recorded in the database.

As if things weren't already bad enough, we also have to keep in mind that a number of periods calculation is itself a semi-additive fact. While it can be summed up over quarters or years, it cannot be summed over *any other dimension*. Ad hoc access to this construct would be quite dangerous; it is easily used incorrectly.

Is There Enough?

The reports shown so far answer business questions about how much inventory was on hand. Many of the things the vice president of Logistics told us were not about figuring out *how much* is on hand, but rather figuring out if *enough* is on hand. The model has two measures designed to help answer these questions: a sales level for the period, and a demand forecast for the next period. These two measures can be used in much the same way. By comparing quantity_on_hand to the actual demand of the previous month or estimated demand for the next month, we provide metrics used by the business to determine the efficiency of its inventory.

Consider the question, "What percentage of the February demand estimate do I have on hand for each product at each region at the end of January?" Report 6.6 answers the question. This report is very similar to Report 6.1, but demand estimate and percent of demand have been added. The Percent of Demand column in the report is calculated by dividing the quantity on hand by the demand estimate.

Report 6.6 Inventory versus forecast.

January 1997 Inventory
Bandage Category

SKU Number	SKU Name	Region	Quantity on Hand	Demand Estimate	Percent of Demand
928474	SaniShield 2"	North	201	804	25%
		South	172	621	28%
		East	32	137	23%
		West	153	805	19%
928247	SaniShield 3"	North	478	1775	27%
		South	56	112	50%
		East	18	96	19%
8593023	MediMax 2"	North	489	2621	19%
		South	108	511	21%
		East	55	208	26%
		West	47	121	39%
8593083	MediMax 3"	North	304	1427	21%
		South	382	1909	20%
		East	101	596	17%
		West	94	205	46%

Which levels in Report 6.6 are good? In a high-volume business like this one, it is not uncommon to find disagreement. The vice president of Logistics implied a desire to maintain a 30-day supply. The executive who requested this report told us that for items in the bandage category, there are weekly deliveries to the warehouse, and it is never necessary to have more than about 25 percent of a month's supply on hand. He considers less than 20 percent dangerously low, while over 30 percent is inefficient. At the executive's request, rows in the report that fall above or below these tolerance levels have been bolded. In his opinion, these rows will require special attention by the business, though others may disagree. We're more likely to find organizationwide agreement about optimal levels of inventory in businesses that do less volume, like car dealers, or businesses with limited shelf space, like retail.

Note the wide range of percentages we see in the report. The numbers dip as low as 17 percent, and as high as 50 percent. This range might be explained by looking at when each warehouse took deliveries for each product. Inventory is sampled on the last day of the month. Products that have just been delivered are likely to have a higher inventory level than those due to be received the next day.

Does the dependence of percent of demand on the sampling date make this report less useful? The answer depends on who you ask. The buyers, who place weekly orders for products with each supplier, may be very happy to get this information. They can use it to control how much will be delivered during the next shipment. They are likely to complain that the data mart is not refreshed often enough. They would like up-to-date information each day.

Move up a level and ask those responsible for managing the purchasing and inventory process, and you may get a different answer. At this level, the particulars at the end of one month are not of interest. The numbers will fluctuate wildly based on when products were shipped and what the order cycle is. These managers will be more interested in comparing the *average* inventory with the *average* demand over a period of months. At this level, much of the fluctuation will be smoothed out, and particular products or regions that seem to be less efficient with inventory should be easily identified.

The flip side of the demand estimate is the quantity_sold measure, which can be used in much the same way as the demand estimate. At any point in time, it can be used to calculate what percentage of a month's sales are on hand. Since sales fluctuate, it may be useful to compare the point-in-time inventory with the average quantity sold over several months.

For the medical product supplier, inventory is a stockpile of product to be sold. If there is not enough to meet the demand forecast, more can be ordered. Next, we'll look at a hotel business, where inventory levels aren't easily increased.

Hotel Occupancy

The distributor's product inventory had two distinguishing characteristics. The things being inventoried were physical. You could enter the warehouse and hold a box of tongue depressors, or count the cases of bandages on the shelves. Second, additional inventory could be acquired as needed. If there were not enough sutures on hand to meet the demand of the next 30 days, more would be ordered. Retail inventory and manufacturing inventory share these characteristics. The inventoried items are physical and supplies can be replenished.

For service industries, the product is not tangible, and is usually subject to a maximum limit. As we described earlier, these traits characterize *capacity-based* inventory. Because of the limited capacity of their products, service industries ask a different set of questions about inventory. They don't ask how much inventory they have, or how much they need; instead, they want to know how much they utilize and how to achieve optimal utilization. We'll study these questions in the context of a national hotel chain.

Capacity Management

Our hotel chain operates 500 hotels in 40 states. There are two branded lines of hotels. The primary line of hotels features larger than average rooms, most of which are suites. The target customers are business travelers and upscale vacationers. The second line of hotels features competitive rates, though with reduced amenities. The target customers are price-sensitive travelers.

The hotel chain has many products. Most branches have at least two restaurants, a newsstand, and a health club. Each of these product lines brings in revenues. Even combined, these revenues are dwarfed by income from the primary product line. Customers pay a daily rate in exchange for a room to occupy. For the accommodation revenue stream, the hotel's product inventory is defined by the number of rooms that can be occupied each day.

The hotel chain's capacity to accommodate customers is limited. Each hotel has a set number of rooms. Construction of new hotels requires significant capital investment, so the inventory remains relatively static. Weekly operating expenses for hotels can be quite high as well. The payroll includes registration clerks, porters, housekeeping staff, and maintenance staff. Other costs include power, gas, and electricity. Given the day-to-day operational costs, the hotel strives to maximize use of its capacity.

We've been assigned to work with the senior vice president of Sales and Marketing, who is funding construction of a data mart to help analyze use of the hotel chain's capacity. Here's what he tells us during our interview:

Our primary source of revenue is accommodations in hotel rooms. There are about 400 hotels in our chain, each of which has between 30 and 500 rooms. There are different types of rooms, like standard rooms and suites. We've got size designations we use internally: small, medium, and large. Each room may also incorporate certain optional features, such as a refrigerator or kitchenette.

One of the biggest challenges we face is determining how to price our hotel rooms. We've got a fixed number of rooms that can be booked to customers. I have a team of analysts who work hard to determine the best way to price these rooms. If they are priced low, our hotels will be constantly booked, people will be forced to try the competition out, and we won't make any money. If rooms are priced too high, a lot of rooms will remain empty. We try to price our inventory at the maximum the market will bear at close to 100-percent capacity. When rooms aren't filling, we can modify pricing or market more aggressively to bring customers in.

To determine how to price and market inventory, our analysts need to look at the use of our capacity over time: the occupancy rate *or* utilization. *The flip side of this rate is the* vacancy rate. *We set overall occupancy rate targets for specific hotels, which requires looking at utilization across room types, and then set guidelines for each type of room, which requires looking at utilization across hotels. Rates are also seasonal, so we sometimes look at utilization at very specific points in time. Seasonal rates will vary with the location of a hotel. For example, our rates in southern Florida are higher during the winter months, while rates in Maine and Vermont are higher during the spring and fall.*

We also need to correlate the occupancy rate to revenue. The best way to do this is by looking at the revenues specifically correlated with accommodation. Price-point analysis is not practical because there are so many different customers paying different rates. We'd like to compare the margin dollars associated with our occupancy rates, but how to calculate the marginal cost of an occupied room is a topic of intense internal controversy right now, because not all costs are fixed. By comparing occupancy rate to accommodation revenues, however, we can assess the overall average rate achieved.

Clearly, the questions being asked by the hotel's senior vice president of Marketing are very different from the medical distributor's vice president of Logistics. In this service-based industry, there is an upper cap on the amount of product that can be sold to customers. Let's look at how a data mart can help the hotel study capacity use.

Hotel Utilization Design

We are now ready to design a data mart for the senior vice president of Sales and Marketing. Our primary objectives are:

- For any day, allow capacity utilization (or "occupancy rate") to be analyzed across products or locations. Products are particular room types.

- Over time, allow analysis of average utilization levels for specific hotels, products, or groups.

- For each room type and hotel, capture the accommodation revenues for comparison to occupancy levels.

To support these needs, we have designed the schema shown in Figure 6.2. The fact table will capture daily capacity utilization by hotel and room type. This grain requires three dimensions: day, hotel, and room type. No additional dimensions will be needed to address our objectives.

We have included a standard day dimension, which allows us to ask for different components of the date, from year down to specific date. Common combinations of elements are also provided, such as Year and Quarter, and there is a holiday flag.

The hotel dimension identifies a particular hotel. It includes the standard address, phone number, and manager information. Names and codes by which each hotel is known are included, as well as an indication of which hotel line the branch is a part of.

The room_type dimension enumerates the different accommodation products offered by the hotel. It is analogous to the item dimension in the medical supplier's inventory model. In addition to capturing room type and size, we capture number and type of beds, maximum number of occupants, and other features. A sample room_type table is shown in Table 6.2.

The fact table contains five measures, enumerated in Table 6.3. During our interview with the senior vice president of Sales and Marketing, we learned that he wants to be able to look at occupancy and vacancy levels. These levels may be expressed as numbers, or as percentages of the total number of rooms. Rooms currently unavailable for maintenance reasons may or may not be excluded from the total number of rooms. We have selected a trilogy of measures to accommodate these needs.

Figure 6.2 Hotel inventory utilization.

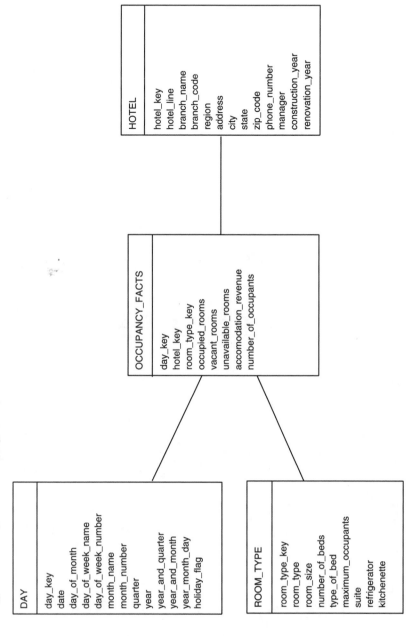

Table 6.2 The room_type Dimension

room_type_key	room_type	room_size	number_of_beds	type_of_bed	maximum_occupants	suite	refrigerator	kitchenette
1	standard	small	2	king	4	N	N	N
2	standard	small	1	king	2	N	N	N
3	standard	small	2	king	4	N	N	N
4	standard	small	1	king	2	N	N	N
5	suite	small	4	king	8	N	N	N
6	suite	small	3	king	6	N	N	N
7	deluxe	large	4	king	8	Y	Y	Y
8	suite	small	4	king	10	Y	Y	N
9	suite	small	3	king	8	Y	Y	N
10	deluxe	large	4	king	10	Y	Y	Y
11	standard	medium	2	king	4	N	N	N
12	standard	medium	1	king	2	N	N	N
13	standard	medium	2	king	4	N	N	N
14	standard	medium	1	king	2	N	N	N
15	suite	medium	4	king	8	N	N	N
16	suite	medium	3	king	6	N	N	N
17	suite	medium	4	king	10	Y	Y	N
18	suite	medium	3	king	8	Y	Y	N

Table 6.3 Occupancy Measures

Measure	Definition	Equivalencies/Notes
occupied_rooms	Number of rooms of a given type booked for a customer on a past date, or reserved for a customer at the hotel on a future date	Not additive across time
vacant_rooms	Number of rooms not sold to a customer on a past date, or not reserved for a future date	Not additive across time
unavailable_rooms	Number of rooms not available for occupancy on a given date for maintenance or other reasons	Not additive across time
accommodation_revenue	Accommodation revenue booked at the hotel on the date in question	
number_of_occupants	Number of guests staying in occupied rooms	

The occupied_rooms and vacant_rooms measures are straightforward. They represent the use of the hotel's inventory. Technically, these measures are not additive over time, or rooms would be double-counted. Some interpretations may relax this restriction; as representations of a day's occupancy or vacancy, they may be considered additive. For example, a forecaster may find it useful to consider a hotel with 50 rooms as having 350 days' worth of vacancies over the course of a week. However, these vacancies are not all available simultaneously. The requirements of the individual report will dictate whether semi-additivity restrictions can be relaxed.

Occupied_rooms and vacant_rooms can be combined to get the total number of usable rooms, calculated as sum(occupied_rooms) + sum(vacant_rooms). By adding the sum of unavailable rooms, we get the total number of rooms, as in: sum(occupied_rooms) + sum(vacant_rooms) + sum(unavailable_rooms).

Occupancy rate is calculated as the ratio of occupied rooms to the number of usable rooms, or to the total number of rooms. Assuming the latter, the following formula yields an occupancy rate:

sum(occupied_rooms) / (sum(occupied_rooms) + sum(vacant_rooms) + sum(unavailable_rooms))

This metric, like all percentages, is not additive; as such, we do not store it in the fact table. By reducing it to additive components, we achieve greater flexibility in calculating occupancy rates. Depending on the conditions and group by clauses of our query, this formula can yield daily, weekly, or monthly use, for a particular type of room at a particular hotel, or across the entire chain of hotels.

High occupancy is not desirable if rates are too low. On the other hand, a slight reduction in rates might lead to increased occupancy. To analyze the effectiveness of utilization, we require operating costs or value, either for used or total capacity. The ratio of capacity used to this number measures the effective use of capacity. Without both cost and value components, we can't assess the profitability of the utilization rate, but a single component allows assessment of effectiveness of utilization in relative terms.

Key Business Term

Occupancy rate. Percentage of available rooms that are booked.

This term can be generalized to *Utilization Rate*, defined as the percentage of available capacity that is sold or obligated. Applicable across service industries, Utilization Rate is expressed as capacity used divided by total capacity.

For the hotel chain, calculating the operating cost of individual rooms is not practical. There are too many components, and the marginal cost of each additional occupancy would require a team of MBAs to estimate. More importantly, we were told that how it is computed is currently a source of controversy within the company. The value of total capacity is also difficult to measure, because in practice, each customer pays a different rate. However, revenue for used capacity is easy to collect from the hotel's computer system: It's the amount customers pay for accommodation, after all the taxes and add-ons are removed from the bill. The ratio of occupied rooms to revenue will be used to gauge the effectiveness of utilization. We've also grabbed the number of occupants, should anyone want to add that metric to the mix.

Why Not Use a Transaction Model?

When designing a data mart to support analysis of capacity utilization, one may be tempted to add customer to the grain of the fact table. Figure 6.3 shows how such a design might look. Each row in the fact table represents an individual customer staying in a particular room type in a hotel on a particular day. By adding customer, the model may be used to answer additional questions.

Several measures are not present in this revised model. Occupied_rooms is conspicuously absent, but it is easy to calculate. Since each row of the fact table represents a customer occupying a room, we can use the SQL count(*) function in queries that require the number of occupied rooms.

The two other missing measures will be more problematic. The change in grain forced us to remove vacant_rooms and unavailable_rooms, which do not make sense in the context of a customer. Their removal means that we are missing one of the key components of the occupancy rate formula: the total capacity. To use this model for capacity analysis, we must find a new place for these measures—since they don't work in the fact table, the only other possibility is a dimension. It doesn't make sense to store them in the Hotel dimension, because we want vacant_rooms and unavailable_rooms at the room-type level. We could break each of the measures down into components for the separate room types, but recall from Table 6.2 that there were at least 18. Breaking these measures into separate numbers for each room type would also make it difficult to calculate total capacity across room types. Similarly, the room_type dimension would not be a good home for vacant_rooms and unavailable_rooms, because at times we will want them broken out by hotel. And neither of these dimensions would allow the changes in capacity over time to be modeled.

None of the dimension tables seem to be hospitable homes for vacant_rooms and unavailable_rooms, because these attributes are not dimensions. Recorded at the intersection of a hotel, a room type, and a day, they are measures, fully additive across two of these dimensions. Since they do not fit in the fact table as modeled in Figure 6.3, we are must add a second fact table to the model in order to capture them. With foreign keys for hotel, room_type, and day, this new fact table will look suspiciously like the original fact table in Figure 6.2, minus occupied_rooms and accommodation_revenue.

Figure 6.3 Adding customer to the grain of the fact table.

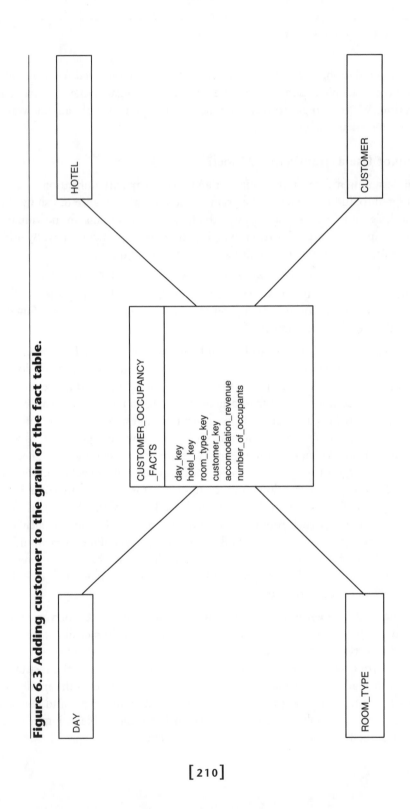

HOTEL

CUSTOMER

CUSTOMER_OCCUPANCY
_FACTS

day_key
hotel_key
room_type_key
customer_key
accomodation_revenue
number_of_occupants

DAY

ROOM_TYPE

With components of occupancy rate relegated to two separate fact tables, its calculation now requires two separate queries and additional local calculation. The first query gets the number of occupied rooms from one fact table, and the second gets the capacity from the other. The application must then compute the ratio locally. While inclusion of customer information seems appealing from a sales analysis point of view, it clearly makes analysis of capacity utilization unnecessarily complex. We'll stick with the original model from Figure 6.2. Let's put it to the test, and see how well it answers the questions of the senior vice president of Sales and Marketing.

Hotel Utilization Reports

We'll test our model's ability to meet each of our design objectives. It needs to support analysis of utilization at a point in time, over time, and in comparison to revenues. Note that these three requirements closely mirror those of the medical supplier.

Point-in-Time Utilization

First, let's look at how well this model supports the analysis of capacity utilization across products. We'll try to answer the question "What was the occupancy rate for each hotel in Virginia last night?" To answer this question, we'll need the hotel_name from the hotel dimension, and the sum of occupied_rooms and vacant_rooms from the fact table. The query is qualified to limit results to the specific date and state. After retrieving the results, we will calculate the occupancy rate using our formula. The result is shown in Report 6.7. The team may decide to focus some marketing efforts on the Richmond market.

Report 6.7 Occupancy rate across products.

**Occupancy Rate
Virginia Hotels, 5-Jul-97**

Hotel	Occupancy Rate
Capital Center	47%
Reston	53%
Old Town Alexandria	59%
Downtown Richmond	35%
Charlottesville	61%

At a glance, this report provides the key metric the senior vice president of Sales and Marketing wants. It is both simple and powerful. Imagine how hard it would be to compare occupancy rates at the various hotels if we had omitted the percentage and supplied Sum of Occupied Rooms and Sum of Vacant Rooms. Executives would be likely to take out their calculators, divide Sum of Occupied Rooms by the Sum of Occupied Rooms plus Sum of Vacant Rooms for each row, and jot the answers in the margin. All too often, developers provide the components of the rate rather than the rate itself. By failing to take this final step, the report is difficult to use.

TIP

Even though we don't store nonadditive measures in the fact table, they are important business metrics that will often be the focus of a report. Reports, after all, are intended to answer business questions. When the components of the answer are delivered in a report, but the answer itself is not computed, the report has missed its mark.

If a ratio is needed, compute it. It is not necessary to present components of the ratio that do not add value on their own. In Report 6.7, occupancy rate has been calculated from the sum of occupied_rooms and the sum of vacant_rooms. The latter two measures are not included in the report; they are not required to answer the business question.

In addition to allowing analysis of the occupancy rate across room types, the model will support analysis of occupancy rate across hotels. "What was last night's occupancy rate for each room type in Virginia hotels?" The process of answering this question is much like the process of answering the previous one. We will retrieve the room_type attribute of the room_type dimension table, and the components of the occupancy rate—occupied_rooms and vacant_rooms. Again, we'll qualify on the date and the state. The result is shown in Report 6.8. Once again, the final report is simple and powerful. By adding different dimensions to our query, we can break occupancy rate out a number of ways—by state, by region, by rooms with and without kitchens, and so on.

Utilization Over Time

The question, "What were the occupancy rates of Virginia hotels for the month of July?" requires looking at utilization over time. To answer this question, we will need all the same data required for the first report, hotel_name, sum of occupied_rooms, and sum of vacant_rooms. This time we'll pull it for a full month

Report 6.8 Occupancy rate across hotels.

Occupancy Rate
Virginia Hotels, 5-Jul-97

Room Type	Occupancy Rate
Standard	47%
Suite	53%
Deluxe	61%

instead of a single day. The astute reader will observe that we seem to be breaking our additivity rules; occupied_rooms and vacant_rooms are not additive across time. However, we are not summing these measures for presentation to the end user. Instead, the sums are required for the occupancy rate formula, which does make sense over a period of time. Our resulting report is shown in Report 6.9.

Notice the parallel to the way the semi-additive fact was handled for the medical supplier. In both cases, a semi-additive fact was summed over its nonadditive dimension. In both cases, this sum was not presented in the report, but rather used in a ratio computation that is valid over time. For the medical distribution report, the ratio was the average inventory level, expressed as the sum of inventory divided by the number of periods. For the hotel chain, the ratio was the occupancy rate, expressed as the sum of occupied_rooms divided by the sum of occupied_rooms plus the sum of vacant_rooms.

Occupancy and Revenues

Last, we need to compare total occupancy levels to revenues. This comparison yields an average price per room, allowing the pricing analysts to judge the

Report 6.9 Occupancy rate across time.

Occupancy Rate
Virginia Hotels, July 1997

Hotel	Occupancy Rate
Capital Center	74%
Reston	79%
Old Town Alexandria	88%
Downtown Richmond	60%
Charlottesville	82%

effectiveness of their capacity utilization. Report 6.10 shows average room price by hotel for Virginia for the month of July. Although the hotel in Old Town posted a very high occupancy rate, average room revenue was significantly lower than any of the other hotels. The analysts might want to reevaluate pricing structures that were in effect in that region.

As always, note that the schema and its associated reports are not a substitute for careful study of the situation by business analysts. The Old Town branch may have posted lower average revenues because it has a proportionally higher number of standard rooms, which command lower rates. It may not be appropriate to compare average room rates due to differences in the various regions. A $130 rate in Charlottesville may be quite unusual, while $139 in Reston is not uncommon. Factoring operating costs of the hotels into the picture might compensate for geographic differences, but the senior vice president of Sales and Marketing told us this is a controversial subject. We would be well advised not to insert our data mart into the middle of that debate. For now, we will have to let the analysts decide what is significant.

Summing Up Inventory

The two case studies in this chapter reveal just how differently inventory can be viewed. The medical supplier looked at inventory to optimize the amount of product purchased, while the hotel chain used inventory analysis to set pricing and target marketing campaigns. Yet the models built bear some striking similarities. Both include product, time, and location dimensions; both have a representation of quantity available. One explanation for these parallels is that in both cases, we modeled *inventory status* of the product.

Report 6.10 Occupancy rate and revenue.

Occupancy Rate and Revenue
Virginia Hotels, July 1997

Hotel	Occupancy Rate	Average Room Revenue
Capital Center	74%	145
Reston	79%	139
Old Town Alexandria	88%	75
Downtown Richmond	60%	135
Charlottesville	82%	130

No single model can answer all the questions a business may have about inventory. Had the medical supplier desired to improve the efficiency with which customers are served, the focus might have been on customer inventory status rather than warehouse inventory. Were there a desire to focus on the shipments received from suppliers, the quality assurance process, and the picking process for order fulfillment, we would have developed a very different model focusing on *inventory transactions* that represent these processes. As we have repeatedly pointed out, it is critical to understand what business objectives are to be addressed before developing the model.

Although we've only scratched the surface of inventory, this chapter has covered a lot of ground. We've learned quite a few things about inventory, how to model it, and how to stay out of trouble reporting on it.

Understand what kind of inventory you are studying. Does the business want to study its inventory of raw materials to improve its manufacturing efficiency, or is it concerned with the stocking levels of product inventory? The measures and dimensions will vary.

Choose the right type of inventory model. The status models in this chapter answer questions about quantities on hand, and can support analysis of value, velocity, capacity, and optimization. A transactional model allows examination of inventory suppliers, quality assurance, and preparations for shipment.

Capture the information needed to address the business questions. Dimensions and measures must be carefully chosen to support business objectives. The model we built for the medical supplier would not satisfy a retailer, to whom the value of inventory is as important as its levels or velocity. Be sure you understand the key indicators and how they are calculated.

Exercise extreme caution when designing inventory reports. Inventory levels are always semi-additive over time. In some reports, it will be appropriate to sum and present these facts, while in others, the sum will only be appropriate if it is part of a larger calculation. Carefully review your use of quantity_on_hand in each report developed.

Don't leave the computation of averages to SQL. We've seen that the SQL average function is problematic. It does not allow us to specify the dimension over which we want to average, and even grain-level averages can be miscalculated due to sparsity.

While the inventory data warehouse can be a challenge to design and build, the project can be quite rewarding to the business. Better information about inventory allows improvements to the purchasing or manufacturing processes, evaluation of suppliers, pinpointing of optimal pricing levels, and effective management of capacity.

QUALITY

Total Quality Management, or TQM, made great waves in the business world in the 1980s. U.S. and European corporations rushed to implement principles and practices that were common in Japan, where they were evangelized by the late Dr. Edward Demmings, an American. Dr. Demmings went to Japan in the postwar period after his ideas were met with skepticism in the United States. The resulting increases in productivity and quality transformed Japan into an economic powerhouse.

As Japanese companies entered and often dominated markets once thought impenetrable, U.S. and European companies began to pay attention to quality. Improvements in manufacturing quality created goods of continually increasing reliability. The quality and reliability of automobiles increased to a level once thought impossible. Warranties, once limited to 12 months or 12,000 miles, now start at 36 months or 36,000 miles. Similar improvements in other consumer and industrial products are common.

Quality, at least in the world of manufacturing, has become a fundamental value. TQM, sometimes grouped with Business Process Reengineering (BPR) and other buzzwords, has become less prominent simply because it is a fact of life for global manufacturers. As such, tracking quality is critical and has been incorporated into many Computer Integrated Manufacturing applications at the operational level. The availability of data on supplier quality, process quality, and costs of nonconformance is continually improving. As more companies adopt integrated manufacturing software applications, like SAP, Baan, and Oracle Manufacturing, ever more data becomes available.

In the service economy, the picture is not as rosy. Delivering a service often requires less structured data than manufacturing a product. The manufacturing process, heavily automated and structured, lends itself to automation and data collection. Moreover, the outcome of the manufacturing process is a physical product whose quality is evident to the eventual consumer. A service is intangible, the result often being an experience for the consumer, who may or may not choose to detail the experience for the service provider.

The nature of providing services also limits the amount of structured data collected by the service provider. The first step in automating a service business is capturing the data about the service transaction. A health care provider must capture diagnoses, treatments, and costs to manage profits. The outcome of a treatment, the obvious measure of quality to the patient, has only recently become financially important to the health care industry. Even if the outcome is tracked, the patient's feelings about treatment, diagnosis, and other interactions with the health care system are rarely captured.

In this chapter, we will begin our discussion of quality by returning to the fulfillment model created for the appliance manufacturer in Chapter 4, "Fulfillment." We will then move on to the software industry and examine the impact of quality on software products, and how a software company might capture quality data and use it to improve results. Finally, we will look at a national hotel chain determined to protect its quality-centered value proposition during an acquisition of another chain.

A Quick Quality Primer

There are hundreds of books on quality and its related subjects, including quality function deployment, TQM, and statistical process control. There is little that your authors could add to this body of work. We are not manufacturing engineers or statisticians, and will steer clear of complex equations that include symbols more commonly found on fraternity houses than calculators. Instead, we will attempt to make quality more accessible to the data warehouse designer, identifying natural design extensions that give considerable lift to the quality efforts of any business.

Key Business Term

Quality. Conformance of a product or service to customer expectations. Quality is always defined by the customer, either internal or external.

This is an adaptation of the classic "conformance to requirements" definition. For production processes, quality is conformance to requirements, but those requirements are determined by internal customers, like product design engineers who interpret customer needs. Our definition is intended to measure quality relative to the customer's expectations.

First we should define *quality*. This is a risky proposition, as some people raise their hackles over how quality is defined. We have chosen a utilitarian definition in an attempt to apply quality principles to a broad segment of the business world, not just manufacturing.

This definition appropriately establishes quality as a standard of interaction in all value-based transactions, whether they occur between two internal business units or a vendor and consumer. Quality in this way becomes an operating principle. A nonmanufacturing specific definition is especially helpful in a world where service and knowledge companies are growing rapidly.

With this definition, we can use a three-step process to identify quality requirements and incorporate those into our data warehouse design. These steps are:

1. **Define the value proposition of the product.** This step is familiar from our fulfillment discussion in Chapter 4. Quality extends the concept of fulfillment, providing more specific measures of product quality.

2. **Determine how nonconformance is measured.** Determine what indicators of nonconformance to expectations are inherent in the product. Again, manufactured goods display nonconformance overtly. Service product nonconformance is more difficult to discern. Understanding how to measure the occurrence and cost of nonconformance determines what data should be collected.

3. **Identify the potential sources of nonconformance.** Examine the process that transforms production assets into the product. Identify dimensions, either process or input related, that could impact quality. This step ensures that our design can help discover the causes of quality problems.

Using these steps, we can incorporate quality management into a data warehouse, capturing relevant data at any point in the value chain. For example, we can measure the quality of the production processes for Fizzy Cola and Pacific Bottling from Chapter 5, "Production." Pacific, a Fizzy customer, expects to be provided with consistent, safe syrup on a timely basis. Nonconformance could manifest itself in returned product from Pacific, or in complaints from Pacific about bad batches of product produced from Fizzy ingredients. The potential sources of nonconformance for Fizzy include the ingredients it uses to makes its syrup, its production process, its packaging and shipping operations, or Pacific's production process. With high levels of automation, Fizzy's production process is likely rich with data that can be used to measure quality. Identifying quality-related data is an additional consideration in the design of the production data warehouse. Quality management may also require its own unique fact tables and dimensions.

Using these steps, we can extend the design from an earlier example of production and fulfillment, incorporating quality management as well.

Washers, Dryers, and Warranties

In Chapter 4, "Fulfillment," we examined the case of an appliance manufacturer with a high-quality value proposition. The manufacturer had increased the warranty period for its washers to gain a competitive advantage. In doing so, the manufacturer made tracking quality an imperative. Our fulfillment model in Chapter 4, presented in Figure 4.10, was designed to track warranty costs over time. This design allowed the manufacturer to continually analyze the financial assumptions behind its high-quality value proposition.

Recall that the manufacturer based its strategy on the assumption that the increase in price associated with quality branding would lead to an increase in revenue greater than any additional warranty costs. The value proposition for the high-quality manufacturer is the production of highly reliable appliances to the consumer at a slight (20 percent) price premium over standard brands. If a standard brand washer with a certain drum size and similar features retails at $350, the company's comparable product would retail at $420. The $70 difference must be enough to more than cover increases in warranty costs, as well as investments in better components and production process improvements.

The first important element of quality to the manufacturer is reliability within an expected service life. The manufacturer covers all repairs through the first three years of service. In the context of the value proposition, we must identify how nonconformance is measured. One indicator of nonconformance first discussed in Chapter 4 is the cost of repairs under warranty. These repair costs, handled by a network of affiliated repair contractors, are a clear indicator of nonconformance. Our design from Chapter 4 tracks costs by product, month, and service month. It does not, however, track the incidence of a repair, which may be as important.

By offering an extensive warranty, the company is offering an insurance policy against product breakdowns, but neither the consumer nor the company expects the product to break down frequently. To the consumer, breakdowns are an inconvenience, while for the company, they are an expense. Our appliance manufacturer is staking out a high-quality market position on the presumption that its products are reliable. Neither the company nor the consumer anticipates a breakdown in the warranty period. A repair incident, perhaps even more than repair costs, is an important indicator of nonconformance. Customers suffering breakdowns are less likely to purchase other company products and will not recommend the company's products to others. Our design must measure both cost and repair incidents to provide a complete solution.

The last step is to identify the potential sources of nonconformance. In manufacturing, the potential sources of product defects can be grouped around the model of production used in Chapter 5, "Production." Bad production inputs or problems in the production process are the most likely sources of nonconformance. For an appliance manufacturer, production inputs consist primarily of components, while the process consists of many assembly steps that could create problems. A fundamental rule of quality and process improvement is to identify and eliminate production problems as early as possible. Our design from Chapter 4 identifies cost problems in finished goods, but the information only supports reactive price changes. To succeed as a quality manufacturer, the company must track quality in the factory and in the postsales market.

Quality at the Back Door

There are four possible outcomes in an assembly production process: We can correctly assemble bad components. We can incorrectly assemble good components. We can incorrectly assemble bad components. Or we can correctly assemble good components—the desired outcome. To address the potential problems of bad components, we will begin at the back door of our production facility. At the back door, components arrive for use on the production line. Some of these components will be tested on an individual basis, others by sampling, and still others not at all.

For example, we may test each primary motor that comes in the back door. This is a large, critical part that could easily hide a flaw until the unit is assembled. It is also easily tested. External metal panels can be visually inspected with little effort. Other parts, such as assembly screws, wiring harnesses, and other small parts may be sample tested. Delivered in production lots, a statistically valid sample of each lot is adequate to ensure overall lot quality. Some items may not be tested at all, for various reasons. Suppose one washer includes a computerized timer. This timer is assembled and tested by the supplier and certified by contract to be functional. The likelihood of damage in transit is low, so the parts are simply accepted. The objective of a data warehouse at the back door is to track component quality and supplier performance over time. The data for this design may come from a variety of sources, including a receiving system, integrated test equipment software, and a supplemental standalone data entry system. The design integrates supplier and component data, and provides a simple structure for tracking results over time.

We need the following dimensions:

Component. A dimension to identify all components to be tracked. The level of tracking will vary by industry. In a continuous process environment, we would track and sample ingredients. An important attribute of this dimension is one that identifies it as either *bulk* or *serialized*. Bulk components, such as screws or wiring harnesses, are sampled. Serialized components, like our electric motor, may be tested individually.

Supplier. The component supplier is identified. Each component may be supplied by more than one vendor. Separating supplier from component simplifies component- and supplier-specific analyses.

Inspection. A dimension to describe the inspection or tests that are performed, it allows for the possibility of sampling or testing in more than one way. For example, we could test an electric motor with automated test equipment as well as visually inspecting it. We might sample a type of screw with a visual inspection, a destructive strength test, and a measurement test.

Time. We include a time dimension at a daily grain.

Lot/serial number. This dimension represents the grouping of items for receiving and testing. Bulk items arrive in lots, while individual items have serial numbers. This dimension, as well as component and supplier, are also linked to a receiving fact table.

We will need two fact tables to track component quality, one to track the quantity received and a second to record quantity rejected and the related defect.

Table 7.1 Sample Defects

Insp_key	Name	Inspection Method	Type	Destructive_flag
1	Wiring harness finish	Visual	Lot sample	N
2	Wiring harness fit	Visual	Lot sample	N
3	Assembly screw tensile	Machine test	Lot sample	Y
4	Assembly screw thread	Instrument	Lot sample	N

The first fact table, comp_receipt_facts, has a grain of supplier by lot/serial by day by shipment by facility by component. Our second fact table has the same grain with the addition of a defect dimension. To illustrate this design, consider a sample of rows, shown in Table 7.1, from the defect dimension.

We must allow for three scenarios in our design. If a component fails a lot inspection, the entire lot is rejected. If our receipt schema records a lot of 500 wiring harnesses, the lot may pass the visual finish test but fail the fit test. Our inspection fact table would have one row recording the quantity rejected as 500. A lot of assembly screws is treated in the same way. A lot of washer lids is handled differently, since the inspections are on an individual basis. These finished panels may be rejected by either a color or form test. A lot of 100 panels might have 80 that are fine, 15 that fail the color test, and 5 that fail the form test. We would need two rows in our fact table to record each inspection failure group. Our final scenario is the individual item failure. These failures, like that of an electric motor, are represented by a single row.

Defect fact table rows for these examples, with foreign keys replaced by reference values, are shown in Table 7.2.

Table 7.1 Continued

Insp_key	Name	Inspection Method	Type	Destructive_flag
5	Finished panel color	Visual	Individual	N
6	Finished panel form	Visual	Individual	N
7	Primary motor power	Instrument	Individual	N
8	Wash drum finish	Visual	Individual	N
...	...	...	...	...

TIP

The alert reader might notice that the occurrence of two defects in the same component would invalidate this design. We are recording only the defect that causes the rejection. It is conceivable that a single lid may have both a form and color defect. In this design, the company must choose a primary defect, perhaps the first discovered. If the company desires to record all defects, then the quantity-rejected measure should be moved to the comp_receipt_facts table. This fact would then represent the number of components rejected from a lot/serial regardless of the reason. The defect_facts table would then identify the quantity of defects found in each lot by type. If this choice is made, remember that the number of defects in a lot does not necessarily equate to the number of rejected components.

Remember, our fact table also contains a foreign key to the supplier dimension. With this design, the ability to monitor supplier and component quality, based on back door tests, is very flexible. We can also easily drill across to the component receipts fact table to calculate the final disposition of a lot. The final design schema is presented in Figure 7.1, and includes the receipts schema.

Using this schema, we can track a variety of information on the quality of components. Using the receipts schema, we can also calculate the disposition of individual lots. An example of the type of report we can generate using this design is shown in Report 7.1.

Table 7.2 Inspection Results

Component	Inspection	Supplier	Lot_or_ser_num	Qty_failed
2mm plastic wiring harness	Wiring harness finish	Acme Harnesses	23-0970A	500
Zinc 7mm assembly screw	Assembly screw tensile	Tunston Corp.	108-988	1000
45WSH9910 lid panel	Finished panel color	Enamel Werks	200199A	15
45WSH99 10 lid panel	Finished panel fit	Enamel Werks	200199A	5
45WSH9910 17hp motor	Primary motor power	Enginecorp USA	120-3400-A261	1
…	…	…	…	…

Figure 7.1 Back-door quality at the factory.

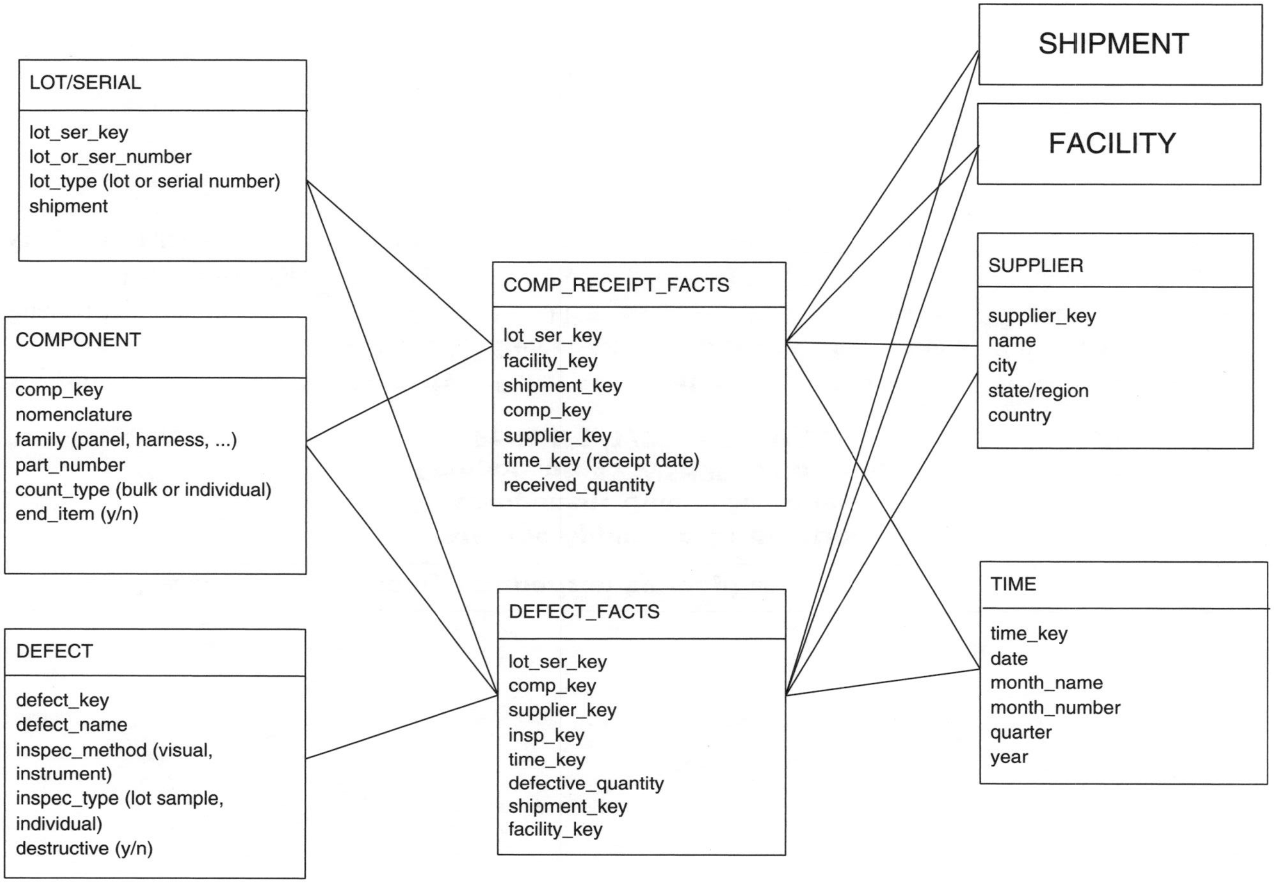

Report 7.1 A component quality comparison by supplier.

Atlantic Appliance Corporation
Component Quality Summary
Component: 45 WSH9910 lid panel
Period: 1/1/97 to 3/30/97

Supplier	Quantity Received	Form Rejections	Fit Rejections	Color Rejections	Total Rejected	% Rejected
Enamel Werks	7,895	11	10	261	282	3.6%
Angeles Metal Fabricators	12,904	28	317	41	386	3.0%
MetalFab Unlimited	3,012	2	19	11	32	1.1%

This report allows the manufacturer to identify suppliers of common components that have provided superior quality lots. In this case, comparing three suppliers of exterior panels shows that one supplier is clearly having difficulty with color conformity, while another is struggling with fit. The third supplier has no significant problems, but is also the lowest-volume supplier. The company must now consider shifting orders to the third supplier, or assisting the other two suppliers in solving their specific problems. Without proactive tracking of component problems, however, such decisions might not be made with the best evidence.

Quality in Production

Now that the appliance manufacturer has a good handle on component quality, we can move to the production line and track production process quality. Process quality is typically monitored by a combination of inline inspection of subassemblies and inspection of end items. For an appliance, inspections would occur at various points in the assembly process, with a final inspection prior to packaging for shipment. Also, a line worker may notice a quality problem and stop the line at an unscheduled point. In Chapter 5, "Production," we accounted for such stoppages in the production activity subject area design. For quality management, the company must track what quality problems are discovered, when in the production process they are discovered, and what are the likely causes. All of our quality management actions should be oriented towards preventing problems as early as possible in the process. That was the reason for our backdoor component quality check.

To understand the requirements for the appliance manufacturer, we can look at the history of a single component through each step of the production process. Remember the enamel-coated metal lid panels from the previous section. These enamel lids, and other enamel-coated parts, are susceptible to damage after the back-door inspection because they are added to the appliances near the end of the production process. Only dials, switch panels, and other finishing touches are performed after the exterior panels are affixed. A panel that passes the receipt inspection can still be damaged before or during assembly. If a damaged panel is not discovered prior to packaging, it probably will not be discovered until a retailer delivers it to a customer's residence. The company will bear a repair cost and the customer will be inconvenienced.

The factory life of a panel is divided into a series of steps, beginning with receipt and inspection. Having cleared this hurdle in the last section, the panel moves to the production line. A quick preinstallation visual inspection will discover any defects caused during movement. A post-installation visual inspection indicates whether the installation process itself caused any damage. A prepackaging visual inspection is the last line of defense. These inspections are logical and not overly taxing on the assembly line personnel. Using this example, we can begin to envision a design for a data warehouse to manage production quality. As in the component quality design, we will encounter many different types of inspections. The data we gather may come from one or more inline production quality systems, trouble-ticket systems, or even standalone defect-tracking databases on a PC. Our job is to integrate the information to give a unified view of production quality.

To do so we will use the following dimensions:

Product. The product dimension from the original fulfillment schema in Chapter 4. Identifies what product is being produced on the production line.

Component. The component dimension is used to identify where the defect is manifested. A component, in this case, comes from the bill-of-materials. Components may be parts, subassemblies, or the end item itself. If the defect affects more than one component, the next higher-level assembly or subassembly is associated with the defect.

Production run. Similar to the production run dimensions introduced in Chapter 5, it identifies the production run and production line where defects occur.

Facility. The facility where the production run is executed. With this dimension, we can look at individual factory quality problems, and compare production operations among facilities.

Time. The time dimension, with a daily grain. The grain of the time dimension could be finer, at the shift or hourly level, if desired. Other companies may find operational systems adequate to manage day-to-day activities, and only track defects on a weekly or monthly basis.

Production step, production step 1. There are two dimensions built from production steps. The first production step dimension identifies at what step the defect was discovered. The second production step dimension is used to identify where the defect was caused, if known by the worker entering the data. For example, if a worker introduces a defect into an exterior panel during the attachment process, the worker should associate the defect with that step. In that case, the production step where the defect is found and where caused are the same. If, on the other hand, the defect goes unnoticed until a final assembly inspection, the inspection step would be used for the where-found value. Also, it is entirely possible that the where-caused step may not be discovered. A broad "production" value is used to cover unknown causes.

Defect. The defect dimension is simply a list of defects found in a component during production. In our design, we will track only a few core attributes, including the type of defect (form, fit, function, visual appearance), a description, and the source (either a damaged component that slipped through production or a production problem). This dimension might evolve based on experience, with similar defects grouped into families. There is also a disposition attribute that determines whether the component was repaired or replaced.

The defect fact table includes the keys from all the dimension tables, providing a broad analytical basis. The only fact is the quantity of defects found. This quantity is additive across components, production runs, products, facilities, time, defects, and production steps. Using this fact, we can internally manage the production process and continually look for production-induced nonconformance. Our final design is depicted in Figure 7.2.

We can use our new design schema to monitor problems across all facilities, production lines, products, and production steps. If, for example, we install new production equipment in a production line at a single facility to automate panel attachment on the assumption that defects would decrease, we might produce the report shown in Report 7.2.

The report indicates the number of defects discovered in the parent process "panel attachment" at three production lines, one in Muncie and two in Columbus. The production line in Muncie has the new production equipment and appears to have fewer defects per 100 units produced. The units produced are found in an adjacent production schema with conformed product, time, and production line dimensions. The initial review of production since the installation of new equipment in Muncie indicates a decrease in defects discovered during the panel attachment process.

Post-Production Quality

Measuring post-production quality requires that we track both the incidence of a breakdown and the cost of repairs. We should also try to carry forward our attempts to identify the type of defect and the defective component. Our design should track repair incidents by product, month, defect, component, and facility. By including these dimensions, we can trace any defects found after a sale back to the time and place of production. This information should be available, because each appliance will have a serial number that is recorded by an affiliated repair contractor on a service call. We will include the channel dimension from Chapter 4's fulfillment schema, as well as a dimension to identify the service contractor.

Figure 7.2 Production quality schema.

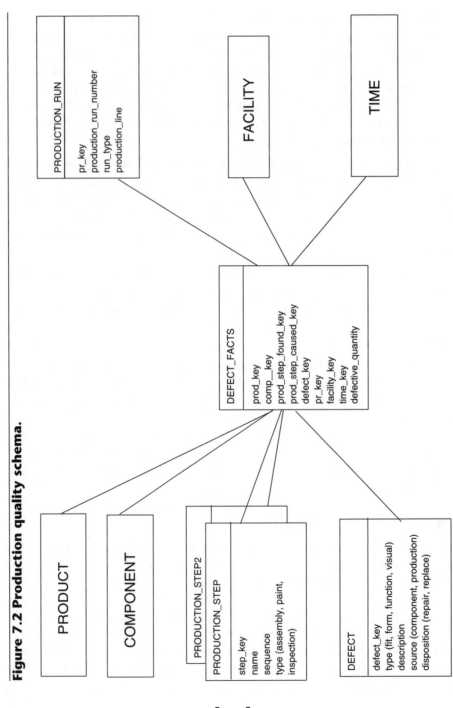

Report 7.2 Comparative defect report—exterior panels.

Atlantic Appliance Corporation
Panel Attachment Defect Analysis
Production Dates: June 1 through July 31, 1997

Production Facility	Production Line	Runs Completed	Units Produced	Defects	Defects/100
Muncie	Automax	47	5,281	312	5.9
Columbus	Blue Line	61	9,420	1,178	12.5
Columbus	Green Line	52	8,112	1,016	12.5

This design gives us a substantial amount of information, but we are missing an important element: the customer. Tracking repair incidents by customer will increase the number of rows in our fact table, with a row for each incident. Does it offer any advantages? First, it will allow us to identify the incidence of repeat breakdowns of equipment owned by any customer. Since washers and dryers are often purchased together, it is likely that some customers have more than one product. A customer experiencing repairs for more than one product is inconvenienced as much as one with a single, chronically broken appliance. In order to retain these customers in the future, the company may want to offer special discounts, rebates, warranty extensions, or even replacements. An additional advantage is the ability to relate sales data to product quality. The assumption behind the high-quality market position is that brand loyalty will increase. The company expects that a customer purchasing one product, perhaps a new washer, will be impressed with the quality and service accompanying it, and be more likely to buy another product. By tracking repair incidents against customers, the manufacturer can examine differences in repeat-buying behavior between customers with repair incidents and those with trouble-free purchases. We include the purchase month, service date, and service age to analyze repair incidents over time. The cost of the repair incident can also be recorded, including parts, labor, and service call charges. A flag in the fact table differentiates between in-warranty and out-of-warranty repair incidents. The final schema is shown in Figure 7.3.

This design allows us to track both cost and repair incidents in many ways, not the least of which is tracking the impact of worn parts. A component that is failing consistently before the end of its projected service life is a serious problem for the manufacturer—each incident creates a repair incident and associated costs. A component used in more than one model or product is even more costly. To monitor such parts, the company might create a report to track repair incidents for high-risk parts used in several models. A portion of such a report is shown in Report 7.3.

Another report can be generated to determine the number of customers with more than one repair incident since purchase. Using this information, the company can project the cost of offering product rebates or other incentives to those most inconvenienced. The analysis shown in Report 7.4 projects the cost of two different rebate programs. Despite similar costs, the second plan touches more customers; still, customers with four or more repair incidents may not be salvageable.

Before we leave the manufacturing example, remember that we have taken great pains to conform the product and component dimensions across all of our quality-monitoring design extensions. The value of such a system is that we can examine the quality history of an individual product or component, including backdoor quality, production quality, and service-life quality. For a specific

Figure 7.3 Repair incident schema.

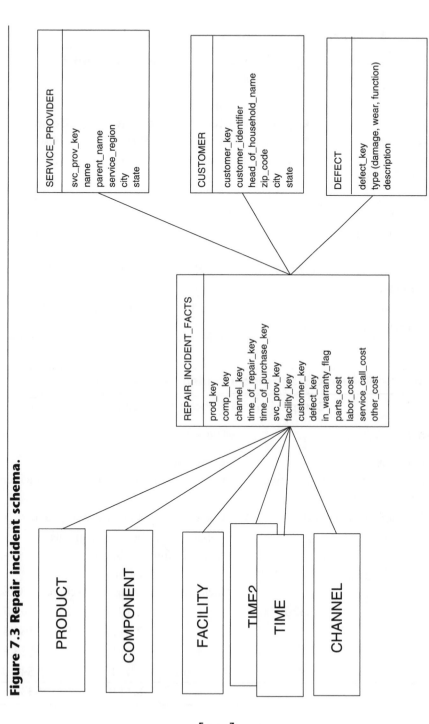

Report 7.3 High-risk component repair summary.

Top Five High-Risk Component Incident Report
June 1997

Component	Qty in Service	Current Month Incidents	Incidents YTD	Lifetime Incidents
High-speed pump/2.8 GPM	76,193	219	884	1,784
Standard spindle balance	52,311	—	2	28
Power conversion/ surge manager	48,970	5	17	31
18cm engine mount brace	28,477	28	112	418
Control timer— Nikkonica	17,639	113	612	612

Report 7.4 Rebate costs for inconvenienced customers.

Comparison of Rebate Plan Costs

Plan 1

Conditions:

Customer must have at least two in-warranty repair incidents

No products owned constraint

Rebate amount	$50
Qualified customers	6,412
Cost	$320,600

Plan 2

Conditions:

Customer has at least one repair incident

Customer owns at least two products

Rebate is $25 per repair incident to a maximum of $100

Incidents	Qualified Customers	Rebate	Cost
1	4,109	25	$102,725
2	3,211	50	$160,550
3	311	75	$23,325
4 or more	480	100	$48,000
	8,111		$334,600

product and component, we can examine the incidence of defects at each stage of the value chain across all plants. Report 7.5 compares three production facilities and the use of a component in a product.

The report analyzes the use of all lots of the component received at each plant in a six-month period. The Muncie plant found the fewest defects during the receipt inspections and production, but its products suffer the greatest incidence of repairs due to component failure after the sale. The likely causes are poor inspection and production quality control practices in Muncie.

Service Quality—Experience Is Everything

Service companies are different: It is simply more difficult to track the quality of a service than a concrete product. Hotels, restaurants, hospitals, insurance companies, and banks all compete on service quality, but measuring the elements of quality for each industry is difficult. The primary problem is that the experience of the customer is difficult to measure. Frequently, service customers simply leave dissatisfied, never to return again. Others patronize a company's outlets less frequently. And the most vocal tell everyone they know about a bad service experience.

The proactive service company recognizes that many customers are reticent about bad service. They encourage customers to complain about bad service through gimmicks, marketing, signs in the bathroom, and guarantees. There are signs in almost every major hotel bathroom or desk advertising the chain's "Make It Right" program. Encouraged to complain, some customers call. Still others, spurned in the past by such gimmicks, ignore the signs and leave dissatisfied. A quality service brand takes a long time to establish and requires constant vigilance.

Report 7.5 Problems in Muncie.

Component Quality Management Report

Component: High Speed Pump/ 2.2 GPM
Product: Wash Master 2100 XL4

	Columbus	East Port	Muncie
Total Received	2,397	1,854	2,108
Receipt Defects	112	119	31
Production Defects	89	61	18
In-warranty Defects	6	7	52

To back up such programs, a company must collect data about complaints and problems, supplement the data with customer surveys, and analyze repeat business. To illustrate, we will use the example of a large hotel chain that has an established quality reputation. The company has never measured quality other than through occasional customer surveys. Recently, the chain acquired the assets of a failing competitor, including several properties with less than stellar reputations for quality. The risk associated with the acquisition is the chain's reputation. Since many customers are frequent business travelers, they will inevitably stay at one of the acquired properties. If the customer suffers a distinctly inferior experience, that individual's loyalty may diminish. The company must quickly retrain staff at the acquired properties and instill service quality ideals.

Management also sees the acquisition as an opportunity to improve service quality measurement in all properties, not just the recently acquired ones. Following the steps used in the manufacturing example, we first identify the value proposition. The chain provides premier lodging for business travelers, with upscale rooms, business centers, and restaurants. Each unit of the chain has superior conference and meeting facilities. The company also offers a frequent-guest program that is heavily patronized. The frequent-guest program allows the company to track customer behavior more closely in exchange for points that can be used for free stays in the future.

The next step is identifying indicators of nonconformance. One positive indicator is the number of repeat visits by guests, probably tracked in the sales and marketing subject areas. With the acquisition, the company will need to be especially watchful of loyal guests who seem to vanish after a stay at an acquired property. A more specific indicator of service quality is the number of complaints and refunds given for various hotel services. While refunds are readily collected from transaction system data, general complaints are not as easily tracked. Such complaints, like a dirty room, broken TV, or cold room-service food, may be happily rectified with no record of the complaint taken. Our subject company decides to install a problem reporting system to track complaints that are resolved absent a financial transaction. All point-of-service employees are trained and encouraged to record all complaints. The system is simplified to encourage use, and organized around services offered. The data from this system is merged with refund data from the sales system into a service quality data warehouse.

With complaints proactively managed, the company decides to go after the most elusive indicator of good or bad service: The opinions of a statistically valid set of guests. Satisfied and dissatisfied guests check out daily without registering an opinion. To track these opinions, the company begins a more active customer survey program. This program augments the usual survey cards found in rooms or given at checkout with follow-up phone interviews designed to measure the experience of customers at all properties. The questions from both the survey cards and phone interviews are designed to validate the company's value proposition and ferret out problems at specific properties or in specific service areas.

Service Problems

The final task in designing the data warehouse is to include dimensions that direct us to the causes of nonconformance. For the appliance manufacturer, this included tracking information about components and the production process. We added dimensions that would narrow our search for a cause, including where a product was produced, what supplier provided each component, and when a product was produced. In the service industry, we can identify similar information. We begin by defining our service products specifically, much like the product dimension for the appliance manufacturer. General service categories include lodging, food and beverage, conference and meeting, and general services. Each of these categories can be further broken down into groups. We divide lodging by type of room. Food and beverage is divided similarly into bar, restaurant, or room service. Conference and meeting is divided into business or social events. General services, like the gift shop, are simply identified by name. The resulting service category and service product lists for the chain might look something like Table 7.3.

The variety of service might vary by each property, but these categories represent the company's general concept of operations. Management is organized along similar lines, and that is where leverage resides in managing service quality. This service listing becomes our product dimension for the hotel chain quality data warehouse. Notice that we have included nonrevenue services like concierge, bell desk, and reception. We want to record complaints and opinions about all services that make up the value proposition.

The breakdown of services gives us a way to think about products and consistently group complaints, refunds, and opinions. A dimension to track where service is delivered is the next logical step. Because some properties have more than one restaurant, gift shop, and bar, we will define a point-of-service dimension. This dimension identifies the point-of-service name, the property where the point-of-service is located, and other details about the point-of-service and property. A sample of rows is shown in Table 7.4.

If we can associate complaints and opinions with these two dimensions, the company can narrow down problems and take corrective action. To track the newly acquired properties, we can add a date-acquired column to the point-of-service dimension, or add a flag to designate the group. Conforming these dimensions among different indicators will allow better correlation of service quality data among the various properties. Also, the property attribute would likely

Table 7.3 Service Categories and Service Products

Service Category	Service Product
Lodging	Executive suite
Lodging	Standard room—king
Lodging	Standard room—two doubles
Lodging	Nonstandard room
Lodging	Business suite
Food & beverage	Restaurant—dinner
Food & beverage	Restaurant—lunch
Food & beverage	Restaurant—breakfast
Food & beverage	Bar—beverages
Food & beverage	Bar—food
Food & beverage	Room service—dinner
Food & beverage	Room service—lunch
Food & beverage	Room service—breakfast
Food & beverage	Catering—dinner
Food & beverage	Catering—lunch
Food & beverage	Catering—breakfast
General services	Gift shop
General services	Bell desk
General services	Parking—valet
General services	Parking—standard
General services	Concierge
General services	Recreation and travel
General services	Registration

Table 7.4 Point-of-Service Rows

Pos_key	Name	Type	Property	City	Region	Date_open
1	Ambassador	Hotel	Ambassador	Los Angeles	CA	1988
2	City of Angels	Restaurant	Ambassador	Los Angeles	CA	1994
3	Dragnet	Bar	Ambassador	Los Angeles	CA	1994
4	Aspen Lodge	Hotel	Aspen Lodge	Aspen	CO	1992
5	Loft Haus	Restaurant	Aspen Lodge	Aspen	CO	1997
⋮	⋮	⋮	⋮	⋮	⋮	⋮

require a separate dimension if the design was targeted for integration with the company's enterprise data warehouse. For simplicity, we will leave property as an attribute in this example.

The Facts of Service Quality

With our two most important dimensions in place, we can focus on capturing the indicators of nonconformance already identified. Recall that some complaints resulted in refunds, extracted from the sales system transactions, while others did not result in a refund. A refund is an artifact of the disposition of a complaint given to repair a customer relationship. Our design can track complaints and refunds together. We will add a disposition dimension and a complaint dimension. The design of these dimensions will be simplified to cover the many situations that may be recorded by the complaint system installed by the company.

The disposition dimension is concerned with three aspects of each complaint. A complaint is a problem, and the dimension should first track whether the problem was solved. If a room was dirty and the housekeeping staff cleaned it to the guest's satisfaction, the problem was corrected. On the other hand, if the customer was given a room with a broken television and the television could not be repaired or another room found, the problem was not solved. A second aspect of the problem is the customer's final attitude about the complaint. The correction of a problem does not always satisfy the customer, especially if the problem was disruptive. Repairing the broken television after the customer's favorite program was over may correct the problem, but leave the customer unsatisfied. Since the goal is to satisfy every customer, the company allows employees to offer compensation in various forms to customers. The guest with a broken television may get a free breakfast, while one with a poor view might be offered a refund. The list of incentives may change over time, but tracking the relationship between compensation and customer satisfaction and eventual return visits is important.

Our complaint dimension details the many categories of complaints. Complaints are identifiable to a service, with rooms having complaints like size, view, temperature (too hot), television reception, and bathroom cleanliness. An attempt is made at the outset to classify all potential complaints, but the list evolves. The design simply groups each individual guest complaint into a more general complaint type. A complaint category is also added to track complaints against elements of the value proposition. Complaint categories include cleanliness, comfort, convenience, condition or quality, and price. Complaints about room size are classified as comfort complaints, while problems with televisions or telephones are classified as convenience complaints. Our final dimension is customer type. Rather than track every customer, we track easily identified customer segments. The dimension is simply a list of all possible combinations of three or four key attributes. This allows the company to examine service trends and opinions among business and leisure travelers, occasional or frequent guests, or any other easily identifiable customer characteristic. Alternatively, the company could collect additional data about complaining customers, but many customers would find attempts intrusive and frustrating when trying to resolve a service problem.

Our fact table tracks the number of complaints for a given combination of complaint, disposition, day, point-of-service, customer type, and service. Sample rows, with reference values replacing foreign keys, are shown in Table 7.5.

The grain of daily is chosen to identify any trends in complaints around specific dates, weekends, or times of the year. We could also use the dates to correlate complaints with staffing levels and occupancy levels. If complaints rise during peak occupancy, the company may choose to increase staffing to improve service levels. The analysis of the data is important, but even more important is the dissemination of the data to the work force that can act upon it. Pricing complaints can be passed to pricing analysts, cleanliness problems passed to property housekeeping managers, and service problems to the respective restaurant managers. The company can also easily watch complaint levels at the newly acquired properties. Even the effectiveness of guest compensation can be measured by correlating this data with repeat visit and defection data from the guest sales subject area. The design of the complaint subject area is shown in Figure 7.4.

The company also introduced a new surveying campaign coincident with increased complaint tracking. The design of a survey schema is best done in the context of the complaint design. The benefits of correlating the results of both types of customer feedback are clear. Survey questions could eventually be tailored to back up complaint trends or look for problems in areas where complaints are rarely reported. A sample of survey questions for the Ambassador Hotel in Los Angeles is shown in Figure 7.5. These questions are used in telephone interviews. These survey questions are derived directly from the general list of complaints found in the complaint dimension. Adding the point-of-service and service dimensions tightens the connection between customer opinions and complaints and the company's concept of operations. This tight correlation is valuable in that it gives structure to the sometimes random collection of customer feedback data.

There is a small problem in tracking the exact date that a customer experienced the opinions expressed in a survey. Respondents may or may not provide the exact dates of the stay, or may have stayed more than one day, but not remember when they experienced a problem. If the survey list is generated from the com-

Table 7.5 Complaint Fact Table

Point_of_svc	Service	Date	Complaint	Disposition	Quantity
Ambassador	Standard room—king	3/14/97	Bed condition	Corrected	1
City of Angels	Restaurant—lunch	3/14/97	Slow service	Not corrected	5
City of Angels	Restaurant—lunch	3/14/97	Poor service	Corrected	2
Ambassador	Parking—valet	3/14/97	Price	Not corrected	1
Aspen Lodge	Parking—valet	3/14/97	Price	Not corrected	1
...				...	

Figure 7.4 The complaint design.

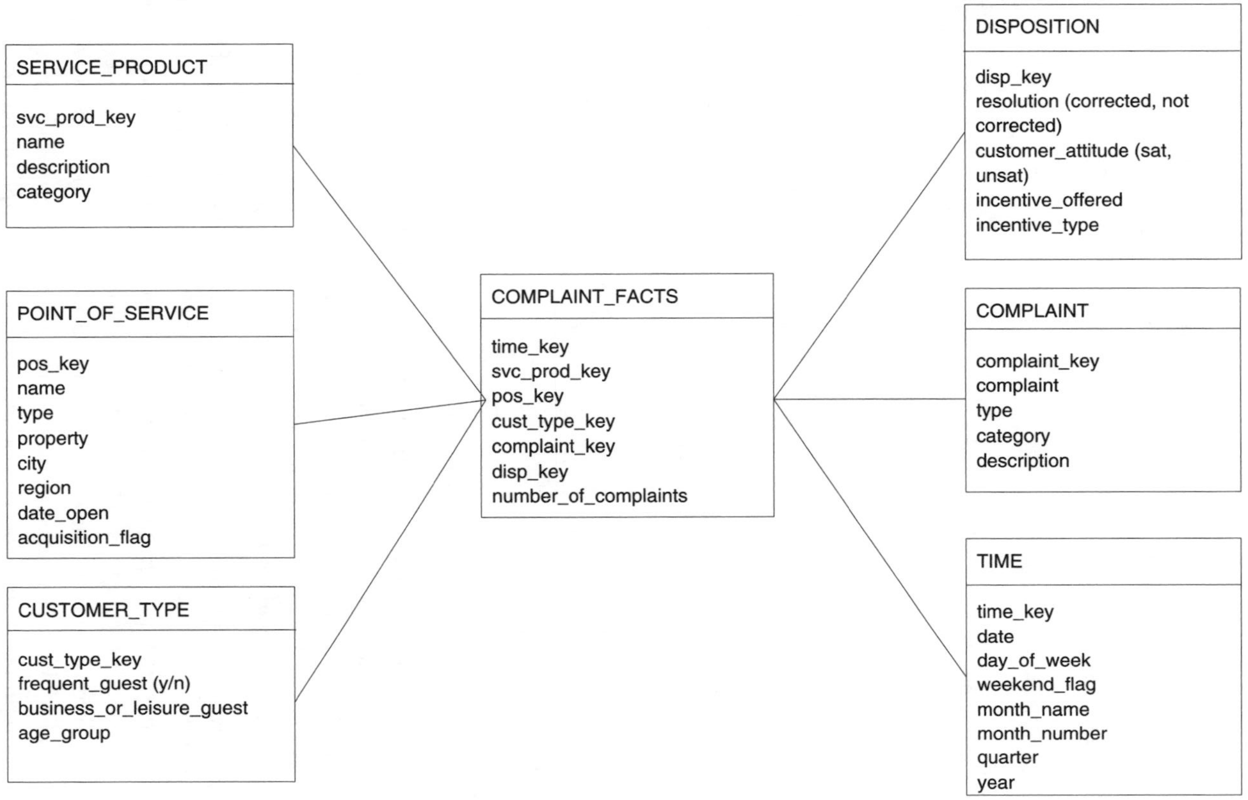

DISPOSITION

disp_key
resolution (corrected, not corrected)
customer_attitude (sat, unsat)
incentive_offered
incentive_type

COMPLAINT

complaint_key
complaint
type
category
description

TIME

time_key
date
day_of_week
weekend_flag
month_name
month_number
quarter
year

COMPLAINT_FACTS

time_key
svc_prod_key
pos_key
cust_type_key
complaint_key
disp_key
number_of_complaints

SERVICE_PRODUCT

svc_prod_key
name
description
category

POINT_OF_SERVICE

pos_key
name
type
property
city
region
date_open
acquisition_flag

CUSTOMER_TYPE

cust_type_key
frequent_guest (y/n)
business_or_leisure_guest
age_group

Figure 7.5 Survey questions.

Category—Cleanliness	Excellent	Good	Fair	Poor	N/A
17. Cleanlineness of room	◯	◯	◯	◯	◯
18. Cleanliness of hotel lobby	◯	◯	◯	◯	◯
19. Cleanliness of restaurant	◯	◯	◯	◯	◯
20. Cleanliness of bathroom	◯	◯	◯	◯	◯
Category—Price					
21. Price of room	◯	◯	◯	◯	◯
22. Price of food/City of Angels	◯	◯	◯	◯	◯
23. Price of food/Dragnet	◯	◯	◯	◯	◯
24. Price of items in gift shop	◯	◯	◯	◯	◯

pany's customer sales database, this information could be provided by the caller. The customer might then be able to narrow down any specific problems to a day. If not, the leakage of opinions into adjacent days, weeks, or months may be considered acceptable. We also include a second time dimension to record the date the survey was conducted, or for a mail or in-hotel survey the date it was received.

Survey questions are structured around the existing dimensions of the business and the value proposition. Each category represents a component of the value proposition, allowing the company to understand where it is out of step with customer expectations. The questions are structured around a service product and point-of-service. The company can also use this opportunity to record any additional problems surveyed customers might have experienced but not reported. These unreported complaints can be included in the complaint fact table. Separating these latent complaints from those already reported would allow the company to measure the effectiveness of the complaint-gathering effort.

The survey fact table records the number of responses in each opinion category, from excellent to N/A. The design of the survey schema is shown in Figure 7.6.

Our integrated design, sharing important dimensions among our quality indicators, will pay off in reporting. As in our manufacturing example, the combined quality data warehouse integrates data from various sources to create a flexible analytical solution.

Reports for Hotel Service Quality

The motive behind the construction of the hotel chain's quality data warehouse was the need to monitor the quality of service at recently acquired properties. The company's management expects complaints to continually decrease at these properties as existing staff is trained and new management is installed. The graph in Report 7.6 plots the daily complaints for two acquired properties for a 60-day period. The plot begins 10 days after the company assumed management of the hotel, and after the installation of the complaint tracking software.

Notice that complaints picked up steadily after the new company assumed control. The initial lag in complaints is no doubt due to the reluctance of both guests and employees to register complaints. After the initial lag, the number increases slowly. While the Minneapolis property appears to have turned the corner, the Dallas team may need more encouragement. The manager of the property could next add the type of complaint to his query to determine what areas demand attention. Report 7.7 is a Pareto chart showing the frequency of complaint type in the category "room" for the Dallas property for the same 60-day period. Most complaints originate over the issue of noise and temperature problems. These problems may be costly to repair, since the noise might be caused by thinly constructed walls, and cooling problems by an inadequate HVAC system.

Our next report presents survey data for restaurants at acquired properties. The report includes a column containing the average score in each category for a chain's original restaurants. Report 7.8 compares the acquired restaurants with the average for the 60-day period since the chain assumed control. Responses are scored 1 through 4, with excellent being 1 and poor being 4. The lower the score, the better the rating.

Our final report compares occupancy rates for the chain to complaint levels. By relating complaints to specific properties and times, the company can determine not only the relationship between occupancy rates and complaints, but also the relationship of specific types of complaints to occupancy rates. The chart in Report 7.9 compares occupancy rates with the occurrence of price complaints.

Figure 7.6 The survey schema.

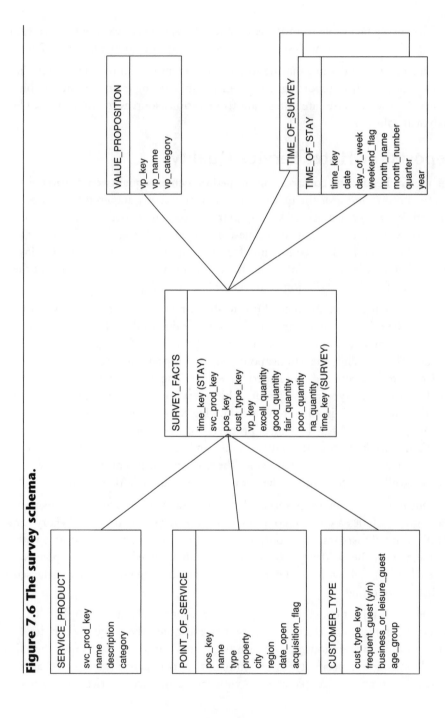

SERVICE_PRODUCT

svc_prod_key
name
description
category

POINT_OF_SERVICE

pos_key
name
type
property
city
region
date_open
acquisition_flag

CUSTOMER_TYPE

cust_type_key
frequent_guest (y/n)
business_or_leisure_guest
age_group

SURVEY_FACTS

time_key (STAY)
svc_prod_key
pos_key
cust_type_key
vp_key
excell_quantity
good_quantity
fair_quantity
poor_quantity
na_quantity
time_key (SURVEY)

VALUE_PROPOSITION

vp_key
vp_name
vp_category

TIME_OF_SURVEY

TIME_OF_STAY

time_key
date
day_of_week
weekend_flag
month_name
month_number
quarter
year

Report 7.6 Complaint trends after acquisition.

Complaint Trends

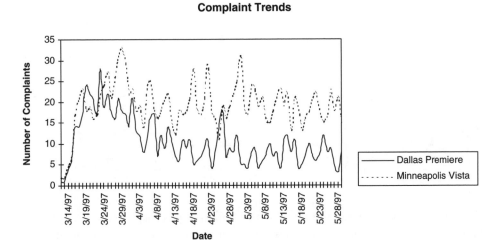

Note that when occupancy is high, indicating heavy demand in the industry, price complaints drop off. The number of possible reports is, of course, infinite.

Report 7.7 Problems in Dallas.

Room Complaints - Dallas

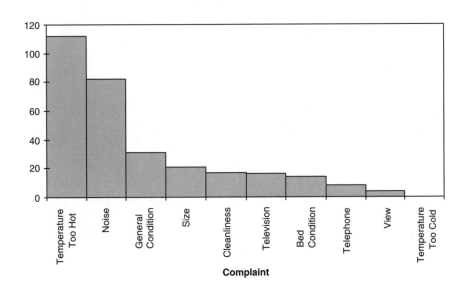

Report 7.8 Restaurant survey results.

	Chain Average	Long River	Tempest	Riverside Café	Richard's Chophouse	Silverado	Beach Villa Café	Med Café
Cleanliness	1.4	2.6	3.1	2.2	1.8	2.1	3.2	3.1
Portion Size	1.3	1.8	2.1	1.7	1.9	2.2	3.1	2.4
Food Taste	1.7	2.2	3.6	2.1	1.5	2.7	3.4	2.6
Food Temperature	1.4	1.8	2.1	2.3	1.6	2.5	2.7	2.4
Service Politeness	1.6	1.9	3.5	2.1	1.9	2.5	2.7	3.3
Service Promptness	1.5	2.4	3.1	2.4	1.8	1.9	2.8	3.1
Food Price	2.5	2.1	2.1	1.9	2.2	2.8	3.2	2.6

The company has a foundation on which to build a repository of service quality data to validate assumptions, improve operations, and successfully manage its new assets.

Summing Up Quality

Service and product quality are *de facto* components of the global competitive environment. Manufacturers are usually adept at monitoring quality throughout

Report 7.9 Occupancy rates and complaints.

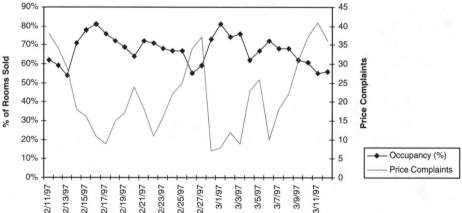

Occupancy Rates and Price Complaints

the production process. In this chapter, we have attempted to extend the view of quality beyond the factory and into the consumer market. With this model, a manufacturer can view the quality characteristics for a product throughout its service life. Service companies are less experienced at defining and measuring quality in their operations. Too often, service quality is measured sporadically, or not at all. Service companies also face the problem of customers who are reluctant to complain about problems.

Including quality-related information in the corporate data warehouse does not require adding many new dimensions and fact tables. Information on quality usually is a natural extension of the design, requiring a few dimensional attributes, an additional fact or two, and perhaps one or two fact tables. In the case of the appliance manufacturer, including quality resulted in only minor changes to the existing production data warehouse design.

Remember also the three steps to identifying quality requirements:

1. Define the value proposition of the product.

2. Identify measures of quality and indicators of nonconformance.

3. Track down as many potential causes of quality problems as possible.

Following these steps should allow the data warehouse team to identify the unique aspects of quality for a specific company or product. Defining the value proposition provides a better understanding of how the company creates expectations in the marketplace for the product. It can be used to derive the measures of quality and indicators of nonconformance. Indicators of nonconformance lead to an analysis of potential causes of quality problems, and identifying causes of quality problems enables the company to take corrective action.

BUDGETS AND SPENDING

The computer systems used by accountants and financial planners are among the most complex in any business. Tucked away in these financials systems are thousands or even millions of transactions, broken down into subcomponents and spread across hundreds of tables. Business managers hunger to study these transactions at a high level of summarization, but super-normalized models make aggregate reporting and analysis nearly impossible. Nowhere is there a subject area that better demonstrates the strengths of the star schema.

The financial workings of a business can be a perplexing topic, and financials systems are equally enigmatic. We've chosen to begin our study of the financial side of the business by looking at a focused piece of the financials landscape: budgeting and spending. An excellent data mart with which to inaugurate the financials data warehouse, this subject area can have immediate benefit while affording the data loaders an opportunity to dip their toes into the uncharted waters of the financials system. In Chapter 9, "Financial Reporting," we'll be asking them to dive in.

Budgeting Demystified

Large and small organizations alike plan their annual spending by creating a budget. The budgeting process begins in advance of the fiscal year. In large companies, budget development can involve many cycles of proposals, reviews, and revisions before approval. The budget may pass through several states before it is considered approved. In smaller companies, the budget may be pieced together fairly rapidly. By the time the fiscal year begins, a final budget is in place. Budget details vary by industry and company, but there is striking degree of similarity in their overall organization.

What's in a Budget

Budgets represent plans for earning and spending money. These components are often considered separate budgets, although they have profound influence on one another. Many organizations break them down even further, producing a series of budgets that roll up into a financial plan. In this chapter, we will focus primarily on the spending side; the same techniques we use can be applied to the revenue side of the budget as well.

The budget we'll look at is a plan for spending money. The particulars of the budget are laid out in a series of *budget lines*. Each budget line represents authorization for a particular *part of the company* to spend an *amount of money* for a particular *purpose* during a particular *time frame*. For example, a budget line might state that the marketing department can spend $200,000 on direct mail campaigns during fiscal year 1999. There is usually a fifth component of the budget line, which we will discuss later.

The specificity of budget lines varies by business. For example, the part of the company authorized to do the spending may be identified at a high level, as in Sales, or Manufacturing. Other businesses may break down spending authority much further, as in Inside Sales, Northern Sales, Product Assembly, and Quality Assurance. One or more levels of summarization are usually found in the organizational component of the budget, mirroring the levels of organizational structure within the business.

Similarly, companies differ in the level of detail at which they identify the purpose of spending. Some companies budget for things like Salaries or Office Supplies. Others budget at a more detailed level for things like Executive Pay, Management Pay, Paper Supplies, and Writing Materials. Businesses that produce detailed budgets usually set up a structure of categories and subcategories, so that the budget can be viewed at various levels of summarization. For example, Executive Pay and Management Pay might be subcategories of the Employee Compensation category. It is not uncommon to find multiple levels of categorization within a budget.

The time frames specified in budgets also vary. Many businesses omit time frames from budgets altogether; these budgets represent annual spending plans. Other businesses break out spending plans by quarter or even month. Not surprisingly, budgets in the latter cases undergo a much larger number of revisions throughout the course of a year.

Along with the organization, purpose, and time frame of the budget line is a budget amount, representing the dollars to be spent. Together, these four components provide the information managers need to know in order to implement the spending plan outlined in the budget. There is one additional component of every budget line of special interest to the accountants: the *general ledger account* from which the budget line will be drawn.

Key Business Term

General ledger. A ledger in which the financial accounts of a business are formally summarized. Often referred to as *G/L*.

The heart of double-entry accounting, the general ledger remains balanced through offsetting transactions to debit and credit accounts. The list of accounts is often referred to as the *chart of accounts*.

Because it is of limited interest beyond the accounting department, the G/L account is often omitted from budget reports. Frequently, a budget line is drawn from more than one account, making the relationship a complicated one; however, this link is critical in placing expenditures into the overall financial picture.

Commitments

Once a budget is established, the business is ready to spend money. Along the way, people will ask how much has been spent and how much remains to be spent. The answers to these questions will vary depending on who is doing the asking. Consider the simple case of an office manager, who has ordered $200 worth of paper for the photocopier. Has this money been spent the moment he places the order, or is the $200 spent a month later when the accounting department sends a check to the office supply company? Both of these events have significance to different factions within the business. The office manager is more concerned with the initial order, while accountants are concerned with the order as well as the payment, and maybe even an event or two in between.

Separate terms are used to distinguish the two events. First, let's look at what happened when the office manager ordered the paper. After phoning in the order, he probably sent a purchase order to the office supply vendor. The purchase order represents the business's intention to pay the vendor, providing the proper paper is delivered under agreed-upon terms. Nothing has been delivered yet, and no money has changed hands. However, the event holds significance from the budgeting perspective because $200 of the office supplies budget has now been promised, or *committed*, to a vendor. The purchase order is usually referred to as a *commitment*.

Key Business Term

Commitment. A formal agreement between two parties to exchange goods, services, or money under specific terms.

An organization commits funds out of its budget when it issues purchase orders, signs work orders, or awards contracts. Commitments can be made to an organization outside the business, or to another organization within the business. Commitments are sometimes referred to as *obligations*, but not within the U.S. Government, where the term *obligation* has special meaning.

The office manager must consider the $200 commitment when determining how much he has left to spend in his budget. What "remains" in the budget is the difference between the total amount budgeted and the total amount committed. In the event that the order is canceled or the paper is returned, the office supply manager will cancel the purchase order. This action results in a negative commitment of $200, effectively placing $200 back in the uncommitted category.

When commitments are made, managers consider the money "spent," and they usually don't pay much attention to the financial details of a purchase after the order has been placed. The office supply manager who ordered the paper notes a $200 reduction in his remaining budget, and moves on to other work. For the accountants, the commitment is only the beginning. Eventually, they will have to pay the office supply vendor, assuming the correct paper is delivered under the terms of the purchase order. In order to track this outstanding commitment, a $200 *payable* is set up in the accounting system.

Payments

The copier paper is eventually delivered to the office. Soon thereafter, accounting receives an invoice from the vendor. After verifying that there was a purchase order and that the paper has been received, accounting cuts a check and sends it to the vendor. This event holds little significance to the office manager, who has already taken the $200 out of his budget. To accountants, it is a significant financial event; $200 has been paid to the vendor, depleting the amount of cash on hand and reducing outstanding payables. Accountants often call this transaction a *cash outlay* or *disbursement*, but we're going to use the more friendly term *payment*. We're going to model this activity, and we want it to be easily understood throughout the organization.

Key Business Term

Payment. A transaction in which funds are distributed from one party to another.

Payments may be made to external organizations, or to an organization within the business. Sometimes referred to as *cash outlay* or *disbursement*.

Payments typically happen in a number of ways. A check may be issued, as in the preceding example. It is also possible that payment may be made by credit card or wire transfer. Some organizations enter into barter transactions, where goods and services are exchanged for goods and services of equal value.

The Need for a Data Mart

While the budgeting and spending processes may sound simple, the financial systems that track them often exhibit mind-boggling complexity. There are numerous ways in which people and organizations enter into financial transactions, and numerous ways in which various parties must report on them. In mapping these activities to abstract accounting principles, the resultant systems contain hundreds or even thousands of tables. Financial systems often have multiple layers of nested menus, and a bewildering array of screens and reports. They can require intensive training, both for accountants and for managers with budget responsibilities.

Because of their complexity, financial systems are the most popular of packaged database applications. Package implementation is an appealing alternative to the prospect of building a financial system from the ground up. Of course, not all businesses operate in exactly the same way. The implementation of a financial package is usually accompanied by a long and expensive customization process. There are few consultants willing to dedicate their lives to these complex applications, so those who do command an impressive hourly rate. As a result, many business questions that can only be answered by intricate reports languish in the backlog of requested enhancements.

To a CFO, a data mart is an appealing way to stem the backlog. It represents an alternative to the endless stream of money spent on the development of custom report after custom report. A well-designed data mart can make a large number of reports in the backlog significantly easier and faster to produce. With a database designed for analysis, questions about budgets and spending can be answered quickly and precisely.

Budget Design

The primary business objectives to be addressed by our budget model are:

- Capture current budget and its history
- Capture commitments of budgeted dollars over time
- Capture payments made against budget commitments
- Facilitate comparison of budgets, commitments, and payments at any point in time, by budget line, account, or department

Based on our discussion of budget, it should be clear to the reader that we are actually modeling three processes: budgeting, commitments, and payments. One would suspect that each process has its own set of details, which may translate into fact tables of different grains. We'll take the processes one at a time, and identify the facts and dimensions involved in each. After we've looked at all three, we'll revisit the grain issue and reevaluate the need for separate fact tables.

The Budget Star

We've already learned that budgets are composed of budget lines, each of which has five components: an amount, an organization, a purpose, a time frame, and a relationship to the general ledger. We also know that the budget changes over time, and that we must capture the history. For our example, we will assume this information is required on a monthly basis. Based on this information, we've put together the star schema shown in Figure 8.1. There are some important nuances of this model, so don't skip over the discussion!

Grain We can't define the grain of our fact table at the budget line—we need to relate the general ledger to the budget, and a budget line may draw from more than one general ledger account. This requirement forces us to set our grain at a slightly deeper level. Each row of our fact table represents a budget line amount for a particular account. Where a budget line relates to more than one account, we will break it down as appropriate.

Recall our example budget line, which stated that marketing could spend $200,000 on direct mail activities during 1999. If one-fourth of this budget line is drawn from the 98-01-0027 account, and the rest from 98-01-9929, our fact table will represent it in two rows. Both will hold the same keys for budget period, department, and month. One row, with an amount of $50,000, will have a key to the 98-01-0027 account, while the second has a budget amount of $150,000 and a key to the 98-01-9929 account.

Figure 8.1 The budget star.

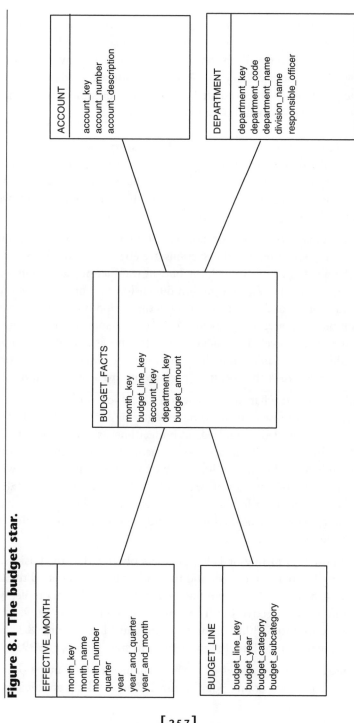

ACCOUNT

account_key
account_number
account_description

DEPARTMENT

department_key
department_code
department_name
division_name
responsible_officer

BUDGET_FACTS

month_key
budget_line_key
account_key
department_key
budget_amount

EFFECTIVE_MONTH

month_key
month_name
month_number
quarter
year
year_and_quarter
year_and_month

BUDGET_LINE

budget_line_key
budget_year
budget_category
budget_subcategory

The way in which a budget line relates to the chart of accounts will vary by system. The relationship may be resolved by an intersect table between accounts and budget lines expressing allocations in dollars, or there may be an indication of weightings. It will be necessary to sort this out prior to loading the budget star. The way the relationship is represented in the financials system will impact the way we load the data, but will not impact our design.

Measures Because we need to capture budget *history* and report on *monthly adjustments* to the budget, we've chosen to build a *transaction model* of the budget. Instead of recording actual budget levels at the end of each month, we will record the changes to the budget that happen each month. The sole measure in the fact table is budget_amount, which is fully additive.

There are actually two time components of interest in this transaction model: the period during which budget transactions are effective, and the spending period for the budget. In this model, the budget transactions are summarized at a monthly level; we use the effective_month dimension to represent when budget changes occur. The second time component is the period during which the budgeted amount is designated to be spent. Our model assumes that budgets are planned at the annual level. The budget_year attribute is placed in the budget_line dimension table. For organizations that plan their spending by quarter or month, we might choose to break the spending period out into a separate table.

Let's take a look at what our transaction model looks like, complete with two time components. Suppose that the initial budget for 1999 is established during November 1998. Amidst the hundreds of budget lines, there is one for $200,000 to be spent by the office management department on office supplies, shown in the first line of Table 8.1. This budget line receives a row in the fact table with a budget amount of $200,000 for budget year 1999, effective November 1998. Note that there is no requirement for the effective_year and budget_year to match; as we have seen, it is perfectly normal for the budget to be approved prior to the beginning of the fiscal year.

Now suppose that in July of 1999, planners observe that the business is using more office supplies than predicted, and the budget line is increased to $250,000. This increase is shown in the second line of Table 8.1. In the fact table, we record a $50,000 transaction effective July 1999, again for budget year 1999. In October, the budget is reduced to $230,000, shown in the third line in Table 8.1. We record a –$20,000 transaction for budget year 1999, effective October 1999.

The transaction model allows us to show changes to the budget over time and calculate the total budget at any point in time. When looking at adjustments to

Table 8.1 Budget Transactions

Account	Department	Budget Line	Budget Year	Effective Month	Budget Amount
98-12-1092	Office management	Office supplies	1999	November 1998	$200,000
98-12-1092	Office management	Office supplies	1999	July 1999	$50,000
98-12-1092	Office management	Office supplies	1999	October 1999	–$20,000

the budget over time, we can group the sum of budget_amount by month. Using our office supplies example, this approach allows us to show the history of the budget, showing the changes much as they are shown in Table 8.1. When looking at the total budget at a particular point in time, we simply aggregate all budget entries up to that month. To show the total budget for office supplies in October 1999, we simply sum the three budget transactions, and get $230,000.

Not all accounting systems record the budget history via transactions. Instead, some systems record a change in a budget line by writing an entirely new line flagged as *current* or marked with a revision number. The method by which the budget changes are recorded in the accounting system should not influence our ability to construct a transaction-oriented star. If the accounting system records budget line status levels, we can deduce monthly transactions as part of the load. We'll look at this process in more detail later when we discuss the *budget status model*.

Observe that we are modeling only approved budget lines. Our fact table will not capture budget proposals, nor will it track the approval process. This process could be easily modeled, but is not among the objectives of our current task: to track and compare approved budgets, spending, and payments.

Dimensions Let's take a closer look at the remaining dimensions in the budget star. We've already touched on the effective month dimension, which is used to record the time of a budget transaction. The account dimension captures the G/L account from which the budget line is drawn. Recall from our discussion of grain that we will need to split some budget lines when they are loaded into the fact table based on G/L information. The remaining dimensions are budget_line and department.

The budget_line dimension is where we store information about the purpose of the budgeted amount. As we have mentioned, there are often many levels of categorization. In this model, we capture two levels of categorization: category and subcategory. Each budget transaction in the fact table is recorded at the subcategory level and can be rolled up to the category level as needed.

As a general rule, multiple levels of categorization deserve the careful attention of the design team. Each fact must be recorded at the lowest level of detail. If the number of levels varies, it will be necessary to record Not Applicable in some cases. For example, if there are some spending categories with no subcategories, we record Not Applicable as the subcategory for pertinent transactions. As a consequence, a report showing budget amounts by subcategory may show a high Not Applicable subcategory, representing all categories that are not broken down.

For example, the Employee Compensation category might be broken down into subcategories for Salary and Benefits, while the Facilities Management and Promotions categories are not broken down. The subcategory fields for Facilities Management and Promotions will read "Not Applicable." A report that breaks budget amounts out by subcategory will show a Not Applicable subcategory that combines the budget from these two categories. This anomaly is generally acceptable, because it can be corrected through the inclusion of Category in the report. A popular alternative is to replicate, or "pad," the category data into the subcategory dimension when subcategory detail is not present. This prevents an unusually large Not Applicable figure in many reports.

The budget_line dimension table also contains budget_year. This attribute represents the spending time frame for which the budget_amount is planned. For organizations that break budgets down by month, we might move this attribute to a budget_period dimension. The decision would be based on the number of budget lines and expected query profiles.

The department dimension table captures the organization within the business responsible for the budget line. We've included two levels of departmental rollup: Departments roll up to divisions, and each division falls under the preview of an executive officer of the company. Building a detailed organizational structure into a model like this one can be a risky proposition, because organizations restructure. Renaming of departments may be handled by simply overwriting a row in the dimension, assuming the business is willing to look at past history under the new name. But if the department is moved into a different division, we will need to add a new row into the dimension table *and* add some transactions.

Suppose that in July 1999, the business decides that product management should be a function of the Sales and Marketing organization rather than

Manufacturing. The department is moved to the new area, but keeps its name and number. Although the department name and number have not changed, the identity of the department as defined in our dimension table *has* changed. Remember that this is a transaction model. If we simply insert a new row into our dimension table the next time the budget changes, our model would incorrectly imply that there were still budget dollars under the Manufacturing division.

To prevent this inaccurate representation of the state of affairs, we must generate a new pair of budget transactions in July. The first will be used to close out all uncommitted budget for Product Management under Manufacturing. The second applies the amount closed out to the new Sales and Marketing department. The last two lines in Table 8.2 show the transaction pair generated by moving the department. Note that the complexity does not end here. If an outstanding commitment is canceled by Product Management subsequent to July 1999, an additional deallocation/allocation pairing will be required so that the funds can be made available to the new version of the department. We'll look at commitments shortly.

Now that we've nailed down a budget model, let's look at how we will capture spending against budget amounts.

The Commitment Star

Capturing the history of the budget is only part of our objective; we also need to measure how money is committed over time. By comparing budgets with commitments, managers can track their spending levels over the course of the year. The question "How much do I have left to spend?" can only be answered when both budgets and commitments are available.

The commitment model is shown in Figure 8.2. Once again, we have built a transaction model with a single measure: commitment_amount. Each row in the

Table 8.2 Budget Transactions Generated by Corporate Restructuring

Division	Department	Effective Month	Budget Amount
Manufacturing	Product management	November, 1998	$20,000
Manufacturing	Product management	July, 1999	–$15,000
Sales and marketing	Product management	July, 1999	$15,000

TIP

Organizational changes may stress the data loading effort. To the extent that the budget star mirrors the way organizational changes are handled in the accounting system, loading the appropriate transactions should be fairly simple. The required transaction pairing will be present in the accounting system and easily loaded into the star. However, if the accounting system handles the reorganization differently, there may be no source transactions to force the reallocation of budget. The complexities required to maintain an accurate star may send developers screaming bloody murder. In such cases, it may be best to continue with the old structure, or simply overwrite the department record with the new division name. The team should address how organizational changes will be dealt with during the design process. Luckily, many of the changes that would be problematic for a star schema will also be problematic for financials systems. Most organizations, therefore, make changes only with the new fiscal year.

fact table represents dollars committed during the effective period, not the year-to-date total of commitments. We've included the budget line in the grain of the commitment star. Any commitment matched to more than one budget line will be broken into multiple rows, similar to the way in which the budget star broke out budget lines that drew from more than one account.

Four Familiar Dimensions All four of the dimensions from the budget star are present in the commitment star. The effective_month dimension represents the period during which the commitment is made, and the department dimension shows who is doing the spending. The account dimension represents the account specified as the source of funds for a commitment. These attributes are almost always available from financial systems; however, the budget line can sometimes be a problem.

In general, spending happens according to a plan. Most businesses require purchase orders to reference the budget line from which the finds will be drawn. We've represented this in the commitment star by including the budget_line dimension. The relationship between commitments and budgets should be accessible in the accounting system. However, financial systems and/or business rules may permit the relationship to remain unspecified for a period of time, or in the worst case, never specify it at all.

Figure 8.2 The commitment star.

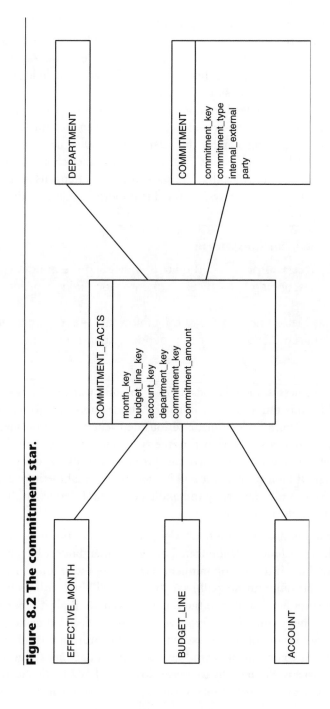

In some businesses, a commitment's relationship to the budget is optional; it is not specified at the time of the commitment, but will be required later. Through a periodic *accrual* process, managers reconcile all their commitments to lines in the budget. In cases like this, we will be forced to include an Unbudgeted row in the budget_line dimension. The budget line will be identified at a later point in time, so we also need to monitor the change history of the budget source of commitments in the accounting system. When a change is observed, we will update the budget line key for the existing row. Some users may not like the fact that we are "rewriting history," but there is no other choice; this is how the business operates. In the event that the accrual process happens in a different system, we'll source the other system for this important relationship.

Key Business Term

Accrual process. The act of indicating the budget lines corresponding to each commitment made during a period of time.

Businesses that do not require budget information at commitment time rely on an accrual process to track spending against budgets.

In some businesses, the relationship of a commitment to a budget line is never enforced. This omission means it will be just about impossible to report on spending versus budget for a budget line, a serious deficiency from a business perspective. Usually, there is a structure within the system to account for it, but it is not used. While a data mart cannot solve this problem, it is likely to serve as the catalyst for change. If built properly, it will immediately reveal the implications of the lax business rule, and stand ready to handle new data if and when the business begins to enforce the relationship.

The key lies in not omitting the budget line dimension from the commitment star. Instead, we include an Unbudgeted or Unspecified budget line in the budget dimension, and use it for all commitment facts where the relationship is not specified. Initially, all commitments will have "unspecified" budget lines because the information is not being added to the financials system. Budget reports coming out of the data mart will raise several eyebrows—key decision makers were probably not aware that the financials system was not capturing this information. The huge amounts of commitments with "unspecified" budget lines trigger a change in the business process. Six months to a year down the line, the financial system will begin to be used to capture the relationship, and the data mart will reflect it.

If budgets and commitments are handled in different systems that interface poorly, make every effort to nail down a relationship, however complex the activity may be. If it is not possible to relate a commitment to a budget line, it is necessary to omit the budget_line dimension from the commitment star. The data mart will *never* be unable to aid the business in comparing budgets against spending for a budget line—one of the primary project objectives. Budgets and spending can still be compared by account, but this may have less business value, and could be a good reason not to build the data mart. This is a decision the business must make, not the data warehouse team.

TIP

Upon discovery that source systems do not support objectives of the data mart, developers all too often cut a piece out of their model and forge ahead. The system will be met with disappointment, the project considered a failure, and the reputations of all participants damaged. All these outcomes can be avoided by speaking out as soon as it becomes clear that key objectives cannot be met. Never lose sight of the primary functional requirements of the data mart. If they prove untenable, it is pointless to build it. Doing so transforms a business problem into a major and unnecessary project failure.

One New Dimension In addition to the four familiar dimension tables, the commitment star contains one dimension table that was not present in the budget star. We've called it *commitment*. The commitment_type indicates whether it is a purchase_order, work_order, contract, and so forth. The internal_external column indicates whether the commitment is made to another part of the company (internal) or to an outside organization (external). The party column indicates the name of the party to whom the commitment is made. Some businesses may choose to drive to a lower level of detail, including a comment on the actual product or service being bought, or even the number and line number from the commitment.

There will be times when items are purchased without a commitment. Company checks, charge cards, and petty cash are routinely used to purchase certain goods and services. Overhead costs like electricity and telephone service often have no associated purchase order. Although there is no formal commitment, all these disbursements impact budgets. Many financials systems generate a commitment when such disbursements are made. The pseudo-commitment makes calculation of remaining budget easier because it removes the need to factor in payments without commitments. We will include a "Paid without commitment" row in the commitment star any time there is a payment with no corresponding commitment.

This will be easy to do if the financials system already generates the necessary commitments. If not, there will be some extra work involved in loading the commitment star.

Using the Commitment Star   The commitment star on its own will be of little interest. Reporting on the number of purchase orders is not useful to managers if they cannot tell how much money is left to be committed, nor is it helpful to accountants if they cannot tell how many of the commitments are yet to be paid. The key to successful use of the commitment star lies in its relationship to the budget star we've already designed, and the payment star we're about to look at. Because these stars share several common dimensions, we'll be able to build reports that combine their contents in useful ways.

The Payment Star

The transaction set up with a commitment culminates when the party to whom the commitment is made gets paid. Managers with budget responsibility will have lost interest by this point, because the money has been long gone from their available funds. To accountants, however, the payment is an important moment when the payable can be closed out.

As you've probably expected, once again we will build a transaction model. This approach allows us to break payments out by period, or aggregate them over time. The grain for this star will include the payment as allocated to accounts, budget lines, and commitments. Some of these relationships may be difficult to flesh out; we'll look at the issues in detail. Shown in Figure 8.3, our single fact is the payment amount.

Just as commitments happen at a more detailed level than budgets, payments happen at a more detailed level than commitments. For the commitment star, we took the four dimension tables of the budget star and added a fifth; for the payment star, we'll take the five dimension tables of the commitment star and add a sixth.

In addition to the familiar effective_month, account, budget_line, department, and commitment, the payment star includes the payment dimension. Here we record information specific to a particular outlay made by the company. The payment type indicates if the disbursement was made by check, electronic transfer, or other means. The payee indicates the actual recipient of the funds. If this payee is another part of the business, the internal_flag is set to Internal; otherwise, its value is External.

The relationship of a payment to an account should never be in question, but there may be situations in which the budget line or commitment is difficult to identify. First, let's consider the commitment. Usually, it *is* possible to relate

Figure 8.3 The payment star.

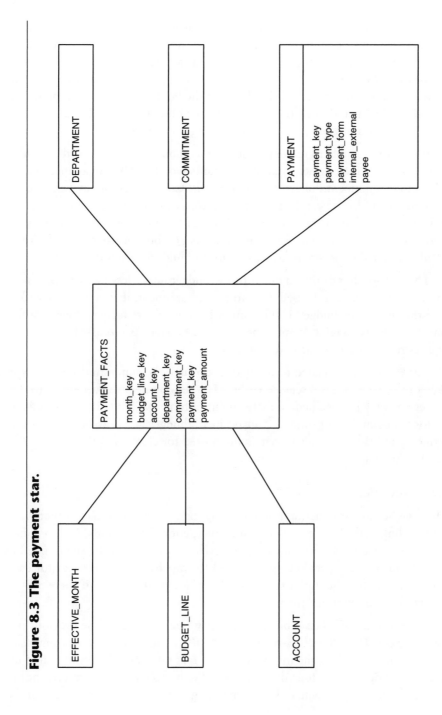

payments to commitments. Generally, a payment must have associated payables, which are set up by commitments. It may be difficult to trace the relationship, particularly when payments are made based on several invoices from the same vendor that have stacked up and aged in such a way that particular products or services are no longer specified. But because the books must balance, the relationship will be defined, though the process may be obscure. Understanding the details of the relationship is critical for loading the payment star.

If it is *not* possible to relate payments to commitments, it is worth considering not building the payment star. Accountants won't be able to compare payment dollars to commitment dollars *by commitment*. Comparison of payment dollars to commitment dollars can be made *by account*, as in Report 8.4, but there may be little perceived business value in this form of analysis. Even if the business does choose to drop the payment star, commitments and budgets together still provide useful functionality—there is no reason not to build these stars.

The relationship of the payment to the budget line is less likely to be a problem. If the payment can be tied back to the commitment, it should be easy to trace through to the budget. If this cannot be done, we're facing a bigger problem: the inability to relate commitments to the budget. As discussed earlier, this requires reevaluation of the entire project.

If the payment is related to the budget through the commitment, we may face some of the same issues discussed earlier. The commitment's relationship to the budget line may be specified at a later point in time. We'll handle this just as we did for the commitment star. An "unspecified" budget line is associated with the payment, and the financials system is monitored for changes in the status. When detected, the payment row is updated.

Grain Revisited

When we began constructing the budgeting data mart, we observed that we were dealing with three processes: budgeting, committing funds, and making payments. Since we suspected each successive process would be surrounded by more detail than the previous, we decided to start by modeling a star for each process. Now that the initial stars have been designed, let's see if there are opportunities to combine them.

As modeled, each fact table has a slightly finer grain than the previous one. The matrix in Table 8.3 cross-references the three fact tables and six dimension tables. A check mark at the intersection of a fact table and dimension table indicates a relationship. All four dimensions in the budget star are also present in the commitment and payment stars. The budget star includes effective_month,

Table 8.3 Budget and Spending Fact Tables and Dimension Tables

	budget_facts	commitment_facts	payment_facts
effective_month	✔	✔	✔
budget_line	✔	✔	✔
department	✔	✔	✔
account	✔	✔	✔
commitment		✔	✔
payment			✔

budget_line, department, and account. The commitment star includes these four dimensions, plus commitment. Finally, the payment star includes all five dimensions from the commitment star, plus payment. Because the grains differ, each process requires its own fact table, confirming our original assumption.

The reader may observe that if the information contained in the commitment and payment dimensions is not deemed critical to the business, these dimensions can be omitted from the model. Commitments and payments would be rolled up to a higher level of summarization. At this point, all three fact tables would share the same four dimensions, or grain. The possibility of merging the fact tables might look more appealing, but recall that in Chapter 1, "The Business-Driven Data Warehouse," we pointed out that the grain was only one reason why different processes deserve different fact tables. The second reason has to do with the sampling of the measurements. Our budget_amount, commitment_amount, and payment_amount measures represent changes to the budgets, commitments, or payments each month. In any given month, one measure may not have changes, while the others do. If recorded in a single fact table, we are forced to record a zero for the measure that does not change.

For example, the budget is set up prior to the fiscal year. During that time period, there will be only budget_amount transactions. Each row in the fact table will record a commitment_amount and payment_amount of zero. During the first couple of months of the year, there may be commitments, but little or no payments. A commitment value is recorded, with budget_amounts and payment_amounts of zero. Through the course of the year, other combinations of zero and nonzero transactions will probably be encountered as well.

The zero values do not reduce the accuracy of the data mart in any way, but they do impact reports that don't require all three of the transaction types. A report listing budget_amount by category by month will now include many rows indicating an amount of zero. These rows appear because zero values have been recorded in the fact table for months when there were no budget changes, but commitments and/or payments occurred. Similarly, reports on commitments and payments may include zero rows for months in which there were budget transactions, especially those prior to the fiscal year. Accountants reviewing reports of payments by month will be puzzled by all the payments of zero dollars that crop up in their reports.

What Happens at the End of the Year?

When the budget year ends, there are often many commitments that have not yet been paid. It is important that the data warehouse team understand how the business deals with such commitments and the subsequent payments, and ensures that the model is able to accurately represent them.

When the goods or services have been delivered and an invoice is received, a payment is likely to be forthcoming. The issuance of a payment may take place during the subsequent fiscal year, but is related to the previous budget year's budget line. The model developed here is able to account for this situation; the payment can be effective during one fiscal period, but tied to a budget line for another fiscal period. This means, however, that to build an accurate picture of commitment status at a point in time, the entire fact table must be aggregated, since multiple budget years may be involved. Instead, it is useful to close out the unpaid commitment, and create a new one relating to a budget line for the next fiscal year. This makes status reporting much easier.

Accounting systems often take this approach. The goods or services on a commitment may not be provided until long after the fiscal year has ended. Because the accountants will need to close their books at some point, these commitments are likely to impact the budgets of the year that has ended as well as the new year. In order to balance the books for the year that has ended, the unpaid commitment is carried over to the next budget year. The prior year's commitment is offset with a matching negative carryover commitment, so that the books balance.

In a variation on the theme, Not Applicable rows are added to the payment and commitment dimensions. In lieu of rolling these dimensions out of the model, each budget fact is tied to Not Applicable rows, and each commitment fact is tied to the Not Applicable payment row. By allowing the grains of the three transaction types to be artificially equalized, the facts can be merged into a single table. This tactic results in transaction reports strewn with a similar preponderance of zeros.

Clearly, combination of the three types of transaction into a single fact table does not make sense, even if the grains remain the same. Our reports would be

There will be some mechanism by which one can determine which commitments were carried over from previous years, and this mechanism will be important should the commitment be canceled, as we will see in a moment. The new commitment will be matched by an increase in the current year's budget to cover the expense. Usually, this additional budget will reflect the appropriate spending category, though some organizations will work around the limitations of their financials systems by creating a Carryover budget line.

The details of these year-end maneuvers, both in the financials system and in the star schema, must be clearly understood by the design team. If the decision is made to handle year end in the data warehouse differently from the way in which the financials system handles it, the load process will be complex. If both systems will handle year end as described previously, but books are left open on the financials system for an extended period of time, the reporting process must take this into account. For a brief period, total outstanding commitments might include current and previous budget years. One alternative is to build a status model, as discussed at the end of this chapter.

If commitments are carried over, cancellation of commitments made during a prior year must be handled carefully. Unlike current year commitment dollars, prior year commitment dollars do not usually go back into the budget when canceled. The transaction that reduces a commitment carried over from the previous year should be accompanied by one that reduces the budget. Here, the carryover attribute of the commitment comes in handy.

subject to a large degree of special processing to filter out the extraneous rows. In contrast, isolation of each transaction type in its own fact table maintains the appropriate sparsity, and these anomalies are avoided. Reports not requiring budget_amounts will not be littered with zero rows for periods in which there were no commitments or payments. Regardless of the granularities used, each transaction type should remain in its own fact table.

Budget Reporting

Now, we'll look at how our model supports the needs of the business. First, we'll demonstrate the capability of our budget transaction model to support year-to-date and time-series reporting. Then, we will show how it can be used to compare budgets with commitments, and commitments with payments.

Basic Reports

At any point in time, a manager with budget responsibility is not likely to be concerned with changes that have taken place in the budget that month, but rather with the total budget as it currently stands. In November, a manager may be working on accruals for the month of October, and want to know what his total budget amount by category and subcategory was that month. We can answer this question by summing the budget_amount in budget_facts, breaking the result out by budget category and subcategory. We'll constrain on the budget year 1998, and only choose rows where the effective month is October 1998 or earlier. We don't need to select a starting month—our budget year constraint will be enough. To limit the results to the particular manager's budget lines, we constrain on his organization in the department dimension. The results are shown in Report 8.1.

Note that by varying the upper limit on effective_month, this technique can be used to reconstruct the total budget at any point in time. Point-in-time status of commitments or payments can be derived using the same approach: constrain on a particular budget year and all effective_months up to and including the month in question. Budgets, commitments, and payments can be broken out at different levels in the budget categorization scheme or departmental hierarchy simply by adding the dimensions of interest into the query.

In addition to providing the point-in-time status, our transaction-based stars also allow us to break dollars out by month. The vice president of Finance is keeping an eye out for departments that may be spending money unnecessarily in

Report 8.1 Year-to-date budget.

Budget Status FY 1998
Office Management
as of October 1998

Budget Category	Budget Subcategory	Total Budget
Facilities	Office space	$200,000
	Utilities	$20,000
	Office furniture	$20,000
	Cleaning	$50,000
Facilities	**Total:**	**$290,000**
Equipment	Copier/FAX lease	$5,000
	Maintenance costs	$5,000
Equipment	**Total:**	**$10,000**
Office supplies	Standard supplies	$140,000
	Consumables—copier	$14,000
	Consumables—paper	$10,000
	Consumables—computer	$17,000
Office Supplies	**Total:**	**$181,000**
Telephone	Equipment lease	$12,000
	Maintenance	$6,000
Telephone	**Total:**	**$18,000**

order to avoid a budget cut for the coming year. She asks for a report that outlines commitments by month for each department, so that she can look for departments with significantly increased spending levels during November and December. To create the report, we select department, month, and commitment amount from the commitment star, constraining on budget year. The results for two departments are shown in Report 8.2.

Because the vice president of Finance is looking for upticks in spending at the end of the fiscal year, we have taken the dollar amounts and computed monthly percentages by department. This extra step makes it much easier to spot the type of trend she is trying to identify. It is clear that both departments shown in the

Report 8.2 Commitments by month.

Departmental Commitments
Distribution by Month
Budget Year 1998

Department	Month	Percentage
Human Resources	January	6.4
	February	8.9
	March	9.1
	April	6.6
	May	6.2
	June	7.2
	July	5.9
	August	7.4
	September	8.3
	October	6.8
	November	9.1
	December	18.1
Human Resources	**Total**	**100%**
Marketing	January	7.2
	February	8.7
	March	6.1
	April	5.3
	May	4.9
	June	7.0
	July	5.6
	August	9.0
	September	8.4
	October	6.5
	November	14.9
	December	16.4
Marketing	**Total**	**100%**

report have increased spending levels at year's end. The vice president knows that the marketing department had a legitimate reason for the disproportionate end-of-year spending, as they were preparing for the rollout of a new product in the first quarter of the next year. There is no similar explanation for the upswing in spending by Human Resources—the vice president may decide to look at their spending more carefully.

Crossing Process Boundaries with Ease

Our trio of stars makes the reports in the previous section easy to produce, but similar reports are probably available directly from the financials system. Drawn from transaction tables, these reports are moderately complex, and their customization may be little more than a minor nuisance. Although the budget and spending data mart makes these reports easier to produce and modify, it duplicates capabilities that are already in place.

The data mart was not designed simply to report on budgets, commitments, or payments. One of our key objectives was to facilitate comparison of these processes. Tracking commitments against budgets, or payments against commitments, is exceedingly difficult in the financials system. The individual transactions in question have been broken down and spread throughout a large number of tables, the relationships between processes are intricate, and there are often numerous alternatives that depend on specific attributes of transactions. The development of reports that trace out these relationships and aggregate the results over large numbers of transactions is a monumental process. In addition, they require significant system resources and processing time, and are very difficult to customize.

The budget and spending data mart makes these comparisons easy. By sorting out the intricacies of transactions one at a time and loading them into star schemas designed to support our analytic objectives, the data mart has removed all the complexities. Simple reports involving two or more of our fact tables provide answers to important questions that would otherwise be extremely difficult to address.

First, consider the needs of managers with budget responsibility. They must continuously monitor their spending levels in comparison with the budget and ensure they are tracking properly. Above these people are senior managers, for whom this information fuels decisions about adjustments to the budget. Report 8.3 provides a detailed status of budget versus commitments for the office management department that serves all these needs.

Report 8.3 Budgets versus commitments.

Budget Status
Office Management Department
October 1998

Budget Category	Budget Subcategory	Total Budget	Commitments	Remaining Dollars	Remaining Percentage
Facilities	Office space	200,000	170,200	29,800	14.90%
	Utilities	20,000	13,598	6,402	32.01%
	Office furniture	20,000	14,920	5,080	25.40%
	Cleaning	50,000	43,515	6,485	12.97%
Equipment	Copier/FAX lease	5,000	4,179	821	16.42%
	Maintenance costs	5,000	4,085	915	18.29%
Office Supplies	Standard supplies	140,000	96,012	43,988	31.42%
	Consumables—copier	14,000	10,878	3,122	22.30%
	Consumables—paper	10,000	7,311	2,689	26.89%
	Consumables—computer	17,000	10,984	6,016	35.39%
Telephone	Equipment lease	12,000	8,519	3,481	29.01%
	Maintenance	6,000	4,003	1,997	33.29%

A tedious manual process in the past, the budget and spending data mart makes creation of this report easy. It requires two queries: one involving budget_facts, the other involving commitment_facts. In both queries, we retrieve the budget category and subcategory, constraining for all months up to October for budget year 1998. In one query, we retrieve the sum of budget_amount, and in the other, we retrieve the sum of commitment_amount. We then combine these result sets, being careful not to eliminate any data where there is a budget but no commitment, or vice versa. The Remaining Dollars column is a simple calculation involving the subtraction of the amount committed from the amount budgeted; the Remaining Percentage divides this number by the budget amount.

Because they span fact tables, reports constructed in this manner are referred to as *drill-across* reports. We've already encountered drill-across queries in Chapter 4, "Fulfillment." The technique of querying each fact table separately and combining result sets ensures accurate results and minimizes response time, and this approach is easily applied by report developers. Care must be exercised to ensure that:

- Each SQL Select statement retrieves the same dimensional attributes.
- The "group by" clauses of the queries are identical.
- Identical constraints are applied in each query's "where" clause.
- Resultant data sets are merged using a reciprocal outer-join process based on the common dimensions, substituting a null whenever one result set does not have a corresponding row in the other.

Drill-across queries can also be used to compare commitments to payments. In accounting, managers are trying to project required cash flow for the coming months, and they would like to get an idea of the level of unpaid commitments, organized by G/L account. We use the same approach as in the previous report, this time combining information from the commitment and payment stars. Two queries are assembled, both of which include the account_number attribute from the account dimension and constrain on budget year 1998. In one query, we retrieve the sum of commitment_amount; in the other, we retrieve the sum of payment_amount. Result sets are combined and laid out in Report 8.4.

Either of these reports would require significant effort, expense, and processing time when run against a database in third-normal form; however, the star schema model makes them simple. Variations in the scope of the report are easy to achieve, simply by changing the dimensions used. We can also compare budgets to payments, or all three types of transactions, computing differences among any of the values.

Report 8.4 Commitments versus payments.

Outstanding Commitments by Account
Budget Year 1998
as of October

Account	Total Commitments	Total Payments	Outstanding Commitments
98-80-1098	$1,204,973	$826,130	$378,843
98-81-1098	$2,361,849	$1,624,959	$736,890
98-82-1098	$804,472	$803,372	$1,100
98-80-1023	$4,283,381	$3,153,719	$1,129,662
98-81-1023	$1,738,332	$845,593	$892,739

The Other Side of the Budget

As we mentioned at the beginning of the chapter, spending is only one side of the budget. It can be thought of as the flow of money *out* of the organization. Equally as important is the flow of money *into* the organization. The same techniques we have used to model spending can be used to model revenues: one fact table representing plans, another representing recognized revenues, and a third representing cash receipts. As on the spending side, each will likely have successively finer grain. Because each process is separate, each deserves its own fact table.

The revenue side of the budget can be used much the same way as the spending side. Managers can compare budget versus actual, and accountants can compare recognized revenues with receipts. In addition, the revenue schema can be combined with the spending schema to provide a comprehensive picture of the budget at any point in time. Together, this set of stars can answer the questions always on the mind of every CFO: "Did we make our quarter?" and "How are we doing so far this quarter?"

The Status Model

The budget and spending model presented in this chapter is characterized by its transaction focus. Rows in the fact table record changes to budgets, commitments, or payments. An alternative approach, which we call the *status model*, is largely a concession to the limitations of many of today's ad hoc query tools. By recording status levels, it makes certain types of reporting easier; however, the status model introduces a new set of complications. After presenting the standard status model, we will suggest a compromise that affords the best of the transaction and status models.

As was shown in the previous section, out trilogy of transaction stars allows us to easily construct reports that break out budgets, commitments, or payments by month, or to summarize their total level over a period of time. Often, accountants and budget managers want to do *both* in a single report. Reports like Report 8.5 are commonly requested. This report requires aggregating dollar amounts in three different ways: The second column represents the sum of all budget transactions through October 1998; the third column represents the sum of all spending through September 1998; and the fourth column represents spending only for the month of October 1998.

This report can easily be assembled using the transaction-oriented budget and commitment stars we have already designed. Like previous reports, this one requires multiple queries. Unlike the previous reports, however, each query will require a different set of constraints. We need some information summed through September, some through October, and some for October only. This is not a problem for the savvy developer with a good report development tool, but it is a problem for users attempting to build it with an ad hoc query tool. As we have already noted, very few such tools support multiple queries in a single document; still fewer permit the individual queries to have differing sets of constraints.

When an organization insists on ad hoc access to the budgeting data mart, and reports like Report 8.5 are deemed critical, an alternative to the transaction model may be required. The budget status model makes it easier to create this kind of report using an ad hoc tool with drill across capabilities; however, as we will see, the model also has some significant disadvantages.

Status Levels to the Rescue?

The budget status model, shown in Figure 8.4, looks very much like the budget transaction model. There are fact tables for budgets, commitments, and payments. The grains of these tables are identical to those in the transaction model, and the same dimensions are present. The only difference in the models is the facts themselves. Each fact represents a budget-year-to-date amount for the current month, rather than the changes during that month. In addition, a second fact records the same information for the previous month.

Using the budget status model, Report 8.5 is easily constructed without requiring multiple queries with differing constraints. This report is now within

Report 8.5 A report requiring three forms of aggregation.

Budget Status
Office Management
October 1998

Budget Category	Total Budget YTD	Spending Through 9/98	October Spending	Remaining Budget
Facilities	290,000	215,214	27,019	47,767
Equipment	10,000	7,527	737	1,736
Office Supplies	181,000	106,125	19,060	55,815
Telephone	18,000	11,197	1,325	5,478

reach of ad hoc users, providing their tool has drill-across capabilities. However, there is now a new set of problems.

Problems with the Status Model

By moving from a transaction focus to a status focus, one problem is solved, but three new problems are introduced. First, all facts are now semi-additive. Second, the density of the fact table must be substantially increased. Third, reports that isolate monthly transactions will be infested with unnecessary zero rows. Let's look at each of these problems in detail.

Semi-Additivity

Because the facts in the budget and spending status model represent budget-year-to-date summaries, each is semi-additive across effective months. Suppose a $100,000 budget line for office supplies remains unchanged throughout the course of the year. At the end of each month, the same $100,000 total budget amount is recorded in the fact table. Summing these budget levels over time would greatly misrepresent the amount that is in the budget. Over a 12-month period, our office supply budget will look like $1.2 million.

Because all facts are semi-additive, it is now easy for a novice business user to make grave errors in ad hoc queries. An errant or missing constraint will result in a substantially erroneous report. Withholding ad hoc access to the data mart avoids this problem, but defeats the purpose of the status model, which was developed primarily as an aid to ad hoc users.

Density

Under a status model, we cannot maintain sparse fact tables. It is necessary to record all status information, even when no activity has occurred; if we do not, important status information disappears from reports. This was not the case with the transaction model, where year-to-date status was derived by aggregating monthly transactions. Although the fact tables were sparse, the aggregation guaranteed that the correct status could be calculated, even for months with no activity. With the status model, we cannot rely on this phenomenon.

To understand why, consider the usage patterns that can be expected with the status model. Each row represents a status level as of a particular month. To find a budget during a particular month, we constrain on the month in question, For example, to look at the marketing department's budget as it existed during the month of October 1998, we query budget_amount, constraining for the marketing department and October 1998. This means that the budget status for

Figure 8.4 The budget status model.

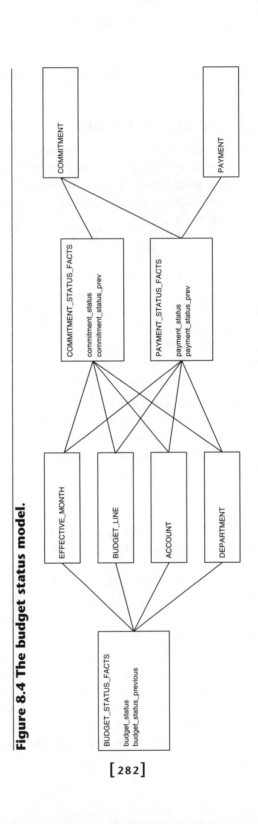

marketing must be recorded for October, even if the budget did not change during that month.

To prevent data from "falling out" of reports, we will need extremely dense fact tables. Each budget_fact will be repeated for each month. We will also need to repeat each commitment and payment fact in all months after their initial occurrences. In the end, we can expect significant increases in the size of our fact tables. Recall the $100,000 office supply budget that went unchanged throughout the year. Our transaction model contains a single row for the $100,000 budget line, for the effective_month in which it was established. No subsequent rows are required. The status model, however, requires the $100,000 budget line to be repeated monthly; otherwise, a query constraining on a subsequent month will not include this sizable portion of the office management department's budget.

One Measure for the Price of Two

In attempting to facilitate year-to-date status reporting, the budget status model renders identification of monthly changes difficult. It is now necessary to subtract the previous month's status from the current month's to capture the increase or decrease. Comparisons across rows are very difficult, so the previous month's value is included with each month. Monthly transactions can now be derived, but each month's status is stored twice: once during the month for which it is effective, and a second time as the previous month value during the current month.

Although we've made it easier to compute the net change in any given month, our reports will be cluttered with unnecessary data. Where the transaction model contained no rows for months with no transactions, the status model does. Comparison to the previous month will net these additional rows out to zero, but the zeros will be displayed. The office supply budget that goes unchanged for a year will generate a single $100,000 transaction followed by monthly transactions of $0.

A Compromise

The status model was proposed to simplify the ad hoc reporting process when multiple levels of aggregation are required. At the same time, it introduced several new issues, including semi-additivity and density. The new problems introduced by the status model can be avoided in a compromise solution that involves both a status model and a transaction model.

In the compromise solution, the budget status model is maintained only for the current month. In addition, a complete transaction model is constructed. The six fact tables are made available to ad hoc users with a query tool capable of performing drill-across queries. They can now combine monthly transactions with year-to-date and year-to-previous-month status by drilling across the transaction and status fact tables. Because the status model only contains a single month's worth of data, the perils of semi-additivity are avoided, and the density of the status table does not become a major storage issue. Ad hoc users are limited to producing reports like Report 8.5 for the current month only, but developers can construct the report for any past month simply by ignoring the status tables and aggregating the transactions as required.

Note that the combination of transaction and status facts in a single fact table will not be appropriate. The status facts require a dense fact table, which would generate a large number of zero-valued transaction facts. Although these zero-valued facts will not impact the accuracy of the data mart, they will generate unwelcome rows on reports that focus on the transactions. Earlier, the same effect led us to conclude that it would not be wise to merge fact tables for the different transaction types.

The Federal Government

Our three-tiered model of budgets, commitments, and payments can be used by almost any organization that spends according to a budget. There will be minor variations in dimensional attributes from organization to organization. There is one type of organization with unique needs: agencies of the Federal Government of the United States.

Individual government offices manage their books much like a business, most even using the same kinds of financial systems. However, their funding comes from the government agency of which they are a part. The agency, in turn, receives its funding from Congress. These processes are unique to the Federal Government, but can be modeled using a similar approach.

Government Funding

Agencies of the U.S. Federal Government receive all of their funding via appropriations from Congress. Even programs that generate money must be approved by Congress. Each appropriation is designated for a particular federal agency, for a particular program, complete with limitations. These appropriations wind up in treasury accounts from which the agency will spend the money. The combination of appropriations and other fund sources allocated by a government agency to various programs is often referred to as a *funding plan*. Funding plans break out into line items, much like budget lines.

Loading the Budget and Spending Data Mart

In this chapter, we have proposed a budget and spending model that represents changes in budgets, commitments, and spending by summarizing transactions on a monthly basis. In some cases, this approach may require a creative approach to loading the data.

All financials systems represent commitments and payments as transactions, but some do not represent budgets in this manner. Instead, budgets are sometimes represented via a status model, where budget lines are entered as total amounts. When a budget is revised, the old budget lines are flagged as "superseded," and an entirely new set of budget lines is added to the database. Although this approach differs from the transaction-based approach used to represent commitments and payments, it should not prevent developers from constructing a transaction model of the budget. Each month, the current budget lines in the financials system are simply compared to the value of the current budget the previous month. A simple subtraction operation yields the transaction amount.

Similarly, the fact that financials systems represent commitments and payments as transactions need not prevent the development of a status star. Should the team actually find benefit in the problematic status model, it can be constructed simply by aggregating transactions up to the current month. It is not even necessary to go to the transaction system to build the status stars; they can be sourced directly from the transaction stars.

The government agency determines how the money will be used by establishing *obligations*. For example, some of the money from a particular funding plan line item might be obligated to a particular contractor to perform a particular service. The obligation is a necessary step in the spending process for the U.S. Government. Contractors are painfully aware that they have no hope of getting paid if money has not been obligated. Managers at government agencies and program offices are interested in comparing their funding plan with their obligations. The difference is referred to as *unobligated* money, which can be used according to the parameters of the funding plan. This number is very important to government programs. They work to ensure that it reaches zero by the end of the year, so that their appropriations will not be reduced by Congress.

At the same time, the agency must make sure that obligated funds are actually being used. Most of the actual spending takes place at much lower levels, within the accounting systems of program or field offices. The details of bill paying are of little interest. Beholden to Congress, the agency compares obligations with *costs* that have been reported against them. Costs represent expenses that will be paid, usually under a contract or commitment. At any point in time, the difference between obligations and costs represents *uncosted obligations*. A high level of uncosted obligations at the end of a budget year may be grounds for suspicion; the program may be attempting to bury money not spent in an obligation that it intends to de-obligate in the future. Such maneuvers might be attempted by a program in order to carry money over to the next year. Government agencies prevent this by requiring that de-obligated funds return to the agency level, where they will be included in a new funding plan, potentially for a different program.

Funding Model for a Government Agency

Funding plans, obligations, and costs can be tracked through a set of transaction tables, similar to those developed earlier in this chapter. Figure 8.5 shows a funding model for a government agency. The structure of this model should look familiar. Like our original budget transaction model, it contains three fact tables, each with successively more detail.

Funding_plan_facts represents the budget for a particular government agency. The appropriation dimension contains information on the source of the funding and the treasury account in which it is located. The funding plan dimension represents how the program will spend the money. It includes information on the program. The office dimension identifies who will be doing the spending. It looks a lot like the department in the business model.

Obligation_facts details how the money in the funding plan is committed for use. To the four dimensions of the funding_plan_facts star, it adds an obligation dimension. This dimension includes information on the type of obligation, the contract under which it is awarded, the contractor, and other details about the obligation.

Last, cost_facts is used by the agency to track the reporting of costs incurred by offices against the obligations that have been established. The cost star includes the

Figure 8.5 Government agency funding and obligations.

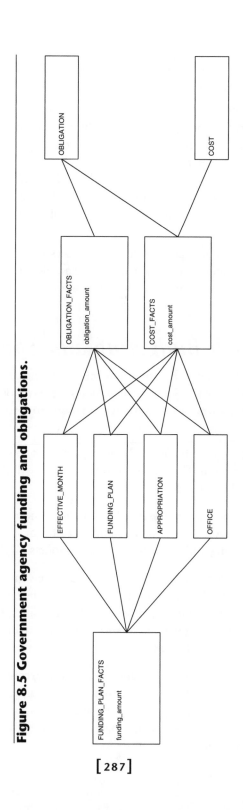

five dimensions of the obligations table. Additional details on the particular type of cost incurred are recorded in an additional cost dimension.

These star schemes permit analysis of agency funding. They work in much the same way as our original budgeting stars. Each can be used to report on changes over time, or aggregated to report on status at a certain point in time. Drilling across tables permits comparison of funding to obligations, or obligations to costs. As with the original budgeting model, the end-of-year processes must be understood and addressed. Once again, a status model can supplement the transaction model to aid in some forms of reporting, complete with the same issues discussed earlier.

The three processes here are not the only processes of interest to a government agency. Commitments and payments, for example, are also of interest. Analysis of these processes can be facilitated by adding the appropriate fact tables to the data warehouse.

Summing Up Budgeting and Spending

In this chapter, we have learned a lot about the budgeting process and how it can be supported by a data mart. Some of the reports we have looked at are very difficult to extract from a transaction system, yet simple to retrieve from the trilogy of stars.

Choose the appropriate budgets. Do managers want to study revenues, expenditures, or both? The answer to this question will determine which processes should be modeled.

Focus on the individual processes. To study the spending budget, we identified three processes: budgeting, commitment of funds, and payments. A successful budgeting and spending data mart models all three processes.

Don't fudge the grain. Each transaction type belongs in its own fact table. Creation of Not Applicable rows in unrelated dimensions confuses the grain and contributes to lopsided reports. Aggregating transactions to the same level and merging them into a single fact table will cause extra zeroes to clutter transaction reports.

Work hard to tease key relationships out of the source system. Remember that the success of the budget and spending data mart hinges on the ability to compare budgets to commitments, and commitments to payments. Some of the necessary relationships may be quite difficult to tease out of the financials system, but without them, the data mart will fizzle.

Drill across for powerful reports. The most powerful reports combine data from two or more of the budget and spending fact tables. A query tool that supports drill-across capability will make these reports easier to produce.

Beware of the pitfalls of the status model. Speedy access to a year-to-date summary can be tempting, but the status model has its downside. Don't combine periodic and summary columns in the same fact table, and be sure you're able to deal with the semi-additivity and density issues of the status model.

FINANCIAL REPORTING

Business is a competition; somebody needs to keep score. Because score keeping is a complex task, we have given it over to accountants and large software systems. These systems, as mentioned in Chapter 8, "Budgets and Spending," are very complex. We do not contend that this complexity is unnecessary, only that it complicates the analytical tasks of business. Sorting out and simplifying the contents of the accounting system is a worthy goal for a data warehouse. Chapter 8 described how to simplify the budgeting world using a family of stars. In this chapter, we apply the techniques of dimensional design to financial reporting.

First, we need to make an important distinction between *managerial* and *financial* accounting. Managerial accounting is less demanding than financial accounting, but equally important. Many data warehouses and data marts are designed for managerial accounting tasks. A data warehouse designed for financial accounting is a serious undertaking because of the potential use of its contents.

Key Business Terms

Managerial accounting. Accounting intended for internal consumption, used in planning and operating the organization by managers and employees.

Managerial accounting is timely, and some degree of imprecision is often accepted. Managerial accounting has countless uses and the data may come from many sources, not just the approved, audited financial accounting system. Many companies use sales force automation software to forecast and record sales for the sales subject area. These forecasts and results, recorded by the sales team, are not the official expectations

Continues

Key Business Terms *Continued*

and results for external consumption, but instead are used internally to manage the sales force.

Financial accounting. Accounting for external consumption, used in reporting financial results on a periodic basis to shareholders, creditors, and government entities.

The source for financial accounting is a company's approved, audited accounting system. This system is protected by well-defined procedures to ensure that data is entered correctly. These procedures and the design of the accounting system are carefully designed to prevent irregularities and thwart fraud. The financial accounting system is the scorecard a company shows to the world, especially shareholders and creditors. Those with an equity position in a company use the information to monitor the performance of their investment. Creditors use financial reports to monitor the security of their debt.

In this chapter, we will design a data warehouse for financial reporting. The design is intended to supplement a company's existing financial accounting system, not replace it. Rather than replace the financial reports produced periodically by the financial system, a financial reporting data warehouse provides simplified access to the detailed data behind past results. To ensure that this data warehouse is reliable and meets the high standards demanded of the financial system, we follow two strict guidelines:

- The financial reports produced from the data warehouse must be as reliable as reports from the existing financial reporting system. All changes and reversals in the financial system must be reflected in the financial data warehouse.

- The sources for the financial data warehouse must be the approved, audited systems recognized as the official source for that data in the corporation.

A financial data warehouse requires that both guidelines be followed. If not, it is still a valuable managerial accounting asset, as are most of the designs in the book, but should not be used to detail or supplement the company's standard financial reports.

Tracing Financial Transactions

To illustrate the importance of an approved, audited source, consider the case of an automotive parts supplier. The company sells parts to manufacturing plants across the country. Information about sales is recorded in no fewer than three operational applications. The first is the sales force automation (SFA) system. Sales team members record forecasts and the status of various opportunities in this system. Using the system, a salesperson records the record shown in Table 9.1.

This record represents the salesperson's forecast that Panda Motors intends to purchase 3000 door locks in December 1998. As the forecast month approaches, the salesperson may visit the customer several times, adjusting the forecast accordingly. By November, the original forecast may have changed to look like Table 9.2.

The anticipated order has decreased from 3000 units to 2000 units. If the SFA system records each change in a forecast, the company can monitor the forecasting skills of the sales force. If not, the company can create a simple forecasting data mart to answer that question. The SFA system allows the company to track expected revenue, or pipeline, as the forecast month approaches. This is information is managerial, not financial accounting. It is forward looking, not a report of what has already happened. While it is useful in projecting results, the company must report such information carefully—outside analysts might overreact to either positive or negative projections. Most SFA systems associate a status with an opportunity, either open or closed, and a resolution of won or lost. As December approaches, this opportunity is closed and reported as won. Can the company count $100,000 in revenue? Is that amount appropriate for financial reporting?

Obviously not. Financial systems have strict controls about revenue reporting, and the company likely has policies in place regarding revenue recognition. The order resulting from this opportunity, and the revenue associated with it, must be recorded in other systems before it's counted. To illustrate, we will track the order through the next two systems. If Panda Motors places an order in December, the company will create the order entry system record depicted in Table 9.3.

There are obvious differences between the order and the forecast. First, the price has changed from $50 per unit to $48 per unit. This difference might be the result of last-minute negotiating by the salesperson, or due to volume discounting the salesperson knew nothing about. It might even reflect an erroneous price in the SFA system. The order also has a different product identifier than the SFA system. While the sales team works with generic product identifiers, the sales order entry system uses an identifier that is associated with a specific production

Table 9.1 The Forecasted Sale

Salesperson	Entry Date	Forecast Month	Customer	Product	Quantity	Sales Dollars
Smith	7/7/98	12/98	Panda Motors	Trunk lid lock X11	3,000	$150,000

Table 9.2 The Forecasted Sale—November

Salesperson	Entry Date	Forecast Month	Customer	Product	Quantity	Sales Dollars
Smith	11/9/98	12/98	Panda Motors	Trunk lid lock X11	2,000	$100,000

facility. Note also that the name of the salesperson is not recorded. This is not always true, but it can happen. The gaps and discontinuity in identifying orders and products across systems are more common than the IT industry likes to admit. These gaps and differences in information are often impossible to overcome, especially in an organization dealing in thousands of transactions per month. There will usually be differences in the sum of sales closed reported in the SFA system and in the official order entry system.

The order also generates additional chargeable items for Panda Motors, including sales tax and freight. Such items are rarely recorded in an SFA system, since the calculations are often obscure and changeable. The order entry system likely includes additional items at both the line item and summary level for each order. In our case, the order totals to $101,926. The order entry system may be linked to the accounts receivable (AR) module of the financial system. This is the system where the money owed to the company by a customer is tracked. This order creates a receivable record, depicted in Table 9.4. When we enter the accounts receivable system, we have reached the financial accounting world.

The specific design of a company's receivable system determines what information it contains. Our receivable record has a billing date in the middle of the month. The company may gather all receivables for Panda Motors, including other orders for different products, and send a bill on the 15th and 1st of each month. Terms describe when the bill is due; in this example, 30 calendar days from the billing date. The receivable is the first piece of information that is guaranteed to be in the accounting system. A receivable that includes nonrevenue items, such as the freight and taxes, usually has associated detail records to delineate each amount.

Why is this $101,926 receivable considered the entry point to the financial accounting world? A receivable is a material asset with recognized value in the marketplace and, as such, can be sold. When negotiating a line of credit, a bank only values a company's receivables, not the orders behind the receivables. The accounting world only recognizes information that can be audited for reliability. The system of double-entry bookkeeping was created to ensure that once a business creates an asset like a receivable, it cannot adjust the value of that asset without recording the change somewhere else. I might be able to delete an order from the order entry system or change a forecast in the SFA system; however, it is difficult, if not impossible, to delete a receivable. If Panda Motors returns some parts, goes out of business, or otherwise takes action to reduce the value of the receivable, the company can only devalue it. Once in the accounting system, it is indelible. The resulting audit capability is critical to investors and creditors. Receivables

Table 9.3 The Order

Customer	Order Date	Product	Delivery Date	Quantity	Price	Sales Dollars
Panda Motors	12/6/98	X11-T96	12/19/98	2,000	$48.00	$96,000

Table 9.4 The Receivable

Customer	Account	Entry Date	Terms	Bill Date	Due Date	Amount
Panda Motors	PDMX001394	12/6/98	Net 30	12/15/98	1/15/99	$101,926

also represent the recognition of income. Once a company credits an order to the receivables system, it counts as revenue. Any devaluation of a receivable results in a restatement or adjustment to revenue, and such adjustments are usually not good news. The indelibility of receivables, payables, and other records in the financial system is important, because it complicates the task of cooking the books.

The distinction between managerial and financial accounting is important to the data warehouse design team. Managerial accounting's demand for timely information sometimes results in approximations of revenue, sales, and income. Product margins based on managerial accounting information are useful for internal decision making. Sales force projections and opportunity probability scores are commonly used to compute expected revenue forecasts during an accounting period. However, neither figure is of value to a shareholder or creditor absent the complete picture provided by periodic, audited, reliable financial accounting information. Terms like *revenue*, *income*, and *margin* have specific meanings in financial accounting that should not be ignored; in fact, there is no greater corporate sin in the financial and credit markets than restating past results. The team constructing a financial data warehouse should take these high expectations of reliability to heart.

Why It's Called Accounting

Accounting is a noun. The verb *account* is the root of the word *accounting*, and means literally to explain. The accounting function in any business is deemed the objective arbiter of results. The accounting department reports what is going on in a manner that is unquestionably accurate. The desire for objectivity is manifested in the auditing of financial statements every year. The accounting department, the most fastidious crowd in the organization, hires an outside group of accountants to validate its own fastidiousness. This is done on the off chance that one of the accountants in the organization has gone on a financial bender and cooked the books. The outside accountants come in to taste the soup, check ingredients, and look for dirt under the other accountants' fingernails—so, accounting is really just explaining. The foundation of a good explanation is a set of facts. In accounting, the facts are the accounts and the transactions against those accounts.

Accounts are what must balance in the accounting world. For each action in accounting, there must be an equivalent action. The Panda Motors receivable account in the previous section is an asset account that increases in value when an order is received. This increase is recorded as a debit. When Panda Motors makes a payment, the receivable account must be decreased, or credited, by the amount of the payment. The company's cash account is debited for the equivalent amount. These assets are balance sheet accounts, a set that includes assets, liabilities, and owner's equity. The balance sheet is used to present the current financial position of the company. Using a scorecard metaphor, the balance sheet is the roster of the team and its strengths and weaknesses at a point in time.

> **Key Business Term**
>
> **Account.** An account is a defined entity of financial importance to the business.
>
> Transactions are recorded against accounts. Examples of accounts include a corporate checking account, line of credit, salaries, vacation, and taxes. The chart of accounts for any business is the current set of valid accounts against which transactions may be recorded. Accounts are categorized as either *balance sheet accounts* or *income statement accounts*.

The order also represents income for the company and is recorded in an income account assigned to Panda Motors. There are other income accounts, primarily dealing with gains from investments, but the most important ones record sales. Income accounts and expense accounts are used to build the income statement. Expense accounts include sales expense, cost of goods sold, salaries, taxes, and office supplies. For any period, we should be able to quickly subtract the sum of all expense accounts from the sum of all income accounts and arrive at profit. The income statement is the scorecard for a specific accounting period, indicating how well the company used its assets to create profit.

If you are not an accountant, you may be dozing off about now. Accountants, on the other hand, are ready to offer an opinion on the perils of oversimplification. We acknowledge those perils and apologize in advance to the accounting community for flying through these topics. We assume some understanding of accounting on behalf of the reader, and think the brief illustration of financial reporting that follows is a safe overview.

The Balance Sheet

The balance sheet is sometimes called the *statement of financial position*. It is less accessible to most people than the income statement. One place where the average developer may encounter a balance sheet is in personal financial software. The balance sheet represents the accounting equation—Assets = Liabilities + Owners' Equity—at a point in time. A monthly balance sheet is like a snapshot, and a series of monthly balance sheets is a photoplay. The figures in a balance sheet are not additive over time; in a balance sheet, we are looking for relative changes. The balance sheet can be thought of as an inventory of assets, liabilities, and owners' equity. The reader may wish to skip ahead and review Figure 9.8, a comparative balance sheet example. The changes in specific balance sheet accounts over time can be useful in understanding how the business is performing. Receivables cycles are useful in planning for cash flow needs, while growing liabilities like unused vacation may augur trouble for the company in the future. Changes in owners' equity represent changes in the value of the business.

The three categories of accounts on the balance sheet are:

Assets. Items that have inherent value. Some assets are created by business activity, such as accounts receivable and inventory. Other assets enable business activity, like factories, production equipment, and working capital. Some assets are short term, meaning they can be readily converted to cash—examples include quality receivables and convertible securities. Others are long term, like production equipment or real estate.

Liabilities. Items for which the company must eventually use cash to reconcile. Short-term liabilities include unpaid bills for operations and current salaries. Long-term liabilities include lines of credit and term loans. Accrued liabilities represent obligations to make future payments, such as deferred bonuses or unused vacation.

Owners' equity. The capital invested in the company and retained earnings make up this category. Owners' equity changes as the values of assets and liabilities vary.

Balance sheet accounts are carefully defined and recorded by the accounting staff. The total set of accounts from both the balance sheet and income statement is known as the *chart of accounts*. The chart of accounts is the ultimate reference table for the accounting system, linking transactions together for integrity. A company's chart of accounts can be large, detailed, and hard to navigate for the average user. Some accounting systems allow little room for describing the account. To overcome this descriptive limitation, companies embed intelligence in the account number or description. The data warehouse team can, with some work, decode the intelligence and create meaningful dimensions for analysis. Simplifying the reporting process and decoding some of the information that may be encoded in account numbers is a common reason for building a financial data warehouse.

With these basic building blocks—the asset, liability, and owners' equity accounts from the chart of accounts—we can design our balance sheet-based schema. We will build the balance sheet schema in two steps: In the first step, we will create fact tables to store the base transactions to calculate asset values. The product of the first step, a set of transaction fact tables, is used as the source for summary tables that provide balance sheet account balances at specific points in time.

Balance Sheet Granularity

The first choice we face in building the balance sheet schema is choosing a grain for our transaction-level fact tables. The general ledger of the accounting system records all transactions against an account. We can take each general ledger transaction for balance sheet accounts, apply reversals, and create a very detailed grain for our transaction fact tables. The general ledger transaction serves as the grain, but this transaction in the general ledger may have limited descriptive data. This data may be encoded in the account number, or accessible by linking the account to related payables and receivables records. As we extract the transactions, we can create dimensions to include this extra data. The basic dimensions typically found for a general ledger transaction are:

Time. The effective date of the transaction is the obvious first dimension, and because we are recording individual transactions we need a grain of day for this dimension.

Category—credit or debit. Debit an asset to increase its value. Credit an asset to decrease its value. Debit a liability to decrease its value. Credit a liability to increase its value. We may also add some additional typifying information to call out depreciation transactions, payments, dividend payments, and so forth.

Account. The account dimension contains the most interesting information, including the type (asset, liability, or equity), a name or description, and other identifying characteristics. Accounts can be further delineated in a variety of ways. For example, we can separate long-term and short-term assets or liabilities. We may add a flag to denote cash asset accounts. The amount of detail added depends on the requirements of the business and the availability of source data.

Other dimensions can be added depending on the specific business model and the depth of the financial accounting system. The granularity of the account information may include the associated owner or customer. We could associate receivable accounts with specific customers, and liability accounts to creditors.

These details are typically not presented in the official summary balance sheet even though they exist in the financial source system. One of the advantages of enabling detailed reporting is to allow end users to drill into the usually bland balance sheet line items. Accounts receivable could be classified by customer, age, quality, and other relevant information. Long-term liabilities can be presented by creditor and interest rate. Lines of credit can be assigned to different operating divisions. These details are invaluable for internal analysis of financial results, and go well beyond traditional financial reports.

In adding additional dimensional attributes, the design team must avoid creating details that are not well understood. It is important to ensure that the details created survive the transition from the operational system recording the detail to the general ledger transaction. Consider the 3NF (third normal form) entity model presented in Figure 9.1. This model depicts the financial system relationship between Division and Account for our parts manufacturer.

Note that general ledger transactions are related only to the account; there is no direct relationship between a Division and a GL transaction. An account may be used by more than one division. Assume it is a cash account used to purchase production materials. The division crediting or debiting the account is not reflected in the GL transaction. It may be available in the source payables system, or embedded in the account number, or it may be a mystery. Unless the design team is absolutely sure that a consistent and reliable method is available to make such an association, then the GL transactions cannot be associated with a division.

Such limitations in design are not unusual, nor are companies always willing to accept these limitations. Workarounds are common. First, look for intelligence in the account key. This key may be encoded with characters that identify divisions, customers, or other relationships between the transaction and other entities. Figure 9.2 shows an exaggerated example of embedded intelligence in an account number.

Notice that the meaning of each character varies even by type of account. For a cash account, the owning division is defined in the first 3 characters, while the depository institution is determined by the characters 4 through 7. For a liability account, the division remains the same, but characters 4 through 7 now identify the creditor. The values in these positions—for example, the 3-character division code—may be kept internal to the account system, derived from the master division table, or under the glass on someone's desk. The last account type, receivables, uses characters 4 through 7 to record the customer for the receivable. The resulting account code creates a level of granularity for the transaction that is not available in the base design of the general ledger transaction table. This type of

Figure 9.1 The financial system ERD.

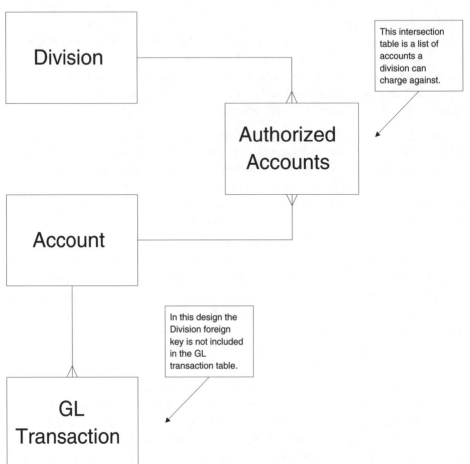

decoding increases the value of the data warehouse, but has inherent risks. First, the team must ensure that changes in these decode values are correctly managed. The team should also ensure that the system of assigning account numbers is clear, well documented, and consistent.

Based on the analysis and decoding of the intelligent account key, we decide that the information captured about each type of account varies widely between assets and liabilities. To arrive at a forthright design, we create separate fact tables for each account type. The resulting design would look something like Figure 9.3.

Figure 9.2 The very intelligent key.

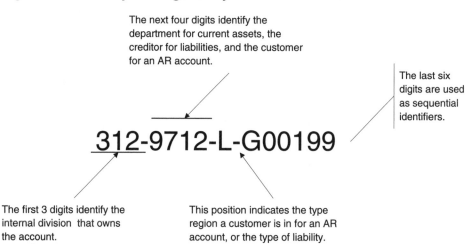

This base transaction schema is the first step toward building our balance sheet summaries. It is to some degree a copy of GL transactions for balance sheet accounts; however, the decoding of account numbers makes it easier to navigate than the source system, and query performance should be better. The advantage to both end users and report designers is that information embedded in the account codes has been revealed. While it is possible to build the balance sheet summaries directly from the GL transactions, this intermediate schema has inherent value.

Consider the history of a $50,400 piece of production equipment used by the parts maker. The purchase of the equipment is a debit transaction in the asset fact table, with a transaction type of "fixed asset purchase" and an asset type of "production equipment." We can add other columns to the asset dimension, perhaps from the fixed assets module of the accounting system, to provide further detail about the equipment. The asset has a seven-year useful life, and is depreciated using the straight-line method. If the company computes expenses on a monthly basis, the asset will be depreciated in 84 monthly expense transactions that record the history of the asset. While an individual asset may not be analytically important, the mix of fixed assets, the balance of value in production equipment, and the ratios between fixed asset value and other assets often are revealing. We can now easily look at all depreciation expense transactions for a period, as well as calculate the balance for an asset, a group of assets, or all assets at any given time. Depreciation is important to businesses because it is a noncash expense, one

Figure 9.3 Candidate balance sheet transaction facts design.

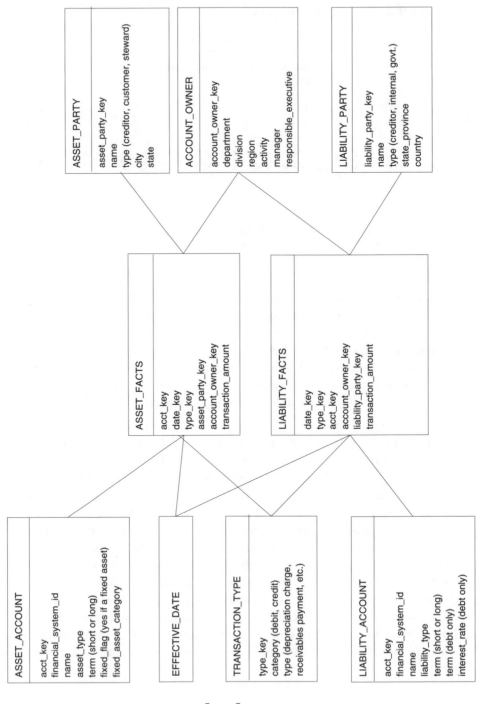

that reduces income but does not reduce available cash. It effectively spreads the impact of profit from an asset across its useful life. Other asset relationships, such as the balance of accounts receivable for a customer, industry segment, or division, affect cash flow and are equally interesting.

Accounts receivable are also useful to analyze over time. A data mart built only from accounts receivable records would provide details on the timeliness of payments, but the balance sheet data warehouse supports comparison of accounts receivable activity with asset value cycles. If the company experiences an increase in slow payments from customers, we would expect the value of accounts receivable to increase. As operating expenses continue to be paid, the balance of cash accounts decreases; eventually, the company would be forced to draw on credit sources to replenish cash supplies. The use of credit is reflected in increases in liability accounts. The interrelationships in this example are shown in Figure 9.4.

The simplified navigation of asset and liability accounts, enhanced readability of financial dimensions, and improved query performance are the principal advantages of building the transaction fact tables. We would supplement our liabilities and assets fact tables with a third fact table, one that captures owners' equity account transactions. These are either stock accounts that capture capital flowing in and income flowing out to investors, or retained earnings. We reuse the transaction type and effective date dimensions, and add the unique dimensions of owners_equity_account.

Figure 9.4 The relationship among accounts receivable, cash, and credit.

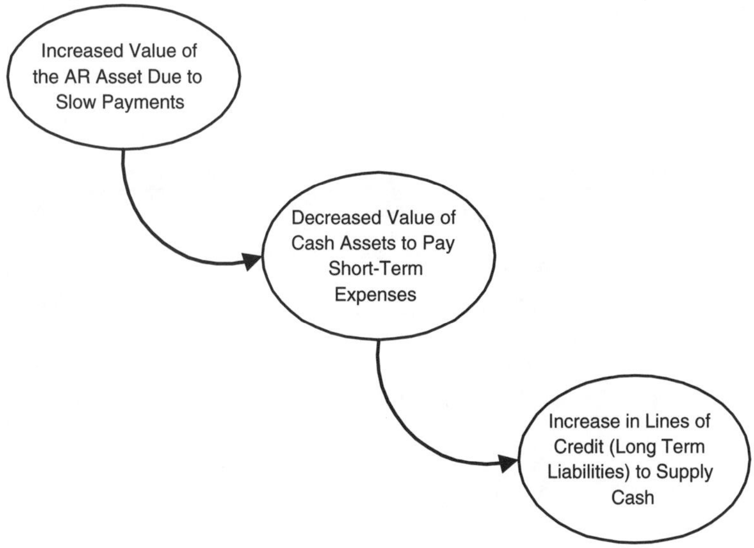

Producing a Balance Sheet

With a trio of transaction fact tables, we can now create a complementary set of summary tables that store the balance of all the accounts associated with the balance sheet. The most common requirement is the creation of balance sheets for each financial period. With our base fact tables, this is a relatively simple process: We simply record the balance of all accounts at a given time interval. Remember that the balance sheet is a snapshot of the asset's value at a given point in time. Our facts in the summary tables represent the account value at a specific point in time. To illustrate, consider the value of the production equipment described previously. The value of the asset at monthly and quarterly increments is shown in Figure 9.5. The equipment was purchased and placed in use in March 1996.

Each month, a credit of $600 is charged to the fixed asset account for the equipment. There are three options for recording the balance sheet value of the asset for each month and quarter:

- Construct separate snapshot tables for quarter and month.

- Modify the month dimension to indicate when a month is the last in a quarter. Fact table rows relating to these dimension rows would be valid for both month and quarter.

Figure 9.5 Snapshotting an asset value at different times.

Asset:	Production Equipment		
Purchase Price:	50,400		
First Use Month:	Mar-96		
Use Periods:	84		
Month	**End of Month Value**	**Quarter**	**End of Quarter Value**
Mar-96	49,800	Q1	49,800
Apr-96	49,200		
May-96	48,600		
Jun-96	48,000	Q2	48,000
Jul-96	47,400		
Aug-96	46,800		
Sep-96	46,200	Q3	46,200
Oct-96	45,600		
Nov-96	45,000		
Dec-96	44,400	Q4	44,400

Figure 9.6 The balance sheet summary design.

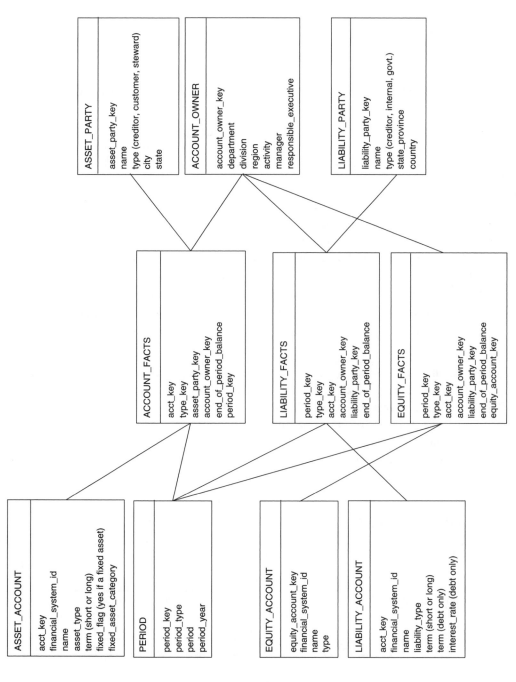

- Create a period dimension that includes month, quarter, and year rows. In this case, a year of balance sheets would require 17 fact table rows: 12 for monthly, 4 for quarterly, and 1 for yearly.

The last solution increases the number of rows in the fact table by about 40 percent, but reduces the number of fact tables required to create the various balance sheets. The proposed solution, summarizing by month, quarter, and year, as well as by account, is shown in Figure 9.6.

Remember that facts in the summary are not simply sums of the transactions for a given period; instead, the beginning value for an account must be calculated and then transactions applied. The actual calculations for an accounts receivable asset in the first six months of use is shown in Figure 9.7. Again, these numbers are not additive for any meaningful balance sheet purpose.

The final design combining period summaries and the raw transactions provides the company with a great deal of detail about balance sheet account activity. For internal, managerial uses, the company can examine balance sheet data by division, examine changes in asset and liabilities by type, and do a myriad of other analyses. A highly summarized balance sheet is presented in Report 9.1.

The asset section of the balance sheet is shown in Report 9.2 with additional summaries at the division level. With the design depicted in Figure 9.6, the company could drill into assets by asset party name, asset type, asset term, and transaction type.

Similar analysis can be performed on the liabilities and owners' equity balance sheet lines. Each line can be explored by the dimensions associated with the respective fact table. Because such analysis draws data from three fact tables, an interactive drill report would be difficult to construct with most ad hoc query tools. Emerging report interfaces can handle such a requirement artfully, allowing the user to drill through the balance sheet line into the account balances that make up the total.

Figure 9.7 Changes in the value of an asset account.

Summary of Tinker Motors Accounts Receivable Account Value						
	Q2 April	Q2 May	Q2 Jun	Q3 Jul	Q3 Aug	Q3 Sep
Beginning Balance	$ -	$ 28,900	$ 83,500	$ 141,800	$ 202,300	$ 125,400
Debits	$ 28,900	$ 54,600	$ 112,900	$ 89,400	$ 36,000	$ 65,900
Credits	$ -	$ -	$ (54,600)	$ (28,900)	$ (112,900)	$ (125,400)
Ending Balance	$ 28,900	$ 83,500	$ 141,800	$ 202,300	$ 125,400	$ 65,900

The Account as a Slow-Changing Dimension

Account numbers are artificial keys, often with some embedded intelligence. This intelligence can be obvious, like the inclusion of a fiscal year, or meaningless. The intelligence can be simple or complex, as our previous example showed. Regardless of the structure of the account number, there is an inherent problem with any artificial key. These keys represent a semantic object, in this case, a specific account. These keys often take on a meaning and life of their own that obscure the underlying semantic object. Software developers involved in legacy system conversions are often faced with users who cling to cryptic artificial keys, demanding that they be converted to a replacement system. The level of comfort and attachment is understandable, and often the development team gives in to these demands. The data warehouse team is also faced with this dilemma as users seek familiar anchors to source systems on which to base queries.

A different issue, and one that is much more important, is the reuse of artificial keys in the source application. This problem is more common than one might think ,and often goes unnoticed in the operational world. Account numbers may be reused, and the consequences may go unnoticed by the operational system managers. We encountered this situation on one occasion. Our customer, upon discovering the reuse of account numbers, went valiantly to the financial system manager and explained the problem. The managers of the operational system denied there was a problem. This denial was in spite of clear evidence that the problem existed, and the resulting changes could adversely impact historical financial reporting.

When building a financial system, a company creates several account numbers to record financial transactions. As time passes, some of the account codes fall into disuse. Reorganizations, new projects, new policies, and closed business units all result in a stream of extinct artificial keys. In a well-run system, these retired account numbers are taken out of service except for use as a report parameter, but in many older accounting systems, many of which are still in operation today, the set of available accounting numbers is finite. The managers of the operational system may eventually run out of numbers. If so, the company may resurrect old

Continues

Report 9.1 Dover Auto Parts, Ltd., balance sheet.

Dover Auto Parts Comparative Balance Sheet
1996 and 1995

Assets	1996	1995
Current Assets		
Cash	$ 1,200,000	$ 1,400,000
Accounts Receivable	$ 3,450,000	$ 2,900,000
Finished Goods Inventory	$ 890,000	$ 1,100,000
Prepaid Expenses	$ 34,000	$ 68,000
Total Current Assets	$ 5,574,000	$ 5,468,000
Property, Plant, and Equipment		
Land	$ 12,000,000	$ 9,000,000
Production Facilities and Equip.	$ 38,500,000	$ 34,900,000
Other Facilities and Equip.	$ 650,000	$ 575,000
Total PPE	$ 51,150,000	$ 44,475,000
Total Assets	$ 56,724,000	$ 49,943,000
Liabilities and Owners' Equity		
Current Liabilities		
Accounts Payable	$ 420,000	$ 720,000
Accrued Payables	$ 311,000	$ 181,000
ST Notes Payable	$ 2,600,000	$ 2,100,000
Total Current Liabilities	$ 3,331,000	$ 3,001,000
Long Term Liabilities		
LT Notes Payable	$ 2,600,000	$ 3,900,000
Capital Equipment Loans	$ 450,000	$ 124,000
Property Loan	$ 8,100,000	$ 8,300,000
Total LT Liabilities	$ 11,150,000	$ 12,324,000
Total Liabilities	$ 14,481,000	$ 15,325,000
Owners' Equity		
Common Stock	$ 40,183,000	$ 33,798,000
Additional Paid In Capital	$ 1,200,000	$ 400,000
Retained Earnings	$ 860,000	$ 420,000
Total Owners' Equity	$ 42,243,000	$ 34,618,000
Total of Liabilities and Owners' Equity	$ 56,724,000	$ 49,943,000

The Account as a Slow-Changing Dimension *Continued*

account numbers. These are dug up and given a new semantic meaning, associated with new organizational units, and new transactions are

Report 9.2 Drilling into the balance sheet.

Dover Auto Parts Comparative Balance Sheet
1996 and 1995

Assets				1996		1995
Current Assets						
	Cash			$ 1,200,000		$ 1,400,000
	Accounts Receivable			$ 3,450,000		$ 2,900,000
	Finished Goods Inventory			$ 890,000		$ 1,100,000
	Prepaid Expenses			$ 34,000		$ 68,000
		Total Current Assets		$ 5,574,000		$ 5,468,000
Property, Plant						
	La					
	Pr					
	Ot					
Total Assets						
Liabilities and						
Current Liabilit						
	Ac					
	Ac					
	ST					
Long Term Lia						
	LT					
	Ca					
	Pr					
Total Liabilities						
Owners' Equity						
	Common Stock			$ 40,183,000		$ 33,798,000
	Additional Paid In Capital			$ 1,200,000		$ 400,000
	Retained Earnings			$ 860,000		$ 420,000
		Total Owners' Equity		$ 42,243,000		$ 34,618,000
Total of Liabilities and Owners' Equity				$ 56,724,000		$ 49,943,000

Assets		1996	1995
Current Assets			
Cash			
	US Manufacturing	$ 300,000	$ 400,000
	European Manufacturing	$ 250,000	$ 200,000
	Other Divisions	$ 650,000	$ 800,000
Total Cash		$ 1,200,000	$ 1,400,000
Accounts Receivable			
	US Manufacturing	$ 1,900,000	$ 1,600,000
	European Manufacturing	$ 1,100,000	$ 850,000
	Contract Engineering	$ 450,000	$ 450,000
		$ 3,450,000	$ 2,900,000
Finished Goods Inventory			
	US Manufacturing	$ 620,000	$ 800,000
	European Manufacturing	$ 270,000	$ 300,000
		$ 890,000	$ 1,100,000
Prepaid Expenses		$ 34,000	$ 68,000
	Total Current Assets	$ 11,114,000	$ 10,868,000

charged against them. In the late 1990s, it is still possible to come across systems reusing accounting codes. Because the window of financial reporting is narrow compared to the financial data warehouse, the

Continues

The Account as a Slow-Changing Dimension *Continued*

financial system team may not even be aware of the problem, but the data warehouse stores historical data and must reconcile changes in the accounting system dimensions. If not, a report that spans two uses of the same account number for different semantic purposes would be erroneous. To prevent this, we must look for changes in the account number:name combination. In doing so, we treat the account number as a slow-changing dimension and define its semantic context independent of its use as an operational system primary key.

We will use our auto parts manufacturer to illustrate the problem. The Dover accounting system includes the tables shown in Figure 9.8.

Figure 9.8 Dover Auto Parts' financial system.

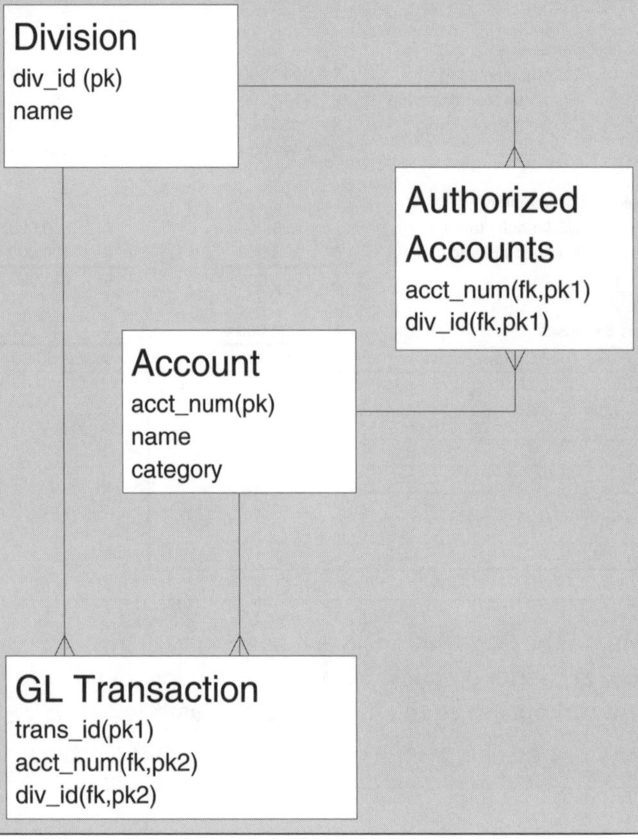

In the past, the company had used a standard set of accounts for plant construction, which were retired after the last domestic plant was constructed in 1994. In 1997, the company began construction of a new plant in Naples, Italy. The company had a new financial system manager who asked the executive team how to segregate costs for Naples. The plant construction director gave the manager a report from the last domestic construction effort to illustrate the type of cost structure needed. The financial system manager and the database administrator (DBA), the third DBA the company had had since 1994, were running low on account numbers—the use of the old numbers was blocked in the application via a current flag constraint. The financial system manager advised the database administrator to change the flag from N to Y for a series of old account numbers and overwrite the old descriptions. He also sent an email to the application manager describing the change. The application manager, a recently hired employee distracted by the installation of a new Materials Requirements Planning package, paid little attention to the reuse. The construction manager and his team began to record Naples construction costs against the resurrected codes. The new and old values are presented in Table 9.5.

Table 9.5 The Reused Accounts

Account	Old Description	New Description
312-8121-C-R09321	Legal charges—real property	Contract construction labor
312-8122-C-R09322	Property repairs—US Ops	Contract engineering
312-8123-C-E04441	HVAC equipment purchases	Corporate engineering
312-8199-X-X00021	Accrued unused vacation	Architectural charges
312-0034-R-E91001	Site preparation—Tulsa	Environmental studies
311-0041-T-E-90012	Site studies—Tulsa	Plant location studies
...	...	...

Continues

The Account as a Slow-Changing Dimension *Continued*

The new descriptions changed the meaning of the account numbers in the operational system, designed for period summaries (the income statement) and snapshots in time (the balance sheet). The impact on operational reporting was minimal, since the codes had gone unused for a long period. The executive team could now easily trace the costs of the Naples plant, and the IT team had minimized the disruption in the account structures.

Even in cases where internal controls are in place to approve creating and changing account codes, these are sometimes short-circuited for expedient, short-sighted reasons. Downstream from all the production system activity is a data warehouse team that has been operating a financial system data warehouse since 1994. With a five-year historical window, the team must be alert to changes in all source dimensions. The new semantic meanings for the old account numbers must be detected by the extract routine so that new dimension rows can be created. The account number can be carried into the data warehouse design, but cannot serve as the key to the dimension. The combination of the account number and the description is the true logical key, while an artificial warehouse key is used for indexes and joins.

The Income Statement

The income statement is a summary of revenue, expenses, and income for a given period of time. Revenue accounts include sales and earnings from investments. Expense accounts include depreciation expenses, salaries, monthly rent, and travel expenses. Because the income statement is a summary of activity, not a snapshot, the measures that make up the line items on the income statement are additive.

Refer back to Figure 9.7, where we tracked the value of a receivables asset over two quarters. The sum of the debits against the account, assuming no cash sales to Tinker Motors, also represents revenue for the respective month and quarter. Revenue from all sales is called, not surprisingly, *sales revenue*. Revenue from interest-bearing accounts and other investments is recorded and presented separately from sales revenue. Sales revenue is also sometimes referred to as *revenue from operations*. This distinction is important for industries such as insurance, in which substantial gains and losses can result from nonoperational investment activity. Conversely, if a typical company was to break even on operations but make a large gain on stockholdings, it would not claim a profit on operations; after all, the company is not in the investment business. Mutual funds, on the other hand, report primarily on gains from investments and management fees, their only sources of revenue.

Expenses are categorized as either costs incurred in producing a product or costs incurred operating the business. In manufacturing, the cost of materials, factory labor, plant depreciation, and other related expenses are grouped together and called the *cost of goods sold*. For a retail store chain, the cost of goods sold is simply the cost of the products sold in the various stores. For a professional services firm, the product is labor, and the general rule is to use the cost of the billed labor as the cost of services sold. If we subtract product costs from sales revenue, we arrive at gross income. From gross income, we subtract sales, administrative, and general expenses to arrive at EBIT, or earnings before interest and taxes. Net income is EBIT less taxes and interest.

To create an income statement data warehouse, we create two fact tables: one for expenses, and one for income. These fact tables will share the time and account owner dimensions from the balance sheet subject area. Other dimensions are added to each fact table based on the analytical requirements of the business and the level of detail captured in the source systems. For sales revenue, the source of income is usually identifiable by tracing a ledger transaction back to the receivables application. For cash expenses, the payee can be retrieved from the payables application. For noncash expenses like depreciation, the specific chargeable fixed asset might be available from the fixed asset application. The design of the two fact tables, with common and unique dimensions, is shown in Figure 9.9.

In this case, it is not necessary to create summary tables for period income statements—the additive facts in the revenue and expense fact tables are simply aggregated by period to produce the income statements. The income statement relies on the expense_type and revenue_type dimensions to categorize transactions. These dimensions contain the desired breakdown of revenue and expenses. For our manufacturing company, revenue is categorized by product family, industry, and division. Revenue from investments and other offbeat sources is also identified. Expenses are broken into specific categories (cost of goods sold, sales and administrative, interest, and taxes), types, and subtypes. Sample rows are shown in Tables 9.6 and 9.7.

The company generates most of its revenue from sales of automotive parts, only some of which are represented here. Revenue is also generated by performing contract plant engineering and setup for other manufacturers. The last row in the

Figure 9.9 The income statement schema.

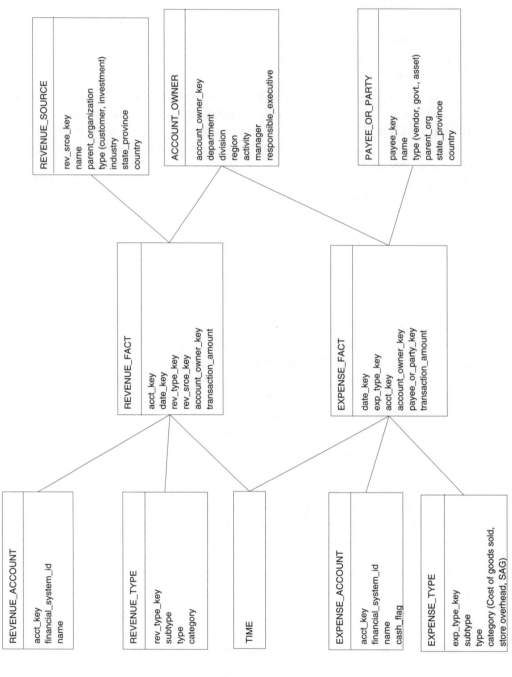

REVENUE_SOURCE

rev_srce_key
name
parent_organization
type (customer, investment)
industry
state_province
country

ACCOUNT_OWNER

account_owner_key
department
division
region
activity
manager
responsible_executive

PAYEE_OR_PARTY

payee_key
name
type (vendor, govt., asset)
parent_org
state_province
country

REVENUE_FACT

acct_key
date_key
rev_type_key
rev_srce_key
account_owner_key
transaction_amount

EXPENSE_FACT

date_key
exp_type_key
acct_key
account_owner_key
payee_or_party_key
transaction_amount

REVENUE_ACCOUNT

acct_key
financial_system_id
name

REVENUE_TYPE

rev_type_key
subtype
type
category

TIME

EXPENSE_ACCOUNT

acct_key
financial_system_id
name
cash_flag

EXPENSE_TYPE

exp_type_key
subtype
type
category (Cost of goods sold,
store overhead, SAG)

Table 9.6 Revenue Types

ID	Product Family	Industry	Division
1	Vehicle seats	New vehicle manufacturing	U.S. manufacturing
2	Vehicle seats	Mass transit	U.S. manufacturing
3	Vehicle seats	Vehicle replacement parts	U.S. manufacturing
4	Plants	New vehicle manufacturing	Production engineering
5	Plant engineering	New vehicle manufacturing	Production engineering
6	Interior fixtures	New vehicle manufacturing	U.S. manufacturing
7	None	None	U.S. finance

dimension is associated with income from investments or other activities. No product or industry is associated with this income; it is credited to the headquarters finance entity.

Table 9.7 Expense Subtypes, Types, and Categories

ID	Subtype	Type	Category
1	Component parts	Direct materials	Cost of goods sold
2	Production sheeting	Indirect materials	Cost of goods sold
3	Unpaid receivables	Bad debt	Sales, admin, and general
4	Disputed charges	Bad debt	Sales, admin, and general
5	Production equipment depreciation	Manufacturing overhead	Cost of goods sold
6	Plant depreciation	Manufacturing overhead	Cost of goods sold
7	Headquarters building depreciation	Property depreciation	Sales, admin, and general
8	Officers' salaries	Indirect labor	Sales, admin, and general
9	Corporate income tax	Federal taxes	Taxes
...	...	...	...

The actual breakdown of expenses will be determined by the way in which each organization's accounting system is structured. In this example, there are two categories of expenses that include depreciation expenses. The company's cost of goods sold calculations include the depreciation of production equipment and manufacturing plants. Depreciation on the headquarters building, unrelated to production, is considered a sales, administration, and general expense. Cost of goods sold is a complex figure that takes into account costs from throughout the organization. The categories and amounts are usually precalculated in the financial accounting system, and the data warehouse team can simply extract and load these values.

With the expense and revenue fact tables populated, the company can create the income statement seen in Report 9.3. The amounts in each fact table are additive, with positive revenue values and negative expense values. The income statement can be created for any period.

Report 9.3 Dover Auto Parts' income statement.

Dover Auto Parts Income Statement For the Month of March 1997		
	March	**YTD**
Sales	$ 17,800,000	$ 49,700,000
Cost of Goods Sold	$ 14,500,000	$ 41,000,000
Gross Income	$ 3,300,000	$ 8,700,000
Operating Expenses		
Sales Expense	$ 1,400,000	$ 3,400,000
Admin. Expense	$ 1,200,000	$ 4,100,000
Other Expenses	$ 340,000	$ 780,000
Total	$ 2,940,000	$ 8,280,000
Operating Income (EBIT)	$ 360,000	$ 420,000
Interest Expenses	$ 29,000	$ 68,000
Pretax Income	$ 331,000	$ 352,000
Income Taxes	$ 109,230	$ 116,160
Net Income	$ 221,770	$ 235,840

As in the balance sheet example, we can drill into the income statement to see more detail. We can also take a slice of specific expenses or revenue across time. If the company is interested in revenue-to-cost ratios, the income statement detail is the best place to get a broad perspective. It is possible to discover interesting relationships among cost and revenue categories using these fact tables. In Report 9.4, we see the relationship between revenue and bad debt expenses.

From this chart, we may surmise that the company has pumped up revenue to customers less inclined to meet their debt obligations. For example, the company may have expanded into overseas markets without establishing sound credit policies in foreign countries. Perhaps many of the customers in one region have been beset by currency problems and economic stagnation. The company can easily calculate the ratio of revenue to bad debt and drill into operational details by customer or division.

Income Statements for Other Industries

A retailer's income statement will have different revenue and expense categories. A large electronics chain store will have income from sales, service contracts, delivery, and interest on credit extended to customers. Where a manufacturer's expenses are chiefly related to producing products, the retailer's are related to operating sales outlets. Expenses include a cost of goods sold for products sold in a given period, store labor, store rent and other overhead, indirect salaries, and advertising. Cost of goods sold is simply the wholesale cost of merchandise paid by the retailer to suppliers. Many expenses will be charged to a specific store location. There is a great deal of complexity involved in allocating all costs and revenue to specific stores and products, and the design of the income statement schema can be more complex as a result. For now, we will simply add an attribute

Report 9.4 Revenue and bad debt—questionable customers?

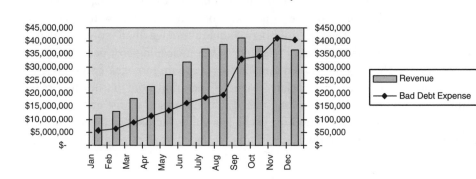

Revenue vs. Bad Debt Expense

to the account owner dimension to track store expenses. The assumption behind this design is that expenses are allocated to stores either directly or through an allocation methodology. The design for the retailer's income statement schema is shown in Figure 9.10.

Allocating Costs: The Challenge of Segment Reporting

The proper allocation of costs in a manufacturing, retail, or project accounting environment is the most vexing problem when designing the financial data warehouse. Companies would like to track revenue and costs in a consistent manner. The typical company has two or three operational concepts that are of most interest. These operational concepts include markets, products, brands, geographic regions, divisions, customers, retail units, channels, and suppliers. From this list, a company can choose the way it manages and organizes its operations and then attempt to track revenue and costs specific to each operational concept. These concepts are often referred to as *segments*. In Chapter 10, "Profitability," we will discuss profitability and profitability reporting. As a foundation for that discussion, we will examine cost allocation issues here. The objective is not to create a comprehensive design for every situation, but rather to provide a framework from which readers can build meaningful models for specific businesses.

A retailer views the world through operating units: stores, restaurants, kiosks, or other outlets. Each unit is treated as a microcompany, with revenue and expenses. While it is usually easy to separate revenue by store, separating expenses is more challenging. Some expenses, like utilities, janitorial services, fixtures, and store employee labor are obviously associated with the store, but these expenses may or may not be easily assigned to a store specifically. A company may sign an agreement with a local firm to clean all its locations. The contract price may be negotiated at a single monthly charge for all stores in an area. If the vendor does not separate the price of cleaning each store, the company must choose an allocation method. The most reasonable method is probably an equivalent allocation, contract price divided by the number of covered stores, assuming that all the stores are similar in size. If not, the company may choose to allocate costs by square footage. The total number of square footage in all stores is calculated and divided into the cleaning price to arrive at a cleaning cost per square foot per month. This amount is then applied to the square footage of an individual store. In the case of expenses related to store operations, the journey to a reasonable allocation is not always a long one. Table 9.8 presents a list of store expenses and an allocation method for each. The value "actual" means the store will be charged the actual amount, discernible in the company's records or accounting system.

Figure 9.10 Retailer's income statement schema.

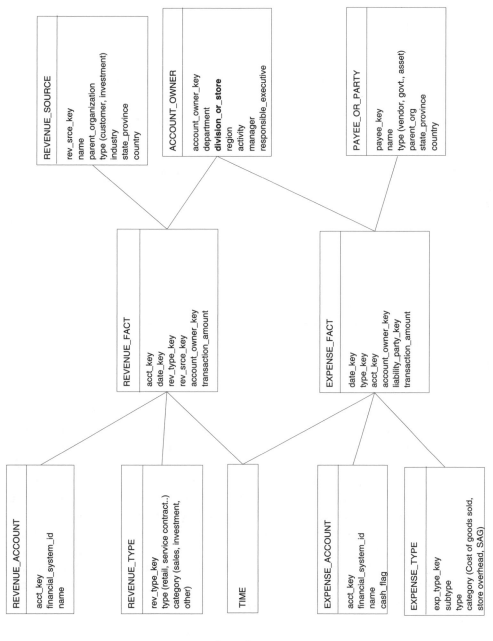

REVENUE_ACCOUNT

acct_key
financial_system_id
name

REVENUE_TYPE

rev_type_key
type (retail, service contract..)
category (sales, investment, other)

TIME

REVENUE_SOURCE

rev_srce_key
name
parent_organization
type (customer, investment)
industry
state_province
country

ACCOUNT_OWNER

account_owner_key
department
division_or_store
region
activity
manager
responsible_executive

REVENUE_FACT

acct_key
date_key
rev_type_key
rev_srce_key
account_owner_key
transaction_amount

EXPENSE_FACT

date_key
type_key
acct_key
account_owner_key
liability_party_key
transaction_amount

PAYEE_OR_PARTY

payee_key
name
type (vendor, govt., asset)
parent_org
state_province
country

EXPENSE_ACCOUNT

acct_key
financial_system_id
name
cash_flag

EXPENSE_TYPE

exp_type_key
subtype
type
category (Cost of goods sold, store overhead, SAG)

Table 9.8 Cost Allocation Methods

Cost	Allocation Method	Expense Type
Cost of goods sold	Monthly FIFO valuation	Cost of goods sold
Store electricity	Actual	Administrative
Cleaning services	Retail square	Administrative footage
Store fixtures	Store revenue	Administrative
Employee labor	Actual	General
Land lease expenses	Actual	General
Rent and mall charges	Actual	General
District manager salaries	Store revenue	Administrative
Regional advertising	Store revenue	Sales
Store-specific advertising	Actual	Sales

Cost of goods sold is calculated using the FIFO method of inventory valuation. This method assumes that goods sold in an accounting period were the ones that had been in inventory for the longest period of time. For our electronics store, televisions that entered the merchandise inventory in January are assumed to have sold before those that entered in February. This method is useful in valuing inventory without capturing the cost of each specific unit as it is sold at retail. Manufacturers use similar techniques to value raw materials and finished goods inventory. Today, many companies calculate cost of goods sold at a much finer level of detail, although these calculations may only be used for internal pricing decisions and not for financial reporting. The improvements in inventory costing are possible because of improved information technology, especially bar-coding and scanning of inventory items from receipt to final sale.

Other costs are allocated to stores at the actual cost. These include general, sales, and administrative expenses. It is important to recognize that the determining factor in allocation is the traceability of the cost itself, not the type of cost. Most companies would like to trace costs to the lowest level of detail practical without creating undue operational or technical burdens. The allocation method should also be a fair representation of reality. Consider the advertising cost types presented in Table 9.8. The first, regional advertising, is allocated to stores based on the revenue each store generates in the month the advertising is presented. Store-specific advertising is charged directly to the store that incurs the cost. With this model, the company can provide some autonomy to store managers to boost location revenues and complement regional advertising. Because the cost is tied directly to the store, the company has a good foundation of accountability. Store revenue may or may not be the ideal allocation method for this cost, but it has the advantage of being readily available. While surveying individual customers about whether they were drawn to a store by a regional advertisement might determine which store received the most benefit, it is costly and intrusive to operations.

In manufacturing, cost allocation methods apply to both manufacturing overhead and SAG costs. Activity-based costing has gained favor in the manufacturing community as an effective way to manage and apply overhead costs more objectively. Traditionally, factory overhead was applied using broad-based measures like machine hours, or direct labor hours charged to a job or product. Today, such methods are either supplemented by or replaced with more refined activity based allocation methods. Service industries as well can use allocation methods to better apply SAG costs to revenue. In all cases, it is imperative that the company first develop a clear understanding of what operational concepts must be supported. This allows both operational system managers and data warehouse managers to configure their environments to collect the proper data and provide meaningful analytical capabilities.

Remember that a business will likely need to model and manage more than one operational concept. The retailer may manage primarily by store, but there may be a need to manage also by geographic region, country, division, or chain. A manufacturer may consider product, brand, and market to be the most meaningful segments to manage, while a bank considers product, market segment, and region to be of paramount importance. Regardless of the operational concepts considered vital, no reporting can be done from the data warehouse unless the data is first captured in the operational systems. Chapter 10, "Profitability," describes the two most important operational concepts: products and customers. Chapter 15, "Interviewing," provides a framework for designing an enterprise-wide analytical environment—some might call it a *data warehouse*—using these operational concepts as guideposts to success.

Professional Services

Two differences come to mind when examining a professional service or contracting firm. The professional services concern has a different income statement line for cost of goods sold consisting primarily of direct labor and travel expenses. Gross income for a professional services firm is calculated by subtracting direct labor from sales. Both professional services and contracting firms are religious about project accounting codes, and most costs are tracked against specific projects within the organization. Their accounting systems usually contain project codes that are used to record project costs and revenue. While these systems approximate building project- and customer-level income statements, users and data warehouse designers should be mindful that some costs will not be directly charged against a project. An allocation method must be developed for these costs as well; the most significant difference in the design of the income statement schema for these businesses other than the inclusion of a project dimension. Other differences are simply reflected in the revenue_type and expense_type dimensions. Table 9.9 depicts sample rows from the revenue_type dimension of a consulting company.

This dimension represents the various services the company offers. The company is organized into vertical industry practices and offers service lines across those practices. Within each service line, specific services are sold to customers. This design assumes that revenue transactions are traceable to both the practice and service.

Table 9.9 Consulting Company Revenue Types

ID	Service	Service Line	Practice
1	Process design	Management consulting	Oil & gas
2	Process assessment	Management consulting	Oil & gas
3	SAP installation	Technology consulting	Oil & gas
4	Baan installation	Technology consulting	Oil & gas
5	Audit planning	Tax and audit	Oil & gas
6	Process design	Management consulting	Financial services
...	...	...	...

Cash Flow Statement

Our final financial report for this chapter is the cash flow statement. Both large and small businesses require cash to operate. Cash is constantly flowing into and out of the business, often in ways that seem unrelated to operations. Goods sold in April may not be paid for until May, June, or July. The income statement and balance sheet give a perspective on operations that is cash neutral, whereas the cash flow statement attempts to describe where cash is coming from and going to in an organization. Fortunately, the information required for the cash flow statement is already recorded in our financial reporting data warehouse.

The cash flow statement usually contains three sections, each with a different purpose. These sections are:

Cash flow from operations. Summarizes the cash impact of operations. There are three methods for presenting and calculating this figure: *direct*, *indirect*, and *reconciliation*. The Financial Accounting Standards Board recommends the direct method, and as nonaccountants, we would be foolish to question the Board's guidance on this one. The basic formula is net income plus depreciation less any changes in the value of short-term assets and liabilities. These include accounts receivable, inventory, prepaid expenses, and accounts payable. All of these items are carried in our balance sheet design.

Cash flow from investments. Summarizes investment activity, including purchases and dispositions of long-term assets. The sale of long-term securities and payments received from creditors, like a subsidiary, are also included. Changes in these values are tracked on the balance sheet.

Cash flow from financing. Summarizes increases in obligations to creditors and stockholders, including increases in lines of credit, dividends, and changes in retained earnings. These are tracked in either the liabilities or owners' equity balance sheet summary fact tables.

The cash flow statement combines information from the balance sheet and income statement for a period and creates a snapshot of changes in the cash position of the company. We can create a cash flow statement using the information in the balance sheet summary fact tables and the revenue and expense fact tables. The 1996 year-end cash flow statement for Dover Auto Parts is presented in Report 9.5.

Report 9.5 Statement of cash flows for 1996.

Statement of Cash Flow - 1996 Year End
Dover Auto Parts, Ltd.

Cash From Operations

Net Income		3,100,000
Depreciation Expense		1,500,000
Net Income and Depreciation		4,600,000
Changes in Short Term Operating Assets		
AR	(800,000)	
Inventory	(300,000)	
AP	124,000	
Other	28,000	
Cash Flow from Operations		**3,652,000**

Cash Flow from Investments

Sale of Factory	250,000	
Fixed Asset Purchases	(600,000)	
Cash Flow from Investments		**(350,000)**

Cash Flow from Financing

Decrease in long term debt	(1,700,000)	
Distributions to shareholders	-	
Cash Flow from Financing		**(1,700,000)**

Net Change in Cash Position	**1,602,000**

The cash flow statement is an important financial analysis tool. It assists investors and other stakeholders in the quest for understanding by revealing the ebb and flow of cash among the various accounts of the company. In the case of Dover Auto Parts, we see that the company had a substantial positive cash flow from operations that was not passed along to shareholders; instead the company used the money to decrease long-term debt. This may not have satisfied some shareholders who were looking for dividends, but other factors may have required the company to otherwise make use of this inflow of cash. For example, the company's operating line of credit may have a covenant requiring a certain ratio of assets to long-term liabilities. Paying down this long-term debt may have been unavoidable.

Summing Up Financial Reporting

This chapter described constructing a data warehouse to support financial accounting needs. Remember that financial accounting is more concerned with accuracy than timeliness. The data must be right, because the audience for the data is demanding. In building the financial accounting data warehouse, the team must use only approved sources, resolve all extract and loading issues with certitude, and work with accounting experts to prepare reports and configure ad hoc tools. This chapter also gave short shrift to the complexity behind some important accounting concepts like inventory costing, prepaid expenses, overhead allocation, and profit from cash flow. The data warehouse professional working on an accounting data warehouse will encounter concepts and topics that are simply beyond the scope of this book. The design presented here is a framework for simplified financial reporting and analysis. It requires adaptation and customization in every case.

The world of accounting is changing rapidly to adapt to new competitive business demands. New methods for allocating costs are being developed to manage markets more aggressively and in shorter time increments. The future will demand income statements of greater detail and frequency. Balance sheets for knowledge companies will include intellectual assets that must be valued and depreciated, like factory equipment. The breadth of data visible to the members of the data warehouse team often exposes them to the untold complexity of operational data that complicates this future vision. Ironically, it also exposes them to the potential of an integrated view of corporate information. The data warehouse team sees the value of integration first, but also witnesses the complexity and confusion of source data firsthand. Understanding the fundamental requirements of financial reporting will help the data warehouse team adapt to changes in financial accounting, with a minimum of pain.

PROFITABILITY

"**W**hat is our most profitable product?" "Who are our most profitable customers?" The ability to answer these questions represents a significant competitive advantage, but a surprising number of companies can only take guesses. A data warehouse designed to analyze profitability can deliver tremendous value to managers.

Whatever the value proposition of a business's product is, the business must realize enough revenues in delivering it to cover the associated costs. Successful businesses are able to quickly identify products for which this balance can be established. Steps can often be taken to tip the scales in favor of profitability for products that are in the red, but if allowed to continue, the delivery of a losing proposition will eventually result in financial ruin for a business. The sooner successful and unsuccessful products are identified, the better.

We refer to the process of studying and controlling product profitability as *Integrated Product Management*, because it requires an integrated view of many processes within the business. In the first part of this chapter, we will study the product management needs of a retailer, and learn how a carefully designed series of data marts can be used to serve these needs.

For some businesses, profitability analysis can be extended beyond the product to incorporate the customer. It is worth the cost of taking steps to retain a good customer, but the same effort is wasted on one who does not generate revenue. When a business factors the customer into its study of profitability, we call it *Integrated Customer Management*. In the second part of this chapter, we will learn how a bank can make use of a data warehouse to meet its customer management needs.

Product Profitability

At its most basic, the profitability of a product is measured as the difference between the revenue generated by the product and the costs associated with the product. While product revenues are obvious and easily identified, the cost components are complicated. Costs are broken down in a number of ways, depending on reporting purposes. Since we are interested in product profitability, we will focus on the costs that the business associates with products. This association may be direct, or it may be an indirect association accomplished by one of several allocation approaches.

We will break costs down around major business processes. The first category is perhaps the most obvious: the cost to produce or acquire the product. These costs are usually referred to as *product costs*, because they are maintained in inventory accounts until the product is actually sold. At the time of sale, these costs are recognized as *expenses*. They appear on income statements as *cost of goods sold*.

Key Business Term

Product costs. Costs incurred in producing or acquiring items in finished goods or merchandise inventory.

Product costs, sometimes called *manufacturing costs*, are recognized as expenses only when the product is sold. At that time, they are itemized as *cost of goods sold*.

For a manufacturer, product costs include the cost of raw materials used to create the end item, the cost of labor contributing to the production process, and manufacturing overhead. Manufacturing overhead may incorporate a number of indirect costs. Businesses that do not manufacture products still have product costs. Distributors and merchandisers have acquisition costs, representing the price they pay to acquire the goods they will resell. Value-added processes introduce additional product costs as well.

There are many nonmanufacturing costs. Although some of these costs can be associated with products, the business recognizes the expense when the cost is incurred, rather than at the time of sale. For this reason, they are often referred to as *periodic costs*. One category of periodic costs centers around the cost of selling the product.

Cost of sale includes expenditures on efforts to generate consumer interest in a product, expenditures involved in actually selling the product, and expenditures involved in the fulfillment process. Examples of these costs include product advertising and promotion, commissions paid to salespeople, and shipping or delivery charges. Our next category of costs centers around activities that take place after orders have been fulfilled.

Nonconformance costs are incurred when a customer is dissatisfied with the product, requires assistance or replacement, or returns the product for any reason. Situations where nonconformance costs are incurred include returns of defective merchandise, exchanges for different size or color, warranty service for a malfunctioning product, and technical support.

Key Business Terms

Cost of sale. Costs incurred in selling and delivering the product to customers.

Nonconformance costs. Expenses incurred when a customer returns or exchanges a product for any reason.

The specifics to be found in each of these cost categories will vary by industry, and even by business. The degree to which costs can be identified determines how well a business will be able to assess product profitability. There are three factors at work that make cost identification and profitability analysis challenging.

First, measuring cost factors can be difficult, and allocating them to individual products still harder. For example, how does a business compute the costs incurred by keeping a product in inventory? The formulas for this measurement can be complex. If a retailer produces a newspaper advertisement promoting 10 products, how does it allocate the cost of the promotion to individual products? Here, the decision may be based on prominence or the number of inches of copy devoted to each product. In both examples, convincing cases can be made to take a cost measurement in a number of ways. Luckily for us, these are managerial decisions and not systems decisions. The approaches chosen by the business often evidence themselves inside a number of transactional systems.

Second, some cost elements may be available at different grains than others. For example, sales and return data include store location, while warranty service does not. When studying a particular combination of cost and revenue components, the analyst must set a scope of analysis common to all elements involved.

Comparison of sales and warranty costs will require aggregating sales data across stores, while a study of sales and returns alone can be performed at the level of the store. For the data warehouse design team, profitability analysis will require careful planning of multiple subject areas with conformed dimensions and appropriate aggregations.

Third, accurately modeled cost data can be easily misused. For example, not all components of product cost become available simultaneously. To accurately study product profitability, the analyst must use a suitable time frame. Production costs are usually known at the time of sale, but marketing and fulfillment costs will not be available until later. As such, it may be more appropriate to study product profitability at the quarterly or annual level, rather than by the week or month.

The sophistication of profitability analysis depends on the degree to which cost measurements can be taken, the quality of the data warehouse design used to record them, and the care with which profitability reports are constructed. We will study these three components of product profitability as they apply to the department store introduced in Chapter 2, "Sales."

Retail Revisited

In Chapter 2, we observed that merchandisers are concerned with effective utilization of resources to move products. Department stores have limited space in which to display the items they sell, and it does not make good business sense to dedicate a lot of space to slow-moving items, unless they carry high margin. Low-margin products are also not worthy of precious shelf space, unless they are fast movers. Some items, such as winter coats, can only be expected to sell during certain times of the year.

The department store's sales data mart, depicted in Figure 2.4, serves as the foundation for profitability analysis. The sales schema has significant impact, enabling the retailer to study movement of product and how it is influenced by factors like price, supplier, and time of year, but the sales data mart alone cannot tell the retailer which products are more profitable. The profitability of a product can be assessed only when sales revenues are compared with costs.

What are the costs associated with the products for sale at the department store? We can identify costs in each of the major categories we have discussed. Product costs are the most obvious. The department store purchases all of its products from suppliers. There are also costs associated with keeping items in warehouses prior to their placement on the retail floor. Acquisition requires a significant amount of human resources, but the number of products and number of transactions make it very difficult to accurately allocate these indirect costs to individual products. Some activity-based costing techniques were discussed in Chapter 9, "Financial Reporting."

Cost of sale for the merchandiser includes marketing, and may include floor space and labor. The department store advertises products, promotes them with "giveaways." Some marketing costs cannot be directly attributed to individual products, but many can. Floor space and labor appear to be relevant to the cost of sales, but merchandisers are likely to categorize these as administrative or overhead costs. No matter how they are categorized, they usually cannot be attributed to individual products.

The primary nonconformance costs for the department store are generated by returns. Already discussed in Chapter 4, "Fulfillment," the return of defective items offsets sales amounts, particularly when a refund is given. When a store credit is issued, the return may not have significant impact on the overall profitability of the business, but it does impact the profitability of the product that was brought back. Returns also generate labor costs, which the department store managed to quantify in Chapter 4.

By combining each of these cost components with sales revenue, the retailer can develop a clear picture of product profitability. As we will see, each cost stems from a particular process with its own set of unique detail. One by one, the business can bring on line data marts centering around the individual processes. Together, these data marts form a data warehouse enabling integrated product management.

Modeling Department Store Costs

We've suggested that each of the cost categories deserves its own data mart. How did we come to that conclusion? Consider the dimensional detail that would be available with each cost category. Table 10.1 cross-references several of the cost categories we have identified with dimensional detail that would accompany cost measures. Each type of cost has an associated time component; we have indicated the level of detail to which time data is available or meaningful.

Each cost category includes product and time detail, but the level at which the time component is available varies, and none of the remaining three dimensions are shared across all cost categories. Were we to model all these cost components in a single fact table, we would be forced to choose the lowest common denominator for

Table 10.1 Dimensions Associated with Cost Categories

	Dimension				
	Time	Product	Store	Return Reason	Promotion
Cost of goods sold	daily	✔	✔		✔
Marketing costs	monthly	✔			✔
Nonconformance costs	daily	✔	✔	✔	

our grain. Any dimension not shared by all processes would be eliminated, and time would be summarized at the monthly level. While this lowest-common-denominator approach would facilitate product profitability analysis, it would eliminate other forms of cost analysis that focus on the individual subject areas. For example, it would not be possible to analyze the reason for a return.

If construction of a single fact table saved time and money, these deficiencies might be acceptable, but as we pointed out in Chapter 3, "Marketing," the time it takes to build a subject area is not a function of the number of dimensions or facts; rather, it is a function of the number of source systems. Whether we build several fact tables or one, our cost data is likely to take about the same amount of time to load into the data warehouse. It is therefore logical to choose the solution that can deliver more answers: separate fact tables.

We've also seen in previous chapters that combining information associated with separate processes into a single fact table leads to reporting problems—because measures are sampled at different times, a large number of zero values will be recorded for each measure. One method for working around this problem is appropriate in limited situations, but would render our profitability reports difficult to produce. See the sidebar later in this chapter for details.

We expect a single source system for each of our cost components. Since we are delivering them in separate fact tables, it means we can bring them online incrementally. This approach has the added benefit of making some of the cost data available sooner. We will prioritize them in terms of their benefits to the business to maximize initial impact.

Figure 10.1 shows the set of fact and dimension tables that will be necessary for integrated product management. As you can see, diagrams that include multiple star schemas can become intricate. In the name of readability, we have omitted dimension attributes and measures not directly related to profitability.

Figure 10.1 A data warehouse supporting integrated product management.

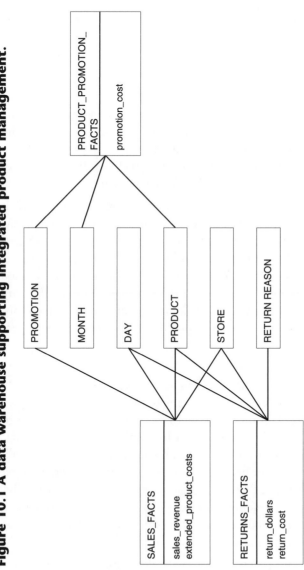

* Only measures relevant to profitability are shown.

TIP

When diagramming a schema that includes many fact tables, it is often useful to produce a matrix like the one shown in Table 10.1, or the one in Table 8.3. Alternatively, diagram only the names of the tables, without detailed attributes, using different symbols to differentiate fact tables and dimension tables. The matrix or diagram can be supplemented by detailed diagrams of the individual star schemas.

Product Costs

By definition, product costs are recognized at the time of sale. This means that we can record the product costs within our existing sales_facts table. They occur at the same grain, and are measured simultaneously with the sale. We've added extended_product_cost to the table. We have included the extended cost, rather than a unit cost, because it is a fully additive measure.

Since the business recognizes this cost at the time of sale, the work in computing this cost is already being done, and is available in our financials system. In many situations, very sophisticated processing is required to produce this number. Overhead costs including indirect labor and the cost of keeping the item in inventory may be represented in this computation. The financials system must correlate quantities purchased with quantities sold in order to compute the proper cost, and incorporate formulas to compute the indirect components. After verifying its validity with managers, we'll use the computation that is already being performed.

Return Costs

The returns fact table should look familiar. As we saw in Chapter 4, "Fulfillment," the return_dollars measure shows the amount refunded or credited to customers returning products. This dollar amount is an important part of the profitability picture of a product. We must deduct it from sales_revenue so that we do not credit products with revenue that was subsequently lost. This is equally important, whether the customer got his or her money back or took a credit toward the purchase of something else. Either way, the original product purchased has been returned, and the sale amount must be deducted. When a customer exchanges a product for the same product, the revenue from the original sale can stand; the return_dollars amount is zero.

In Chapter 4, we pointed out that the department store also tries to quantify the processing costs of a return. Returns require maintaining a customer service desk, a restocking process to return undamaged items to the shelves, and interaction with suppliers when items are found to be defective. The department store had a standard list of costs per return for each of the types of return, as computed by management consultants, and we used these numbers to calculate total cost of a return in some of our reports. Because it is a valid indirect cost that can be used in evaluating the profitability of products, we have added the cost of a return to the returns_facts table. These costs will now be computed during the load rather than in reports. It will be important to keep the formulas up to date.

Marketing Costs

Our next fact table, product_promotion_facts, contains marketing costs that can be allocated to products. A promotion such as a newspaper advertisement typically promotes more than one item. The costs of the promotion are allocated to the items promoted in the product_promotion_facts table. The allocation of costs to products is a manual process, so it is only practical for the merchandiser to collect these costs at a monthly level. If store were to be included in the grain of the product_promotion_facts table, the cost must also be allocated to a store.

It can be tempting to store the promotion cost directly in the promotion dimension, bypassing the need for an additional fact table; however, we want to be able to exploit the additivity of the promotion costs. If placed within a dimension table, we would be forced not to include information from other tables when aggregating the measure. To do so would potentially cause SQL to count a single promotion multiple times.

TIP

Never query the sum of a value in a dimension table; relationships to other tables may cause it to be counted multiple times. Measures should always be stored in a fact table.

Product Profitability Reports

Let's assume that the various costs will be brought online one process area at a time. The data warehouse team works with managers to determine the cost categories with the most immediate benefit. Based on their consultations, the first cost category to be brought online is product costs, which are simply added to the existing sales schema. At this point, a rudimentary margin calculation can be made, and we produce Report 10.1.

A Costs Fact Table?

Businesses incur many different kinds of costs associated with their products. Because a different combination of dimensional attributes surrounded each cost, we made a case for treating each type of cost in its own fact table. Detail not common across cost types is not lost, and there is likely to be little difference in the amount of time required to build the solution.

We also suggested that when the business sacrifices dimensional detail in order to create a single fact table, a large number of zero values will make reporting difficult. Assuming each cost measure is recorded in its own column, we must record all measures whenever one is available. We encountered this situation in Chapter 8, "Budgets and Spending," when considering combining budgeting, commitment, and payment measures.

In limited situations, an alternative design approach makes the single fact table more appealing; rather than record each cost category in its own column, our fact table has a single cost measure. An associated dimension records the cost type. Now, each row represents a single cost, and the sparsity of the different processes can be preserved. We considered this approach for our telco schema in Chapter 3, "Marketing," and rejected it because it would make reporting quite difficult. Report column headers representing different costs would be extremely difficult to produce, since the data would be returned in different rows, rather than columns. A report like 10.3 becomes difficult to produce, even when using tools that support pivot tables.

In other situations, however, cost categories in separate rows are exactly what is needed. An income statement, for example, usually itemizes costs on separate lines. A design incorporating a single dollar amount and expense type may be appropriate. This is the approach we took in designing Chapter 9's income statement schema. Shown in Figure 9.9, it includes an expense fact table with a single dollar amount; the cost category is found in the expense_type dimension. In combination with an income star, the expense schema is used to produce the income statement. Note that many reporting tools can produce such a report even when costs are returned in columns.

Report 10.1 The beginnings of profitability.

Product Profitability
Winter Coats
1999 Season

Brand	Sales Revenue	Product Costs	Margin	As % of Revenue
Duck South	$41,093	$39,000	$2,093	5%
NHL Logo	$4,674	$3,830	$844	18%
Chimney Rock	$240,125	$181,542	$58,583	24%
Templeton	$60,603	$47,222	$13,381	22%
USFL Logo	$18,384	$14,768	$3,616	20%
Wee Kids	$94,956	$79,668	$15,288	16%

This simple report is constructed by querying the sales_facts table, retrieving brand and the sum of sales_dollars and extended_product_cost. Margin is computed as the difference between the two, and expressed as a percentage of sales by dividing by sales_dollars.

Once return_facts and product_promotion_facts are brought online, we can complete the profitability picture. In Report 10.2, the profitability of the same products is recalculated using the additional cost data. Most of the profitability metrics look lower now; two products have fallen into the red. We also see that the relative profitability of our products has changed: Templeton now falls behind NHL Logo and Wee Kids.

Like the fulfillment reports found in Chapter 4, this report requires drilling across fact tables, only this time we have three: sales_facts, return_facts, and product_promotion_facts. The drill across is performed via three queries. Each query retrieves brand and the sum of the appropriate measure—sales_revenue, extended_product_cost, return_dollars, and so forth. Each of the three queries is constrained for the same time period. Return_facts has two time dimensions; we choose the return date for this report because the return is a period cost. In the report, the cost categories have been laid out. A subtotal for all costs is provided, then each cost is subtracted from the revenue amount to yield profitability in dollars. Lastly, profit as a percentage of sales is calculated by dividing the profit dollars by sales.

The retailer's data warehouse has been architected so that it can be built incrementally. One by one, data marts representing new cost centers are brought

Report 10.2 Complete profitability.

Product Profitabilty
Winter Coats
1999 Season

| Brand | Sales Revenue | Product Costs | Nonconformance Costs | | | Sales Costs | | | As % of |
		Product Costs	Return Dollars	Return Processing	Return Costs	Promotion Costs	Total Costs	Profitability	Revenue
Duck South	$41,093	$39,000	$1,650	$248	$1,898	$4,800	$45,698	($4,605)	-11%
NHL Logo	$4,674	$3,830	$84	$14	$98	$0	$3,928	$746	16%
Chimney Rock	$240,125	$181,542	$4,367	$888	$5,255	$6,200	$192,997	$47,128	20%
Templeton	$60,603	$47,222	$2,465	$422	$2,887	$6,200	$56,309	$4,294	7%
USFL Logo	$18,384	$14,768	$848	$124	$972	$3,200	$18,940	($556)	-3%
Wee Kids	$94,956	$79,668	$2,865	$505	$3,370	$2,000	$85,038	$9,918	10%

on line, providing new analytic capabilities and providing an increasingly accurate picture of product profitability. The retailer is able to make new judgments about which products it should and should not be selling to whomever walks into the store. Next, we'll look at how profitability is managed by a business in which the customer relationship is more formal and enduring.

Customer Profitability

The retailer carries a large number of products at significant cost. Little is known about the customers who purchase these products. Some may be repeat buyers, but repeat business is sporadic. In this situation, the profitability of individual products is an appropriate subject for analysis. When the identities of customers are known, and the nature of the product places them in continuous relationship, profitability analysis can be extended to the customer level.

Customer profitability, like product profitability, is defined as the difference between revenues and costs; however, instead of aggregating revenues and costs by product, they are aggregated by customer. A composite picture of a customer's profitability allows the business to work smarter. The demographic attributes of the most profitable customers can be used to focus sales efforts. Conversely, profitability analysis may reveal that seemingly successful marketing campaigns have attracted unprofitable customers.

Once again, the key to profitability analysis will be the degree to which the business can pinpoint costs. For businesses performing integrated customer management, we will organize costs into three categories: the cost of customer acquisition, execution costs associated with the customer relationship, and customer retention costs.

We include most marketing activities under acquisition costs. As for the merchandiser, sales costs are periodic. The money spent on marketing an offer becomes a part of the cost of any prospect who responds. For example, consider an insurance company that conducts a telemarketing campaign to acquire new customers. The cost of the campaign represents the acquisition cost of the total number of new customers enrolled.

Acquisition costs also include the costs of efforts to sell additional products to existing customers. In Chapter 3, "Marketing," we referred to this technique as *cross-selling*. A campaign for term life insurance targeted at customers with auto policies may result in the writing of 200 new policies. The cost of the campaign is part of the cost of intensifying the relationship with these 200 customers.

Execution costs are incurred in providing the customer with the goods or services that have been sold. They represent the fulfillment of the business's value proposition. A life insurance company's execution costs include sending quarterly statements to the insured, providing semiannual consultations, distribution of the prospectus or annual report of any investments made under a policy, billing and processing monthly premiums, and making distributions when necessary. The execution costs are similar to the manufacturer's product costs; they are incurred in delivering the insurance company's product to customers. Some of these costs may not be treated as product costs by management, but they can still be associated to a product and customer.

Key Business Terms

Customer acquisition costs. Expenses associated with the procurement of new customers, or with selling additional products or services to existing customers.

Execution costs. The cost of providing goods or services to the customer.

Retention costs. Costs incurred in the process of ensuring that desirable customers remain customers.

A business that is able to identify profitable customers will want to make sure they remain customers. Marketing efforts designed to keep these customers happy are known as *retention efforts*. Retention efforts may involve premiums, such as a free gift or reduced interest rate, or special products.

As was the case for Integrated Product Management, the accurate identification of individual costs will be challenging. It is also one of the keys to successful profitability analysis. Integrated customer management will bring a new challenge: accurately identifying the revenues associated with customers. Although straightforward in many service industries, this process may be difficult for many financial services companies. We're going to study integrated customer management in the context of a bank.

Banking Revisited

In Chapter 3, "Marketing," we introduced a retail bank, and produced a schema that allowed analysis of household customers over time and by account. The schema shown in Figure 3.5 was useful in establishing a picture of the customer across accounts and time. A rich set of demographic data was included so that marketers could focus their efforts.

Missing from this schema is any detail about what the customers are worth, or what they cost. The measurements required to answer these questions are not included in the model. Some banks might not even know where to begin to measure either side of the profitability equation.

We will show two ways in which the bank's schema can be extended to permit customer profitability analysis. We will start with a common, rudimentary approach to profitability assessment, which provides some benefits, but only allows customer profitability to be viewed in the context of a single product. Next, we'll develop a more comprehensive model that allows customer profitability to be measured continuously, across products. Although much more complicated, this second model will prove significantly more powerful.

Profitability Dimension: A Single-Product Approach

Many institutions, not ready to fully quantify their costs and revenues, opt to construct thumbnail profitability assessments based on simple formulae. Our bank has chosen to do just this, and it is going to begin by assessing the profitability of its credit card customers.

The bank's credit card products generate revenue on two fronts: First and foremost, a finance charge is levied against the outstanding balance under certain terms. Most banks are delighted to have customers who use their card regularly, but routinely make only the minimum payment. These customers quickly rack up finance charges, which benefit the bank. Second, the merchants who accept the card are charged a fee based on the amount of the transaction. Heavy use of the card, even by customers who tend to pay their balance in full, generates revenue for the bank.

Recall that the banking schema in Figure 3.5 captured end-of-month balance and status information for all bank products a household customer holds. In order to study the profitability of customers using bank cards, we need some information specific to credit card products. We will require the transaction dollars, and either the balance carried over from the previous period or the finance charges assessed. In terms of dimensional attributes, we will want to capture the type of card, the interest rate on the card, the grace period, and the type of grace period.

These attributes are relevant for credit card products only, and are not applicable to other types of accounts, such as deposit accounts or loans. We will

Figure 10.2 Custom credit card schema.

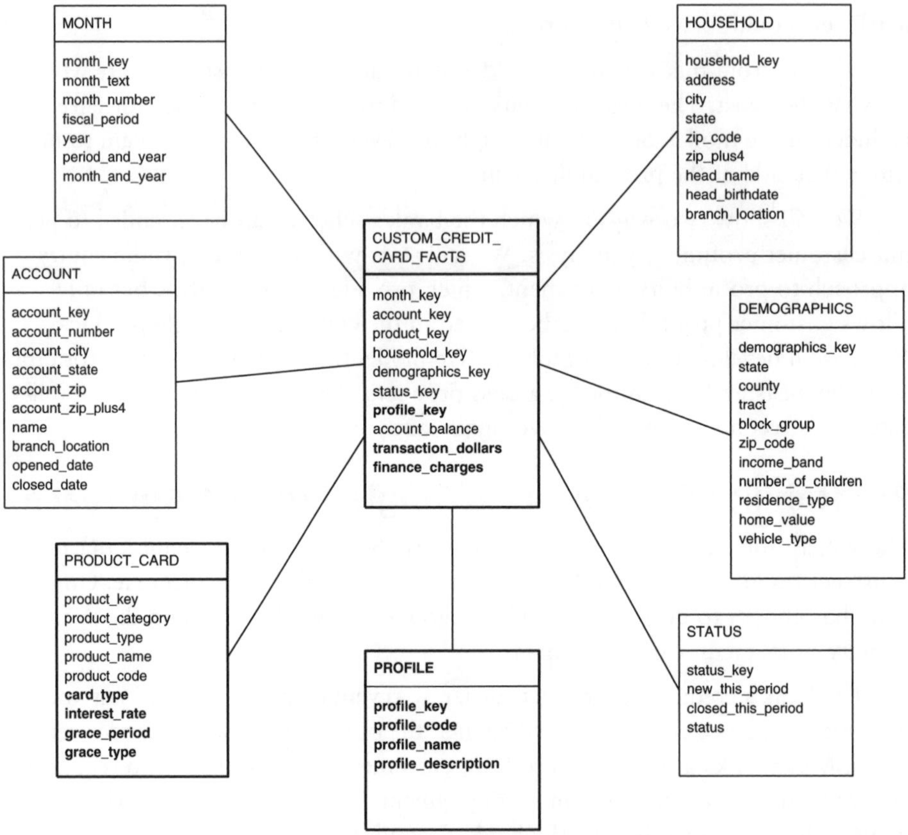

Custom credit card attributes are shown in bold.
The core schema is shown in Figure 3.5.

leave the original schema untouched, and develop another schema specifically for the analysis of credit cards, containing all the attributes of the original schema, plus the custom attributes required for card products. The schema in Figure 3.5 is the *core* schema; it carries attributes shared by all products and nothing more. The credit card schema, shown in Figure 10.2, is a *custom* schema; it includes all the attributes from the core schema, plus additional attributes specific to the credit card product type. There are likely to be custom schemas for other product types as well.

Using the information about balance carried over and transaction dollars, the bank intends to construct a rough estimate of profitability. Based on a formula determined by the bank's analysts, the bank assigns each customer a profile measure each month. The profile rating is determined by looking at finance charges and transaction dollars over a period of time culminating in the current period. The calculation is not a precise measure of profitability, nor was it concocted by the data warehouse team. It is a metric already in use by the business.

The profile information is captured in a new dimension table, added specifically for the custom credit card fact table. It assigns the customer one of four profiles: *borrower, revolver, transactor,* and *dormant.* Each of the profiles is described in Table 10.2. They are listed in order from most profitable to least profitable.

The profile dimension is a rudimentary measure of profitability. A customer's profile may change from month to month, based on changes in his or her usage patterns. The profile calculation is already being performed by the business, and can be drawn from our source system. Its formula is documented and accepted internally. By storing the transaction dollars and finance charges used in the calculation, we can recompute the values, should it be modified. Keeping the components on hand also gives us the option of computing profitability at load time rather than drawing it from a source system, which may be useful if there is a difference in grain.

Reporting with the Profitability Dimension

Using the profile dimension, the bank can assess the value of its customers. Each of the marketing activities identified in Chapter 3 "Marketing," can be refined. Undesirable, or dormant, credit card holders can be excluded from the sample

Table 10.2 Credit Card Customer Profiles

Revolver	A customer who uses the card frequently, and maintains roughly the same balance each month. Revolvers generate transaction and finance charge revenue.
Transactor	A customer who uses the card, but generally pays the balance in full.
Borrower	A customer who quickly runs up a large balance, then reduces it by making monthly payments. Borrowers tend to generate some finance charge revenue, but low transaction revenue.
Dormant	A customer who does not use the card very often and does not carry a balance.

when identifying the demographics likely to respond to a marketing campaign. Retention efforts can be focused on the more desirable customer profiles, bringing better return on the dollars invested in marketing.

The profile dimension also gives marketers a new way to measure their effectiveness. Consider a mailing promoting a particular card offered by the bank. Three months after the mailing, the schema is used to produce some reports showing that they have achieved a 3.1-percent response rate—a very successful campaign. Six months later, Report 10.3 is generated. It shows the profile of the respondents of the original campaign.

A full 26 percent of the respondents to the campaign are undesirable dormant customers, and an additional 2 percent have since closed their accounts. The third column shows that as percentages of the original mailing list, these groups represent .81 percent and .06 percent, respectively. Deducting these amounts from the originally assessed 3.1-percent response rate yields a new measure for the mailing: 2.23 percent of the recipients became *profitable* cardholders.

Marketers can look at the characteristics of the revolvers and transactors among the group of respondents. A study of their characteristics can lead to improved selection criteria for the next mailing, which in turn should increase the response rate and reduce marketing costs.

Drawbacks of the Profitability Dimension

While the profile dimension enables analysis not previously supported by the banking schema, the approach has three shortcomings:

Report 10.3 Profitability profile of campaign respondents.

**Auto Plus Co-Branded Card
September 98 Rollout Mailer
Respondent Profiles as of July 1999**

Profile	Percentage of Respondents	Percentage of Mailer Recipients
Revolver	12%	.37%
Transactor	43%	1.33%
Borrower	17%	.53%
Dormant	26%	.81%
Closed Account	2%	.06%
Total:	100%	3.1%

- The profile rating is a very rough estimate. It places an entire continuum of customers into four buckets based on a formula that only roughly approximates execution costs.

- The profile rating is formulated based on the two sources of revenue from card products. It does not include costs associated with acquisition, execution, or retention.

- We do not get a true picture of customer profitability because it is a single product metric.

On the revenue side, the profile rating provides a rough estimate at best. It does not account for the wide range of possible cardholder usage patterns; instead, it separates customers into four groups. The actual profitability of an individual customer account is not provided.

Earlier, we identified several categories of *costs* that factor in to the profitability assessment of a customer. The profiling done by the bank focuses on revenues and incorporates *none* of these costs. Efforts to obtain and retain the customer are not a part of the formula, nor is the cost of doing business with the customer. Inclusion of this information may provide a different picture.

Last, the measure only applies to a credit card account held by a customer. Consider a customer who falls in the *dormant* category. Perhaps she saves the card just for emergency purposes. Looking at her card business alone, she may seem like an unprofitable customer, but she may hold a second card, under which she has the status *transactor*. Perhaps she also holds a mortgage and auto loan, each with significant balances. On the whole, she is a profitable customer. The unprofitable product is worth maintaining, so that she does not turn to another institution.

A cross-product picture of profitability is necessary for true customer profitability analysis. What is the profitability of the customer holding two cards, one that is *transactor* and one that is *dormant*? What if this customer also has several other profiles for other account types? Assuming the bank had a suite of 15 product types, we're looking at a lot of individual profitability or profile measures. There is no way to add these together for a composite assessment of the profitability of the customer. When profitability is reduced to a series of dimensional attributes, this composite picture of a customer's profitability cannot be constructed.

Happy with the results of the profitability profile, but hungering for a more comprehensive profitability picture, the bank has decided to do some more work on the model. In the next section, assisted by the bank's team of management consultants, we will build a model that can truly be used for integrated customer management.

TIP

It may be tempting to represent a key business measure, like the profitability measure in this example, using a dimensional attribute that takes on one of a set of values. Another common example of a business metric represented through dimensional values is an inventory velocity dimension that takes on the values High, Medium, and Low. While this approach can provide some value, it tends to fall short in many respects. In particular, the measure cannot be grouped across other dimensional attributes, such as product or branch in our example. In general, it is worth pursuing a way to represent key business measures using additive facts. These can always be "bucketized" as a dimensional attribute if and when it is convenient.

Profitability Measured: Integrated Customer Management

Financial products are complex instruments. Cost and revenues associated with a credit card, checking account, or mortgage loan can be difficult to identify, but the work involved in isolating costs and revenues and allocating them to individual customer accounts can be rewarding. A clear picture of costs and revenues can save the bank money in a number of ways:

- Profiles of profitable customers can be used to target prospects for acquisition activities. Instead of attracting customers, the bank attracts profitable customers.

- Retention and cross-selling campaigns can be focused on profitable customers, improving the bottom line in the long run.

- The bank can eliminate retention efforts aimed at unprofitable customers.

Each business has its own approach to evaluating the costs and revenues associated with financial products, and some styles of measurement are more sophisticated than others. The method used to identify costs and revenues and allocate them to individual customers and accounts should not be developed by the data warehouse design team. While the team can suggest that a more sophisticated approach can have a bigger impact, it should not force a new approach on the business. To do so would risk a design that is not built on a financially solid paradigm.

TIP

The data warehouse team's job is to model the business in a manner consistent with the way it is run, even if the current approach lacks sophistication. It is appropriate to point out potential benefits of alternative approaches, but not to force new ones on the business.

The top costs identified by the financial planners of the bank are shown in Table 10.3. We have organized them by cost category. Notice that acquisition and retention costs apply to all types of products. By contrast, execution costs tend to differ by product.

Table 10.3 Costs

Cost	Description	Category	Product
Introductory checking mailer	Marketing campaign targeted at acquisition of new customers.	Acquisition cost	All products
Bonus rate credit card offer	A mailing sent to existing customers and prospects who fit the profile of responders to a similar campaign.	Acquisition cost	All products
Bonus checking offer for high-balance savings customers	This marketing program is designed to keep profitable customers.	Retention cost	All products
Interest paid	The monthly interest paid on savings account balances.	Execution cost accounts	Deposit
Check processing	Cost of handling checks written by customers.	Execution cost	Checking products
Teller transaction	Cost of transactions such as deposits or withdrawals done in person.	Execution cost	Deposit accounts

Continues

Table 10.3 Costs (Continued)

Cost	Description	Category	Product
ATM transaction	Costs associated with usage of automated teller machines.	Execution cost	Deposit accounts
Monthly maintenance	The cost of monthly account maintenance, including statement processing.	Execution cost	Deposit accounts, card products

For profitability analysis, we will also need to quantify the revenues realized by the bank. Table 10.4 shows several forms of bank revenue as identified by management. We've grouped the revenue types by product. Much like execution costs, revenue types are product specific.

From the few examples we have given, it should be clear that the methods used for identifying execution costs and revenues should be left to the experts. Our bank's financial planners have identified these categories, and supplied the data warehouse team with the information required to compute them on a monthly basis. We now need to enhance our model to accommodate them.

Profitability Design

Acquisition and retention activities are measured in much the same way across all product types. These costs will reside in a fact table that conforms with our existing account_facts star schema. Our execution costs and revenue categories are product specific. They will integrate with custom product stars like the credit card schema developed earlier, just as the merchandiser's product costs integrated with its sales_facts table.

First, we will look at the acquisition and retention costs, and develop a contact and response model that will integrate with our core account_facts table for drill-across queries. This schema will have additional benefits for marketing. Second, we will analyze the execution cost and revenue components. These detail costs will be stored in custom product fact tables, and summarized in the core account_facts. When everything is in place, we will be ready to analyze the profitability of customers across products.

Table 10.4 Revenue

Type	Description	Product
Revenue on reinvested deposits	The bank reinvests a portion of the deposits in checking and savings accounts. The average return on a dollar deposited is measured by the bank on a monthly level. Its calculation is very complicated, but is already done by the financial planners.	Deposit accounts
Financing revenues	The primary source of revenue on credit products is the finance charges assessed each month against unpaid balances. Because merchants must be reimbursed regardless of the card-holder's payment, there is an associated opportunity cost. This may be factored into the finance charge measure as is done here, or broken out as a separate cost.	Card products and line of credit product
Check charges	On certain types of accounts, the bank charges a fee for each check written by the account holder. Note that there are associated costs of check handling, which have been broken out separately. Banks typically have a wide range of fees, each of which may be offset by a cost.	Checking
Transaction revenues	The bank's share of the percentage of card transactions deducted from merchants' receipts.	Card products

Acquisition and Retention Costs Acquisition and retention costs are generated by marketing campaigns. In order to allocate the cost of a marketing campaign to a customer, we will require a method for tracking the marketing activity and responses over time. The cost of a marketing campaign cannot be determined until after it has ended. For example, a cross-sell mailer offering a new card product to existing customers may involve 100,000 pieces of mail. The total cost of the mailing, and even some of the marketing activities involved in its production, are available. The total cost of the campaign is divided by the number of respondents to determine the promotion cost per new account; however, the cost per account cannot be accurately computed until the campaign is over and the number of respondents is finalized.

To calculate acquisition and retention costs, we will build a contact model that can be used to monitor marketing activities. Shown in Figure 10.3, this pair of fact tables can also refine some of the activities surrounding campaign assessment. Because these tables track all marketing activities, they can be used to ensure that individual households are not "over-contacted." Too many phone calls or mailings can sour a customer's relationship with the bank. See the sidebar in Chapter 3 for more information on how contact management aids marketing activities.

Each time a prospect is contacted under a marketing campaign, regardless of the type of campaign or method, we record a row in contact_facts. The grain of this table is the month of contact, household party contacted, and offer.

The contact dimension table identifies the type of marketing activity, method of contact, and name of the offer. The contact_types include Retention and Acquisition. Examples of contact_methods include Telemarketing, Mailer, and Bill Stuffer. Each marketing activity has a name, such as "Free-Checking Retention," or "8.7 APR Co-Branded Card Offer," which we will store in the offer_name column.

Every offer is associated with product, represented by a foreign key to the same product dimension used in our account_facts star. There are three foreign keys in contact_facts to time dimension tables. Although exact dates are available, a monthly grain provides sufficient detail for our analysis needs. The contact_month table represents the date of the mailing, offer_begin_month and offer_end_month represent the time period during which the campaign takes place.

The prospect dimension contains the name and address of the household contacted for each offer. Marketing efforts may involve contacting existing customers, noncustomers whose names and addresses were acquired from an external source, or both. When an existing customer is contacted, the internal household_number from the existing household_dimension is included. For externally identified prospects, this attribute takes the value Not Applicable. The Source attribute identifies how noncustomer data was obtained.

Figure 10.3 Contact facts.

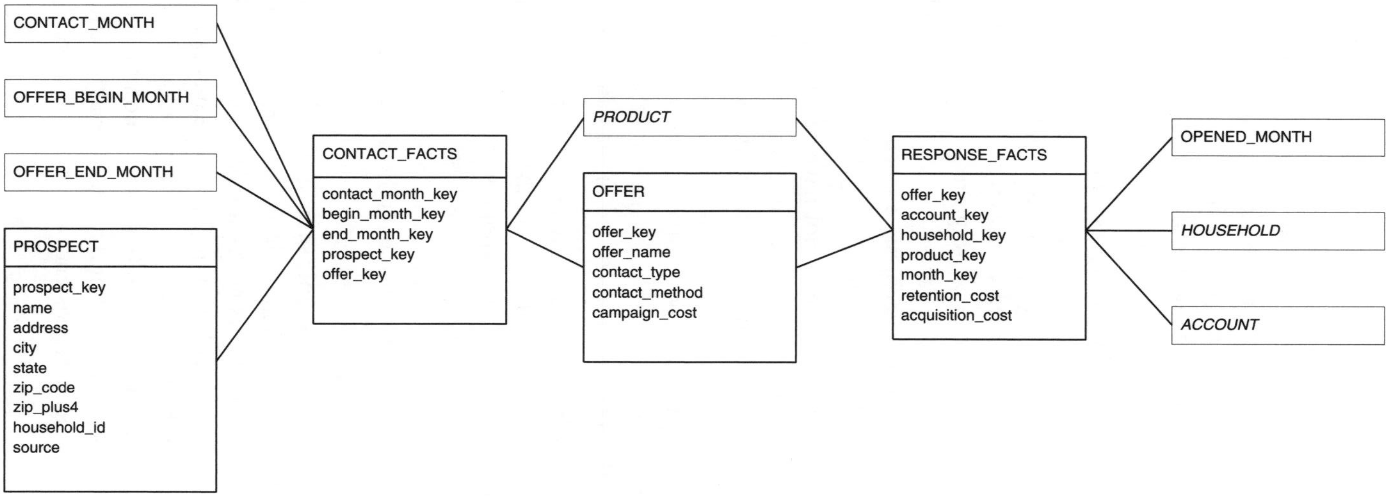

Our contact_facts table may not contain a row for every prospect contacted with an offer—sometimes, the bank does not have information on the individuals contacted via a campaign. This restriction is often a requirement when the company purchases prospect data from an external source. The source may provide a list of names and addresses to the bank's direct mail house under the condition that the names not be passed along to the bank, or stipulate contractually that the bank is not to archive or reuse the list for another mailing.

As part of the offer fulfillment process, the bank records the fact that an account was opened in response to the offer. This can be easily accomplished when the offer is made over the telephone or involves returning an application to a fulfillment center. We record a row in response_facts each time this happens. Some offers may require the prospect to go to the nearest branch and open an account—these responses may be harder to identify. We can look for them by scanning account_facts for new accounts opened by prospects of an offer during the time period covered by the offer.

As previously mentioned, we may not have detailed data on all prospects. The prospect dimension is likely to be dirty; names and addresses may be duplicated, or not match the name used to open the account. In cases where prospect data is not available and the response to the offer is not tracked by the business, it may not be possible to identify the new accounts as responses to the mailing. This issue must be dealt with by the bank; the data warehouse team can only identify responses where sufficient data is recorded in the bank's systems.

Initially, the acquisition_cost and retention_cost columns in response_facts are not populated. These columns will contain the cost of the acquisition or retention effort as allocated to the individual respondent. The cost will not be known until the offer expires, when it is not possible to have further responses. At this time, the total cost of acquisition or retention can be computed. The total cost of the campaign, stored in the offer dimension, is divided by the total number of responses as counted in response_facts.

Notice that only one of these measures is populated: whichever is appropriate for the campaign. By isolating acquisition costs versus retention costs, we will make reporting on these costs easier. As we saw in Chapter 3, "Marketing," recording a single measure with a "type" attribute makes reporting difficult. We might choose to place these numbers in separate fact tables (acquisition_response _facts and retention_response_facts), but there is no practical reason to do so. These costs will not be the subject of marketing analysis efforts, which will be more concerned with the mere existence of rows in response_facts. The zero values will not be of concern.

Although we have placed these cost measures in response_facts, they could also be located in the account_facts table. However, the average account will remain open for many years. Assuming accounts have an average life of five years, there will be 60 monthly rows for each account in account_facts. For each account, a maximum of 1 out of the 60 rows would have an acquisition cost. Many accounts are not open in response to an offer; these will have no acquisition costs recorded. Retention costs would appear a bit more often, but would also be very sparsely populated. We will therefore keep these costs in response facts, and involve them in reports as needed by drilling across. Execution costs, by contrast, recur on a monthly basis. As we are about to find out, they will fit nicely into the monthly account_facts snapshot.

Execution Costs and Revenues The remainder of the bank's costs, along with all its revenues, break out into categories that are product or product category specific. The execution costs occur on a monthly basis, and the bank is already recording a row in account_facts every month for every account, zero balance or not. Since they are measured at the same grain and at the same period, we can place execution costs directly into account_facts.

In order to accommodate detailed, product-level analysis, as well as overall cross-product analysis, we will capture specific types of execution costs within the custom product stars, and summarize them in the core account_facts star. Similarly, our revenues can be tracked at the category level within custom product fact tables, and summarized in account_facts.

Table 10.5 shows an updated version of the credit_card_facts table from Figure 10.2. We have included new attributes for profitability analysis in bold. For this example, we have shown two costs and two revenue types. The execution costs are added together in the total_execution_costs column, and revenues are added together in total_revenues.

For each banking product, we can include a similar set of customized cost and revenue attributes. Deposit accounts, for example, do not incur the same costs and revenues shown in credit_card_facts. The deposit accounts will have their own custom cost and revenue components. Each custom product fact table will include the total_execution_costs and total_revenues attributes.

The core account_facts table will be modified to include the total_execution_costs and total_revenues attributes. These columns summarize the costs and revenues that are present in each of the custom fact tables. This scheme of recording detailed cost and revenue types in the custom product schemas and summarizing them as total_execution_costs and total_revenues in the core fact table allows us to analyze

---

Table 10.5 credit_card_facts with Costs and Revenues

---

credit_card_facts

month_key

account_key

product_key

household_key

demographics_key

status_key

profile_key

account_balance

transaction_dollars

carry_over

finance_charge_revenues

vendor_transaction_fee_revenues

monthly_maintenance_costs

default_costs

total_execution_costs

total_revenues

---

product-specific costs in detail using the custom schemas, or overall costs and revenues using the core schema.

Integrated Customer Management Reporting

Now that each of our cost and revenue categories is represented, we are positioned to perform true customer profitability analysis. In Figure 10.4, we consolidate the components of the retail bank's data warehouse needed for profitability analysis. Marketing costs are broken down in response_facts as retention_costs and acquisition_costs. Execution costs are present in the revised account_facts table as total_execution_costs. Together, these three attributes represent the cost of a particular customer account.

Figure 10.4 A data warehouse supporting integrated customer analysis.

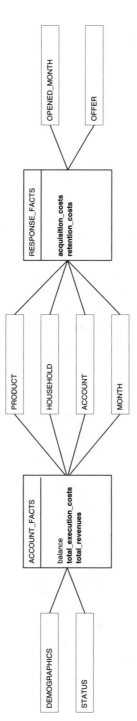

Measures required for profitability analysis are shown in bold. Keys and dimensional attributes have been omitted. See Figure 3.5 and 10.3 for detail.

The other component of profitability is revenue. Revenue has been summarized in the total_revenue column of account_facts. The profitability of a customer account can easily be calculated at any point in time, or over time, simply be subtracting costs from revenue. Because the costs and revenue are fully additive dollar values, we can now assess the profitability of a customer across products.

Demographics and status do not impact the grain of account_facts. If profitability analysis is being performed for a single month, these tables can safely be used, even though response_facts is part of the mix. However, customer profitability will be better assessed over time. Only by looking at quarterly or annual periods do the spikes generated by periodic marketing activities begin to level off. Demographic and account status attributes can be included as long as the attributes selected correspond to those in effect at the end of the period. It will be prudent to select these attributes in a separate query.

Consider the credit card customer described earlier. One of her credit cards was used infrequently, earning her an undesirable profile rating of *dormant*. However, she also held another card that was used more frequently, as well as a mortgage and auto loan. Now that the profitability of this customer can be measured across products, it can be determined that, overall, she is a desirable customer. Report 10.4 shows that she is a very profitable customer, thanks primarily to her very high savings balances.

Total profitability of a customer at a point in time or over a period of time can be studied in conjunction with demographic attributes to fine tune mailing selection criteria. The characteristics of profitable responders are profiled and used to select prospects for future campaigns. Unprofitable customers are screened out of new offers, unless the additional product is likely to transform their profile into a profitable one. Customers who are profitable overall can be included on the list for retention offers. As we encountered in Chapter 3, "Marketing," the banking schema may not be used for a large number of paper reports, but the analysis it allows provides major benefits to the business.

Summing Up Profitability

Profitability analysis helps businesses make decisions that directly impact the bottom line. In this chapter, we have looked at integrated product management, or the study of product profitability, and integrated customer management, or the study of customer profitability. We've learned many important points about the business of profitability analysis, and how it can be supported by a data warehouse. In particular:

Report 10.4 Profitability across products.

Profitability by Product and Overall
Customer Number 6860318
1998

Product	Acquisition Costs	Retention Costs	Total Execution Costs	Total Costs	Total Revenues	Profitability
Eagle no monthly fee card	95	0	20	115	0	–115
Co-branded low APR	0	0	30	30	268	238
Interest checking	0	75	40	40	864	824
Max Equity Loan	0	75	20	95	2,147	2,052
Auto Finance Plus	0	0	20	20	416	396
Total	95	75	130	300	3,695	3,395

Know your focus. Does the business you are supporting maintain a regular, ongoing relationship with customers, or is the focus specifically on products? The perspective will impact your design.

You're building more than a data mart. Profitability analysis requires combining cost and revenue data from several subject areas. If individual subject areas are to be developed one at a time, the overall design and implementation approach must be developed up front.

Dig deep for costs, but don't define new ones. Remember that it must be left up to the business, not the data warehouse team, to identify the costs and revenues tracked, and determine how they will be measured.

Find the right home for each component of profitability. The cost and revenue components of profitability may belong all together, or in separate fact tables. It may also be appropriate to include some at a detailed level in a custom schema, and summarized in a core schema.

Include the components of an assessment. Dimensional attributes like the "Profile" in this chapter are a common first step toward profitability analysis. When a simple formula is used to compute the value of the dimensional attribute, measures involved in the calculation should be stored in the fact table.

Construct additive profitability measures whenever possible. A profitability dimension has limited use. Profitability analysis can have more impact when fully additive cost and revenue measures are available. These can always be used to construct profitability dimensions when convenient.

KNOWLEDGE AND INTELLECTUAL CAPITAL

11

The Information Age and the increased importance of knowledge to business success are accepted facts. During the Industrial Age, the acquisition and investment of capital to produce goods was paramount. In the Information Age, capital is subordinate to knowledge. The very fact that you are reading this book is a manifestation of the Information Age. Computer professionals have increased in ranks in the last 20 years much as the ranks of miners and factory workers increased at the onset of the Industrial Age, but the computer and software industry represent only one facet of the Information Age. The increased communication of information in the economy—the telecommunications revolution—is equally important. Together, these technologies have made the storage and exchange of information inexpensive.

The discontinuous force unleashed by advances in telecommunications and computing is change. Continuous, unpredictable, and often wildly profitable change is an established force in the economy. Everyone recognizes that change is causing the competitive storms that sweep through the global economy. What often goes unrecognized is the basic reason for all this change: the application of knowledge. With more information about the business, stored and easily retrieved with computers, companies can innovate more quickly than ever before. And with more telecommunications channels, a company can share information internally, or with business partners, more easily. We know more and we share what we know much more quickly than in the past.

Consider the agricultural inputs industry, consisting of seed, fertilizer, pesticides, and herbicide products. Largely seen as a collection of factories and distribution channels in the past, agricultural inputs is a knowledge business. Companies compete to develop innovative products, secure patents, and sell them to growers around the world. The process of developing a new agricultural chemical is knowledge intensive, while automated production equipment makes manufacturing increasingly less labor intensive. The application of knowledge to product design, production, planning, marketing, and sales, is unlimited in scope. It permeates strategic and tactical decision making and is enabled by the revolution in technology.

The application of knowledge for competitive advantage is now the foundation of success for large companies in most industries. While the application of knowledge has always been important, it has only recently gained equal status with capital. In his seminal book, *Intellectual Capital* (Doubleday, 1997), Thomas Stewart fixes the official start of the Information Age as 1991. It was in this year that corporate spending for computers, software, and telecommunications exceeded spending for production equipment, and investment in gathering, exchanging, and sharing information has continued to increase since then. Operational processes in both service and manufacturing have been heavily automated. ERP software, automated voice response phone systems, call centers, and sophisticated manufacturing equipment are all artifacts of the growing importance of information and knowledge. Originally intended to reduce operational process costs and increase productivity, these information-based assets capture a huge amount of data. Data about current operations, used to manage daily activity, are widely available. Data warehousing is a natural result of the desire to make sense of the growing store of enterprise data. From this data, companies hope to create information and glean knowledge from capital investments in computers and telecommunications originally intended to improve operations. The resurgence in data warehousing is a harbinger of a future competitive environment where market, customer, and operational knowledge comprise the cornerstones of competition.

If knowledge and intellect are important assets to the corporation, however, where are the values of these assets recorded? Most current applications that manage activity, costs, and investments were designed with the physical, industrial world in mind. This legacy mind set means that the information required to measure intellectual capital, knowledge, and the return on these intangibles is not systematically tracked. The data warehouse may be the best place to stitch together

Key Business Term

Intellectual capital. Intellectual assets, including corporate knowledge, patents, databases, and process structures that can be used to increase the value of an organization.

Intellectual capital is a term popularized by John Stewart, a well-known proponent of knowledge management. Intellectual capital, unlike other information from across the company, and provide measures of return on intellectual capital that are often overlooked.

It is useful to categorize intellectual capital to further understand how it permeates the activity of a modern corporation. One of the more useful categorizations, developed by Hubert Saint-Onge and Leif Edvisson, divides intellectual capital into three types: human capital, structural capital, and customer capital. We will use these, including a broader definition of customer capital known as *relationship capital*, to frame our discussion. Each type of intellectual capital provides a different set of measures for a company competing in the emerging knowledge economy.

Human Capital

Human capital is not the sum total of the brain power of a corporation. It is better described as the potentially valuable knowledge of a company's employees that is relevant to its business. This is a subtle but important distinction in that it focuses our effort to measure human capital. Interestingly, the brain power of many employees, while substantial, may not be relevant to the business. Imagine a production line worker with a strong inclination and knowledge of computers. At home, the worker assembles, repairs, and tinkers with computer hardware and networking equipment. It is a hobby to the worker, a rare skill for the employer. The worker's production line activity, perhaps working an automated lathe, uses only a fraction of the knowledge available. At the same time, the factory IT director is frantically recruiting a hardware engineer to help manage the increasing number of automated equipment and backroom computers. Would the IT director think to look on the production line for a candidate? In one scenario, the company spends several months recruiting and training a new hire. The cost of recruitment could easily be $20,000, and the new worker might spend the first six months learning the work environment and tasks of the specific position. If the new worker costs $10,000 per month in labor and benefits, the company has spent

capital assets, is tucked away inside of companies, more difficult to find and measure than a computer or office space. For example, the information technology industry suffers today from a severe labor crunch. Replacing an IT worker is costly. Recognizing this reality is easy; measuring a company's ability to deal with it is not. It requires careful monitoring of employee retention and the impact of different employment stewardship actions by the company.

$80,000 to staff a position that might have been filled by an internal worker. The internal worker is not recruited by a headhunter, is familiar with the plant environment, and would likely be productive in half the time. The difference in cost is at least $50,000, the sum of the recruiting fee and the three additional months of unproductive labor. How proactive should a large company be in searching for knowledge among its work force to fulfill critical positions?

Another type of human capital ignored by American business until the quality revolution is the process knowledge of the production employee. The catalyst for most process improvement is the unused process knowledge of production workers. In a classic industrial setting, the worker passively produces, performing repetitive tasks, but is never asked how to improve them. The worker has eight hours a day to study the production process, observe, and understand it. It seems obvious today that the worker is an invaluable pool of process knowledge, and that a group of workers is even more valuable. Today, companies train and condition employees to study and improve processes. Even factory workers see more and more of their work going from touch labor to process improvement.

In the new age of knowledge-based competition, companies must innovate, and the wellspring of innovation is the collected knowledge of the workforce. Whether this knowledge is applied to product design, production processes, marketing, sales, or finance, the result is a more competitive entity. But human capital needs a path to follow. It must be harvested and applied using structural capital.

Structural Capital

The term *structural capital* refers to the underlying assets that enable the capture, storage, and exchange of information. It also encompasses the underlying business processes and methods that provide a company with competitive advantage. Structural capital is represented in manuals, techniques, even patents and copyrights. The importance of structural capital is that it provides context to the human and relationship capital that exist in the organization.

Smart people—human capital assets—must be able to cultivate the company's collected body of knowledge. They must be able to create and act in the context of proven techniques, strategies, and known constraints. A database of customers, for example, is not constructed without a significant amount of structural capital. The discipline of designing a process that carefully tracks customer attributes and behavior is part of the structure, as is the hardware and software used to store the data about customers. Analytical methods and supporting software create the final piece of structural capital. This set of structural intellectual assets—a process, a database, and an analysis capability—enables the company that owns it to leverage its customer relationships.

Because much of structural capital is technology related, the first impulse might be to count up IT assets and stop. This is a serious mistake. Technology is the fastest depreciating structural asset. A company with a proven customer attrition model has a valuable asset of enduring value. The software used to implement the attrition model might change every one to three years.

Relationship Capital

Relationship capital refers simply to the value of relationships a company has with other entities. The most obvious relationship that has inherent value is with the customer. The cost of acquiring a customer can be amortized over the life of the customer relationship. In many businesses, like long distance or utility services, the cost of acquisition is much higher than the revenue likely to come from a customer in the initial service period. An existing loyal customer with a history of profitable and frequent purchases provides a greater return on the acquisition investment. Many companies spend as much effort coaxing more business out of existing customers as they do on finding new customers. A loyal, profitable customer base is an extremely valuable asset.

Supplier relationships are also increasingly valuable. A reliable supplier, able to respond quickly to changes in demand, is an important partner for a modern manufacturer. Many manufacturers include suppliers in the product design process, viewing them as full partners with valuable knowledge to share. Some companies reduce the number of suppliers to strengthen relationships. In exchange for a preferred status, these suppliers are expected to invest in technology, share data, and respond nimbly to changes in requirements. Effective suppliers are often courted by competing manufacturers who clearly recognize the value of a supplier relationship.

Another common type of relationship is the channel relationship. In Chapter 2, "Sales," we examined the importance of channels for a database software vendor. Possessing an efficient set of channels to distribute new products is extremely valuable. Knowledgeable channel partners know their respective customer base and can rapidly introduce a new product to the marketplace. We can think of the channel salesperson as a high-level door-to-door salesperson, continually making the rounds of customers and prospects in an assigned territory. Each visit is an opportunity to introduce new products or services. This "feet on the street" advantage is even more important in markets in which the cycles of innovation and product displacement are quickening.

Cooperative partner relationships are especially important in the technology industry. Companies must work together to ensure that their products are compatible. Technology companies also seek partners that allow them to stitch together complete solutions from pieces of generic technology. An interesting example is the value of the partnership that Oracle Corporation has with the various ERP vendors. Oracle is the world's largest database company, and its relational database product has the greatest market share in large organizations. As ERP vendors like SAP, Baan, and PeopleSoft have grown, Oracle's database sales have been partially driven by the popularity of these packages. Even though Oracle offers its own ERP solution, it still works hard to ensure that other competing ERP software works well with its database. This shotgun marriage of competitors is driven by the value of the relationship between the products, not the companies. If a company can make its technology compatible with other technologies, it is a much safer bet for risk-averse buyers.

Some technologies are so pervasive that they create markets for other products. The obvious example is Microsoft, whose PC operating system technology has paved the way for its own office automation, networking, and Internet software. Interestingly, Microsoft's prepotency on the desktop has made a relationship with Microsoft incredibly important to other software vendors. Because of Microsoft's importance, many software companies have abandoned efforts to develop for Apple or any other platform. Relationships with other operating system providers are unimportant to the vast majority of vendors. None of these relationships, however, are found in the typical balance sheet.

Assembling information on the intellectual assets of a company is not always an easy task. Operational systems may or may not have the right information. Gathering information on a company's human capital requires information from human resources, project staffing, and the accounting system. Analyzing the impact of structural capital requires that a business analyst assemble information on the cost and return from the asset, be it an information system or an improved manufacturing process. It is not necessary for a company to build a data warehouse for measuring intellectual capital. It is more important to infuse the data warehouse team and the business community with an awareness of intellectual capital's growing importance. Once alerted to the importance of these assets, the team can begin to include relevant data in the design of the data warehouse. The taxonomy of intellectual capital presented is intended to frame the discussion of these assets in the course of a project.

Simplifying Intellectual Capital Analysis

The data warehouse exists to increase the value of the corporate body of information, while operational systems exist to support the execution of ongoing activity. Operational data often is known only by workers who perform the processes that capture it, and because operational processes must be controlled, security and access to operational systems is tightly monitored. Imagine being assigned the task of analyzing labor turnover and cost trends for a multisite manufacturer. The task requires gathering and correlating data from several implementations of ERP software. What challenges are faced absent a data warehouse?

Access to the ERP systems probably is controlled by a system administrator at each plant. You must convince each of them to give you an account, which can be difficult even with an executive mandate. Secondly, assuming you're not an IT wizard, you must get your requirements to the front of the queue for processing. These requirements, which are likely to generate suspicion among plant management, are competing with daily production reports and other time-critical operational needs. Multiplied over several production sites, the barriers to quickly and accurately completing your task are significant.

Undertaking the task in a company with an integrated manufacturing data warehouse is not so daunting. The data in the data warehouse is organizationally neutral, and its ownership is not physically constrained. No single plant manager, uncooperative database administrator, or production requirements queue will delay your work; instead, you are able to pool information from across the organization and complete your analysis in less time than otherwise would be possible. One might contest, however, that one study of labor trends, the needs of one junior MBA working on a project for the CFO, does not justify the cost of the data warehouse. One study does not, but the accumulation of questions, studies, analyses, and the resulting insights surely does.

Knowledge and the Value Chain

We can also examine the impact of knowledge and the value of intellectual capital using the value chain framework first introduced in Chapter 2, "Sales." A generic view of the value chain is presented in Figure 11.1, from which we can develop a mental model of almost any business.

From this admittedly simple picture of the business cycle, it is possible to define, measure, and perhaps value the impact of knowledge on business performance. Understanding the impact of knowledge, the amount applied, and the cost to develop it, is not always straightforward, but approximations and internal standards can take the place of formal accounting procedures until knowledge and intellectual capital measures are standardized.

Improving Process Inputs

The concept of managing inputs to the production process builds on the production and quality discussions in Chapter 5, "Production," and Chapter 7, "Quality." First we will consider the standard production inputs, raw materials, and components. Raw materials are transformed into finished goods in the production process. A refinery transforms crude oil, a wood products company transforms logs, and a steel company transform ores. One of the interesting results of the

Figure 11.1 The simplified value chain.

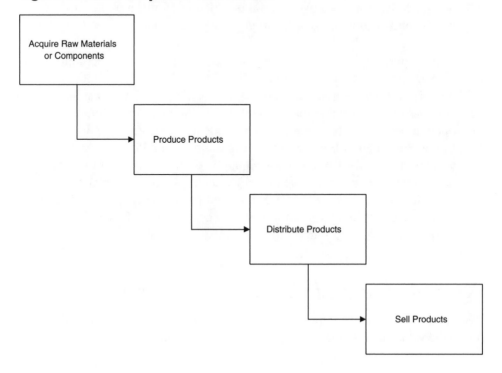

knowledge economy is the decline in the cost of raw materials. While resources in the world are finite, civilization has continually improved methods and processes for extracting and processing these resources. These improvements and the resulting unit cost reductions are attributable to the application of knowledge to these processes.

To further illustrate how knowledge can be applied to purchasing raw materials, consider a wood products company that processes timber into construction products. We can divide the company's concerns into three areas that can be improved by applying intellectual assets:

Raw materials cost and quality. What is the relative cost and quality of the various raw materials used in the production of finished goods? Elements of quality include strength, flexibility, value of scrap, and consistency. The cost of raw materials—in this case, timber—can be tracked to identify changes in demand. To balance cost and quality, the company must continually monitor the impact of raw materials on finished goods.

Supplier performance. Understanding supplier performance is equally valuable. The quality of raw materials from a supplier may be high, but if the supplier continually misses delivery schedules, production interruptions can ensue. Combining quality, cost, and timeliness gives the company knowledge about the supplier that can be used in sourcing decisions.

Materials handling. Another important category of knowledge is materials handling. The form, packaging, and size of raw materials can be manipulated to push costs outside the producing company. For the wood products company, timber may arrive raw, with bark still on. The company could spend a significant amount of money removing bark and trimming the raw timber down for processing. The bark and scrap may even be used in other products; however, if these products generate less revenue than the cost of preparation, the company could negotiate with suppliers to trim the excess before delivery—a production step of limited value to the company can be pushed out the back door.

With these areas of concern in mind, we can identify some needs that could easily be satisfied in a planned data warehouse. The requirement is essentially to gather data about the subjects listed and apply the knowledge gleaned from that data to improve decision making in each area. It is better to have these issues in mind during the design. For example, the schema in Figure 11.2 is used to track quality inspections for incoming timber. Defects are noted and tracked by material, supplier, and type.

Figure 11.2 The timber inspection schema.

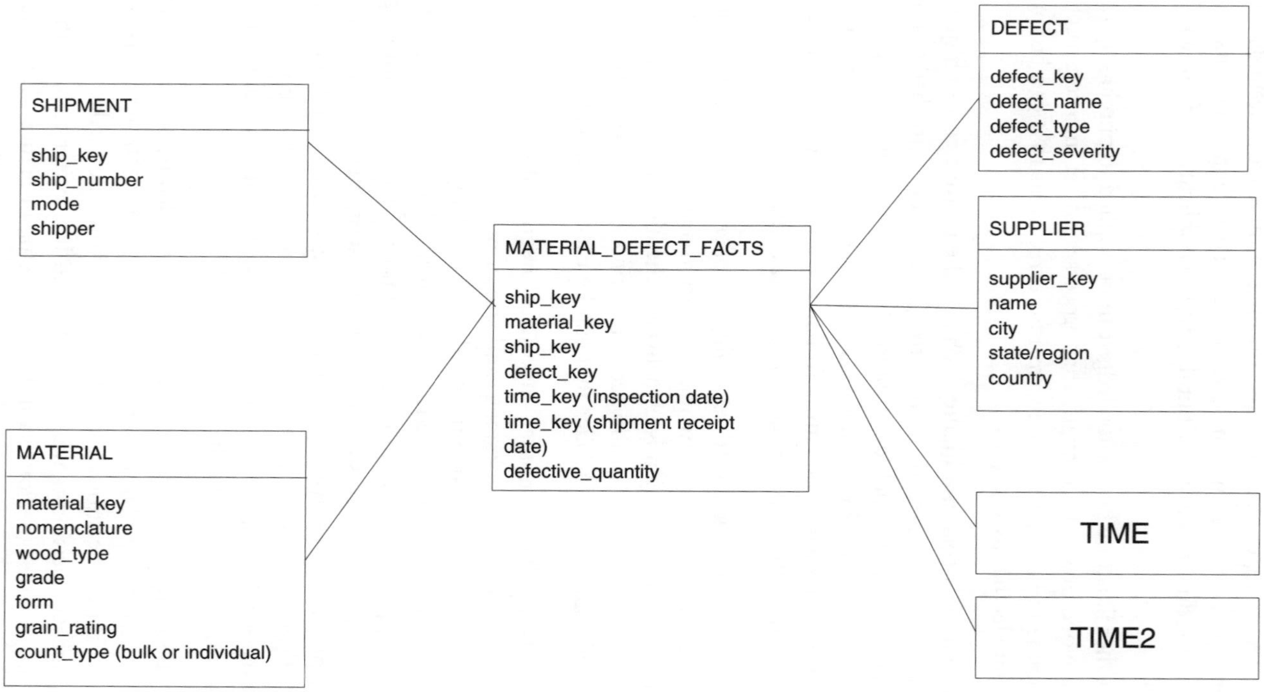

DEFECT
defect_key
defect_name
defect_type
defect_severity

SUPPLIER
supplier_key
name
city
state/region
country

TIME

TIME2

MATERIAL_DEFECT_FACTS
ship_key
material_key
ship_key
defect_key
time_key (inspection date)
time_key (shipment receipt date)
defective_quantity

SHIPMENT
ship_key
ship_number
mode
shipper

MATERIAL
material_key
nomenclature
wood_type
grade
form
grain_rating
count_type (bulk or individual)

The information gathered provides valuable information to the company. The company can internally monitor and manage supplier performance and build contract clauses that provide incentives for high-quality materials. The company can also share material quality problems with suppliers, who may be able to correlate the errors with certain tree stands, ages, species, or even transport methods. The supplier can then use the data to save the manufacturer time and money. As more and more defects are prevented, raw materials quality continually improves. A company that assembles computer parts is in a similar partnership with component suppliers.

While the previous design provides some data on supplier performance, the company must also track material deliveries and quality. Tracking material deliveries must include the expected and actual delivery date, and in some very demanding industries, delivery time. We also track quantity and cost. The resulting schema, presented in Figure 11.3, can be used in conjunction with the quality schema to provide a comprehensive view of supplier performance.

Materials handling issues can also be considered in our design. Tracking the utilization of raw materials provides insight into the amount of material inventory carried in the manufacturer's warehouses, the amount of damaged inventory, and the impact of receiving raw materials in different forms and lot sizes. Suppose the wood products company proceeds with the decision to change the form of material, from raw timber to stripped logs. A stripped log is more susceptible to damage from exposure to the elements. Including form in our definition of material in an inventory schema would allow the company to monitor inventory damages as the change is enacted. If the amount of damaged raw material inventory increases, the company may need to improve storage facilities or work with suppliers to reduce inventory levels, thus reducing time exposed to the elements. The chart in Report 11.1 presents data on damaged material by form.

These examples show the value of accumulating data and deriving knowledge from it. To produce these results, we need human, structural, and relationship capital. The human capital is the knowledge of the people involved in managing inventory quality. The structural capital includes the data capture mechanisms, the data warehouse itself and the associated costs, and the inspection processes that support the improvements in quality. The relationship capital involved is that with the suppliers. A relationship with a supplier that improves quality, cost, and responsiveness is considerably valuable to the company. The actual value may be difficult to calculate, but the quantitative analyst interested in doing so can use the raw data in the data warehouse to build a valuation model.

Figure 11.3 The supplier performance schema.

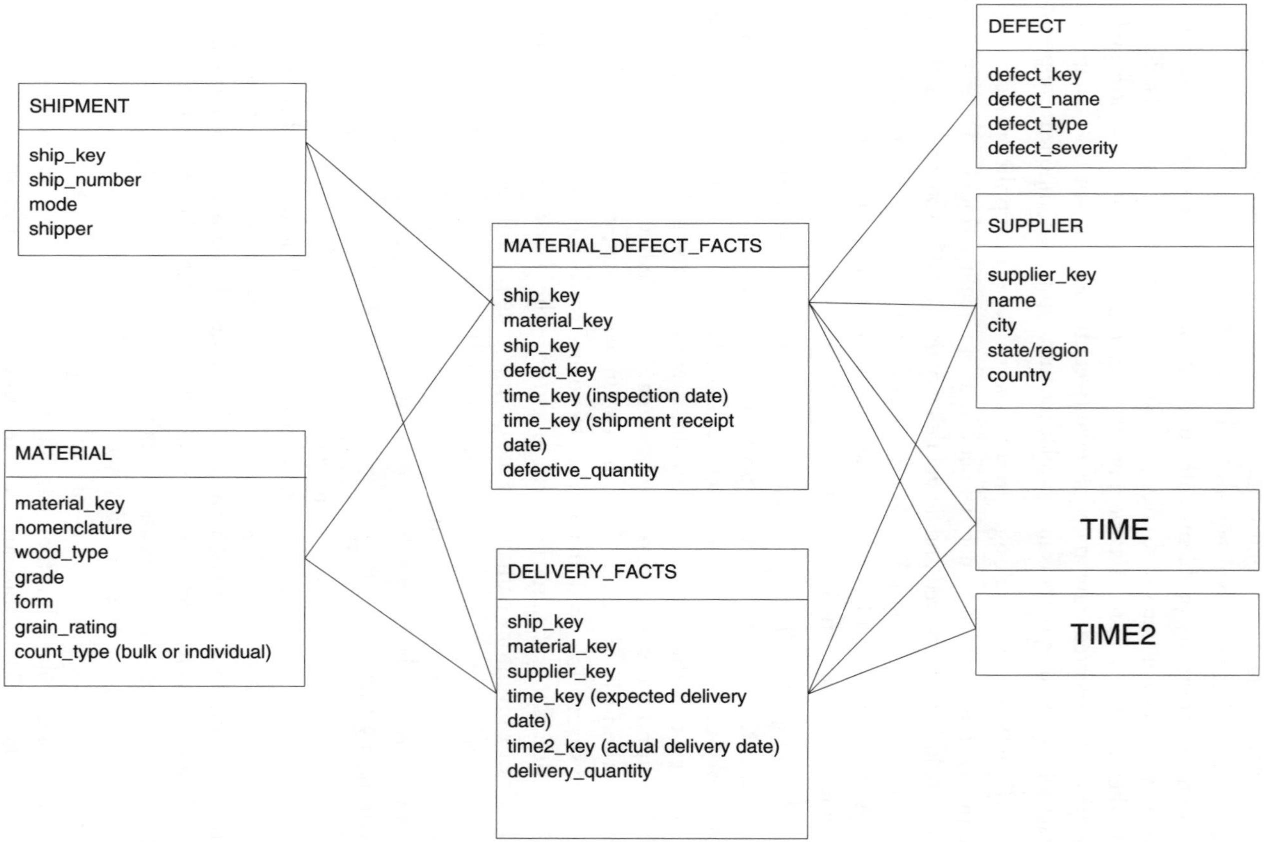

Report 11.1 Increasing damages to raw materials.

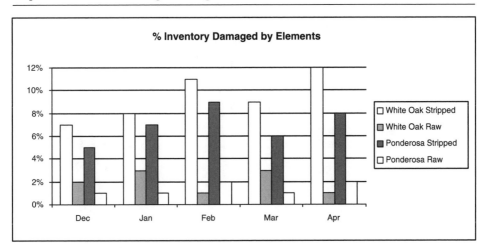

Improving the Process

Process improvement is the area in which knowledge is most frequently applied in both manufacturing and service industries. Remember that a process is essentially a type of structural capital in the intellectual capital world. By managing processes and keeping historical records of process performance, we build a basis for calculating the value of processes in the organization. We will examine two examples, one from service and one from manufacturing.

The Value of Improved Manufacturing Processes

What is the value of a process to an organization? Improving a process in a manufacturing company can impact labor costs, quality, capacity, and factory utilization. In Chapter 5, "Production," we introduced a computer manufacturer with production facilities around the world. Each production facility had one or more production lines used for different products. The company has a proprietary production process, a structural asset, supported by a sophisticated ERP package and data warehouse. Remember that these are also structural assets that support the process. The value of this process asset resides in its ability to produce increased earnings by reducing cost per unit of production over time. While competitors may own the same ERP software, hardware, production equipment, and have a data warehouse, the ability to exploit these in the process structure can still yield competitive advantage.

Figure 11.4 The computer maker's production data warehouse.

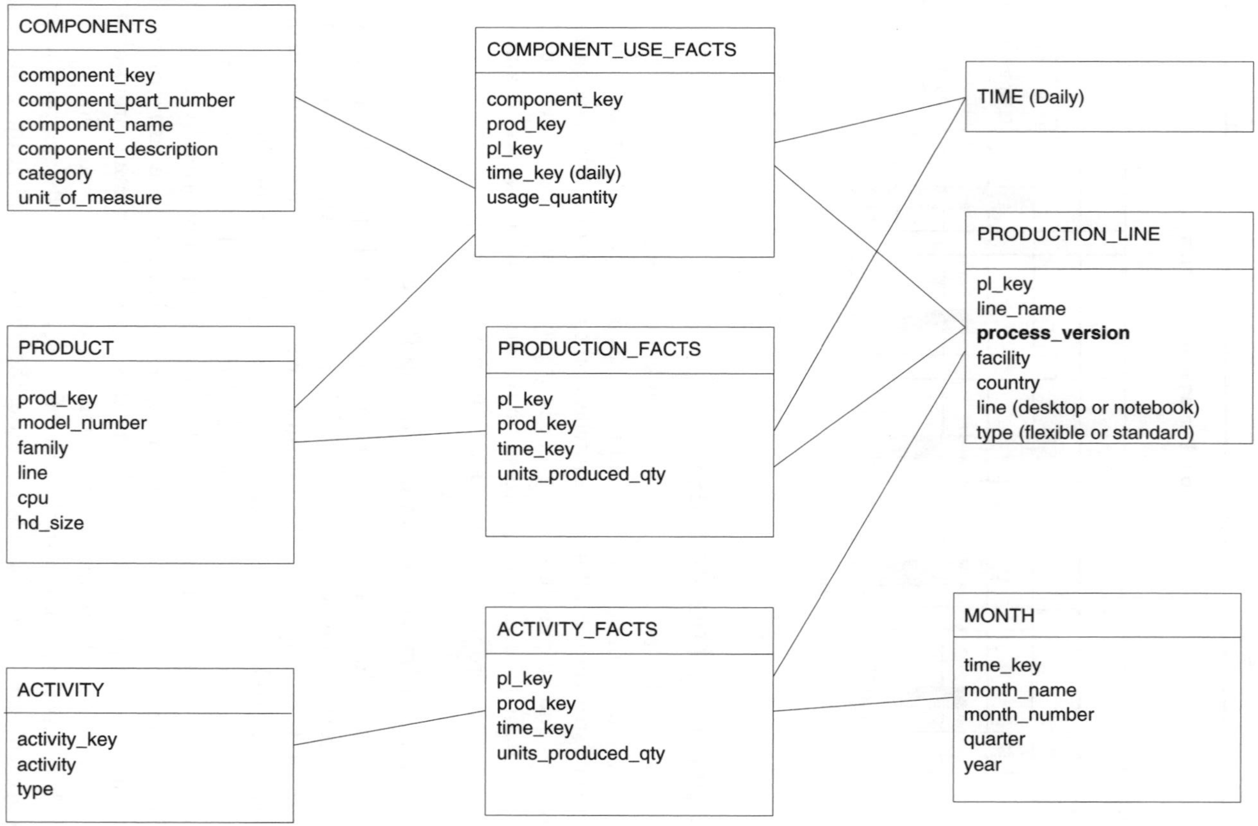

COMPONENTS
component_key
component_part_number
component_name
component_description
category
unit_of_measure

PRODUCT
prod_key
model_number
family
line
cpu
hd_size

ACTIVITY
activity_key
activity
type

COMPONENT_USE_FACTS
component_key
prod_key
pl_key
time_key (daily)
usage_quantity

PRODUCTION_FACTS
pl_key
prod_key
time_key
units_produced_qty

ACTIVITY_FACTS
pl_key
prod_key
time_key
units_produced_qty

TIME (Daily)

PRODUCTION_LINE
pl_key
line_name
process_version
facility
country
line (desktop or notebook)
type (flexible or standard)

MONTH
time_key
month_name
month_number
quarter
year

With this in mind, we return to the computer maker's data warehouse schema, depicted in Figure 11.4. While we have a good handle on production line activity, we have no representation of process changes. Without a measure of process change, we cannot objectively gauge improvements in the process and develop any valuation model. To do so, we can add a process version number to the production line dimension, allowing us to track production facts by the specific process version used at that time. We assume that a rigorous process management discipline exists in the company.

If we capture this data we can monitor changes in unit production costs across process versions. A quantitative analyst might use the data to calculate the net change in unit production costs during a year for two process versions. First we define the beginning and end unit standard costs; then we define the difference as the standard unit cost reduction, as shown here:

Notebook production process V 1.7   Standard unit cost: 1,196.41
Notebook production process V 1.8   Standard unit cost: −1,165.30
                                       Reduction in costs: **31.11**

This reduction should increase gross margins in future years, and the amount of increase expected can be determined by multiplying the reduction by forecasted output, depicted in Table 11.1.

The analyst would then apply a discount rate to future earnings improvements to arrive at a final determination of change in value of this manufacturing process. The process is becoming more valuable, and the money and time devoted to process improvement are the expense of maintaining this asset. Such a baseline valuation formula may also include an allowance for any competitive advantage the process provides in the marketplace. The actual valuation process must be clearly defined and consistently applied so it gains internal acceptance.

Another interesting aspect of intellectual capital management in manufacturing is the measurement of knowledge labor versus touch labor over time. Process improvement, quality training, and improved production equipment should

Table 11.1 The Value of an Improved Process

V 1.8	1998	1999	2000	2001
Production forecast	30,000	42,000	61,000	75,000
Earnings increase	995,458	1,368,809	1,959,930	2,395,501

decrease touch labor per unit of production, and over time, a company should see increased production with less touch labor, as well as improvements in quality. To measure this information, a company can track labor costs by activity, with an eye toward identifying efforts that are geared to increasing the knowledge component of each product. This might be done through project accounting codes in the financial system, and transferred to a labor costs data warehouse. A few rows of the task dimension might look something like Table 11.2.

Tasks are classified in a standard manner, with IC_Flag identifying tasks that contribute to intellectual capital. Task types allow the company to further break down these tasks into specific types of IC activity. Using this information, the company can prepare the chart shown in Report 11.2, which indicates that touch labor per unit of output is decreasing. And the money spent building intellectual capital assets like improved processes should be capitalized and depreciated over time. This is a radical change in perspective from standard accounting practices, but it may become common practice in the future.

This measure is valuable in showing the change in knowledge content for the company's products. The reduction is probably attributable to a combination of factors, including improved production equipment, process improvement, and better training. Correlating increases in these activities with production improvements is possible in this design.

Service Process Improvement

Service processes also have value, although they change more often than production processes and may be more loosely defined. An excellent example of proprietary

Table 11.2 The Sample Task Dimension

Task ID	Task Name	Task Type	IC_Flag
1	Lathe operation	Production	N
2	Lathe maintenance	Maintenance	N
3	Process team meeting	Process management	Y
4	Seminar attendance	Knowledge management	Y
5	Vacation	Comp. time off	N
6	Cross-training	Knowledge management	Y

Report 11.2 Touch labor per unit of production.

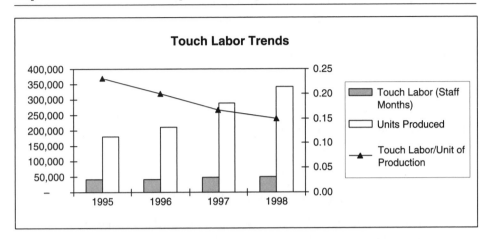

service processes that have incredible value are those that implement customer profitability models. Whether a company is a credit card issuer, catalog retailer, or airline, identifying and accommodating profitable customers improves operating results. An example from the lodging industry is the growing array of frequent-guest programs, aimed primarily at business travelers wielding expense accounts.

Major hotel chains first introduced these clubs in the 1980s, following the model of airline industry frequent flier programs. While upgraded rooms were sometimes offered, the primary reward was a free stay in the future based on accumulating credits for paid nights. In recent years, however, most hotels have begun to offer room upgrades, express check-in, and other amenities to increase the perceived value of these programs. One amenity, express check-in, is a structural process that requires technology and labor to implement. The process is an asset that can span the organization, improving the earnings of each member hotel. It also costs money to implement. Much like an item of production equipment, the cost of developing and operating the express check-in process should be carefully measured against the value to customers. Understanding and managing these structural assets is an aspect of service operations management that should not be overlooked. The company should define the value of the structural asset with some reasonable method *before* incurring the costs to implement and operate it.

Another example of the application of knowledge to structural processes and the resulting change that can sweep through an industry is Internet stock trading. Built entirely upon structural assets, Internet stock trading is altering the way people buy and sell stock. The storied brokers of Wall Street are losing market share to companies that offer customers the ability to buy and sell equities without talking to anyone. E-Trade, a public company that offers such services, is valued by the marketplace on the quality of its online trading process and the technology behind it. The company's book value is far less than its market value, and the difference is made up of these intellectual assets.

When knowledge is a key competitive advantage and a company is built on structural assets, what type of information must be collected to manage the business? Trading volumes, customer loyalty and lifetime value, and operational costs are all important. A company that relies on structural assets must try to incorporate as much information about the cost and value of these assets into its operational and analytical systems.

Improving Inventory and Distribution

By now, the reader can begin to picture the role of knowledge and intellectual assets before an example is presented. There is no doubt that one of the biggest changes in manufacturing over the last 20 years is the obsession with inventory control and supply chain management. While the cost of storing excess inventory is one driver, the opportunity cost of mistiming the use of working capital is more important. Excess inventory is a misuse of working capital, which is too scarce to use building products that languish in warehouses, distribution centers, or retail stores for weeks or months. The capital used to produce those languishing products might have been used to produce other products, design new ones, or increase dividends.

The desire to reduce finished goods inventory has created fortunes in the software industry. It is a principal cause of the ERP software revolution, and has spawned niche market players that help companies anticipate demand and balance supply. Remember our medical distributor from Chapter 6, "Inventory and Capacity." The company was less interested in how much inventory was on hand than in whether enough was on hand. Aggressive inventory managers drive down the "enough" figure to as low a number as possible. The balance of factory output and market demand is a tightrope walk best accomplished with some structural capital in place.

Consider the question of balancing factory utilization with demand in the case of our computer manufacturer. Each factory has an ideal utilization level that minimizes overtime costs. Ideally, we can balance production across the company to keep utilization as close to ideal as possible. What we want to avoid is the case of over-utilizing when finished goods inventories are higher than demand. Report 11.3 shows the quantity on hand at the end of a production week, the demand forecast for the next week, and factory utilization rates for two products.

Report 11.3 Unbalanced production.

Product	QOH	Demand Forecast	Production Line Utilization
Z2000-996-X	2,412	1,191	126%
Z2000-211-X	1,241	2,680	62%

Each row in the report represents a different problem. The first row shows that the demand forecast is significantly less than the quantity on hand. The company has produced too much product, and factory utilization is 126 percent of the ideal, meaning the cost to produce the excess products was driven up by overtime labor charges. Demand forecasts for this product should be improved. The second row presents a case of failing to meet demand for the next week, and not working very hard to do it. The 62 percent utilization shows that the production lines were not used to full capacity. Remember also that our company can produce these two products on the same line by reconfiguring the equipment. Better forecasting might have enabled the company to reduce production on the 996 model to less than 100 percent, reconfigure the line to produce 211 models, and get a better balance at reduced costs.

Stitching together the data to answer these questions, and the expertise to manage the inventory process, represents a major investment for the company. But the investment in a superior demand forecasting process has a measurable impact on earnings as surely as the purchase of a new piece of production equipment or other more traditional capital investments.

Improving Sales

The final step in the business cycle for a product is the sale. The importance of knowledge in sales and marketing is quite obvious. Since we spent a good deal of time on sales and marketing structural assets in Chapters 2 and 3, we will examine the value of relationships in this section. Our example is the database software vendor from Chapter 2. A typical database software vendor is interested in the following types of relationships:

Customer:vendor. The purchasers of the company's products are the first type of relationship. These customers represent the vendor's installed base, its most valuable relationship asset.

Vendor:cooperative partner. The database company is likely to have relationships with other vendors, including both complementary software providers and service companies that assist customers in implementing the software.

Vendor:channel partner. Another type of business partner that deserves separate consideration is the channel partner. A channel partner is an extension of the company's sales force, and in some cases, a replacement for it.

Each type of relationship provides the company with an opportunity to increase revenue and earnings. The installed base is a ready market for future versions of the core product, as well as the best place to introduce new products. To measure the value of the installed base we can distinguish between new and existing customers in the sales subject area. A report of cross-selling effectiveness is generated by product, as shown in Report 11.4, where a cross sale is defined as selling a nonupgrade product to an existing customer.

The exploitation of existing relationships for increased sales is an obvious use of existing customer relationships—the incremental cost of a sale to an existing customer is lower than that for a new customer. The amount of knowledge than can be gained and applied to customer relationships is enormous. Much of the data mining activity going on today is designed to extract more value from the relationship capital of existing relationships. Companies are increasing efforts to track both the cost and value of each customer relationship. This is true for our database vendor, as well as a bank, stockbroker, or aircraft manufacturer. Repeat buyers need less convincing, assuming the last buying experience was positive.

Vendor:cooperative partner relationships are valuable because they create an environment of success for products. The database vendor must create a sense in the market that a customer will meet with success when implementing a new product. The cooperative partners include operating system and hardware vendors on which the product will run, packaged application companies that commit to the database as platform, and consulting companies that help customers implement the product. In the current labor climate, the scarcity of skilled technical staff makes the customer

Report 11.4 Cross-selling effectiveness by product.

Product	Version	Total Units	Cross Sales	Percentage
Interbase	3.7	128	19	14.8%
Interbase web	1.1	67	45	67.2%
Interbase tools	1.2	31	19	61.2%

base wary of products that have a small pool of expertise. And the value of these relationships should be measurable. For example, the database vendor may do joint marketing with two different packaged application providers in the call center market. If the company is diligent in identifying sales driven by those packages, the relative value of each relationship can be estimated. We can add a dimension to the data warehouse to identify a cooperative partner that facilitated a sale.

The vendor:channel partner relationship was described in Chapter 2, "Sales," and the channel was included as a dimension. Channels exist in many industries and should be viewed as an extension of a company's operations. The power of the channel is unassailable, and our database vendor's use of channels was included in the design of the sales subject area. The value of each relationship is traceable to revenue, and efforts to increase or improve channel relations can be measured against that revenue.

Interbase can create a family of measures to value these relationships by drawing on data from different parts of the organization. Well-designed operational systems allow the company to differentiate between new and existing customers, calculate lifetime customer value, and approximate acquisition costs for each customer. The influence of cooperative partners on revenue, and the cost to develop relationships with each, can also be tracked. And all operational sales systems should track channel data. Once the operational systems are designed properly, the analysis of relationship value in the data warehouse environment is possible.

Corporate Intellectual Measurement

Measurement of intellectual capital today is not impossible, and some standard corporate measures are on the horizon. A common, simple measure of the value of intellectual capital is the ratio of *market value* to *book value*. Market value is essentially the total value of shares times the current share price. Book value is the amount of equity reported on a company's balance sheet. Anyone can easily calculate these figures for a publicly traded company. The difference between market value and book value is the estimated value of a company's intellectual assets, as perceived by the marketplace. The ratio allows you to rank companies objectively regardless of size. To illustrate, consider two fictional software companies, ZigaWeb and MegaWeb. Figure 11.5 shows the calculations to determine the estimated value of intellectual assets for each company and the ratio of market value to book value.

As you can see, ZigaWeb has a higher ratio of market value to book value than MegaWeb. The market believes that ZigaWeb has a more valuable pool of

Figure 11.5 Market value to book value calculations.

	ZigaWeb	MegaWeb
Shares outstanding	10,000,000	25,000,000
Price per share	5.75	3.25
Market value	57,500,000	81,250,000
Book value	12,000,000	24,000,000
Est. of intellectual assets	45,500,000	57,250,000
Ratio of market to book value	4.8	3.4

intangible assets than MegaWeb. Most of these intangible assets are intellectual assets. If these companies compete head to head in some form of Internet product, a knowledge-based business like ZigaWeb may win out due to its greater pool of intellectual capital. The problem with current financial reporting is the paucity of detail about the composition of either company's intellectual assets. In reality, the assumption about who will win is not simple. The market could be very wrong, but no one will find out until the competitive cycle plays out. Wild gyrations and shifting fortunes of knowledge-based businesses occur because changes in the value of intellectual assets are invisible using traditional accounting standards.

Over the next several years, public accounting standards will emerge to better assess and measure human, structural, or relationship capital. The value of the workforce, experience, turnover rates, and employee morale will be monitored. Standard models for calculating process, system, and information infrastructure assets will be developed to better understand the impact of a technically enabled process on future results. Portions of research and development salaries will be treated as assets and depreciated rather than expensed as a period cost.

We can envision a data warehouse designed to track information about a company's human resource assets. In a revolution of sorts, corporations may actually mean it when they say "people are our most valuable asset," and be able to prove it to investors. The design would include fact tables to track employee assignments, experience, education, and compensation. Using this model, a company could continually monitor turnover, looking for trends in assignments, education, term of employment, and perhaps compensation. The company could create aggregate tables to track trends in total experience of the knowledge base. By tracking compensation and salary, the company could create interesting measures of cost per year of experience, total employee value, and distribution of costs by position, knowledge, education, and specialty. These measures of human capital are important to internal management and to external investors.

Today, measures of structural capital are focused primarily on information technology investments. The problem with capturing IT investments absent process context is evident. A bank can spend lavishly on IT, capturing gigabytes of information about its customer base, but absent a coordinated process to exploit a large volume of data is wasteful. In the data warehousing world, size does not matter. A small data warehouse executed in the context of a proactive business process is far more valuable than a large data warehouse developed in a process vacuum. The return is not in the collection of data, but in how the data are applied to improving corporate performance.

Summing Up Intellectual Capital

In the future, intellectual capital may appear alongside capital assets on the balance sheet. Some thought leaders propose restructuring corporate balance sheets and income statements to include intellectual capital. The concept is gaining grudging acceptance in the financial community. This restructuring is important if we are to use financial statements as an objective measure of corporate performance in a knowledge economy. Until that time, companies should develop their own measures of intellectual capital. These measures should be considered in the design of both operational and analytical systems, like the corporate data warehouse. The data warehouse design team can then consider these in the design of each subject area. If the required operational data is not available, the team can at least identify the information gap that must be filled.

Understanding the worth and composition of a company's intellectual capital is the best predictor of future performance in a knowledge economy. If two large software companies have equivalent revenues and a high ratio of revenue to traditional assets, then intellectual assets make up the lion's share of their respective market values. Both external investors and internal managers must focus on increasing intellectual value. No better illustration of the power of intellectual capital exists than in the diverging fortunes of Apple Computer and Microsoft during the 1990s. In the late 1980s, each company possessed substantial intellectual assets, with Apple also possessing traditional assets like production equipment and factories. Apple's intellectual assets lost value rapidly in the 1990s, and by 1997, the company's market share in PC operating systems was below 5 percent. Microsoft, with few tangible assets, is arguably the most valuable company in the world today, with huge margins and marketplace dominance. Feared like no other company since IBM in the 1960s and 1970s, Microsoft is a pure knowledge company. In the end, Apple's capital assets became a burden in its battle for relevance. You would have been hard pressed to find any indication of Microsoft's intellectual power and capital in its financial statements in the late 1980s.

KEY MEASURES AND RATIOS

12

Each day, thousands of people turn to the financial pages of the newspaper and look up the closing price of their favorite stocks. Most people can approximate the stock price of a company in which they have invested, and some may even know the price-to-earnings ratio or market capitalization of the same company. Following a stock price is like following the statistics of your favorite baseball player or the ratings of your favorite TV show. It is a simple and accessible number. Unfortunately, if the only measure you follow is stock price, your first indication of trouble in a company is probably decline in that stock price. In recent years, especially for investors in high-technology companies, relying on this indicator has been painful. Companies routinely lose 10 percent of their value in a single trading session. Single-day losses in value of 20 or 30 percent are no longer rare.

How does an investor foresee such a turn in fortune? The investor must follow a portfolio of measures, supplemented by analyst recommendations, financial reports, and other information from the company. From this information, the market at large projects performance and buys or sells shares in company. The information cycle runs quarterly, with a company forecasting results at the beginning of the quarter and reporting results at the end of the quarter. Interim reports are used to reset expectations, and the stock price often responds to these reports as dramatically as it does periodic financials. If the company meets expectations, the price is usually stable; if it exceeds expectations, the price may go up. However, if the company disappoints the market, punishment is often swift and severe. An investor following only the stock price is relying on fortune rather than fact.

Like investors, companies also need a broad portfolio of measures. This portfolio should include measures of revenue, cost, income, value, and operational performance. Some measures, like those derived from the company's official financial statements, are for external consumption. Others are used only internally. The principal use of a data warehouse, with its rich store of enterprisewide historical data, is for the development of key measures and ratios from the vast pool of operational data. This book has explored the use of dimensional modeling techniques in many areas of the business. The designs presented are a rich source of measures. This chapter will present a sample of measures from various industries. A framework of guidelines, questions, and categories of measures is provided to help the reader build a sound portfolio of measures in any industry.

Our first recommendation is to be careful. Measures may trigger management action. If a measure is poorly defined, incorrectly calculated, or based on the wrong source data, the action taken is likely to be misguided. In developing measures, a company should use the following guidelines:

Explicitly define each measure semantically and mathematically. The purpose and limitations of the measure should be clearly understood by those who are defining it and those who will use it. The formula used to calculate the measure should be validated with the appropriate business users.

Validate the processing used to present the measure, tracing from the query that presents the measure to the sources of data. Measures often are calculated by combining information in the data warehouse with other information not as rigorously managed. The reliability and consistency of this data is critical.

Present the measure clearly and on a consistent basis. If the measure's calculation or source changes, the users and consumers of the measure must be told. It is also useful to present measures in related groups; for example, opening share price, closing share price, price-to-earnings ratio, and earnings per share may be presented quarterly to investors.

Carefully following these guidelines will result in measures that are reliable. Doing so will also force the data warehouse team to learn more about the business. Understanding the operations, competitive environment, and key measures of the business will result in a more valuable data warehouse.

Building a Portfolio of Measures

In 1997, AT&T hired a new Chief Executive Officer and began the task of reinvigorating company performance. Several actions, including changes in compensation plans, reorganizations, and staff reductions, were implemented as the company prepared for increased competition. Behind the decision to name a new CEO with a proactive reputation was poor performance in several key measures.

Revenue was flat, market share was declining, and income was disappointing shareholders. The new CEO announced several actions, including an increase in overseas investment, moves to compete in the local service market, and cuts in administrative costs.

What type of measures would AT&T need in the coming years to measure progress? To identify a set of measures for AT&T, we would examine the company's concept of operations, business model, strategies, and competitive environment. These subjects help to draw out the unique aspects of the company that need to be measured. AT&T's concept of operations is the profitable provision of telecommunications services for business and residential customers around the world. This may seem obvious, but the company's concept of operations changed dramatically in 1996 when it divested itself of two large divisions. One division, now known as Lucent Technologies, conducts applied research and develops telecommunications products. The other division, NCR, was acquired and then sold by AT&T over a five-year period. In 1995, the company's concept of operations was a multidivision conglomerate with separate operating divisions. By 1998, it planned to be a global telecommunications company. Prior to the divestiture, each division of AT&T operated a different business model, executed different strategies, had different competitors, and different operational profiles. The number of measures required to manage such a diverse company is certainly greater than the number required to run a telecommunications giant. It is safe to say that AT&T's board of directors felt that focus on its core business would accrue greater profits to AT&T than the existing model. Executive management had much less to worry about after the two divisions were spun off. Simply changing the concept of operations simplified the measurement portfolio.

To further illustrate the complexity of maintaining separate operational divisions, consider the measures required to operate three distinct business models. A business model is a simplified view of how a company is designed to make a profit. For example, AT&T's long distance business generates revenue by selling services on its communications network. The revenue generated must cover the high fixed costs of the network, as well as selling and administrative costs. There is a budgeted level of utilization and price required to make a profit. For the long distance business it may be 80 percent utilization of the network at an average rate of 11 cents a minute. By manipulating utilization and average rate, AT&T managers can ensure operational profitability. These measures, derived from the business model, are substantially different than those required for a manufacturer or bank. Each unique business model operated by a company will require different operational measures.

Other measures are related to a company's strategy. The newly focused AT&T plans to expend capital to expand overseas and enter the local service market. Many questions arise from such a strategy. What is the current revenue from foreign operations? What is the change in revenue from last year? How does such growth relate to the amount of capital invested in each market? What is the company's revenue in domestic local service? What markets generate that revenue, and is it growing or declining? How much capital has been invested? Another strategy announced by the company in late 1997 was a plan to reduce the relative cost of sales, general, and administrative expenses to equal that of leaner competitors. The distribution of expenses at that time is depicted in Figure 12.1.

In an era of cost reductions and more aggressive competition, AT&T determined that spending 29 percent of total revenue on administration was excessive. Competitors were reported to be spending substantially less. As administrative cost cutting is implemented, managers will devise new ways of managing and justifying administrative costs. Measuring administrative costs as a percentage of revenue is a simple way to ensure that growth is well managed.

Still other measures are driven by the company's competitive environment. Long distance companies face increased rates of customer attrition similar to those in the banking example discussed in Chapter 3, "Marketing." The company should measure the number of defections, acquisitions, and overall churn in its customer base. It will also need to approximate estimated lifetime value of existing customers by analyzing their calling patterns. This information can be used to

Figure 12.1 Expense distribution for AT&T.

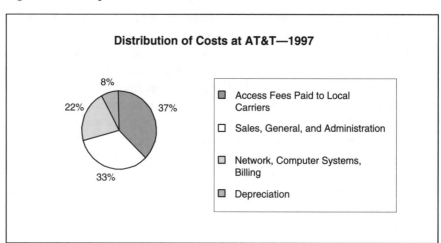

create compelling but profitable calling plans that increase the likelihood that valuable customers are retained.

Finally, we can identify many important measures simply by examining a company's operational environment. For AT&T, such measures are directly related to the performance of core business processes. These include network management, service initiation, customer service, billing, marketing, and financial management. The area of network management could easily generate several operational measures, including network availability, failure rates, signal quality, signal drop rates, and equipment failure rates. These measures reflect the unique operational environment of the company and provide managers and employees with feedback on operational performance.

The skeleton set of measures developed for a telecommunications-focused AT&T is presented in Table 12.1. These measures would likely come from a variety of sources within the company, including operational systems and the data warehouse. Because the data warehouse team often sees data from across the company, spanning operational systems, it may have the first opportunity to satisfy these requirements.

Most companies have an existing portfolio of measures that are consistently reported. Other measures are used only for a specific program, project, or activity. The data warehouse team should research existing measures and assist users in identifying new ones that may be satisfied by a specific data mart or the data warehouse as a whole.

The process of creating an effective portfolio of measures is continuous. Measures gain or lose importance as strategies change in response to the competitive environment. New sources of data create new opportunities to correlate data. The data warehouse is often the first opportunity a company has to compare detailed data from across the enterprise. The concept of operations and business model are the most important factors in choosing and defining measures for a company. The remainder of this chapter describes measurement portfolios for different categories of businesses.

Measures for Manufacturers

Manufacturing companies produce and sell goods to their customers. The manufacturing business is complex, and the measurement portfolio for a manufacturing company contains a diverse set of revenue, cost, income, value, and operational measures. These categories of measures define the framework we will use throughout this chapter to build a measurement portfolio. First, however, we will

Table 12.1 Partial List of Measures for Telecommunications Company

Source	Measures
Concept of operations	Revenue from operations
	Expenses by category
	Income
Business model	Network utilization
	Network capacity
	Price per minute
	Total minutes used
	Price per minute mix
Strategies	Revenue by country
	Revenue by service (local or long distance)
	Local service revenue by market
	Return on capital by country
	Capital investment by country
	Revenue per dollar of sales expense
	Sales expense as a percent of revenue
Competitive environment	Attrition rates
	Total churn
	Average customer relationship in months
	Acquisition rates
	Reacquisition rates
	Acquisition cost per customer
Operational environment	Directory assistance response time
	Service initiation time
	Network availability
	Customers suffering outages
	Equipment maintenance costs
	Equipment failure rate

define the basic business elements that are used as sources for measures. To do so we will use a fictitious manufacturer, Omnicraft Boats, Ltd.

Omnicraft designs and manufactures powerboats for the consumer market in the Americas. The company operates as a single division, multiple product line, discrete manufacturer. The business model is a standard manufacturing model for a durable goods company. Product revenues must cover product and period costs, and target net margin is 5 percent. The company maintains two large job cost manufacturing facilities, one in Canada and one in South Carolina. The company's strategy is to create products for the low-cost market while providing high-market reliability. The company has established a solid reputation for quality at a fair price, and is considered the Toyota of powerboat makers.

In recent years, the company has experienced intensive price competition from a major competitor, Swiftwinds USA. Swiftwinds is a subsidiary of a large European conglomerate and has entered the market with lower prices. Omnicraft suspects that Swiftwinds is able to price aggressively due to lower labor costs and modern facilities. Omnicraft also suspects that Swiftwinds's product line will have a poor durability record in the future. Unfortunately, the company must wait at least two years for the competitive tides to turn. In the interim, Omnicraft is having a difficult time convincing dealers and buyers that its product is superior.

Omnicraft is organized into five major processes that comprise the bulk of company operations. These processes are product engineering, manufacturing, inventory management, dealer sales, and demand creation. Each of these processes is further divided into subprocesses. Manufacturing includes production, material purchasing, production planning, and quality assurance. Each processes requires its own set of operational measures.

Manufacturing Sales Measures

Measuring sales volume and revenue is an obvious requirement for Omnicraft. The company sells its product through dealers on a consignment basis in an arrangement similar to the car manufacturer discussed in Chapter 2, "Sales." Revenue is realized when a sale is completed by a dealer to an end customer. This type of revenue, sales revenue, is the only type most manufacturers experience. Still, the company must also report income from investments and the proceeds of asset sales. It is important when defining revenue measures to clearly distinguish revenue from operations and other nonoperating revenue sources. *Sales revenue* is the term most commonly used to refer to operational revenue.

Revenue is realized in a specific accounting period, usually when a legal document from a purchaser is recorded. For Omnicraft, revenue is realized in the month a purchase contract is signed by a customer. The company may also wish to measure and report on returns or canceled purchase contracts. Returns are usually charged to the period in which they occur, not the period in which the sale is made. This avoids continually restating revenue numbers as returns are made. In a big-ticket industry like powerboats, however, the company may not allow returns beyond a very short time, perhaps five days. If so, the company may wish to wait the five days at the end of each month before calculating final sales revenue. This would allow any returns from the previous month to be subtracted.

Periodic reporting of revenue is the most common requirement in revenue reporting. Revenue is aggregated by the period in which it is realized by the company. The ability to aggregate by period is satisfied by including a time dimension in the data warehouse schema, as shown in Chapter 2, "Sales." The grain of the

Revenue Recognition Controversies

Revenue recognition is rather straightforward for a manufacturer; in other cases, the rules are not so clearly defined. Remember the software company in Chapter 2, "Sales," which sold a substantial amount of software through channels. In that chapter, we discussed the importance of deciding when to recognize revenue. Software companies have been known to ship software to channel distributors and recognize the revenue from those shipments before an end customer makes a purchase. Such a sale to a distributor is encumbered, and counting the revenue from it is very risky. One large database vendor, Informix, had to reduce revenues by almost $200 million in 1996 partly due to "stuffing the channel," as this practice is called.

The software industry is also prone to side letters and other unfortunate practices by aggressive salespeople. A salesperson might negotiate a deal and use all the standard procedures and quotation forms, submitting the sale as an irrevocable transaction to the software vendor. At the same time, the salesperson gives a side letter to the buyer, outlining conditions that would allow the buyer to return the software if not satisfied. From the software vendor's perspective, it has made an unconditional sale, as it is ignorant of the side letter. The salesperson, perhaps under incredible pressure to meet quota, acts recklessly and encumbers the sale. The company again may be faced with a substantial reduction in revenue once the letter is invoked by the customer. Side letters were a major problem for companies, including Oracle, in the early 1990s, but tighter internal controls are making such incidents less common. Nevertheless, Sybase had a revenue restatement due to side letters at its Japanese subsidiary in 1997.

time dimension should be the smallest time period in which revenue accounting is required. The grain is usually daily for the sales revenue subject area. A rich time dimension provides the capability to look at day of week, day of month, holiday, and other revenue increments. Omnicraft may use daily revenue reporting to plan production, cash flow, and promotions.

The reason to track revenue at specific periods is to allow comparisons of this measure over time. The most obvious use is a periodic revenue comparison over consecutive periods. A consecutive quarterly comparison is shown in Report 12.1.

A good rule to follow in presenting sales revenue is to use the standard definitions and controls adopted by the company's financial management. This keeps the data warehouse team out of the pool of material witnesses in SEC actions and shareholder lawsuits. If channel sales are recognized, then recognize them as such in the data warehouse design. If channel sales are only recognized when a final customer is identified, then apply that logic.

If revenue is restated for any period, the likelihood of a major adjustment to the data warehouse is high. The data warehouse must reflect history. Imagine that our software vendor from Chapter 4, "Fulfillment," has a particularly unscrupulous salesperson. This individual closes four site license deals at major corporations in Q3 1996 using side letters. These letters are disclosed by the customers in Q1 1997 as the vendor continues to dun them for payment. The companies refuse to pay and return all software. The impact is substantial, as these three deals equated to 20 percent of Q3 1996 revenue. The company must reverse all benefits from the sales in its financial systems in order to restate revenues. The data warehouse team should ensure that it also records the reversals. Similarly, the company may choose to delete the orders—determining that they did not really exist to begin with—from the order entry system. The data warehouse team must also remove the orders from the data warehouse. The company could decide instead to override system controls and simply cancel the orders with an effective date of Q3 1996. This situation may cause difficulty for the data warehouse team, which may key off effective dates when extracting data. Such instances are rare, but their handling is important and underscores the subtlety behind a simple measure like revenue.

Report 12.1 Consecutive quarter comparison.

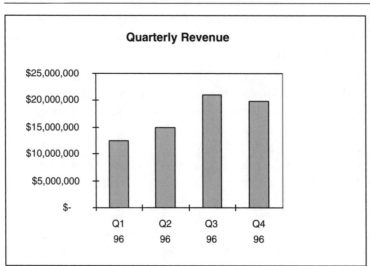

While quarterly revenue is the base measure, the relationship between a quarter and the quarter immediately preceding it is quarterly revenue increase/decrease. The percentage change in revenue is the quarterly revenue percentage increase/decrease.

Consecutive period comparisons are not always as revealing as equivalent quarter comparisons. In the example in Table 12.2, the running comparison shows a 6-percent decline in revenue from Q3 to Q4 in 1996. If the company experiences strong seasonal sales, however, a drop off from Q3 to Q4 may be normal. Table 12.3 presents equivalent quarter comparisons for 1995 and 1996. The drop-off in Q4 may be a normal part of the business cycle. What

Table 12.2 Periodic Revenue Measures

	Q1 96	Q2 96	Q3 96	Q4 96
Revenue	$12,505,000	$14,908,000	$21,050,000	$19,880,000
Revenue increase/ decrease		$2,403,000	$6,142,000	($1,170,000)
Revenue percentage increase/decrease		19%	41%	–6%

Table 12.3 Comparing Equivalent Quarters

	Q1	Q2	Q3	Q4
1995 revenue	$9,450,000	$8,230,000	$13,800,000	$10,700,000
1996 revenue	$12,505,000	$11,908,000	$21,050,000	$19,880,000
Revenue percentage increase/decrease	32%	45%	53%	86%

stands out in the equivalent quarter comparison is the growth in sales from Q3 95 to Q3 96, and the drop-off in Q3 to Q4 sales was not as substantial in 1996 as in 1995.

The company may also wish to track revenue to date for a current, previous, or equivalent period. Month-to-date, quarter-to-date, and year-to-date comparisons are an easy way to snapshot performance compared to previous years. An example of a period to date is Report 12.2, depicting the Prior Year Month to Date Revenue for January 1995 and 1996. The report was run on January 25, 1996 and includes data on sales through January 24, 1996.

Computing average period revenue over a range of time can remove volatility from revenue analysis. Software companies often have wide variability in revenue because new product releases drive sales. Average monthly revenue over a year or longer period gives the company a basis for budgeting and forecasting. Rolling averages are also useful in softening the impact of variability in revenue. For example, 90-day rolling average revenue can be used to balance day-to-day variability in demand with consistent output from production facilities.

Report 12.2 Month-to-date revenue report.

Omnicraft Boats, Ltd.
Month-to-Date Revenue/Prior Year Month to Date
January 1–24, 1996, compared to January 1–24, 1995

Current Month to Date	Prior Year Month to Date	% Change
2,561,702	2,009,112	27.5

Revenue by Dimensions

Revenue measures by dimensions other than time are of obvious value. The relevant dimensions for measuring revenue come from the business model and operational characteristics of the business. We can deduce some dimensions relevant to both revenue and cost measurement by answering a few questions about the company. These questions are:

- What is the organizational basis of the company? Into what operational segments is it divided?

- What is the product organization of the company? What levels of product does it offer? What brands does it manage?

- What is the market organization of the company? What markets does it serve, and how does it segment those markets?

- How does the company sell its products to the marketplace? What channels and methods are used to sell goods to the marketplace? Who are the customers, and how are they segmented?

The answers to these questions are useful in defining dimensional measures for a specific company. For Omnicraft, we can imagine the candidate measures presented in Table 12.4. The problem is that, in many cases, revenue is not tracked at the level of specificity required to create these measures.

If we include these dimensions in the design of our data warehouse, the appropriate product comparisons, division comparisons, and market comparisons are straightforward. Some of the most meaningful measures come from the competitive environment questions. These measures are often unique to a company and change frequently.

Table 12.4 Candidate Revenue Measures for Omnicraft

Category	Measures
Division	None, single operational division
Product	Revenue by product, revenue by product line
Market	Revenue by country, region, state, city, SMSA, demographic profile of customer
Sales channel	Revenue by dealer, dealer type, dealer geography
Competitive environment	Market share, revenue compared to Swiftwinds

Cost Measures

Manufacturers face significant challenges in tracking costs, as seen in Chapter 9, "Financial Reporting." Recall from that discussion that manufacturing costs fall into four categories: cost of goods sold, sales and administration, interest, and taxes. Cost of goods sold, or product costs, includes the cost of direct materials, direct labor, and manufacturing overhead. These costs are tracked over time to value finished goods inventory and look for variances from budgeted costs. Remember that cost allocation can be complex and that measures of profitability presented in Chapter 10, "Profitability," were accurate only to the degree that the costing methods were accurate.

Direct materials costs are tracked for both financial accounting and managerial accounting. Financial reports include direct material costs in the calculation of cost of goods sold for a specific period. Material planners and purchasers monitor the cost of material to create direct material cost standards for budgeting. Product managers track material costs to support pricing decisions, both increases and decreases. Direct labor is of similar interest to the same parties. Direct labor costs are tracked and allocated to cost of goods sold for financial reporting, but they are also tracked as they are incurred for budgeting and pricing purposes.

The final subcategory of cost of goods sold is manufacturing overhead. Remember that manufacturing overhead consists of everything else that is related to manufacturing but not part of direct labor or direct materials. Indirect manufacturing costs include indirect materials, factory utilities, production equipment depreciation, production equipment maintenance, and plant support staff labor.

To review, the three elements of cost of goods sold in manufacturing are direct materials, direct labor, and manufacturing overhead. Each of these costs are valid measures for both managerial and financial accounting. Managerial accounting examines actual costs and compares them to standard costs in each category to ensure the accuracy of financial reports downstream. Manufacturers also like to separate fixed manufacturing overhead costs from variable manufacturing overhead costs. Fixed manufacturing overhead costs are incurred regardless of the level of production, while variable manufacturing overhead increases as production increases. Fixed manufacturing overhead allocations are relatively constant over time, while variable overhead allocations will, as expected, vary with production levels.

Manufacturers carefully monitor the elements of cost of goods sold over time. Combinations of these cost measures are also useful. Direct materials plus direct labor costs are known as *prime* cost. Direct labor plus manufacturing overhead is known as *conversion* cost. In Chapter 11, "Knowledge and Intellectual Capital,"

> **Key Business Term**
>
> **Fixed cost.** Costs that remain constant within a broad range of operational activity. Both product and period costs can be classified as fixed or variable. Fixed product costs include factory rent or depreciation, utilities, administrative labor, and property taxes. Variable product costs include direct materials, direct labor, and indirect materials. Some fixed costs are called *committed* fixed costs because they represent the cost of actually continuing in business and are unavoidable. Business licenses and executive salaries are examples of committed fixed costs. Other fixed costs are *discretionary* and planned in each budgetary cycle. Discretionary fixed costs are usually not product costs. These costs include employee training, company parties, and some administrative salaries.

we discussed how increasing automation and improved processes are continually reducing the amount of direct labor and the cost of direct materials required to produce a product. Cost of goods sold, direct labor, direct materials, factory overhead, prime cost, and conversion costs can be expressed in currency or as a percentage of revenue. Report 12.3 presents quarterly comparisons of these measures for Omnicraft during the 1996 fiscal year.

Report 12.3 Omnicraft quarterly cost of goods sold measures.

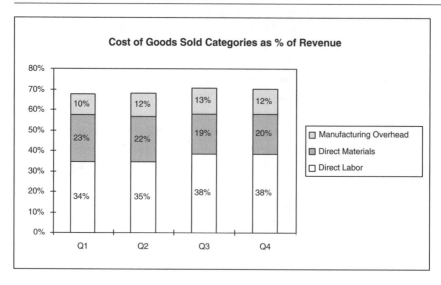

Sales, Administration, and General Costs

In addition to cost of goods sold, Omnicraft incurs various sales, administrative, and general (SAG) costs. These costs are not directly traceable to a specific product and are expensed on a periodic basis. For Omnicraft these costs include office rent, office supplies, dealer relations, sales commissions, administrative salaries, officers' salaries, and advertising. Because Omnicraft is facing intense price competition, it should carefully monitor SAG costs and attempt to find savings in these accounts. This same price competition will require Omnicraft to invest more money in advertising, promotions, and dealer incentives in the coming months. A best-case scenario would be to hold the ratio of sales revenue to SAG costs constant, shifting more dollars to the categories most likely to increase revenue. It is also useful to attribute SAG costs, where possible, to other dimensions. Tracking sales and marketing costs by product and market are common. Tracking administrative costs by organizational unit and cost category is also useful.

Fixed and variable SAG cost measures are also useful to a manufacturer. Committed fixed SAG costs are considered unavoidable since they make up the operational framework of the company. Committed fixed SAG costs for Omnicraft would include office rent, executive salaries, office equipment depreciation, accounting fees, legal fees, and business licenses. The company must incur these costs to operate, regardless of its strategy or business volume. Omnicraft's discretionary fixed SAG costs include advertising and marketing costs, employee training, entertainment, and product research.. Reducing discretionary fixed SAG costs is a common tactic in cost cutting. These costs are the furthest removed from production and can be eliminated. Of course, reductions in discretionary fixed SAG costs may have long-term ramifications.

Income Measures

A full set of revenue and cost measures leads to a good set of income measures, since income equals revenue minus costs. In Chapter 9, "Financial Reporting," we defined the three important income measures: gross income, EBIT, and net income. Gross income is calculated by subtracting cost of goods sold from sales revenue. EBIT, or earnings before interest and taxes, is calculated by subtracting SAG costs from gross income. Net income is calculated by subtracting interest and taxes from EBIT. Omnicraft measures and reports income based on this format. Quarterly income statements for 1996 are presented in Report 12.4.

We can create three additional income measures by dividing each income measure by sales revenue. These measures are margin percentage of gross income, EBIT, and net income. For Omnicraft in 1996, the gross margin percentage for

Report 12.4 Gross, EBIT, and net income for Omnicraft.

	Q1	Q2	Q3	Q4
Revenue	$12,505,000	$11,908,000	$21,050,000	$19,880,000
Cost of Goods Sold				
Direct Labor	$ 4,300,200	$ 4,120,000	$ 8,050,200	$ 7,630,000
Direct Materials	$ 2,900,500	$ 2,600,700	$ 4,100,900	$ 3,890,000
Manufacturing Overhead	$ 1,260,000	$ 1,375,000	$ 2,700,100	$ 2,450,000
Total CGS	$ 8,460,700	$ 8,095,700	$14,851,200	$13,970,000
Gross Income	$ 4,044,300	$ 3,812,300	$ 6,198,800	$ 5,910,000
SAG Costs	$ 3,794,200	$ 3,335,980	$ 5,988,300	$ 5,566,400
EBIT	$ 250,100	$ 476,320	$ 210,500	$ 343,600
Interest Expense	$ 47,900	$ 38,100	$ 62,300	$ 75,900
Taxes	$ 82,533	$ 157,186	$ 69,465	$ 113,388
Net Income	$ 119,667	$ 281,034	$ 78,735	$ 154,312

Q4 is 29.7 percent, EBIT margin percentage is 1.7 percent, and net margin percentage is 0.8 percent. Omnicraft is in a difficult position considering the increased pressure from Swiftwinds.

Note that the income measures calculated in this example ignore proceeds from investments, asset sales, and other extraordinary items; thus, the income measures that we reported are operating measures. Including extraordinary items leads to a different set of measures that should be clearly identified as consolidated or comprehensive in nature. Income measures that include extraordinary items are usually only of interest to external observers and accountants.

One other note on income measures. There is a strong move in manufacturing and other industries to create segment-level income measures. These measures provide income for specific products, divisions, markets, or similar segments of the business. These segments are usually equivalent to the dimensions identified for revenue and cost segregation discussed previously. Segment reporting is the holy grail of data warehouse reporting and requires a significant investment and commitment by a company. We discuss segment reporting in Chapter 10, "Profitability."

Cost, Revenue, and Income Ratios

It is often revealing to track the relationship among costs, revenue, and income. It is equally revealing to compare these individual measures with other measures in a company. We introduced in the previous section margin percentages, which is the relationship between income measures and revenue. Comparing specific categories of costs to revenue is also helpful. The ratios of the direct materials, direct labor, and manufacturing overhead to revenue were presented in Figure 12.5. Remember that Omnicraft is responding to competitive pressure from Swiftwinds by increasing spending on marketing; unfortunately, the company has little room to maneuver due to its thin profit margins. Management is disappointed with the return on its current marketing dollars and has recruited an outside marketing executive to improve that return. How can that return be measured? One simple measure of the value of marketing is the ratio of sales revenue per market dollar expended. This figure can be calculated simply by dividing period sales revenue by period marketing costs. If sales increase, the company is getting a better return on its marketing dollars. Sample figures are shown in Table 12.5.

Relating other fixed-cost categories to revenue and income is increasingly important to manufacturers. Discretionary costs are choices to spend money, and many discretionary costs are expected to impact revenue or income. In a given

Table 12.5 Tracking the Impact of Marketing Costs

	Q1	Q2	Q3	Q4
Revenue	$12,505,000	$11,908,000	$21,050,000	$19,880,000
Marketing expense	$890,500	$900,340	$1,450,000	$1,100,000
Marketing expense as percent of revenue	7%	8%	7%	6%
Revenue dollars per marketing dollar	14.04	13.23	14.52	18.07

year, Omnicraft may choose to increase spending on marketing, quality training, and dealer relations. Each of these cost increases is expected to have an impact on some other measure. Increased spending on dealer relations should manifest itself in increased sales revenue. Increased quality training should result in lower cost of goods sold, since increased attention to quality usually reduces rework and improves productivity.

Revenue, cost, and income measures can also be compared to operational measures used by the company, as well as relatively static statistics. Revenue per direct labor hour is a simple measure of productivity that combines an operational and revenue measure. Revenue per direct labor employee is a similar measure. The increased spending on dealer relations should not only increase revenue, but also increase Omnicraft's revenue per dealer. The company may wish to focus on a selected set of dealers, perhaps those who also sell Swiftwinds products, and measure the impact on revenue per dealer in that group.

Operational Measures

Previously, we described Omnicraft's operations as consisting of five major processes: product engineering, manufacturing, inventory management, dealer sales, and demand creation. The company needs operational measures for each of these process areas, as well as measures that address specific strategies and competitive pressures. Because Omnicraft is a manufacturer, we will develop a set of measures for the production process to illustrate a set of operational measures.

Every process has inputs and outputs. A good set of process measures will measure the volume, quality, and cost of inputs and outputs, as well as the performance of the process. In production, the inputs are raw materials, labor, machine hours, and factory overhead. The outputs are units of products. Candidate measures for the Omnicraft production process are presented in Table 12.6.

This partial list of measures is used to manage the production process. These measures should be tracked by production facility, production line, and product, as well as companywide. Additional measures could be developed for the subprocesses of production. Operational measures are often supported by existing OLTP systems and reports. If so, the data warehouse team should carefully decide which measures it should reproduce.

This rough portfolio of measures for Omnicraft is far from complete. Measures exist at every level of the organization and change continually. Understanding what measures are most valuable in a specific industry or subject area accelerates the requirements definition process and moves important requirements to the top of the list. Understanding measures at a broad level can also help guide the team in scope

Table 12.6 Candidate Production Process Measures

Process Area	Measure
Direct materials	Direct materials quantity consumed by material
	Direct materials usage variance
	Scrap material quantity and value
	Materials cost per unit
Direct labor	Direct labor quantity used by category
	Direct labor usage variance
	Direct labor quantity per unit
	Direct labor cost per unit
	Overhead labor cost
Production equipment	Total machine hours
	Machine hours per unit
	Machine downtime
Production output	Units produced
	Average daily production
	Production capacity versus actual production
Quality	Defective units
	Units reworked
	Units scrapped
	Defect quantity by type

decisions. Many data warehouse teams are operating under intense scrutiny and aggressive time schedules. Pulling in all source data and then deciding what measures are important is a risky approach.

Measures for Merchants

Merchants are companies that sell goods made by others. Examples include grocers, department stores, restaurants, and electronics chains. Merchants do not own production facilities, and because they do not produce a product, they have no direct material or direct labor costs. A merchant typically manages many locations and may even have more than one type of store in its portfolio. Radio Shack and Wal-Mart both operate more than one type of retail outlet, each with separate brand identity. Our example for developing retail measures is Aquarius Electronic Corporation (AEC), a fictitious company operating two chains of electronics stores.

AEC is organized into two divisions, one for each chain. The company operates stores in North America, Japan, and South Korea. The largest chain is ElectraMarket, with 75 outlets worldwide. ElectraMarket offers a wide range of electronics and appliances, similar to Circuit City or Best Buy. The smaller chain, ElectraDirect, is a chain of 10 stores located in malls and featuring specialty electronics for upscale buyers. ElectraDirect stores carry cellular phones, PDAs, pagers, portable electronics gear, portable cameras, and other small but pricey times. ElectraMarket earns revenue from sales, service contracts, and repair services. ElectraDirect's revenue sources are product sales and service commissions paid by pager and cellular phone carriers.

ElectraMarket faces intense price competition in all its markets. The company locates its stores in high-traffic retail areas frequented by midmarket consumers. These consumers frequently use competing stores' prices in negotiations. ElectraMarket prices aggressively to move inventory and keep sales volume up. Conversely, ElectraDirect carries an eclectic inventory that often languishes on store shelves. The chain's price structure is higher to cover the higher price it pays for retail space. ElectraDirect has been unprofitable since its inception in 1992. The company is considering altering the product mix and pricing structure at some stores in the future, as well as closing consistently unprofitable locations.

The company segregates nearly all costs by chain. Only executive salaries and headquarters expenses are treated as common costs. Each chain maintains its own staff of buyers and selects its own product lines.

Measuring Retail Sales

AEC would use the same periodic revenue measures as Omnicraft as a basis for consecutive and equivalent period comparisons. But merchants and the few manufacturers that sell directly to the public face a more volatile revenue arena than Omnicraft. Sales volume varies greatly from day to day and month to month. Retailers must deal with the seasonality of goods, as well as changes in consumer preferences. Most retailers today measure product-level sales volume and revenue on a daily basis. AEC measures sales daily, but also compares sales on a day of week, day of month, and seasonal basis.

The daily sales fact table with product and store dimensions is invaluable for store-specific management actions. Imagine a store manager at an ElectraMarket chain outlet in a town in which the largest employers are a large military installation and an industrial plant. That outlet manager is probably the only person in the organization who is interested in analyzing sales coincident with paydays at these large employers. She may plan promotions coincident with those days. If she knows the plant pays a production bonus on a quarterly basis, she may promote big-ticket items coincident with these events. These store- and product-specific sales measures are imperative to the company's success, especially considering the problems with ElectraDirect.

AEC also needs to measure sales per location. This measure can be used to monitor the general health of the chain and perhaps identify problems in the rapidly expanding business. The charts in Report 12.5 present revenue and revenue per store for the two chains. The numbers indicate that ElectraMarket is managing its growth better than ElectraDirect. The revenue per store number is an excellent indicator to investors and managers of the health of the entire system in a multisite business.

Another measure used to examine the health of a retail organization is the percentage increase in revenue at stores open more than one year. This shows the overall health of the chain by eliminating stores that did not operate for the prior reporting period. Report 12.6 shows sales for ElectraDirect, which opened two new stores in 1997.

The percentage increase in revenue for the entire chain is 25.6 percent in 1996; however, the revenue increase in stores open more than one year is only 2 percent. Roughly 90 percent of the $3M increase in revenue came from new store sales. ElectraDirect is gaining little revenue ground based on same-store sales.

Report 12.5 Revenue per location comparison.

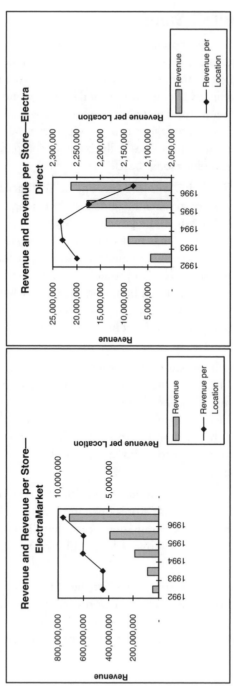

Report 12.6 Sales at existing and new stores.

		1995	1996
Existing Stores	Store 1	2,780,000	2,670,000
	Store 2	1,560,000	1,890,000
	Store 3	2,450,000	2,130,000
	Store 4	2,120,000	2,230,000
	Store 5	2,230,000	2,100,000
	Store 6	2,160,000	1,960,000
	Store 7	1,890,000	2,260,000
	Store 8	1,760,000	2,130,000
Existing Store Sales		**16,951,995**	**17,370,000**
New Stores	Store 9		1,950,000
	Store 10		1,980,000
New Store Sales			**3,930,000**
Total Sales		**16,951,995**	**21,300,000**

Customers, Baskets, and Visits

Interestingly, some merchants have no idea who is buying their products. These anonymous customer industries deal mostly in cash. The typical fast-food restaurant has little information about the demographics, income, and buying behavior of its customers when compared to a bank, airline, or rental car company. Such companies create measures that profile customer behavior by visit rather than by demographic or name. A fast-food chain is very interested in how much people spend in an average visit, what promotions generate increases in revenue, and how much business is generated by what menu items. They may supplement this data with surveys or analyze the demographics around a particular store location, but they have much less customer-specific data than named-customer businesses. A candidate list of dimensional attributes relevant to revenue reporting for a fast-food chain is shown in Table 12.7.

The company would likely be interested in revenue by the various attributes. If the products sold in each are carefully tracked, product

Continues

Customers, Baskets, and Visits (*Continued*)

Table 12.7 Candidate Revenue Dimensions for Fast-Food Chain

Dimension	Attribute
Division	Division name, company owned or franchise, franchisee
Product	Type (food, beverage), type (sandwich, side item, etc.), product name, size, diet, meal (breakfast, lunch/dinner)
Market	Region, state, city, SMSA, demographic profile of location
Sales channel	Location type (mall, pad site, kiosk, airport, retail collocation), store id, drive-through or counter
Competitive environment	Time of purchase, visit

relationships can be discovered. This is a step beyond the classic beer and diapers story famous in data warehousing circles. That story related the discovery of the sales relationship between beer and diapers at grocery stores. This relationship was not discovered by analyzing the items in each shopping cart, but by tracking the correlation in sales between each item on a store-by-store and day-by-day basis. If we can refine the revenue grain to visit—shopping basket in the grocery store—discovering product relationships is even easier.

Other industries have a similar requirement to measure the sales event as well as the revenue. The completion of a call is a process that a phone company executes thousands of times a minute. The completed call represents the output of the process and is the fundamental transaction of

Retail Cost Measures

As a merchant, AEC has both product and period costs, although the cost of goods sold for a merchant consists only of merchandise costs. Merchandise costs replace the direct materials, direct labor, and manufacturing overhead cost measures used for Omnicraft. Using one of the standard cost allocation methods discussed in Chapter 9, "Financial Reporting," AEC can carefully track changes in cost of goods sold by product. Unfortunately, retailers often have little control over merchandise costs.

the business. It encompasses both the basic sales transaction and the fulfillment process for a customer. Measuring the operational volume of this process is critical to the business. We can use the measures from our revenue and cost questions to identify specific aspects of volume that might be meaningful. It is especially useful to be able to compare operational volumes to measures of revenue and costs. In doing so, we can create additional comparative ratios, like average revenue per call and average cost per call. Operational volumes are also useful to compare with quality, customer service, and fixed-cost measures. A sample of these measures from different industries is shown in Table 12.8.

Table 12.8 Sales Transaction Volume Measures

Industry	Sales Transaction Measure	Comparative Measures
Grocery	Basket count or visit	Average sales per basket/visit, average item count per basket/visit
Fast food	Visit	Average sales per visit, average item count per visit
Manufacturer	Order	Average revenue per order, average items per order, average shipping costs per order
Construction	Contract or job	Average sales per job, direct labor per job
Theater	Showing	Average revenue per screen, attendance per screen

AEC cannot reduce product costs, improve processes, or slash overhead for any of its suppliers; instead, the company must cut the best deals it can for the most desirable items in a very competitive marketplace. About the only effective method of manipulating merchandise costs is volume buying. Because Wal-Mart is able to purchase huge quantities from manufacturers, it carries great negotiating weight. Smaller retailers like AEC often have less power and can be left without desired products or with units costing significantly more than larger competitors.

With little ability to affect product costs, merchants often attempt to optimize and aggressively manage SAG costs. Carefully identifying and allocating costs to specific stores and product lines can help the company manage profitability. Measuring these costs over time on an aggregate and per-store basis allows the company to continually fine-tune operations. A sample of AEC's SAG costs for a three-month operational period is shown in Table 12.9, along with the period average.

AEC will likely measure all of these costs over time and continuously look for ways to reduce them without impacting revenue. Notice that most of these SAG costs vary minimally, and the variability is probably unrelated to sales revenue. Rental expense went up slightly in September, probably due to an annual increase in a rent coming due at a few stores. Sales staff salaries vary somewhat, probably due to the number of days in a month and the staffing variances at individual stores. Utilities increased slightly, perhaps due to increased air-conditioning costs in the summer months. The biggest change in costs occurred in advertising, where increased spending may be related to promotions for the back-to-school season. The company may be heavily promoting computers, organizers, and other school-related gadgets.

Table 12.9 Sample SAG Costs for AEC

SAG Cost Category	Jul.	Aug.	Sep.	Period Avg.
Rental expense	139,000	139,000	152,000	143,333
Executive salaries	345,000	345,000	345,000	345,000
IT asset depreciation	260,000	260,000	260,000	260,000
IT salaries	480,000	480,000	480,000	480,000
Sales staff wages	1,290,000	1,450,000	1,390,000	1,376,667
Sales commissions	312,000	427,000	419,000	386,000
Store utilities	56,900	61,800	71,200	63,300
Store maintenance	118,000	211,000	141,900	156,967
Store fixtures depreciation	61,000	61,000	63,500	61,833
Advertising	125,000	311,200	456,700	297,633

Retail Comparisons and Ratios

Merchants have a great affinity for ratios, especially those that relate costs or revenue to other operational measures. These ratios are in addition to the classic income, cost, and revenue ratios we have already covered. We should note that these ratios, including the different types of income and income margin percentages, are calculated in the same way for a retailer. Ratios of costs to revenue are also very valuable to a retailer like AEC with tight margins and aggressive competitors. The company most constantly monitor the relationship between SAG costs and revenue to ensure that increases have the intended effect and decreases do not have unintended consequences. Now on with the ratios.

Merchants like AEC often view the world in terms of square feet. How much revenue and cost is associated with a square foot of retail space is one of the most cherished measures in retail. This measure is important, because space is the retailer's most costly and valuable asset. An idle product is a problem for a retailer because it takes up space that a hot product could be occupying. AEC is having a serious problem with its ElectraDirect outlets because revenue is flat and costs are high. The problem is particularly acute when you compare ElectraDirect's revenue and costs per square foot with those of ElectraMarket. This comparison, shown in Table 12.10, illustrates that ElectraDirect has higher costs per square foot but significantly lower revenue per square foot. Divisional comparisons are easy. The company may also want to examine the cost and revenue per square foot of individual ElectraDirect outlets to determine if any are profitable.

These ratios are useful in managing the use and cost of retail floor space, a precious commodity. The company may want to create measures for specific cost categories in each chain, or other revenue cost relationships that might be revealing. As an example, the company may measure revenue per sales staff hour worked to monitor the impact of an increased sales presence on revenue. This

Table 12.10 Square Footage Measures

Measure	ElectraMarket	ElectraDirect
Revenue/sq. ft.	86.61	73.45
Product cost/sq. ft.	62.12	58.28
SAG cost/sq. ft.	19.02	23.41
Total cost/sq. ft.	81.13	81.69

measure, when tracked with the ratio of sales staff wages to revenue, may indicate lift from increased customer service across the chain.

Another important ratio to merchants is the inventory turnover ratio. This ratio is used to calculate how many times inventory is completely replaced during a particular period. This ratio can be calculated from both a financial or volume basis. For financial inventory turns, AEC divides cost of goods sold for a period by the average inventory balance during that period. For example, to determine the yearly inventory turnover ratio for ElectraMarket, we would find the average of the beginning and ending inventory amounts for the year and divide it by cost of goods sold. Assume the beginning inventory balance was $41,725,000 and the ending balance was $53,900,000, yielding an average inventory balance of $47,812,500. If the cost of goods sold for the year in question was $512,450,000, then the division's inventory turn ratio is 10.7 to 1. This ratio indicates that the company completely turns over inventory 10.7 times per year. The average sales period for the division, calculated by dividing 365 days by the average turns ratio, is 34 days. This measure approximates how long it takes the division to sell the equivalent of its average-inventory balance. Operational measures for a retailer include inventory turns on a product-by-product basis.

Operational Retail Measures

AEC describes its merchandising operation with four major processes: purchasing, inventory management, store management, and demand creation. Inventory, marketing, and purchasing measures are discussed elsewhere in the book. For illustration, we will focus on store management measures.

AEC's ElectraDirect is in dire straits as we have seen from previous measures. The company suspects that poor product mix and poor store management have contributed to these problems. It plans to adopt an aggressive store management program for the ElectraDirect chain to improve performance. It will recruit seasoned retail managers with experience in sales of big-ticket items. The company also believes it can increase revenue from cellular phone and pager service agreements. The company wants to create a good portfolio of operational measures for the new managers. Improving these measures will be the primary basis of store manager compensation above base salary.

Based on these strategies for improving store performance, the company should implement the following measures:

- Store revenue per month, percent change in revenue from previous month, percent change in revenue from same month previous year, store rank by revenue per month, revenue per square foot

- Store costs per month, labor costs per month, variance from budgeted store costs per month, store cost per square foot

- Income per square foot, store contribution margin, service contracts sold

An enlightened store manager from a competing chain was interviewed and commented that the proposed operational measures were all financial. She was wary of taking a position in a struggling chain where financial performance in the past had been poor. Instead, she proposed that the company add measures to the mix that would help the chain's position in the long term. She also was concerned about how store costs were being allocated. She wanted to be sure that only costs under the control of the store manager were included in store cost calculations. For example, store costs as designed by the management team included the cost of goods sold in the store. The store manager had little control over this measure, which is more suited to the purchasing process. In the end, the company added the following measures to focus on other operational areas that were important to success:

- Employee turnover, direct labor costs as a percentage of sales revenue, average length of service for employees

- Theft losses as a percentage of revenue, returns as a percentage of revenue, customer complaints, customer compliments

- Average price of items sold, inventory turns by item, inventory turns by store, store costs as a percentage of revenue

The combined portfolio of operational store management measures, along with measures to improve purchasing and inventory management, should allow AEC to make one last run at profitable operations in the ElectraDirect chain.

Measures for Service Product Companies

The fastest-growing sector of the economy in the United States and much of the developed world is the service sector. The growth of service sector businesses is another indication of the growing importance of technology and telecommunications in the economy. These factors have revolutionized services in banking, insurance, and health care, while generating a healthy chunk of service revenue themselves. Long-term service businesses like banking have entrenched, time-honored measures that may or may not apply to the new competitive environment. Newer service industries, like Internet service providers, must create measures from existing related industries or create their own. Service industry measures differ greatly from industry to industry, much more so than measures in manufacturing and merchandising.

An important step in understanding any service industry is the determination of the basic unit of service for a company. This unit is usually the basis for revenue and cost transactions regardless of the industry. Some service units are continual, like bank accounts and insurance policies. In these cases, customers pay fees or premiums in exchange for the service. The provider of the service incurs costs to maintain the accounts or pay claims on the policies. Other service units are charged for based on usage. Long distance carriers charge per minute or a fraction thereof for service, while lawyers charge hourly rates.

Service Sales Measures

Service company revenue measures vary widely. For our discussion, we will consider three examples of service companies: an auto insurance company, a telecommunications company, and a large law firm. Each company will use traditional revenue measures discussed previously, but each will also use measures unique to their business and defined by the unit of service provided.

For the auto insurance company, revenue is equivalent to premiums received for a given month. Premium revenue may be received in advance of the effective month, such as a six-month advance payment. In this case, the premium is held as a liability until the effective month occurs. The basic unit of service then is a policy month. The sum of premiums paid for a given policy month is the monthly revenue earned by the insurer. The amount of revenue earned in a month is an important measure, as is the number of policies in force in a given month.

Revenue for the telecommunications company is measured differently. The basic unit of service is a fractional minute of phone service provided to a customer. The company probably offers a variety of service types, including long distance, local service, data communications, and wireless communications. This revenue is probably divided into business and residential segments, and further segmented within those classifications. The company's sales measures will include usage minutes and revenue in each of these markets. These markets are further divided into geographies. The granularity of markets in this business may go as far as customer demographics, as in the banking example in Chapter 3, "Marketing." A market definition may be as specific as "18–35 single males with income between 25K and 35K owning homes in San Mateo County, California."

For the large law firm, the basic unit of service is the billable hour, whether provided by a partner or a paralegal; of course, the cost per unit of service varies greatly between these two labor categories. The company must track revenue by labor category, partner, customer, and project to ensure a proper accounting of fees. After all, sending a knowingly erroneous legal bill through the mail constitutes mail fraud.

The company can track revenue in relation to the basic service units. This allows the company to approximate the per-unit revenue and per-unit costs common in manufacturing and merchandising. Sales and service unit totals for each of our businesses are presented in Table 12.11. The measures of service units also provides an actual service measure to be compared with the theoretical capacity of the organization. These measures, known as *utilization*, are discussed later.

Measuring Service Costs

Service companies do not measure cost of goods sold like manufacturers and retailers. They do not sell a tangible product, but rather the provision of a service. These services may be continual, like life insurance, or short-lived, like hair replacement surgery. Capturing the costs of a service is difficult because most of the costs incurred cannot be attributed to a specific service unit. The cost of the capital used by an insurance company to pay the claims against accumulated risk is difficult to allocate to each policy sold. Likewise, the depreciation expense of the specific equipment used to connect a phone call is impossible to track and apply to that call on a continuing basis. Each call made by a customer may be routed along a different connection path, further complicating any futile attempt at costing a specific call. Only the law firm has a good grasp on costs, capturing many costs by customer and project, including the cost of copies, phone calls, and direct staff labor. These costs can be considered the cost of sales, a similar measure to cost of goods sold for labor-based service companies.

Similarly, the auto insurer has an important cost to track, that of claims against policies in force. Insurers carry an allowance for claims in future periods in their financial reports, allowing them to approximate claims costs in future months from the policies likely to be in force at that time. This allowance is usually an average based on actuarial estimates and does not allow for natural disasters or a period of extremely bad driving. If the company discovers that its estimates are sorely out of synch with reality, it may adjust its allowance for future claims.

Table 12.11 Service Sales and Service Units

Company	Monthly Sales	Service Units
Insurance company	$250,000,000	1,700,000 policy months
Telecommunications	$80,000,000	910,000,000 service minutes
Law firm	$2,400,000	22,000 billable hours

At a macro level, service companies need to track costs by the standard categories found in the income statement. These categories include product and product line, market segments, geographies, and other dimensions common to all businesses. Typical SAG costs, including cost of sales, administration, depreciation, and executive salaries, can be allocated as appropriate. As in other companies, the relationship of these costs to revenue should be monitored. The insurance company should measure the cost of claims administration, which is often outsourced to claims service companies. The telecommunications company likely measures the depreciation costs of various types of network equipment and relates it to revenue. The law firm probably tracks the few shared SAG costs, like country club memberships and other clubby perks, against revenue.

The most important cost measurement for the law firm and auto insurance company provider is customer profitability. Customer profitability, discussed in Chapter 10, "Profitability," requires the careful allocation of customer costs to match up with a careful accounting of customer revenue. Auto insurers are often quick to non-renew customers whose claims exceed their premiums.

Ratios and Comparisons

Service companies use revenue, costs, and income measures similar to those of other types of businesses. They will also develop industry-unique measures similar to the per-square-foot ratios used by retailers. For the insurer, the equivalent measure might be based on the number of policies. Table 12.12 presents the measure of revenue, SAG costs, and claims costs per policy for the auto insurer.

This measure can be supplemented by other measures that are based on an asset count. Revenue per agent, revenue per customer, and other asset-based ratios are commonly used. Whether the insurer can drill into these figures by geography, policy terms, customer profile, or other meaningful dimensions will depend on the design of its operational and analytical systems.

Table 12.12 Per-Policy Measures

	Base Measure	Policies	Per Policy
Revenue	941,568,900	328,090	2,870
SAG costs	128,981,822		393
Claims costs	213,800,657		652

The law firm can construct a similar measure using the billable hours service unit. They can also track revenue per associate, revenue per case, and revenue per customer. The phone company might use circuits, customers, and calls as the basis for a set of ratios.

Summing Up Key Measures

The purpose of building a data warehouse is often to improve the measurement portfolio of a company, either in terms of timeliness, historical depth, or quality. Most IT staff are familiar with operational systems and operational reports. The data warehouse team is chartered to build an analytical system that improves performance and financial measurement at the operational and strategic levels.

The data warehouse team is well served by assisting the business user community in defining its portfolio of business measures. In doing so, the team should remember the guidelines of explicit definition, exacting validation, and consistent presentation. The search for measures is best conducted with a clear understanding of the following information:

Concept of operations. Understand how the company is organized. What are the highest-level divisions of responsibility, and how are income and costs aggregated?

Business model. As simple as it may sound, it is important to understand exactly how the company makes money. What generates money and what expense categories are used to divide up costs?

Corporate strategies. Consider the strategies the company is following in order to achieve success in the marketplace. Strategies vary over time, and measures must change with them.

Competitive environment. The competitive landscape is a great source of measures. Competitors usually attack a company's weaknesses. Too often, companies design measures that do not measure their performance against the competition.

Operational environment. A company's operational environment is a source for a great many tactical measures. Understanding key operational processes yields numerous valuable measures.

By fully exploring these aspects of a company's business environment, the data warehouse team and end users should be able to come up with a strong portfolio of measures.

Presenting Information 13

E arly in this book, we said that the data warehouse is all about *getting answers* to business questions. These answers come in the form of reports. The culmination of all the work involved in designing and building the data warehouse, good reporting is imperative. Even the best schema designs cannot guarantee success if answers are not delivered.

Reports must communicate pertinent information clearly and concisely. Throughout this book, we have built models that measure business processes, and we've used them to create reports that answer business questions. In this chapter, we will look at common features that make these reports useful, generalizing them from a technical perspective.

We will explore the implications of several critical reporting elements, and show how they should be implemented by applications. We'll also look at how to choose or build a reporting tool. Support for each of the desired elements is not sufficient; the process by which the tool is used must be considered. We will see that this process varies, depending on who is using the tool.

Three Ways to Present Information

The tools used to produce reports are known by a variety of names, based on a variety of architectures, and serving groups with diverse perspectives. The market is full of "reporting tools," "end-user query tools," "analysis tools," and software classified in a number of other ways. These tools run on client workstations, or on application servers, and some deliver results across the Internet. Some are intended for use by programmers or developers, while others are targeted at "end users." Some are commercially available, while others are developed by businesses for use in house.

Despite the diversity in platform, capability, complexity, and marketing, all of these tools share one thing in common: They can be used to take information from a database and present it in one of a variety of formats. We'll refer to all of them as *reporting tools*.

Most of the reporting tools on the market today present information in three ways: through traditional reports, through charts, and through pivot tables. While tool vendors focus most of their demos on the exciting features that let people spin around pivots and charts, experience suggests that these flashy features are among the least important.

Traditional reports are familiar to everyone. They typically contain columns of data, with headers across the top and one or more levels of subtotaling. Sometimes, the attributes by which a table is subtotaled are elevated into the header, to produce "master-detail reports." These reports have remained a mainstay in most businesses, surviving the transition from mainframe to client-server computing. No longer a six-inch stack of green bar paper, the traditional report can be focused and concise. We have found that almost every business question can be answered in a traditional report.

Pivot tables present measures cross-referenced by one or more dimensional attributes on two or three axes. They are sometimes referred to as *matrix reports* or *crosstabs*. A pivot differs from a traditional report in how it correlates and summarizes measures with respect to dimensions. Because dimension values are enumerated across column headers as well as row headers, they allow summarization in multiple directions rather than just one. Their technical implementation is very different, but the basic concepts are the same.

The favorite presentation mechanism of OLAP vendors, pivot tables are often positioned as "the next step," enabling "analysis" of the data. They often allow the user to drill down into successively deeper levels of detail. We have found these assertions to be misleading. While pivots facilitate speedy drilling, the traditional report, too, can easily serve as a platform for analysis. By adding and removing dimensional attributes to and from any report, a user is analyzing information. We refer to these processes as *drilling down* and *drilling up*. They take place within any kind of report, any time the amount of information in the report is increased or reduced. The concept of analysis therefore has no required link to OLAP, hierarchies, or pivot tables.

Charts depict information graphically. The relationship of one or more measures to one or more dimensions is shown in a number of formats, including pies, plots, lines, areas, bars, and a number of variations. Each chart can be depicted with a variety of options, including the number of axes, scale, and rotation. As we mentioned in Chapter 3, "Marketing," the same data can be charted in ways that lead the mind to make radically different conclusions. Because the presentation of a chart can impact its interpretation, charting options must be used with care.

It shouldn't come as a surprise, then, that we will be focusing most of this chapter on the traditional report. This focus does not mean the other presentation mechanisms are not important; pivot tables in particular can be extremely useful. However, we have found that the overwhelming majority of business questions are best answered in traditional reports. Since tool vendors often neglect the features of this less flashy but very important presentation mechanism, it is the most important one to evaluate.

Reporting Basics

A very basic report is shown in Report 13.1. Drawn from the Shipments schema in Chapter 1, "The Business-Driven Data Warehouse," it shows sales and margin for a set of products during the month of January 1998. The first two columns, Brand and Product, are taken from the product dimension table. The next two columns are sums of fully additive measures in the fact table for the products in question during the time period in question. The final column is an important business metric: margin, expressed as a percentage of sales. It is not stored in the

Report 13.1 The simplest report.

Margin by Product
January 1998

1	2	3	4	5
		Sales	Margin	
Brand	**Product**	**Dollars**	**Dollars**	**Margin**
Captain Coffee	Standard coffee maker	$175,000	$14,000	8%
Captain Coffee	Thermal coffee maker	$96,000	$10,560	11%
Captain Coffee	Deluxe coffee maker	$114,000	$2,280	2%
Kitchen Master	Can opener	$102,400	$6,144	6%
Kitchen Master	Blender	$96,200	$7,696	8%
Kitchen Master	Toaster	$124,000	$11,160	9%
Kitchen Master	Toaster oven	$120,000	$12,000	10%

fact table because, like all ratios, it is not additive. However, it can be calculated from fully additive components that are available.

We refer to the Margin Report as a *simple report* because all the required data can be captured using a single SQL query; no additional processing or calculations are necessary. The SQL statement used is shown next. Comments highlight its major components.

```
Select product.brand,            -- dimensional attributes
    product.product,
    sum(shipment_facts.sales_dollars), -- aggregation of additive
facts
    sum(shipment_facts.margin_dollars),
    sum(shipment_facts.margin_dollars) -- calculate non-additive fact
        / sum(shipment_facts.sales_dollars) as Margin
from product,              -- tables
    date,
    shipment_facts
where product.product_key = shipment_facts.product_key -- joins
  and date.date_key = shipment_facts.shipment_date_key
  and date.month = 'January'         -- conditions
  and date.year = 1998
group by product.brand,            -- level of aggregation
    product.product
```

The first portion of the query, often referred to as the *column list*, selects the dimensional attributes that will appear in columns 1 and 2, and the sum of fully additive measures that will appear in columns 3 and 4. Column 5, margin as a percentage of sales, is computed by dividing the total margin dollars by the sales dollars. The *from clause* indicates the tables involved; in this case, the two dimensions product and date, and the fact table shipment_facts. The date table has not been referenced in the column list, but will be used to constrain the query. The first two lines of the *where clause* contain the joins necessary to relate these tables. The next two lines constrain the query to the month in question. Lastly, the scope of the sum operations from the column list is defined in a *group by clause*, which includes all dimensional attributes that appeared in the column list.

The nonadditive measure in column 5 can also be created via processing within the application. The margin calculation is removed from the SQL statement, but we must keep its components—the sum of sales_dollars and the sum of margin_dollars. Upon receiving the result set, the application performs the margin calculation, rather than the RDBMS. We will see later that the components of some nonadditive measures must be retrieved in *separate* queries. In these cases, the measure *must* be computed within the application.

Simple reports like this one can be produced with any reporting tool on the market. They can also be coded by hand quite easily. In the real world, however, most reports are more complicated. In order to present useful information, we must add reporting elements that aren't always handled well by SQL. We'll start by looking at how something as basic as summary rows can wreak havoc with the most powerful reporting tools. Then we'll also look at other types of business questions that pose reporting challenges, such as comparisons, averages, aggregate calculations, and semi-additivity.

Summary Rows

Any report that contains a measure is likely to contain a "total" at the end. If the report has more than one dimensional attribute, the measure may also be subtotaled. For example, we can add a grand total and brand subtotals to Report 13.1—the results are shown in Report 13.2. The brand subtotals summarize margin and sales

Report 13.2 Summary rows.

		Margin by Brand January 1998		
1	**2**	**3**	**4**	**5**
		Sales	**Margin**	
Brand	**Product**	**Dollars**	**Dollars**	**Margin**
Captain Coffee	Standard coffee maker	$175,000	$14,000	8.00%
	Thermal coffee maker	$96,000	$10,560	11.00%
	Deluxe coffee maker	$114,000	$2,280	2.00%
Captain Coffee	**Total**	**$385,000**	**$26,840**	**6.97%**
2	Can opener	$102,400	$6,144	6.00%
2	Blender	$96,200	$7,696	8.00%
2	Toaster	$124,000	$11,160	9.00%
	Toaster oven	$120,000	$12,000	10.00%
2	**Total**	**$442,600**	**$37,000**	**8.36%**
Grand Total		**$827,600**	**$63,840**	**7.71%**

for all products within the brand, and the grand total summarizes the measures for all products within the report.

We've shaded the subtotals and grand total in this report to highlight them. These rows are variously referred to as *subtotal rows*, *summary rows*, or *break rows*. The rows of data that are not summary rows are usually referred to as *body rows*. This report has one level of subtotaling on brand, along with a grand total for all products. It is not uncommon to have several nested levels of subtotaling. If each product was shipped in several colors, we might add a Color column to the right of Product. With sales and margin being broken out by color, it would now be useful to have a summary row for each product.

The summary rows add value to the report because they show the same information at an alternative level of aggregation. More information is now available to the reader, who is free to decide which parts hold the most value. Report 13.2 contains data summarized at three levels: the product level, the brand level, and for all brands. The reader can review margin at the brand level, but also observe product-level variations that may skew it. For example, the Captain Coffee brand shows a margin just under 7 percent, but also includes a low-margin product. It is left up to the reader to decide how to use this information. By contrast, Report 13.1 forces the reader to view sales at the product level alone.

Unfortunately, Report 13.2 no longer qualifies as simple. SQL cannot be used effectively to retrieve data at multiple levels of aggregation. Although some vendors have offered proprietary extensions, we will suggest two approaches with broader applicability. Each will require some additional work on the part of the application.

Computing Summary Rows within the Application

The fully additive measures in columns 3 and 4 of our sample report can be subtotaled simply by summing the data from the body rows within the query tool. For example, Sales Dollars at the brand level is computed by summing all product sales for the brand. The same approach can be used to compute grand totals for these columns.

TIP

Fully additive measures can be added to compute summary rows.

However, this approach will not work for the nonadditive measure in column 5. It is not appropriate to sum the percentage values; the results will be wrong.

TIP

Nonadditive measures should always be calculated from their fully additive components, even within a summary row. In the case of a ratio, always take the ratio of the sums of the additive components, not the sum of the ratios.

The ratios for the products in the Captain Coffee brand do not sum up to the brand level ratio (8%+11%+2% ≠ 6.97%). The subtotal must be computed as the ratio of the sums of margin dollars and sales dollars.

Computing margin at the brand level will not be a problem for Report 13.2, because the components of the ratio are already present in the report. In fact, we're already subtotaling them, so all that remains is to compute the ratio of the subtotals. This wouldn't have been so easy had we not included Margin Dollars and Sales Dollars in the report. If we had computed the margin within the SQL as shown earlier, and not captured the components of the ratio, it would have been impossible to calculate the summary rows. We wouldn't have the additive components of the measure available to aggregate.

TIP

Computation of summary rows for a nonadditive measure requires access to its fully additive components, even if they will not be displayed in the report.

To construct Report 13.2 using the computation approach, we would take the following steps: First, the data is retrieved for the body rows in columns 1, 2, 3, and 4. Second, we compute the summary rows for the fully additive measures in columns 3 and 4. Last, we compute the nonadditive measure in column 5. For each report row, whether body or summary, the ratio is calculated using the data in the row.

The computation approach to creating summary rows works well for Report 13.2. We've identified three requirements for a tool that computes summary rows locally. Fully additive measures can be summed to compute summary rows. Nonadditive measures cannot be summed to compute summary rows; instead, their additive components are summed, and the measure is computed from the constituent sums. The constituent components of a nonadditive measure must be managed by the application even if they are not present in the report.

Tools designed to allow end users to build queries must manage these details. When a user is required to build a query containing ratio components, and subsequently construct a calculation, the tool fails the ease-of-use test. The most creatively designed tools allow the user to specify the desired ratio as part of the process of building a query, or select it from a group of predefined ratios. The tool can then fetch the components and use them to create summary rows.

Summarizing Averages

In the reports we have looked at so far, the values summarized are either fully additive, or they are composed of fully additive components. For these measures, the application can compute the summary rows, providing that the additive components of nonadditive measures are available. But what happens when the body rows contain averages rather than sums? Let's take a look at how this impacts our ability to create summary rows.

The manufacturer is considering an incentive program, in which rebates are issued to customers whose purchases are above average. The product managers are deciding whether to base rebates on product sales or on brand sales. They want to see average customer sales by product and brand, as shown in Report 13.3. This report is similar to the one in Report 13.2, except that we see average sales rather than total sales.

Report 13.3 Summarizing averages.

	Average Customer Sales **Product and Brand** **January 1998**	
1	**2**	**3**
		Average
Brand	**Product**	**Customer Sales**
Captain Coffee	Standard coffee maker	$3,182
	Thermal coffee maker	$2,233
	Deluxe coffee maker	$2,073
Captain Coffee	**All products**	**$5,833**
Kitchen Master	Can opener	$1,969
	Blender	$2,047
	Toaster	$2,138
	Toaster oven	$2,105
Kitchen Master	**All products**	**$5,289**
All brands		**$9,311**

Averages are shown at three levels in this report. Each body row shows the average sales dollars across customers purchasing a product. Summary rows present average sales across customers at the brand level. The final row shows average sales dollars across customers for all products in the report.

If using the computation approach, how could we compute the summary rows in this report? It should be clear that the individual product averages cannot be summed to come up with brand averages—the evidence in Report 13.3 rules this possibility out. Why is this the case? Mathematically, the sum of the product averages will only add up to the brand average if each product average and the brand average share exactly the same domain of customers. This is not the case for our report.

Careful scrutiny of the numbers bears this out. Consider the Captain Coffee brand. Table 13.1 shows that Standard coffee makers were purchased by 55 customers, Thermal coffee makers by 43 customers, and Deluxe coffee makers by 55 customers. These customer sets overlap, but not completely; the total number of customers purchasing Captain Coffee products is 66. This means two of the product averages, Standard and Deluxe, are taken across 55 customers, while Thermal is taken across 43. Further, the brand average must be taken across the 66 distinct customers. Because the averages do not share a common denominator, the brand average does not equal the sum of the product averages.

Another common error is to summarize the body rows by averaging them. Were we to do this, we would be producing numbers that represent averages of averages. While an average of an average can coincidentally equate to the latter average taken against the original set of values, these numbers will not always match. Again, Table 13.1 illustrates this: The three product averages in the Captain Coffee brand average to $2,496, a far cry from the actual brand average of $5,833.

The astute developer might observe that an average is nothing more than a nonadditive ratio, similar to the percentages in the previous section. It represents the ratio of a sum to a count. Why not break it down into its additive components, and use these components to calculate the summaries? This method will not succeed because the denominator of the average is not additive, and frequently is not a constant.

Recall that we said the customer sets of the individual products in the Captain Coffee brand overlap. Many customers have bought more than one of the products, but some have not. In Table 13.1, we see that the number of customers for each product do not sum to the number of customers for the brand, which is 66. How can we obtain this number when looking at the body rows? It is simply not possible. Having broken the average down into its components, we are still hard-

Table 13.1 The Ratio Components for Captain Coffee Products

Product	Sales Dollars	Number of Customers	Average Sales
Standard coffee maker	$175,000	55	$3,182
Thermal coffee maker	$96,000	43	$2,233
Deluxe coffee maker	$114,000	55	$2,073
All three products	$385,000	66	$5,833
Sum of averages	$7,487		
Average of averages	$2,496		
Average across 66 customers	$5,833		

pressed to compute the brand-level average. The total sales can be summed up, but what number do we divide by? We need the total number of customers buying products from the brand. Unlike the other ratios we encountered, averages are not composed of fully additive components. This means we can't rely on using the components to compute summary rows.

TIP

The cardinality component of an average is not additive. This means that averages cannot be summarized by local computation, even if the ratio components are available. They must be computed from the base data.

Unlike Report 13.2, the summary rows in this report cannot be computed from the data in the body rows; there simply is not enough information. To accurately calculate the summary rows locally, we would have to fetch all the base data that went into the averages presented in the body rows. This represents a large number of transactions, potentially an impractical data set for a reporting application. Luckily, there is an alternative.

Query Again for Summary Rows

The alternative to computing summary is to query the database multiple times. The first SQL query retrieves the body rows. Each level of summarization is then constructed by issuing a more generalized query. The application must then take the results of these summary queries, and interleave them into the correct parts of the report.

For example, Report 13.3 would be constructed as follows: First, we query Product, Brand, and the Average Customer Sales. This query returns the information needed to construct our body rows. Next, we query Brand and Average Customer Sales. This query gives us the information we need for our Brand summaries. Because we are returning to the database, the average can be computed from the base data, rather than the information returned from the first query. Lastly, we compute the Average Customer Sales for all products. This gives us the information needed for the All Products at the bottom of the report. (Note that throughout this process, we will probably not be using the SQL average function to compute averages. See "Dealing with Averages" later in this chapter for more detail.)

The requery approach works equally well with additive and measures. This means that it is not necessary to build an application that constructs summary rows in different ways depending on the measure. But an argument can be made in favor of using computation whenever possible. Why do in three queries what can be accomplished in one? This is a valid objection, but observe that when requerying for summary rows, each query is successively simpler. Further, if the database has a well-designed set of aggregate tables, each successive summary level will enjoy a performance boost over the previous.

TIP

Any measure, including an average, can be summarized through the use of multiple queries. The application must issue an set of successively more general SQL statements and appropriately interleave their result sets.

Choose the Right Approach

So what is the right approach to summarization? The answer depends on your needs. If you are summarizing additive measures, or nonadditive measures that break down into fully additive components, the computation approach offers the benefit of less interaction with the database. However, care must be taken to handle the nonadditive measures properly.

If you are working with averages, or any measure that cannot be reduced to fully additive components, multiple query passes are the only option. Any subject area that involves a semi-additive measure will have this requirement. The semi-additive measure must be averaged when aggregated across its nonadditive dimension. In Chapter 6, "Inventory and Capacity," we saw that inventory levels must be averaged when aggregating them over time. Similarly, the semi-additive account balances in Chapters 3 and 10 must be averaged when studied over time, and the semi-additive basket count in Chapter 3 had to be averaged when aggregated across products.

If your subject area does not include semi-additive measures, you are still likely to encounter the need for multipass computation of summary rows. Even when all measures are fully additive, averages are frequently required to answer business questions. Report 13.3 is a good example; a fully additive measure is averaged across customers by product and by brand.

This last point bears consideration, because most query tools on the market are built around the computation approach. They will *not* be able to produce summary rows in situations involving averages. Worse, they are likely to attempt a sum, or an average of an average, producing *inaccurate* results. We have seen the vendors of popular tools obfuscate this issue by building demo queries that fetch all the data from the database. Their reports contain accurate summary rows because all the data has been brought back from the database, making computation seem to work. But this approach is hardly practical with 400,000 bank account balances!

A final note on the subject of summary rows: Often, the summarization may not be a sum. We've already seen that averages are usually summarized with more averages, but even body rows that represent sums can be summarized with averages. Imagine that the brand totals in Report 13.2 showed the product average rather than totals. Summaries may also include minimums, maximums, counts, count of distinct values, median values, and other forms of computation. Whatever the form, the pros and cons of the alternatives we've studied still apply.

Comparison between Rows

We mentioned in the previous section that SQL cannot effectively be used to retrieve data at multiple levels of aggregation—at least not in a single SQL select statement. By submitting multiple select statements, we were able to work around this limitation and produce summary rows. But what if we now want to compare data in one row of our report with data in another row? Here, SQL fails us as well, and this time, issuance of multiple select statements doesn't solve the problem. We're in a similar bind if we want to prepare a running total or rank the rows of our report.

Business questions that require comparison or aggregation across rows in a report fall into three major categories:

- Report columns comparing body rows to summary rows, or summary rows to grand totals. For example, "For each product, show me total sales, percentage of brand sales, and percentage of the grand total."

- Report columns containing running totals. For example, "Show me monthly and year-to-date sales for the Northern region."

- Report column containing a ranking. For example, "Rank each product by Sales Dollars and Margin."

Each of these questions requires comparison or aggregation of data across rows in the report. Were we to try and answer these questions using SQL alone, we would quickly become bogged down in a series of correlated subqueries, temporary tables, nonstandard SQL, and other tricks. We would also wind up forcing the RDBMS to repeat some of the calculations that are already required for summary rows.

As a general rule, it is best to avoid these SQL acrobatics; however, we should not abandon these questions. Like summary rows, each of these elements is an important tool in the effective presentation of information. Although hard to answer using SQL, these needs can be addressed within the application. We'll look at each type of comparison.

Comparison across Aggregation Levels

We have seen that adding summary rows to a report makes it more valuable to a business. The reader can look at the information at various levels, and make her own decisions about what is important. The utility of the report can be further increased by providing comparisons of each body row to the subtotals and grand totals. These comparisons allow the reader to look for important trends without having to perform calculations in her head or along the margins.

In Report 13.4, we show a sales report to which these comparisons have been added. The first three columns of the report match those from Report 13.2: Brand, Product, and Sales Dollars are shown, along with summary rows for brand totals and a grand total. To this information, we have added columns 4 and 5, which simply compare each row to the summarizations. In column 4, we compare each product's sales to sales for its brand. Within a brand, these percentages add up to 100 percent, as shown in the brand summary rows. In column 5, we compare each product's sales to the grand total. Within the brand summary row, the brand's total is compared to the grand total.

Report 13.4 Comparison across aggregation levels.

Sales by Product
January 1998

1	2	3	4	5
			Percent	Percent
		Sales	of Brand	of Total
Brand	**Product**	**Dollars**	**Sales Dollars**	**Sales Dollars**
Captain Coffee	Standard coffee maker	$175,000	45%	21%
	Thermal coffee maker	$96,000	25%	12%
	Deluxe coffee maker	$114,000	30%	14%
Captain Coffee	**All products**	**$385,000**	**100%**	**47%**
Kitchen Master	Can opener	$102,400	23%	12%
	Blender	$96,200	22%	12%
	Toaster	$124,000	28%	15%
	Toaster oven	$120,000	27%	14%
Kitchen Master	**All products**	**$442,600**	**100%**	**53%**
All brands		**$827,600**		**100%**

We refer to columns 4 and 5 as *interrow comparisons*. These comparisons are ratios that compare the row's data to data at a different level of summarization. These ratios are very different from the margin ratio in Report 13.2, where the components of the ratio were all found within a single row of data, and could even be computed using basic SQL. We could go to great lengths to produce SQL that would retrieve the interrow comparisons, but computing them within the application will prove much easier.

Notice that the first three columns in Report 13.4 can be produced using methods already discussed. First, we retrieve all body rows in the report, using a simple select statement, similar to the one found at the beginning of this chapter.

Next, we produce summary rows, either by requerying the database or by performing a series of computations using the data that has been retrieved.

Once the first three columns have been set up, we have all the information required to produce the interrow comparison columns. For example, column 4 requires comparing a sales for each row to the sales for the brand. Because we have already fetched the body and summary rows for columns 1 through 3, we can easily perform the division calculation. The same calculation that serves within body rows also works within the summary rows. Total sales for the brand compared to the brand's total sales naturally works out to 100 percent. We just need to be careful not to compare data to a row that is *less* summarized. For example, it doesn't make sense to compare the grand total to the brand total. We'll leave that spot blank.

TIP

A report column comparing data at various levels of summarization can only be constructed *after* the summarization is completed. Once all base data and summarizations have been fetched or computed, the data for interrow comparison columns can be computed within the application. If a nonadditive measure is part of the comparison, it too must be computed before the comparison can be made.

Once interrow comparisons have been computed, the report can be displayed without the base data. If Report 13.4 is intended to answer a question about each product's share of brand revenues and share of total revenues, we can omit Sales Dollars by removing column 3. Although we will require Sales Dollars to compute the comparisons, we don't have to include it in the report.

In a variation on this report, the summary rows show averages rather than subtotals. Interrow comparisons are constructed to show percent above or below brand and report averages. The report can now be used to compare performance of a product to other products in the brand, and to all products. Because sales is summarized using averages, the summary rows require a requery of the database. But the interrow comparison columns can still be accurately constructed by comparing each row to the various summaries.

Rankings

Rankings are frequently requested by business people. For example, a business person requests a report showing margin and sales for all products, much like the one in Report 13.1. However, it is also requested that all products be ranked based on their sales dollars. We might achieve this ranking by sorting based on margin dollars and adding a row count. But what if the report requires a second ranking based on the margin percentage? Now we are hard-pressed to produce the report using SQL.

Report 13.5 shows the requested sales report, complete with two sets of rankings. Sales Rank, in column 5, shows the product's position in terms of the fully additive measure Sales Dollars. Margin % Rank, in column 6, shows each product's position in terms of the nonadditive measure Margin Percentage. While challenging to compute in SQL, these ranking columns can easily be added to a report after the base data has been retrieved. The application need only perform a descending sort on the measure and then apply index values. The sort operation need not drive the display of ranked objects. The ranking in column 6, for example, is not being used to order the display of report rows.

TIP

Rankings order dimensional attributes or report rows based on the magnitude of a measure. Rankings can be computed within an application through a sort and index operation.

Alternative approaches to rankings are not as flexible. Many applications perform a ranking by sorting the result set based on the measure being ranked. This approach works if the aim is to provide a single ranking, but cannot be used when multiple rankings are to be included, as in Report 13.5. There is no way to avoid application computation to compute the second ranking.

Some rankings will be based on a measure that is to be computed within the application, rather than returned by SQL. In this situation, there is no choice but to perform the ranking in the application. In "Comparing across Columns" and "Drilling Across," we will find examples of measures that are computed within the application based on data returned by multiple queries. Until this computation is performed, we cannot rank the results.

TIP

Rankings can be performed on any form of measure—additive, semi-addditive, or nonadditive—including those calculated from multiple query result sets. A ranking can only be computed once the measure upon which it is based has been computed.

Report 13.5 Ranking of additive and nonadditive measures.

**Sales by Product
January 1998**

1 Product	2 Sales Dollars	3 Margin Dollars	4 Margin Percentage	5 Sales Rank	6 Margin % Rank
Standard coffee maker	$175,000	$14,000	8%	1	4
Toaster	$124,000	$11,160	9%	2	3
Toaster oven	$120,000	$12,000	10%	3	2
Deluxe coffee maker	$114,000	$2,280	2%	4	7
Can opener	$102,400	$6,144	6%	5	6
Blender	$96,200	$7,696	8%	6	4
Thermal coffee maker	$96,000	$10,560	11%	7	1

As with summary comparisons, we may choose to omit the ranked measures from the final report. In Report 13.5, columns 2, 3, and 4 can be removed. We are still required to fetch the data for columns 2 and 3, and compute the data for column 4, in order to calculate our rankings.

Rankings are usually not placed within summary rows. Suppose that we had chosen to include Brand in Report 13.5, and order products alphabetically within their brand. A summary row for brands cannot include a product ranking value. A brand ranking might be placed in the summary row, but the ranking column will become difficult for the reader to scan, because it contains two different kinds of rankings. As a general rule, a column containing rank values should not include any data within a summary row.

When the report does contain summary rows, we might rank the same measure with respect to the summary group and the entire set. For example, if product sales were summarized by brand, we can rank each product within its brand, as well as with respect to all products.

Running Totals

Many business questions require a *running total*. Most commonly employed in conjunction with a time series, the running total is used to produce columns such as Period to Date or Year to Date. Running totals are required by the following request: "For Standard coffee makers, I would like to see monthly sales with running totals for the quarter and year." The report is shown in Report 13.6.

This report shows Sales Dollars by Month and Quarter, with summary rows for each quarter and a grand total for the year. Column 4 shows Quarter to Date sales, which represents a running total of the Sales Dollars column. Column 5 shows the Year-to-Date summary. Notice that the quarterly total resets at the beginning of each new quarter.

Most databases do not supply an effective mechanism with which to accumulate running totals like the ones shown here; those that do, offer proprietary extensions to SQL. Report columns containing running totals must therefore be computed by the application. They can be placed into the report once the dimensions and additive measures have been retrieved from the database and summary rows have been added.

TIP

Running totals of additive measures can be computed by local computation once the measure had been retrieved and the report rows have been sorted as required.

A more complex running summary requires a new query for each row. Running averages, for example, average a measure over a cardinality that increases with each row. As we have already seen, computation of averages requires a return to the database.

As with interrow comparisons and rankings, it is not necessary to display the measure being summarized; however, we must still fetch it and manage it within the application. We must exercise care when placing running totals into a report that contains summary rows. A running total's value within a summary row is the same as its value for the last body row in that group. Incrementing the running total by the subtotal amount would be a grave error. Also notice that a quarterly running total has no relevance at the annual level—a year summarizes multiple quarters. These cells are left blank, as has been done in the last row of column 4 in Report 13.6.

Comparisons between Columns

In the previous section, we looked at three report elements that require comparison or aggregation across rows of data. Now we will look at situations where we need to compare data across columns. We've already encountered some simple

Report 13.6 Running totals.

Sales by Month
Standard Coffee Makers
1998

1	2	3	4	5
			Sales Dollars	**Sales Dollars**
Quarter	**Month**	**Sales Dollars**	**Quarter-to-Date**	**Year-to-Date**
Q1	January	$175,000	$175,000	$175,000
	February	$104,000	$279,000	$279,000
	March	$125,000	$404,000	$404,000
Q1	**Total**	**$404,000**	**$404,000**	**$404,000**
Q2	April	$95,000	$95,000	$499,000
	May	$85,000	$180,000	$584,000
	June	$101,000	$281,000	$685,000
Q2	**Total**	**$281,000**	**$281,000**	**$685,000**
Q3	July	$115,000	$115,000	$800,000
	August	$119,000	$234,000	$919,000
	September	$110,000	$344,000	$1,029,000
Q3	**Total**	**$344,000**	**$344,000**	**$1,029,000**
Q4	October	$120,000	$120,000	$1,149,000
	November	$135,000	$255,000	$1,284,000
	December	$145,000	$400,000	$1,429,000
Q4	**Total**	**$400,000**	**$400,000**	**$1,429,000**
Total		**$1,429,000**		**$1,429,000**

examples. In Report 13.1, the nonadditive Margin measure in column 5 was computed by comparing Sales Dollars from column 3 to Margin Dollars in column 4. This computation could even be done within SQL.

Sometimes, however, the values to compare are not easily fetched within a single SQL statement. Frequently, business questions require constraining a single measure in two ways and comparing the results. Consider the request, "Show me January sales by brand and product, along with the percent increase over January of last year." Report 13.7 responds to this request.

Report 13.7 This year versus last.

January 1998
Sales by Product and Brand

1	2	3	4	5
		Sales	PY Sales	Percent
Brand	**Product**	**Dollars**	**Dollars**	**Change**
Captain Coffee	Standard coffee maker	$175,000	$169,000	3.55%
	Thermal coffee maker	$96,000	$101,000	–4.95%
	Deluxe coffee maker	$114,000	$102,000	11.76%
Captain Coffee	**Total**	**$385,000**	**$372,000**	**3.49%**
Kitchen Master	Can opener	$102,400	$78,000	31.28%
	Blender	$96,200	$102,000	–5.69%
	Toaster	$124,000	$104,000	19.23%
	Toaster oven	$120,000	$118,000	1.69%
Kitchen Master	**Total**	**$442,600**	**$402,000**	**10.10%**
Grand total		**$827,600**		

Standard SQL is not well equipped to build this report. While we could easily fetch data for January 1998 and January 1997 in a single query, the amounts for each year would appear in different *rows* of the result set, rather than in columns. The application would be forced to do an intensive restructuring of the result set so that the data could be displayed in the desired format. If any component of the result set is semi-additive or nonadditive, computation cannot be used to restructure the result set.

Instead, this report can be created by constructing multiple queries. The first query fetches Brand, Product, and Total Sales Dollars for January 1998. The second query fetches Brand, Product, and Total Sales Dollars for January 1997. Summary rows are produced following one of the methods outlined earlier. We then join the result sets together within the application. We now have the needed components to produce the column containing the percent change ratio, which is calculated from its additive components as discussed in the beginning of this chapter. We might go on to use the percent increase measure to rank the products, by employing the ranking technique discussed earlier.

Many applications approach this problem by querying all the required data in a single pass, then performing internal computations to reorganize the data as required by the report. This approach has two major drawbacks: First, the process of building the query requires the appropriate constraints and dimensional attributes so that the data in all columns can be computed. This will be a counterintuitive process, especially when data sets to be compared are at different levels of aggregation. Second, the effort required to massage the data will be significant. We have seen several tools with facilities to do so, but they quickly become unmanageable as the number of columns requiring recalculation increases. The SQL CASE statement removes the second burden, but the first problem remains.

By contrast, the multiple query approach remains appropriate even as the business questions become more intricate. We are not limited to two passes at the fact table, nor is it required that each pass be constrained for a single month's worth of data. Two columns might be added to Report 13.7 showing total sales for the previous month and previous six-month period. We simply issue two more queries, each retrieving Brand, Product, and Total Sales Dollars for the time period in question. Additional passes can also be employed to isolate sales of a particular product or brand.

This approach can be combined with rankings or other interrow comparisons for more powerful effects. By querying sales data for two periods and ranking the result for each period, we can easily produce a "change" column. For each product, it can show how many spots it has risen or fallen since the previous period.

TIP

When a report includes columns that qualify measures in different ways, such as January 1997 Sales, and, January 1996 Sales, multiple SQL queries are recommended. Each should fetch the same dimensional attributes along with the measures in question, and include any conditions common to all columns of the report. The result sets are joined together within the application.

The method by which the result sets are joined together within the application requires special attention. Most of the time, a *full outer join* is required. If a particular product was present in one period but not another, we don't want to lose track of it. In some cases, this may not be true. For Report 13.7, it may be appropriate to include only products that were sold in January 1998. Products that were sold in the other period, but are now discontinued, are excluded. A left or right outer join might be chosen in this case, so that only products sold in January 1998 are included. It is important to recognize that this approach makes the Previous Year brand subtotals inaccurate; we may not be including all products sold under that brand during the previous year.

TIP

If using any mechanism other than a full outer join to merge result sets of separate queries, pay close attention to the meaning of the summary rows. It may be appropriate to remove them from the report, or include some fine print on the report footer. For example, "Products no longer sold in January 1998 are excluded from Previous Year Sales."

Drilling Across

So far, the examples in this chapter have drawn from a single fact table, such as sales_facts. For many business questions, this is not possible. In previous chapters, we have referred to questions requiring information from more than one fact table as *drill-across queries*. These reports are constructed in much the same way as our cross-column comparisons in the previous section.

In Chapter 1, "The Business-Driven Data Warehouse," we built conformed schemas tracking the orders and shipments processes for a manufacturer. Order_facts measured the order management process, and shipment_facts measured the shipping process. Depicted in Figure 1.3, these schemas contained several common dimensions, including product and date. We posed the business question "By product, what percentage of orders placed in January have shipped?" While each fact table is useful in its own right, only by combining data from both tables can we answer questions like this one.

To answer this question, we require the quantity_ordered and quantity_shipped measures from order_facts and shipment_facts, respectively. We'll also need information from the shared dimension product. Lastly, we need to constrain on the order date. With shipment_facts, we must take care to use the correct date key. The final product is shown in Report 13.8.

Report 13.8 Order fulfillment.

Fulfillment of January 1998 Orders
As of February 15, 1998

1 Product	2 Units Sold	3 Units Shipped	4 Percent Shipped
Standard coffee maker	5,000	3,800	76%
Thermal coffee maker	2,400	1,632	68%
Deluxe coffee maker	2,073	1,658	80%
Can opener	6,827	1,707	25%
Blender	3,848	1,732	45%
Toaster	5,167	3,204	62%
Toaster oven	3,000	1,950	65%

A single query involving all these tables is simply not practical. First, we want to be sure that Products for which there are orders but no shipments do not get lost. We would require outer join processing of both Date and Product to Shipment_facts. Many databases will simply not permit multiple outer joins on the same table. Second, the optimizers of most databases will have a very difficult time resolving this query. Lastly, it is quite possible that the two fact tables are on physically distinct databases, perhaps even on heterogeneous databases.

Instead, it is useful to handle drill-across queries in the same way we approached comparisons. We will query each fact table separately, including the appropriate measure and all dimensions in each of the queries. Then we merge the result sets within the application. As with comparisons, we must perform our application joins with care, and pay attention to their impact on the meaning of summary rows. Also like comparisons, measures gathered in more than one query may then serve as the components of a computation. In this case, our Percent Shipped column represents a computation involving the quantity ordered and the quantity shipped.

TIP

Measures derived from different fact tables should be retrieved in multiple queries. Each should fetch the same dimensional attributes and conditions, along with the appropriate measures. The result sets are joined together within the application.

We've already said that nonadditive measures should be computed after their components have been fetched. Note that these components will not always live in the same fact table. When the components of a nonadditive measure reside in different fact tables, the measure requires drilling across. Each component should be retrieved in a separate SQL query. The business question in our example is not "Show me quantity ordered and Quantity Shipped," but rather "Show me Quantity Ordered and Percent Shipped." Percent shipped is a nonadditive measure, much like the Margin Percentage discussed earlier. Unlike Margin Percentage, the components of Quantity Shipped are drawn from two separate fact tables.

TIP

When the components of a nonadditive measure reside in different fact tables, each component of the measure should be retrieved in a separate SQL query.

When drilling across fact tables, each SQL query usually contains the same constraints. In our example, the queries on order_facts and shipment_facts each constrain for an order date in January 1998. However, there are occasions when the constraints on drill-across queries are not identical. Suppose the business question were modified to "What percentage of orders placed in January shipped within one month?" Our order_facts query remains unchanged. But now we must add an additional constraint on shipment_facts, because we only want to count items that shipped within one month of their order date. This is not a problem, since each shipment fact has associated order dates and shipment dates, but this additional constraint is only relevant on the shipment_facts side of the drill-across operation.

Dealing with Averages

Reports requiring averages present a series of challenges. Earlier in this chapter, we saw that summarizing averages requires special care. We pointed out that you shouldn't average averages; instead, additional trips to the database are required to summarize averages. But even before we summarize an average, there are difficulties to face. In Chapter 6, "Inventory and Capacity," we saw that issues of *sparsity* and *grain* render the SQL Average()function unusable when computing averages. In this section, we'll show how to properly compute averages.

The issue of how to properly compute an average can crop up in *any* subject area. When working with Inventory in Chapter 6, we were forced into the use of averages for reports that spanned time periods. We had no choice; our primary measure in the inventory data mart was not additive across time. We faced the same issues with bank account balances that are not additive across time in Chapters 3 and 10, and with basket counts that are not additive across products in Chapter 3. However, the issues surrounding computation of averages are not limited to subject areas where measures are semi-additive. As we will see in these examples, even fully additive measures are subject to the same difficulties.

Sparsity and Grain Issues

The average of a set of numbers is computed by summing them, then dividing by the number in the set. When a business person asks, "What are Average Customer Sales by Product?" they are actually requesting a series of averages: one for each product. For each product, the "average customer sales" is computed by taking the total sales and dividing by the number of customers.

TIP

Averages are calculated by dividing the sum of a quantity by a cardinality.

In our discussion of summary rows, we pointed out that you cannot add together averages. For example, product averages cannot be summed to produce a brand average. This limitation makes sense in light of our definition of an average—because it represents one number divided by another, an average is a ratio. As we have seen, ratios are not additive.

TIP

Averages are nonadditive measures.

Recall from Chapter 6 that the SQL Average() function produces a sum and then divides by the number of rows that were summed. Using the terms from our definition, we say that SQL uses the number of rows as the *cardinality* component of the average. There are two reasons that this gets us into trouble. In Chapter 6, we referred to them as the *sparsity* issue and the *grain* issue.

The first problem is that there may not always be a row. Recall from the inventory example in Chapter 6 that there is no data recorded for products not in inventory. If a product is not in stock at a particular warehouse during a given period, SQL's Average() function cannot compute the average warehouse inventory level. It uses the number of rows as the cardinality component, but there is no row for one of the warehouses.

We called this the *sparsity* problem. SQL shows us the average warehouse inventory for warehouses that have the product, rather than across all warehouses. This problem may be cured by loading "zero rows," but we would balloon the size of the fact table and still face the second problem of SQL averages.

When we want to compute an average across a set of values at a higher level of summarization than our fact table, we face a new problem. Suppose that we want to see the average monthly inventory of a product for a year across *the company*, rather than for a particular warehouse. Our fact table contains monthly totals for each warehouse, but we want to average monthly totals across the corporation. The grain of our fact table does not match the cardinality component of our average. If we have four warehouses, we potentially have 48 rows in the fact table for the product and year in question—one for each warehouse for each month. SQL's Average() function will dutifully divide by 48, but we need to divide by the number of months: 12.

We refer to this as the *grain* problem. The cardinality of an SQL average is always determined by the grain of the data series being averaged. We want it to be the cardinality of a dimensional value. When the dimensional value in question is time, we say we are trying to take a *period average*. In other cases, we say we are taking a *dimension average*, such as Warehouse Average, Customer Average, or Salesperson Average.

Computing Averages

How then, do we compute an average? We've seen that SQL gets the cardinality of the average wrong most of the time. The secret to successful averaging is to treat an average like any other nonadditive measure. Retrieve the sum and cardinality components separately, then perform the division in the application. Unfortunately, this is not as simple as it may seem. Computation of the cardinality component of an average can be a sticky proposition.

TIP

Averages are best constructed by retrieving the sum and cardinality components, then calculating the ratio.

Depending on the business question, the cardinality of an average is computed in one of three ways: It may be a relative constant, as is often the case with period averages. However, there will be times when the cardinality of an average varies from row to row within a report. These cardinalities may be computed based on dimension data alone, or based on facts.

First, we will consider the simplest case. A business person asks, "What was the average monthly sales for product A by quarter during 1998?" Every quarter contains the same number of months: three. We can easily compute the average monthly sales by dividing by retrieving total sales and dividing by 3.

But what happens when the cardinality of an average is not constant? Suppose that a business person asks for "Average Product Sales by Brand for January of 1998." Because each brand includes a different number of products, we can't simply divide by a constant; instead, we need to query the database and get the appropriate cardinality for each brand. We can compute the cardinality, or Number of Products, by counting distinct product_keys grouped by brand. However, we must be careful. A product that did not sell during January will not be represented by rows in the fact table. We still need to include it in the number of products that make up the brand. The solution is to compute the cardinality of the average in a separate query that does not involve the fact table.

TIP

It is often necessary to retrive the sum and cardinality components of an average in separate queries.

To construct the required average, we first query the brands and total sales for January 1998. In a separate query, we query the brand and number of products. This query only involves the product table, so it does not omit products that don't sell. We then join the result sets together within the application and compute the average.

The process of joining result sets together becomes complicated when the report requires showing an additional dimension. For example, if we had broken out our quarterly totals by region, there would have been multiple rows in the first query for each quarter—one for each region. The results of our second query, which only involves the product table, must be repeated for each region when linked to the first result set. This differs from the join operation of drill-across queries, where we have an optional one-to-one relationship.

There are times when it is acceptable to retrieve the cardinality of an average in a query that involves a fact table. Sometimes, it is even appropriate to do so in the same query that is used to compute the sum component of the average. It may be that the business question takes sparsity into account. Earlier in this chapter, we considered the request, "Show me average customer sales by product and brand." Report 13.3 fulfills the request. Here, we want the average to reflect the sparsity of the facts. We don't want to include a customer who doesn't buy toasters in the cardinality of the average for toasters.

TIP

If you want an average to reflect the sparsity of the facts, compute the cardinality in the same SQL select statement that is used to compute the sum.

It is also acceptable to involve a fact table in the computation of a cardinality when the fact table in question represents coverage. For example, the method we described to produce brand averages will not work if the products in a brand change over time, or if slow changes in the product description force new rows. To accurately reflect the set of products within a brand at a point in time, we might need a coverage table associating rows in the product dimension with rows in a date dimension. We can then compute the cardinality of the average using the coverage table, constraining for the appropriate date. The sum component of the average will be retrieved from the shipments fact table.

TIP

In some cases, a coverage table will be required to compute the cardinality of an average.

Recognizing this limitation, and not wanting to build a separate coverage table, many designers opt to include a *current* flag in dimension tables. They can then compute the appropriate cardinality by counting products where the current flag is Y. However, this solution can only be exploited in reports on the current period; there is no way to compute how many products were in a brand two months ago.

Constraining Queries

Almost any business question asked will require constraining the data returned from the database in some way. The way these constraints are applied will vary according to the business question. The most simple constraints require simply adding a line into the where clause of a query. More complicated questions may require subqueries or correlated subqueries. For some questions, the subquery itself may be a set operation on two queries. Luckily, a simple alternative exists for the more complicated queries.

Basic Constraints

Basic constraints require nothing more than the addition of one or more lines to the where clause of a report. For Report 13.1, we wanted to consider only sales that took place during January 1998. The SQL for the simple report showed how this translated into a pair of lines in the where clause, effectively limiting the result set to the time period in question.

When a business question requires access to multiple fact tables, as in our fulfillment example in Report 13.8, it is important that each query be constrained in the same manner. For Report 13.8, our queries against order_facts and shipment_facts contain the same time constraints on the order date. As noted, in some situations it is appropriate to add additional constraints to one or more of the queries.

In the case of a comparison query requiring separate passes at the same fact table, each pass will always contain additional unique constraints. Report 13.7 required comparison of January 1998 sales with January 1997 sales. Two separate queries were issued, one constrained for January 1997 and one for January 1998. If this report had been focused on sales within a particular brand, both queries would share a common brand condition.

Often, a business question requires constraining the results by the value of a measure. For example, "Show me Sales by Product for January, only for Products that accounted for more than $150,000 in revenue." Because it requires constraint on an aggregated sales value, this query is qualified by adding a *having clause* to the SQL.

Constraining Based on Comparison to Summary or Rank

A slight modification of the previous question leads us into territory not covered well by SQL. "Show me Sales by Product for January, only for Products that account for more than 30 percent of the total in their brand" requires comparison of information at multiple levels of aggregation. We could embark on some advanced SQL heroics involving correlated subqueries, but we've already seen that this type of comparison is easily done within the application. It follows that this constraint can be applied within the application after the comparison.

To answer the question, we query Sales by Product and Brand for January, then retrieve the brand summary, then perform the "percent of brand" comparison for each row. This is the same technique we discussed in interrow comparisons, earlier in the chapter. We now add a final step. After completing the percent of brand for each row, we filter out any rows where this comparison falls below 10 percent. Similarly, we may choose to constrain based on a ranking. "Show me sales for the top 5 customers in each region" requires retrieving all sales, computing the ranking as discussed earlier in this chapter, then filtering out rows in which the rank is greater than 5.

While these constraints can be achieved through SQL, we've already argued that the required SQL tends to be complex. More importantly, performing these calculations within the database can reduce the efficiency of the application, particularly if the ranking or comparison is to be included in the report.

Group Membership Constraints

Many questions require constraining the data based on a set of values that is difficult or impossible to retrieve in a query. For example, a bank marketer might ask, "Show me the average balance of new savings accounts opened by recipients of the January 1998 Super-Saver mailing." If the mailing in question went to several thousand people, it is certainly not feasible to type all their household IDs into a constraint on the SQL.

Instead, we must enumerate the group somewhere in the database. One way to do this is to build a table in the database containing all the household_keys of the mailing recipients. We might call this simple table Jan98Mailer. Our query can now include this constraint:

```
...and account_facts.household_key in (select household_key from Jan98Mailer)
```

Note that the same effect can be achieved by simply joining to the mailer table, as in:

```
...and account_facts.household_key = Jan98Mailer.HouseholdKey
```

The latter approach achieves the same results while offering better performance on most databases. We refer to the table as a *study group*.

This approach can be used by report developers, but also lends itself to a simple user interface when engineered into a reporting tool. Users can be given the ability to save a set of keys into a named table within a database, and then use these tables to perform constraints. They do not need to be made aware of the underlying SQL mechanics.

The study group approach allows us to qualify based on conditions that wouldn't otherwise be reflected in the data warehouse. But it can also be used to save us from having to write a lot of complicated SQL over and over again. Most important, it allows complex questions to be broken down into more manageable questions. We only need to be wary of the impact of slowly changing dimensions on our study groups.

Consider the request, "Show me sales by salesperson for customers to whom we sold something last month." Study groups transform this from a question requiring a subquery to two simple questions about sales. First, "Show me the customer keys for customers who bought something in December 1997, and save the list as a study group." Second, "Show me sales in January 1998 for customers in the study group I just created."

Many applications answer questions like these by generating a *temp table*, which is deleted after the question is answered. But notice that if the table is kept around, it can be reused to answer questions much more quickly. The same business person, or someone else, might come back weeks later and say, "Show me March 1998 Sales for customers who bought something in December 1997." If the study group table is still around, the question will be answered much more quickly. It might even be used to look at behavior a year later. However, we need to be careful about letting study groups persist over extended periods of time. A slowly changing customer dimension might result in a new key for some customers. Storing a date within the study group table, we preserve the opportunity to adjust the keys, but an adjusted table will not be usable when studying past history.

Set Operations

It is not uncommon to discover that the SQL required to answer a business question can be written in three or four different ways. The complexity and performance of each method will vary. Often, the use of *set operations* can boost performance *and* reduce the complexity of the query. Used in conjunction with study groups, set operations can be a very easy alternative to subqueries and correlated subqueries.

Set operations allow comparison of groups of data in various ways. In SQL parlance, set operations are often referred to as *union*, *intersect*, and *minus*. While supported by an increasing number of databases, these operations are simple enough that they can also be effectively performed within an application. Figure 13.1 shows two circles, each representing a set of data. They have been numbered. Set 1 represents "customers who bought something last month," while set 2 represents "customers who bought something this month." It is likely that there will be many people who fall within both of these groups, while there will also be many who only belong to one or the other. We have labeled these regions in the diagram.

Figure 13.1 Two sets of customers.

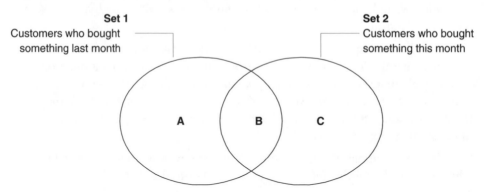

Set operations can be used to compare these sets in very specific ways. We've enumerated the three primary types of comparison in Table 13.2. The minus operator takes a set, and from it removes any values found in another set. Set 1 MINUS set 2 yields "Customers who bought this month and last." The intersect operator takes two sets and gives us only values found in both sets. Set 1 INTERSECT set 2 gives us "Customers who bought last month and not this month." The UNION operator gives us all values that appear in at least one of the sets. Set 1 UNION set 2 gives us "Customers who bought this month or last month."

There is no limitation on how each set is defined. In our example, each set tested the same condition—sales—for a different period. We could just as easily define one set as customers who bought something last month, and the other as customers whose average order is over $10,000. The sets do not have to constrain

Table 13.2 Set Operations

Operation	Results
1 MINUS 2	Customers who bought last month and not this month (region A)
1 INTERSECT 2	Customers who bought this month and last (region B)
2 MINUS 1	Customers who bought this month and not last month (region C)
1 UNION 2	Customers who bought this month or last month (regions A, B, and C)

the same type of condition, but they must each return the same data attribute—in this case, customers.

The set operators can greatly simplify the task of building a report. In conjunction with study groups, they eliminate the need to use complicated subqueries or correlated subqueries, which are out of reach for business users, and prone to errors for developers. For example, "Show me the list of products that sold in January but not in February." Without set operations, this question might be answered using a correlated subquery. For each product sold in January, the database would be required to issue a query to check for the existence of February sales. An SQL wizard would instantly recognize that we can simplify this to a subquery using the IN operator. In either case, it is a bit much for an end user to understand.

Using set difference, the question is answered through two simple requests: "Show me products that sold in January" yields one set of results; "Show me products that sold in February" yields a second. The set difference between the first and second—set 1 MINUS set 2—answers the original question. Each of these questions might result in a study group. The set difference of the two study groups becomes a new study group that can be used in a number of ways. It can be used to qualify additional queries to find out what the January sales dollars and margin dollars were for these products, how much is left in inventory, and which customers bought them in the past.

Similarly, the INTERSECT operator can often simplify the processing required to fulfill a request. For example, "Give me a list of customers who have purchased both color scanners and color printers." The answer is the intersection between customers who purchased color scanners (query 1) and customers who purchased color printers (query 2).

Tool Requirements

The purpose of the data warehouse is to answer business questions. An excellent schema design and efficient load process mean nothing if information cannot be effectively presented to business people. This means that reporting tools are critical components of the data warehouse architecture. Now that we've looked at the components of a good report, we will look at what makes a good reporting tool.

At a minimum, any reporting tool must be able to construct each of the elements presented in this chapter. But equally important as *what* a tool can do is *how* it does it. A tool that produces the desired result through a counterintuitive process will be the source of frustration. We refer to the degree to which working with the tool reflects the user's way of thinking about the process as *ease of use*.

TIP

Reporting tools must be capable of producing all of the required elements, in a manner consistent with the way in which the user thinks about what he or she wants to do.

There are two groups likely to make use of reporting tools: developers and business users. Because each group approaches the process of reporting with a different framework, we can expect that tool requirements for each group will differ. Consider the process improvement report shown in Report 13.9. The report compares percent of orders shipped within one month for January 1998 with percent shipped within one month for 1997 orders. It combines many of the elements we have discussed in this chapter, including nonadditive measures, summary rows, comparisons across columns, drilling across, and rankings.

A business person thinks about building this report as the process of defining what it should look like and what should be in each column. By contrast, a developer is likely to break it down into the various elements we have discussed in this chapter. We'll look at the needs of these two groups individually, but keep in mind that a single tool may satisfy everyone.

Tools for Developers

One of the keys to a successful data warehouse is the availability of a library of predefined reports. Only a small handful of managers will be willing to take the time to learn how to use an end-user query tool, and still fewer will be able to reach the level of mastery required to answer their most important business questions. Most users receive benefit only if prebuilt reports are made available to them. It follows that the successful data warehouse team includes analysts who design these reports. We'll refer to these analysts as *developers*.

The successful developer brings together two areas of knowledge: First, a solid understanding of the business process is required to answer business questions in the form of reports. Second, technical understanding of dimensional modeling and SQL are required to extract the answers from the data warehouse and produce the various report elements discussed in this chapter.

For a developer, it is natural to think about building Report 13.9 by identifying the key elements, breaking them down into the required queries and computations,

Report 13.9 Process improvement report.

Process Improvement Report
30-Day Fulfillment versus Previous Year
January 1998 Orders
As of April 15, 1998

1	2	3	4	5	6	7	8	9
			January 1998			1997	Change	
Brand	**Product**	**Units Sold**	**Units Shipped**	**Percent Shipped**	**Rank**	**Percent Shipped**	**Improvement**	**Rank**
Captain Coffee	Standard coffee maker	5,000	3,800	76%	2	71%	5%	3
	Thermal coffee maker	2,400	1,632	68%	3	60%	8%	1
	Deluxe coffee maker	2,073	1,658	80%	1	79%	1%	5
Captain Coffee	All products	9,473	7,090	75%		71%	4%	
Kitchen Master	Can opener	6,827	1,707	25%	7	60%	-35%	7
	Blender	3,848	1,732	45%	6	55%	-10%	6
	Toaster	5,167	3,204	62%	5	61%	1%	4
	Toaster oven	3,000	1,950	65%	4	59%	6%	2
Kitchen Master	All products	18,842	8,593	46%		51%	-5%	

[453]

identifying dependencies among these steps, and assembling them in the appropriate order. One possible outcome is the process shown in Figure 13.2.

Based on the measures required in the report, four queries are executed. These queries include the fully additive measures that will be displayed in report columns, as well as fully additive components that are necessary to compute nonadditive measures. They have been divided into multiple queries for two reasons: First, we are drilling across order_facts and shipment_facts in order to compute percent shipped for January 1998. This requires two queries. Second, we require the same measures required for a different time period—1997—requiring a second pair of queries. These four queries are shown to the far left of the diagram in Figure 13.2.

Next, the result sets are merged together, producing the information required for the body rows of columns 1–4 of the report. Summary rows are then added, completing columns 1–4. In this case, summary rows were computed, though it is also possible to requery for summary values. Next, the nonadditive measures in columns 5 and 7 are computed for body and summary rows. Rankings and comparison of rankings are constructed, and then the information needed to construct column 7 is removed from the report. Dependencies are shown by arrows.

A developer may use one of a number of tools to develop the report. If writing procedural code using a language like C++ or Visual Basic, good code will reflect the modularity of the processes in Figure 13.2, and their dependencies. Notice that a multithreaded application can execute many of these tasks in parallel. Alternatively, the developer may use a report writing tool intended for programmers, complete with a graphical interface and layout capabilities. Such a tool might be purchased, or developed internally. The more closely the use of the tool reflects the process shown here, the more effective it will be in the hands of a good developer.

Where working with the tool does not reflect this process, its utility is reduced. For example, if comparisons are not handled via multiple SQL passes, the developer must produce queries that place the periods for comparison in a series of rows, then pivot the report to produce comparisons. The process of doing so will be more complex, time consuming, and error prone.

TIP

A tool for use by a developer must reflect the way in which the developer breaks down and solves the problem. The tool should handle reporting elements in a manner consistent with those described in this chapter, rather than in an obtuse or counterintuitive fashion.

Figure 13.2 Building the process improvement report.

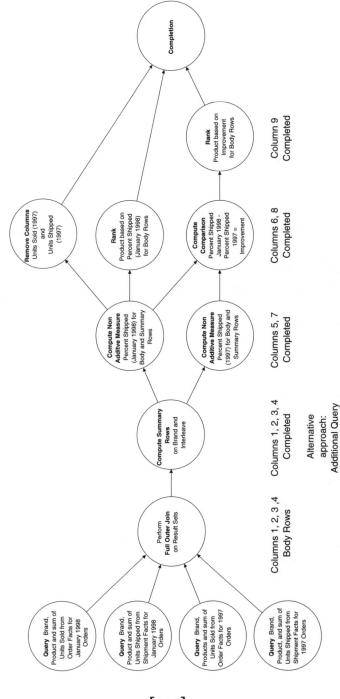

Tools for Businesspeople

When a piece of software to be used for construction of reports is to be given to a business person, we face a different set of requirements. Because the businessperson thinks about building the report in different terms, it is appropriate to look for a different set of features. As before, we'll look at ease of use, or the degree to which the tool reflects how the businessperson thinks about creating a report.

Ease of Use

There is much more to ease of use than a flashy user interface. Widgets for rotating pivot tables or changing the elevation of a chart look great in a demo. However, if a businessperson cannot easily drill across fact tables, compare this year to last, rank sales, or compare detail to group averages, the query tool quickly becomes an encumbrance, and the potential of the data warehouse will be unfulfilled.

As we have said, ease of use can be measured by comparing how a business person thinks about building the report to how the tool requires him or her to do so. The closer these processes match, the easier it is to use the tool. Unlike developers, businesspeople do not break a report down into additive and nonadditive elements, identify processes needed to query the data, compute summaries, perform comparisons, and so forth. Instead, business users think of building a report as the process of specifying what it is they want to see. If a businessperson were to break down Report 13.9, he or she might do so as follows:

- Show me brands and products.
- Show sales, shipments, percent shipped, and a ranking of percent shipped for January 1998 orders.
- Show percent shipped for 1997 orders.
- Show the change in percent shipped from 1997 to January 1998, and a ranking of the change.

Unlike developers, business people do not specify *how* to construct the report; instead, they define *what* they want to see. The closer a tool comes to reflecting this perspective, the easier it will be to use, and hence, the more successful it will be. As we will see, this does not necessarily require a different tool.

Businesspeople should be able to say, "Show me this. . . ." and receive the desired report. The tool must therefore have an interface that allows them to indicate what the report should look like—allowing them to choose what should be placed in each column: dimensions, additive and nonadditive measures, comparisons, and rankings. Measures from different fact tables, perhaps even different databases, can be placed within report columns. The interface must allow them to reuse the same measures, qualified in different ways to facilitate comparisons. From the business user's point of view, they are identifying what they wish to see.

Based on their input, the tool determines the approach to be used to construct the result. This approach might look much like the plan a developer constructed in Figure 13.2, but must be completely invisible to the end user. The tool executes the necessary queries, performs the needed computations, and assembles the results for presentation as requested by the business person.

Because the underlying process of building the report is ultimately the same as the one created by the developer, it is possible for a single tool to satisfy both developers and businesspeople. To the developer's tool, we add a user interface that allows the businessperson to define the end result, then generates the process steps by which the report is constructed. The developer can bypass this interface, directly manipulating the construction process.

Too many of today's "end-user query tools" make report creation a two-step process: define the query, then build the report. Operations not suited to SQL are done in the second phase, often through complicated calculations and variables. If a report requires multiple queries, it is usually the user's responsibility to assemble these queries, especially if the queries require differing constraints or execute on different databases. To the businessperson, this separation of functionality seems arbitrary and counterintuitive.

TIP

For businesspeople, ease of use necessitates a single interface allowing them to specify what they want to see, completely shielding them from having to know how to construct the result.

Here are just a few examples of how this rule can be applied to the key reporting elements described in this chapter:

Additive, semi-additive, and nonadditive measures can be freely requested by the user. They do not bear the burden of breaking down a nonadditive measure into its fully additive components, nor of figuring out how to compute an average. To a businessperson, a measure is a measure.

Summaries are simply requested. The tool computes them appropriately, aggregating fully additive measures, requerying to summarize averages, and computing summaries of nonadditive measures through recourse to their fully additive components.

Comparisons across rows are easily added to a report. A businessperson can compare body rows to summary rows, add running totals, and rank rows based on one or more measures. Construction of a calculations or variables interface is not required to perform these comparisons. Any interface that separates the construction of the query from the calculation of column contents or the layout of the report will fall short of being usable.

It is possible to include the same measure in multiple report columns, qualified in a different manner. This form of comparison must not require the user to construct variables or computations. Instead, a user request should trigger multiple SQL statements transparently.

Drilling across fact tables should be transparent. The businessperson should not have to be aware that a particular question requires more than one query. The tool must decompose a request whenever necessary, without the intervention of the end user. Neither should the location of the fact tables be a concern. Whether all on a single database, or distributed across multiple, heterogeneous platforms, drill across should remain transparent.

Constraints are applied through a single interface. Some may find their way into a where clause while others will performed within the application, but this distinction is not relevant to a businessperson. A constraint is a constraint.

To some, these requirements may seem extreme, but we have seen each element described in this chapter implemented in such a way that these requirements have been met, though not in a single tool.

Prevention of Inaccurate Results

If it's easy to use, businesspeople will quickly come to rely on the reporting tool for information to support business decisions. If a tool gives the wrong answer, results can be disastrous. For example, an average computed incorrectly might lead to dangerously low inventory levels. While it can't be expected to prevent a businessperson from asking the wrong question, a good reporting tool should help avoid the pitfalls we have already discussed.

TIP

In addition to meeting ease-of-use requirements, a reporting tool for businesspeople must prevent actions that would result in inaccurate reports.

Many of the techniques we have suggested for handling key report elements aid in preventing inaccurate results. Using a full-outer join when merging result sets from a drill across query, for example, prevents loss of data when a dimension value is measured in one fact table but not another. However, there are several categories worth revisiting, if only because so many of today's "end-user query tools" don't prevent serious errors. Here are some of the most common problems.

Nonadditive Measures Most nonadditive measures are ratios, such as the Margin Percentage from Report 13.1. Typically, these ratios are considered key indicators, of central importance to the business. They must be constructed as the ratio of component sums, and not the sum of ratios.

Even where properly defined, the nonadditive measure risks incorrect summarization. Query tools that produce summary rows based on the computation approach often sum ratios, producing meaningless and inaccurate results. This behavior must be prevented.

Summarization of Averages Averages should never be summarized by aggregating them further. As we have seen, the summarization of an average requires access to the source data. This simple rule is frequently violated by tools that use the computation approach to produce summary rows. The tool should not permit averages to be summed or averaged.

Semi-Additive Measures Semi-additive measures present the most serious dangers for reporting tools. We have encountered many such measures throughout this book, including inventory levels, basket counts, and account balances. In each case, at least one dimension existed across which the measure was not additive. Inventory and account balances were not additive over time; the basket count was not additive across products.

The reporting tool must prevent reports from presenting semi-additive measures summed across the dimension in question. For example, a reporting tool should prevent a user from producing a report that sums and displays account balances. The result would be disastrous. Although the sum must not be displayed, the tool may choose to compute it. For example, the sum of balances might be used in the computation of an average balance.

In practice, this requirement means that the tool must ensure that when summed, the semi-additive measure is either constrained by a single value at the grain of the dimension in question, grouped by multiple values at the grain of the dimension in question, or used only in a computation of a nonadditive measure.

These restrictions must be placed on the SQL the tool issues, as well as any computations that take place after results are fetched by the application.

Summing Up Effective Reporting

Building a data warehouse is all about delivering reports. Report design and construction is as important as any other part of the project. Without good reports, the data warehouse project will fail, regardless of the quality of the design.

The most important reporting elements require going beyond the capabilities of SQL. Rankings, comparison across summary levels, and running totals should not be omitted from your repertoire simply because SQL won't handle them. Tools must support all the elements presented in this chapter, using one of the approaches we have identified.

Summary rows must be handled with care. Fully additive measures can be aggregated, but nonadditive measures require aggregation of their additive components. Averages can only be summarized by returning to the database.

Comparison across rows is best accomplished within the application, rather than through SQL heroics. Comparing levels of summarization, construction of running totals, and rankings are all achieved through computation.

Comparison across columns requires multiple queries that qualify the same measure in different ways. The results of these queries are merged within the application carefully. Comparisons are a critical mainstay in business reporting.

Drilling across subject areas also requires multiple queries, this time against different fact tables, potentially against heterogeneous databases. Failure to support drill-across queries will leave you unable to answer business questions that cross subject areas.

Averages must be constructed carefully. The cardinality of the average may be a constant. If it is not, care must be taken to fetch it appropriately.

Ease of use is determined by how well the tool mirrors the way its user thinks about building a report. For developers, ease of use means that the tool allows them to specify how the report is built, by breaking it down into processes surrounding the elements we have identified.

For the businessperson, ease of use means that the tool allows them to specify what they want to see, and determines how to produce the desired results on its own. The tool must allow construction of all the reporting elements in this chapter without becoming too complicated. A single interface and invisible multipass SQL are critical.

Shield business users from common pitfalls like averaging averages, summing ratios, and adding semi-additive measures across a forbidden dimension.

BUILDING AN ENTERPRISE DATA WAREHOUSE

14

We have taken great pains in this book to be helpful without being particularly controversial. Other than our obvious preference for the star schema design techniques first popularized by Dr. Ralph Kimball, we have attempted to avoid the great debates of the data warehouse world. It has been our professional experience that much of what passes for debate is simply an attempt to gain favor for certain products under the guise of impartiality. In this chapter, we will reveal, as is only fair to the reader, our opinions. The purpose of the chapter is to present a coherent approach to constructing an enterprise data warehouse that has a reasonable chance for success. It is not the only approach, but it is one that we have seen work. The ideas in this chapter are drawn largely from the work of Dr. Kimball, our colleague Greg Jones, and our own experiences.

What is an enterprise data warehouse? Rather than burning brain cells in a jargon-laced recitation, we will instead lay down a simple definition and use it to frame our discussion.

Key Business Term

Enterprise data warehouse. A planned, integrated, managed store of relevant corporate data optimized for analysis, query, and reporting functions.

The optimal design for an enterprise data warehouse is an integrated series of conformed dimension tables and transaction-grained fact tables that provide the business with a comprehensive analytical repository. Building an enterprise data warehouse does not require that dimension and fact tables be populated from an intermediate 3NF operational data store. While some staging of data may be necessary, directly populating fact and dimension tables is the least complex and costly solution.

The most important goal in designing and building an enterprise data warehouse is to provide value to the organization. This simple, obvious, unavoidable truth is too often avoided by the gurus and pundits. Proving value in a relatively short time frame is increasingly important to data warehouse teams. The data warehouse team carries a heavy burden of proof because too many businesspeople remember the last great movement to integrate the world's data.

The Golden Age of Data Modeling

It has been apparent for years that we are collecting vast amounts of operational data. As more processes are automated, more data is stored in a variety of formats and technologies. Today, many large corporations keep their operational data in relational databases, legacy hierarchical databases, and old flat files. The arrival of relational databases in the 1980s promised improved access to information, data integration, and eventually improved business operations. But the transition to relational databases took longer than we expected—remember, that job is still not finished—and relational databases did not immediately solve the problem of information access. What was supposed to happen and what did happen are different things. To understand why, we must return to the Golden Age of Data Modeling.

When companies began moving to relational databases, they were told to create entity relationship models (ERDs) of the entire business and build new relational systems based on these models. Companies got bonus points if they signed up for a client/server solution. The data models were almost always done without looking at the existing source systems. Consultants schooled in the art of information engineering told the IT managers of the 1980s to ignore old systems and ask the business users what the data would look like in an ideal world. When the ERDs were complete they were passed off to technical folks to implement. The result was not unlike moving from a college apartment to a $1,000,000 mansion. There was plenty of room in the house, but the old stuff just did not seem to fit. No one had thought about where all the new data would come from or how the old data would be reformatted to the new relational tables. Of course, the old stuff was the information the business ran on. If denied the use of that information, the company would simply cease to operate. Implementation projects in this age were often disastrous.

The data modeling consultants took a very useful and practical tool for requirements gathering and turned it into the holy grail of systems design. This misguided approach, along with the poor performance of early GUI development tools, networks, and relational databases, made the 1980s one of the least productive times in the computer age. While many technology companies and consulting firms made money, few customers were able to predictably implement systems and realize the underlying promise of integrated operational systems. And as projects slipped off the right edge of the Gantt chart, IT managers faced a hostile world. The crusade to integrate disparate legacy systems into a single, integrated database was replaced with survival tactics. Business users began to abandon internal resources and develop their own applications. Others bought turnkey packaged applications and paid consultants to install them. Internal projects were chopped into manageable pieces that could be completed in six months or less. Some companies found that in the face of continuing project failures caused by poor execution and buggy development tools, the best path was to sit out the decade and live with the old systems until the industry sorted itself out. Amidst the turmoil, few companies got much more data out of their hodgepodge environments than before.

What about a Data Warehouse?

Those companies that sat out were rewarded in the mid 1980s. A few perceptive people, the most vocal at the time being Bill Inmon, proposed a radical solution to the problem of integrating data. Like most great ideas, the data warehouse concept solved not just the problem of data integration, but also that of temporal inconsistency. Inmon and others proposed moving operational data from different systems into a single data warehouse where it could be accessed more easily. Inmon solved the temporal inconsistency problem by proposing that the data warehouse contain both historical facts and historical descriptive data, all carefully timestamped so the business could recreate the past at will. In today's dimensional designs, this is done by including a time dimension and carefully managing slow-changing dimensions.

The data warehouse concept made sense for three reasons:

- Data from various systems could be integrated regardless of where the company was in the process of integrating operational systems.

- Data in combination was more valuable and people could ask questions of the data warehouse that were unanswerable by operational systems, whether integrated or not.

- The data warehouse was updated periodically. The underlying architecture could evolve to support query-only processing at a higher level of performance than any existing OLTP environment.

One of the authors worked on a data warehouse project in late 1989. Mr. Inmon actually came and spoke to our project team at one point. As he scribbled away on an overhead projector, it was obvious that he had uncovered something conceptually important. At the time, there was no specialized data warehouse technology. On that project, the data was moved from COBOL flat files to an Oracle database with COBOL programs. Rather than a graphical ad hoc query tool or a data discovery product, we implemented a character mode, canned query interface. And when the data warehouse was finally implemented, the DBA at the first site refused to free up adequate system resources to make performance tolerable. It was a failure from a business perspective.

The project failed for at least four reasons:

- The data was to hard to move.

- Querying and analyzing the data was difficult.

- The design was a 3NF database with timestamps. It was not optimized for analysis.

- The project lasted too long and never delivered answers to business users.

Despite integrating historical and current data from across the organization, that data warehouse faded away with little interest from the business. In the end, the reason for failure that mattered most was the failure to show businesspeople any answers. The technological challenges could be addressed in time, but the failure to prove the value of the solution was the big omission, an omission too often made by IT managers and consultants. Good ideas are often presented poorly, with too much emphasis on technology. In the years since this project failed, the industry has solved the first three problems. New data movement and analysis tools simplify the technical challenges of building a data warehouse. The dimensional modeling and star schema design techniques used in this book simplify and speed analytical processing. However, a data warehouse can still fail if it does not provide answers to businesspeople after a reasonable investment of time and money.

An Incremental Approach

Our colleague, Greg Jones, spent a considerable amount of time over the last few years studying the field of data warehousing with particular attention to project failure issues. Based on this work, he developed an incremental approach to developing an enterprise data warehouse that has proven to be quite successful. The methodology was developed at the height of the controversy over data marts versus data warehouses. Rather than becoming embroiled in that controversy, Jones focused on developing the optimal low-risk path to an enterprise data warehouse. This approach was designed around two immutable laws of data warehouse development.

The first immutable law is that of loading complexity: *The most complex part of building a data warehouse is loading the data.* Poor source data quality, missing source data, poor system documentation, multiple source loading, and redundant, conflicting source data contribute to the difficulty of this task. Much of the complexity is hidden, only coming to light as data is loaded into the data warehouse. Automated data movement tools can help, but the underlying semantic complexity of transformation cannot be engineered away.

The second immutable law is that of design uncertainty: *It is impossible to evaluate any data warehouse design until legacy data is loaded and shown to users.* A successful data warehouse design must accurately reflect the business needs of the company using data from a variety of sources. Uncertainty in the design is guaranteed during the design process, as data quality issues from various source systems become apparent.

The traditional approach to data warehouse design requires that a large, comprehensive design be completed before loading begins. Data is then loaded into the entire data warehouse in a late stage of the project. The effect of this approach is to ignore the two immutable laws until late in the project. The scale of design uncertainty and load complexity are unknown until data is loaded and shown to business users. Projects frequently blow up at this stage. In recent years, as projects failed to meet time and cost predictions, business people quickly recalled the golden age of data modeling.

Jones proposed two simple changes to the process that to some are still heresy. First, following the ideas of Dr. Kimball, he proposed that you could build an enterprise data warehouse a subject area at a time. He further asserted that you should load the first subject area design as soon as technically possible and iterate the design through an aggressive feedback cycle with business users. Using the latest data movement and analysis tools, Jones argued, project teams could load and evaluate a single subject area in weeks, not months. This design could be moved into production in less than six months. Subsequent subject areas could be designed the same way and deployed even more quickly, since some of the dimensions would have been defined in the previous subject area. This approach drags design uncertainty and load complexity from late in the project to the first stage, as shown in Figure 14.1.

Perhaps the most controversial aspect of this incremental approach was that it did not mandate the building of a large, comprehensive data warehouse prior to building star schemas for individual subject areas. A single subject area star schema looks a lot like a data mart to many people. In creating a more practical solution than either a series of data marts or a 3NF enterprise data warehouse,

Figure 14.1 Loading early.

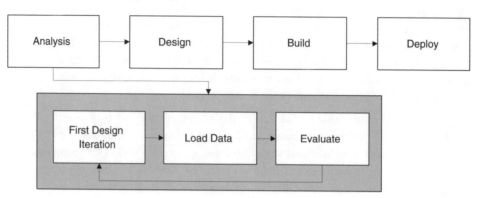

Jones had blurred the distinction between the advocates of each concept. Of course, not everyone has endorsed this new approach. Many observers still cling to the idea of a large, 3NF data warehouse as a mandatory first step in developing an enterprise data warehouse. From this 3NF data warehouse, the business can then create dependent data marts. This camp—we are going to get a little controversial here—is stuck in the technology of the past. To understand why, we must consider the two most common objections to a dimensional enterprise data warehouse.

First, members of the 3NF enterprise data warehouse camp claim that a dimensional EDW creates redundancy. They view the dimensional EDW as a series of independent data marts. Their belief that a data mart is valid only when sourced from a 3NF EDW makes it difficult to accept the concept of interlocking star schemas with conformed dimensions. Consider the architecture presented in Figure 14.2, which is our discrete manufacturing design from Chapter 5, "Production," viewed through the eyes of a 3NF EDW advocate.

The 3NF EDW view forces us to recreate every dimension that is common to more than one fact table; however, nothing in the design of an interlocking series of star schemas, the approach used throughout this book, requires or even suggests this. In fact, the approach to building a dimensional EDW advocated in this chapter is intended to avoid redundancy and improve the consistency of data across the enterprise without a 3NF EDW.

The second common objection to the dimensional EDW approach is that the load process is redundant and unnecessarily complex. To get to this point of confusion requires that you first believe entirely in the first objection, that redundant dimensions are rampant in the dimensional EDW design. Redundant dimensions

Figure 14.2 3NF EDW view of production design.

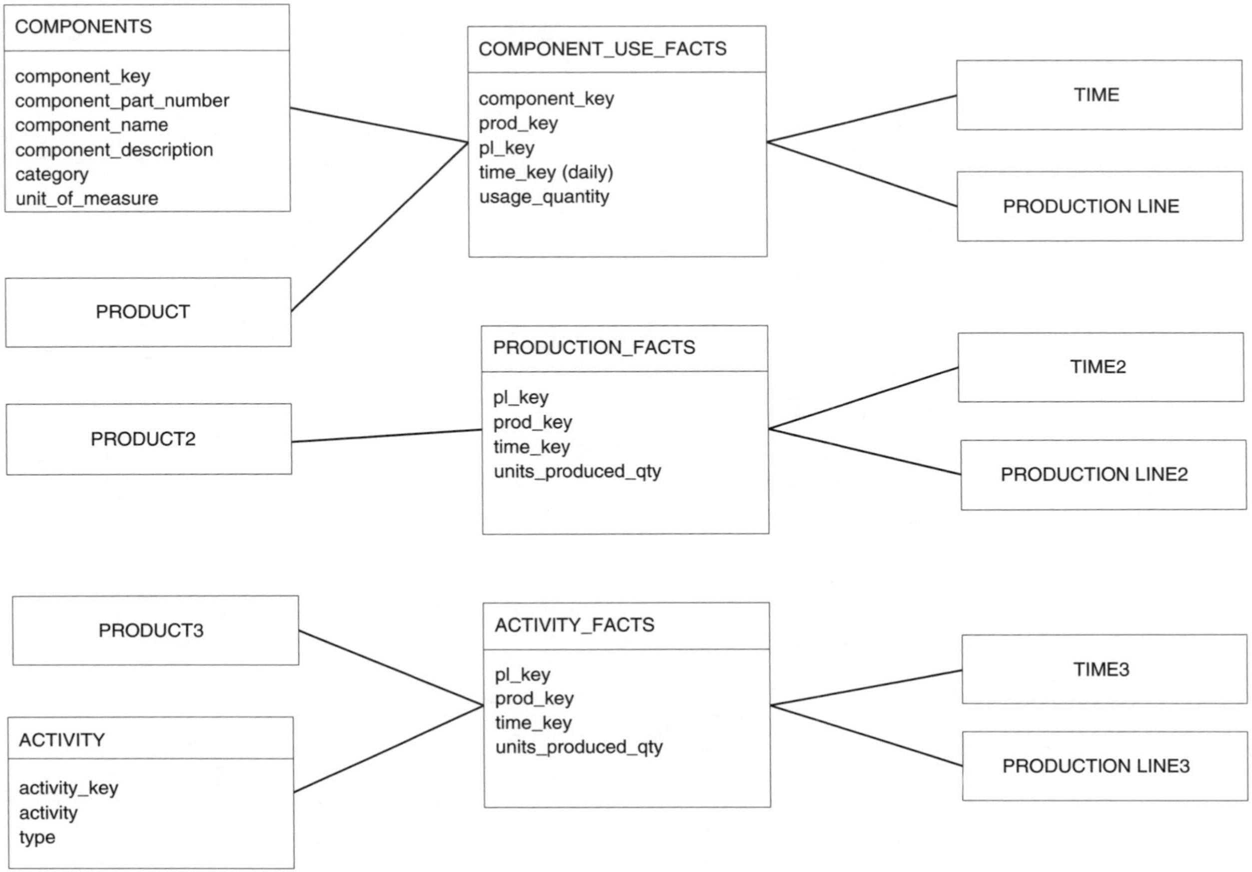

COMPONENTS
- component_key
- component_part_number
- component_name
- component_description
- category
- unit_of_measure

COMPONENT_USE_FACTS
- component_key
- prod_key
- pl_key
- time_key (daily)
- usage_quantity

TIME

PRODUCTION LINE

PRODUCT

PRODUCTION_FACTS
- pl_key
- prod_key
- time_key
- units_produced_qty

TIME2

PRODUCTION LINE2

PRODUCT2

ACTIVITY_FACTS
- pl_key
- prod_key
- time_key
- units_produced_qty

TIME3

PRODUCTION LINE3

PRODUCT3

ACTIVITY
- activity_key
- activity
- type

require redundant loads, perhaps even from different systems. The product dimension for the sales subject area must come from the order entry system, while for manufacturing, it must come from the manufacturing system. Again, our design approach for the dimensional EDW would not use this approach to loading. Instead, the dimensional EDW requires a single conformed dimension to which all source data transactions (represented by fact tables) can be correctly associated. Figure 14.3 compares the 3NF EDW myth of redundant loading with the dimensional EDW reality.

With these two objections out of the way, we can focus on the reality of building a dimensional EDW using a series of interlocking star schemas. This overall design strategy, coupled with the tactical use of early loading to address the risks associated with design uncertainty and load complexity, provides a safe, sure course to success. The approach also has the distinct advantage of proving value early, facing the most difficult issues immediately, and leveraging recent advances in data movement and presentation software.

Changes in the Operational Environment

This is going to be a big project. An enterprise data warehouse is going to touch many operational systems, involve business users from across the organization, and require aggressive project and risk management. It will take longer than anyone wants to complete the first complete pass through the business. It should also be noted that the data warehouse is an environment of continuing change and adaptation.

Changes in source systems are the most obvious cause of changes in the EDW. An EDW that covers all principal business areas will use several source systems. A company planning an EDW over a two-year time frame cannot ignore upheaval in the OLTP world during that time. Future changes must also be considered. The operational system evolution of a typical company is presented in Table 14.1.

The company must consider the impact of each system when planning for an EDW. Because much of the OLTP environment will change over the next three years, the company may choose to delay data warehouse development. The cost of reworking data movement software might be considered prohibitive, especially when using hand-coding and a 3NF EDW approach. But the obvious benefits of data warehousing can not be delayed. The pressure to build data marts for existing systems and then rework them as new OLTP systems come on line is the most common reason that stovepipe data marts are built. The need to provide historical data overwhelms the desire to design and build the data warehouse correctly.

Figure 14.3 Redundant loading debunked.

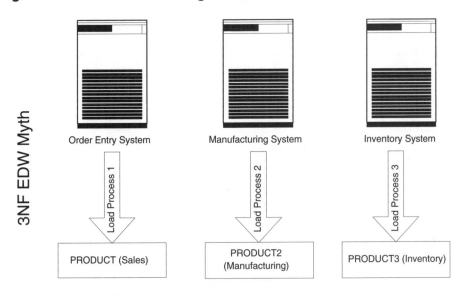

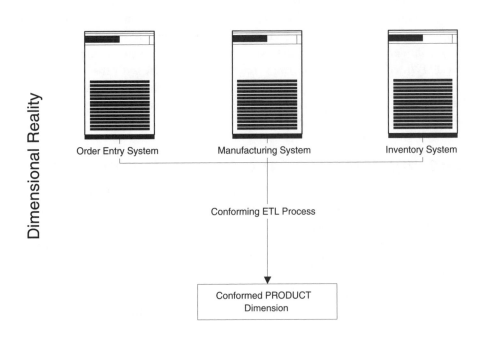

Table 14.1 Evolving OLTP Environment

System	Year 1	Year 2	Year 3
Financial accounting	Inhouse		Baan installed
Manufacturing	ASK	Baan installed	
Sales force automation	None	Siebel installed	
Call center	Inhouse		Clarify installed
Administration	PeopleSoft installed		

The criticisms of stovepipe data marts are legitimate and are the same as those used to incorrectly criticize the dimensional EDW approach.

Remember, we are not proposing stovepipe independent data marts as a solution; instead we advocate a dimensional EDW approach that allows for change in the operational environment, simplifies the integration of new technologies, and provides a consistent analytical framework for the business. A 3NF EDW with dependent data marts offers no advantage for managing change in the operational environment over the dimensional EDW approach. These changes impact the 3NF EDW just as they do the dimensional EDW. In fact, the complexity of the 3NF EDW design makes such changes more difficult to quickly implement. Moreover, the extra layer of data movement required for a 3NF EDW/dependent data mart approach is unnecessary with the improvements in data movement software. Continuing to use the 3NF EDW/dependent data mart approach is akin to going to the river for water after the pipes are run to your house. Why make the trip?

Dealing with Change in the Business

An enterprise data warehouse should provide a consistent view of corporate data that is relevant to analysis. Does this include every single data element in the corporation? Does it include every operational source system? More heresy: It is not necessary that an EDW contain every bit of corporate data nor address every operational system. While much has been done to push data out to end users over the last several years, the thought behind the resulting systems was limited. We have encountered ad hoc query environments designed with the best of intentions that presented, in a single encounter, a choice of over 1000 possible data elements to include in a query—surely we can do better than that as an industry. Many ad hoc tools allow developers to slap together query environments with too many objects, and these tools are still limited to standard SQL in developing queries. The limitations of SQL in analytical processing are well documented.

Providing confusing data in a timely manner through powerful ad hoc query tools causes more confusion for the business user. The mission of the EDW team is to provide a consistent analytical framework of important corporate data that is useful for analysis. This includes a navigable schema, a reliable and consistent data movement capability, and easy-to-use analysis and reporting tools. What is important among a company's data varies greatly from industry to industry and even company to company within an industry. Companies have different levels of analytical sophistication. The latest, coolest analytical application described in an industry rag or vendor white paper may be incomprehensible or irrelevant to your company. The clearest indication of a requirement is the expressed and documented need of a businessperson, preferably in the form of a question or series of questions.

In every business there are constants, elements that are steady state or change only rarely. Operating today's modern corporation is like flying a large airliner. The corporation and the airliner have a predetermined course with clear waypoints. The pilot, with the assistance of onboard computers and air traffic controllers, avoids bad weather and seeks favorable winds to speed the plane to its destination. As the plane flies, the automatic pilot makes minor corrections with the various control surfaces. There are two things that a high-speed airliner reacts poorly to: big, sudden changes and small, unexpected changes. In either event, the airliner is very prone to lose control. Companies also react poorly to big, sudden changes and small, unexpected changes. They operate within an environment of operational parameters that guide process execution.

In today's competitive environment, companies are attempting to react to change more rapidly than in the past. The pace of change has quickened, forcing companies to constantly reevaluate elements once thought relatively stable. In Chapter 12, "Key Measures and Ratios," we identified five elements of a business that were defined to come up with key measures. These elements were:

Concept of operations. How a company is structured and organized, whether around products, divisions, or geographies.

Business model. How a company makes money and how costs are allocated.

Corporate strategies. Specific strategies used to execute the business model and gain competitive advantage.

Competitive environment. A company's competitors and how they attack the company's position.

Operational environment. Key operational processes that are executed in service of the business model.

In the past, a company's concept of operations, business model, and even strategies were remarkably stable. For years, AT&T operated under the same concept of operations and business model, executed the same strategies, and lived in a competitive vacuum. Only operational changes, mostly driven by technology, were common. After the initial round of deregulation, the only change was that AT&T and the regional Bell operating companies (RBOCs) divided up the business by service type and geography—the business model changed hardly at all. Corporate strategies and the competitive environment were also unchanged. Today, both AT&T and the RBOCs face changes in their business models, corporate strategies, and competitive environment. Providing wireless service, competing with cable companies, and responding to the growing use of the Internet have altered the business model, competitive strategies, concept of operations, and competitive environments of the RBOCs and AT&T. The upheaval makes the design and deployment of an EDW a complex undertaking. Other industries face similar cycles of change and upheaval.

The enterprise data warehouse development process must adapt to changes in the business environment. The EDW team has an advantage in that changes must occur first in the downstream operational systems. This reality ensures that such changes will not happen overnight. Still, these changes must be evaluated for the impact on the EDW, whether partially or completely implemented. Examples of changes and the resulting impact on the EDW are shown in Table 14.2.

In each case of business change, the EDW team must be ready to alter the basic design, change data movement software, and add supporting analysis capabilities. But the effort to do so is generally far less than the effort required to implement the operational system and process change for the business.

Building the Dimensional EDW

Building a dimensional EDW is a multistep process that consists of first defining the overall target design, conforming primary dimensions, selection grain for primary transaction fact tables, and then building a series of interlocking star schemas. The execution of each subject area build—a single subject area star schema—is accomplished using the incremental methodology described previously. The approach is described more completely in the white paper "A Practical Guide to Building Data Marts," included on the CD that accompanies this text.

Table 14.2 Impact of Changes on EDW

Element	Change	EDW Impact
Concept of operations	Add several international subsidiaries	• Modify organizational dimension to include international organizations • Handle multiple currencies
Business model	Change from per-minute to flat-rate pricing for Internet access	• Evaluate revenue fact table to ensure that customer minutes are easily calculated • Create usage profile dimension to group customers into profitable and unprofitable groups
Corporate strategy	Change from a high-margin retailer to a discount retailer	• Add price points to sales fact table • Add fact table to track competitor prices over time • Ensure inventory model supports closely monitoring day's sales outstanding
Competitive environment	Increased competition in a low-margin business	• Improve customer behavior tracking • Add the ability to track competitor sales and pricing strategies • Gather data to track customer profitability and lifetime value
Operational environment	Outsource call center operations	• Track wait time, resolution/order time, and volumes before and after cutover • Track customer service ratings before and after cutover

Viewed at a high level, the dimensional EDW process consists of a comprehensive planning stage that should last only a few months. This stage can precede or run concurrent with the first subject area build. During this initial planning stage, the EDW team should accomplish the following major tasks:

Identify and conform the primary dimensions for the entire business.
These dimensions provide the framework for cross-process analysis using drill-across queries.

Identify key transaction grain fact tables for the entire business. These fact tables describe the fundamental transactions of the business and are a wealth of analytical data.

Create a high-level dimensional EDW design, showing the relationship between primary dimensions and key fact tables. This design is used to coordinate development across subject areas and ensure consistency with no redundancy.

Prioritize subject areas for development based on business need. This is done by businesspeople, not by the EDW technical team. If you have done a good job of describing the benefits of a dimensional EDW and convinced everyone that they could be less than six months away from those benefits, prioritizing will be a challenge. If not, you have not sold the project well enough.

Determine any source system changes planned for the EDW project time frame and include them in project and risk management plans. These changes may be ignored or used to make tie-breaking decisions when prioritizing subject areas.

Select data storage, movement, and analysis software. We recommend a relational database with star schema awareness for storage, a multi-threaded data movement tool—not a code generator—and an analytical tool that is aggregate aware and can handle multipass SQL.

Document requirements that require specialized technology, especially for analysis. These include high-speed MDDBs for very real-time analysis, data mining tools, data cleansing tools, and other esoteric segments of the data warehouse tools marketplace.

Completing these steps will provide a road map to a completed dimensional EDW. The conformed primary dimensions ensure that redundant dimensional data is unnecessary, and future changes to these dimensions can be accomplished with minimal rework. Identifying primary transaction grain fact tables ensures that all basic measures of the business will be captured at a high level of granularity. Prioritizing subject areas will ensure that the most important business answers are provided early in the project, while considering operational system changes can reduce rework in the data movement tasks. Finally, the selection of a standard technology for data storage, movement, and analysis reduces product swapping and evaluations during the EDW project. Specialized requirements for data mining and visualization, data cleanup, and multidimensional online analytical processing

(MOLAP) can be addressed as the EDW project moves forward. Selection of these specialized tools must not delay the overall, time-critical task of building the dimensional EDW.

Creating a High-Level Design

Primary dimensions are those that describe the core operational concepts of the business. These are the principal entities that are related to key transactions and are used to describe the concept of operations. The set of primary dimensions includes product, component/part, supplier, customer, channel, and time. Most businesses can be described using a combination of these dimensions. The defining characteristic of these dimensions is that they are common to more than one fact table and form the basis of drill-across analysis. Figure 14.4 depicts the primary dimensions for a manufacturer, retailer, and software company.

Although these companies do not share all the primary dimensions, each one uses a familiar set of concepts. Conforming these dimensions in the dimensional EDW is the first step to a successful implementation.

Along with primary dimensions come key fact tables. These fact tables represent the basic transactions of the business and vary by industry. Key fact tables are designed at the transaction level to ensure a high level of analytical capability.

Figure 14.4 Primary dimensions.

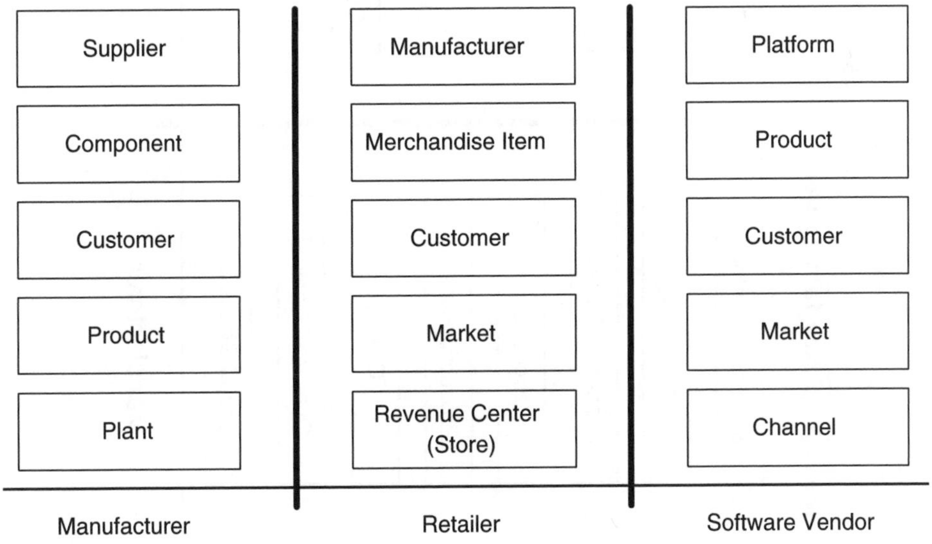

Supplier	Manufacturer	Platform
Component	Merchandise Item	Product
Customer	Customer	Customer
Product	Market	Market
Plant	Revenue Center (Store)	Channel
Manufacturer	Retailer	Software Vendor

Figure 14.5 Key fact tables.

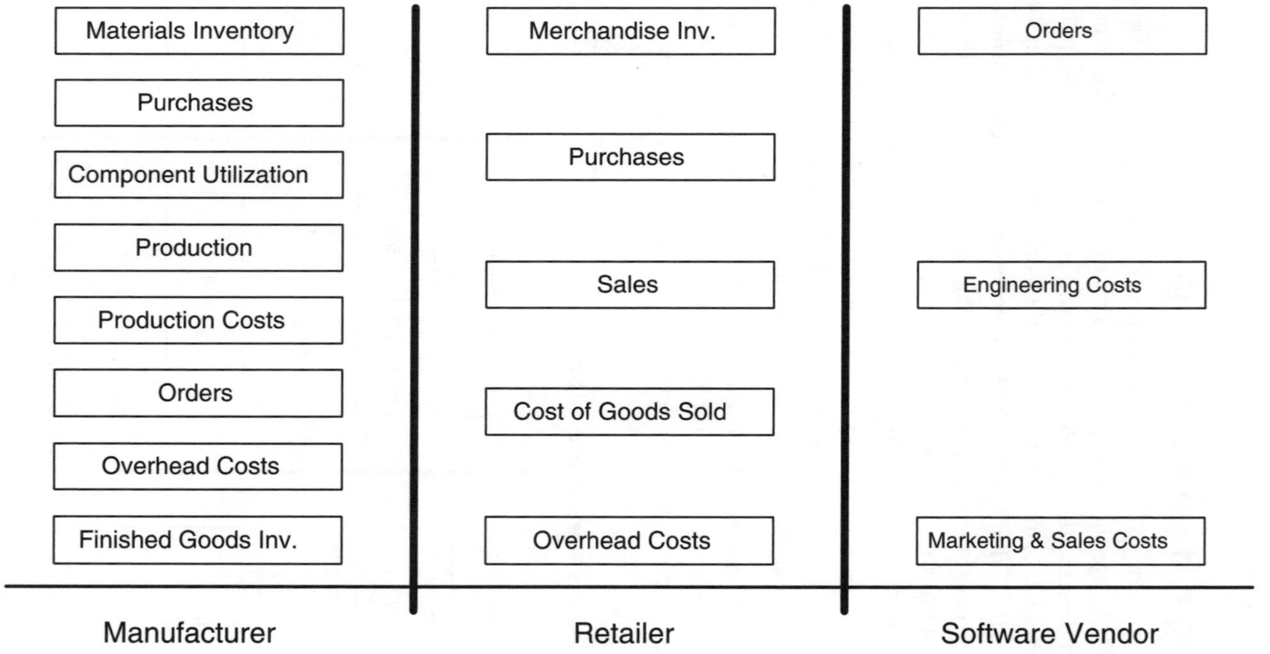

Manufacturer	Retailer	Software Vendor
Materials Inventory	Merchandise Inv.	Orders
Purchases	Purchases	
Component Utilization	Sales	Engineering Costs
Production	Cost of Goods Sold	
Production Costs	Overhead Costs	Marketing & Sales Costs
Orders		
Overhead Costs		
Finished Goods Inv.		

While there may eventually be many fact tables in the dimensional EDW, these first fact tables should provide measures of sales dollars, sales volume, order volume, labor costs, labor volume, material or merchandise costs, and other costs. Using these transaction-grained fact tables along with conformed primary dimensions will provide a sound analytical framework for the business. Figure 14.5 presents the key fact tables for the manufacturer, retailer, and software company whose primary dimensions were presented in Figure 14.4.

Using the primary dimensions and key fact tables we can create a high-level design for the dimensional EDW. This design, in practice, should be fully attributed with primary sources for data identified. A high-level design diagram for the retailer is presented in Figure 14.6. The design team will add subject area specific dimensions and fact tables as the EDW project proceeds.

From this high-level design the EDW team can identify the first subject area for development and begin to implement the iterative methodology described previously. To do so requires that the team interview business users for analytical needs in the first subject area. From these interviews, the dimensions and facts that are unique to the subject area and not represented in the high-level design can be added. The first subject area for the retailer is presented in Figure 14.7.

Figure 14.6 Primary dimensions and key fact tables.

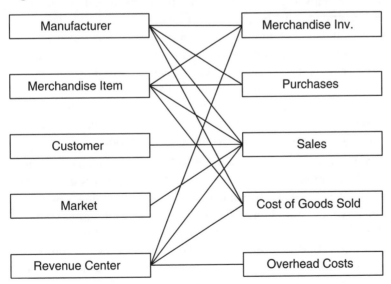

As this subject area is completed, work can commence on additional subject areas. As additional subject areas are designed and implemented, the EDW team can reuse dimensions already loaded to relate to new fact tables. Additional unique dimensions are also discovered as new subject areas are added. For our retailer, Figure 14.8 shows the addition of the inventory subject area to the design.

Subsequent subject areas can usually be developed and deployed in less time, since much of the design in the form of primary or common dimensions is already completed. The design process evolves to a process of determining the associated primary and unique dimensions, loading the facts, and training users.

Scheduling Subject Area Implementations

Concurrent with developing a high-level design, the EDW team can also work with decision makers to prioritize subject areas. While it is not impossible to work on more than one subject area at a time, assuming the high-level design is completed, most organizations experience best results when the first subject area is used to shake out technical and process issues. Once the first subject area is completed, the business is usually in much better shape to tackle concurrent development efforts, manage changes in operational systems and analytical requirements, and implement specialized technologies as required.

Probably the most common subject area selected first is sales. It seems that everyone is interested in analyzing sales. The sales subject area usually includes the product, customer, and channel primary dimensions, so it is a good place to start when seeking to validate data movement assumptions. The next logical extension when sales is the starting point is the inventory subject area. Inventory uses the product and channel dimensions, and comparing sales to inventory is often a valuable drill-across query. Other companies may choose to tackle cost-related subject areas instead, including direct labor and cost of goods sold. Neither course is right or wrong, as the company and its decision makers are in the best position to prioritize the subject areas for implementation.

As the EDW project continues with a series of subject area implementations the overall analytical environment will take on a life of its own. Users in the first subject area will request additional dimensional attributes and perhaps new measures. Some will even request entirely new dimensions or fact tables after seeing the value of the first design. The more interesting requests will be those for data not stored in the current OLTP environment and data from outside the company's databases. When faced with a request for data not stored in the OLTP world, the EDW team should tell the business user exactly why the data cannot be provided,

Figure 14.7 The first subject area—sales.

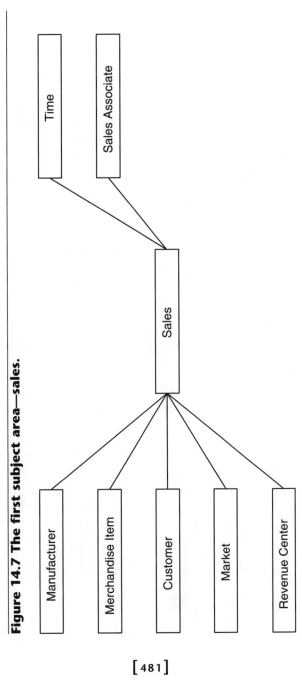

Figure 14.8 Adding inventory.

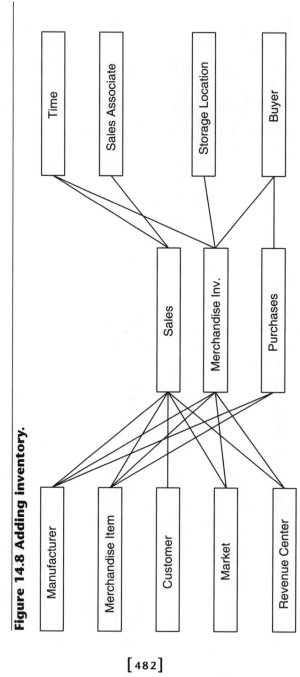

as well as notifying the OLTP development teams of the request. Requests for outside data should be taken very seriously and accommodated whenever possible. In short, the EDW will become an integral part of the company's information technology infrastructure. Over time, the novelty of data warehousing will fade away as more and more organizations treat the concept as a normal activity required to compete in today's information-based economy.

Summing Up The EDW

Building an enterprise data warehouse successfully requires a combination of foresight, business knowledge, and superior project execution. The EDW design team can choose between several possible approaches, some old and some new. These approaches include:

3NF enterprise data warehouse. First popularized by Bill Inmon and now advocated by NCR and other large box vendors, the 3NF data warehouse is constructed by moving operational data from various systems into an integrated 3NF query-only database.

3NF enterprise data warehouse with dependent data marts. An extension of the original 3NF concept to address the poor performance and navigation issues of a large 3NF EDW, this approach creates dimensional data marts sourced from the EDW. The dimensional data marts can be star schemas or MDDB implementations.

Independent, unintegrated data marts. An architecture that results from an unplanned, hasty approach to data warehousing, this approach ignores the cost associated with redundant loads and benefits associated with creating an enterprisewide architecture of common dimensions.

Integrated, dimensional enterprise data warehouse. The approach recommended here, which eliminates redundancy, allows cross-process analysis, and supports evolving OLTP environments. The dimensional EDW consists of a series of interlocking star schemas that share common, conformed primary dimensions.

If you select the last approach, we are confident you will arrive at the destination of an enterprise data warehouse. This approach, if executed correctly, can reduce the cost of development and maintenance. Perhaps most importantly, the dimensional EDW approach proposed here accelerates the time to value for the business.

INTERVIEWING

This book has been all about the delivery of answers to businesspeople. To provide answers, the designers of the data warehouse must possess a solid understanding of the way the business is run. Without it, the design will not reflect the way people look at the business, nor will it provide answers to pressing questions. A deep understanding of the business can only be gained by talking to people. In this chapter, we'll look at how to prepare for and conduct interviews.

The discussions of data warehouse and report designs throughout this book are of interest to many different groups of people, including data warehouse designers, information technology managers, and the businesspeople who use the data warehouse. This chapter centers around cultivating an understanding of the business, and is specifically directed at the data warehouse designer, whose job is to link the technical design to business requirements. Interviewing techniques apply in many areas of life, but the examples in this chapter center around the needs of the data warehouse designer.

The key to successful interviewing may surprise you. We've provided insight into the ways in which a number of businesses are run, and you've probably had enough contact with the people in your business to form a general notion of how they work. However, if you want to learn anything by talking with someone, *you must forget what you know*. Forget about the key business terms you have read in these pages; forget about your past experience with the business; forget what someone told you in an interview yesterday. *What you think you know will only color your interpretation of what you hear.* Throughout this chapter, we will return to this crucial point.

Successful interviews require a little bit of up-front planning. While a structured agenda for an interview can be counterproductive, it is important that the interviewers have a clear understanding of the project scope, the roles of the interviewers, and any outstanding business questions; otherwise, the interview will not advance the design of the data warehouse.

The beginning and end of every interview should be used to provide the person being interviewed with some insight into the project and its current status. For the remainder of the interview, your objective is to learn as much about the business as possible. The best way to maximize this valuable time is by practicing a technique called *active listening*, which we will explain in detail.

You Don't Know Anything

A businessperson has sacrificed valuable time to talk with you—time during which he or she could be doing very important things. This time is a precious resource for both of you. The businessperson deserves your gratitude for this time, and you need to maximize its benefit. Never lose sight of your primary objective for the interview: to learn about the business.

If you want to learn something, you must begin by realizing that *you need to learn*. If you are convinced you know the business well, there is no point in conducting an interview. Whether you are right or wrong about what you think you know, the interview will not add value. If there is something to be learned, you won't learn it. Your preconceived notions about the business will color what you hear; assumptions you make about what is said or not said will remain untested.

To maximize the use of your time, you must start from a position of ignorance. You need to admit to yourself that your understanding of the business is imperfect, and that the person you are going to speak with can provide valuable insight. The more interviews you conduct, the harder it will become to do this. As you develop your picture of the business process, your growing knowledge will become your biggest obstacle. Each time you walk into an interview, you must throw away your experience within the organization, the knowledge you've drawn from other businesses in the industry, and anything you've read in books like this one.

The needs in every business vary, and you will not catch crucial details if you are not ready to learn. Even within an industry, organizations exhibit differences in how they are run. These differences may be striking, but are often subtle. Something as seemingly obscure as how accountants recognize revenue can have profound impact on a sales schema like those in Chapter 2, "Sales," a budgeting schema like the one in Chapter 8, "Budgets and Spending," and financial schemas like those in Chapter 9, "Financial Reporting." You must be open to learning if you are to sense these crucial subtleties. You will overlook them if you think you know the business already.

Even within a single organization, it is possible to find variations in how processes are viewed, or in the meaning of terms. You must keep your confidence in check if you are to detect these variations. Something as simple as the term *sales* can mean different things to different people. For example, a sales manager considers something sold only once the product ordered is fulfilled. An inventory manager may think of sales as past demand for a product. In the former case, *sales* refers to *shipments*; in the latter case it refers to *orders*. You are more likely to pick up on these distinctions if you have no assumptions coming into the interview.

TIP

Your objective for the interview is to learn. Clear you mind of any preconcieved notions about the business. The less you think you know, the better off you will be.

Do not treat an interview as a chance to impress someone with your knowledge of his or her business. At best, this approach will stand in the way of learning. At worst, it will offend the person being interviewed. If you succeed in impressing the interviewee with your grasp of the business, he or she won't bring up important details—and you won't learn. For example, you walk into a sales manager's office and preface your questions with a lengthy explanation of the compensation plan for salespeople. Believing you understand this complex process, the sales manager will assume there is no need to mention the need to exclude prepayments when computing commissions. Don't allow hubris to prevent you from learning something important.

More likely, any attempt to impress a businessperson will fail. Every person you interview is a professional with training and experience, living daily in the business process you are studying. You are an information technologist. Who do you think is likely to know more about the business? Your efforts to convey your vast business knowledge may seem arrogant, and are likely to offend the person you are interviewing. If you doubt this, reverse the roles for a moment. How would you react if a businessperson showed up for a meeting with you and told you how a system should be designed? Remember: No one knows more about how the person sitting across from you thinks than that person.

Instead, you must be open to being wrong. You must patiently allow people to explain things to you that you think you already know, and you must *listen* as if it is the first time. You will be surprised how much you can learn. Later, we'll discuss a technique that will help you get the most out of an interview, but first, you need to prepare for it.

Planning Interviews

As we pointed out in Chapter 14, "Building an Enterprise Data Warehouse," data warehouse designers actually conduct two kinds of interviews. Interviews with businesspeople serve to identify the analytic requirements for the data warehouse. Interviews with database administrators and developers of OLTP systems determine what answers can be delivered to businesspeople. Although this chapter focuses on the former set of interviews, the same principles apply in each situation. It all begins with preparation.

The Interview Schedule

The first consideration when planning interviews is whom to interview. Staying within the scope of the subject area, there is usually a very large number of people with whom one might talk. In Chapter 1, "The Business-Driven Data Warehouse," we pointed out that OLTP systems are transaction or event focused, while data warehouses are process focused. It important to find those individuals who are focused on the process, usually someone in "management." The best place to focus is one or two steps up from the operational level and one or two steps down from the CEO.

In planning the list, keep in mind that the same person may have concerns that are both operational and process focused. Don't be too quick to rule someone out. For example, a salesperson may spend a good deal of time placing orders into the order entry system, or pulling reports on particular orders or shipments. In addition to these operational concerns, the same salesperson may have analytic questions. She may be interested in how much of a particular product she is selling over time, or what the characteristics of her best customers are. These are questions best answered by a data warehouse.

It is reasonable to expect the interview list to change throughout the course of the project. After interviewing three regional managers, the team may decide that the perspective of the fourth can be accommodated via a short telephone call rather than a two-hour interview. Also be open to the possibility of expanding the list. Conversations with a senior vice president may reveal that an administrative assistant does a lot of the important number crunching. This person is worth interviewing. A change in project scope may also require reorganizing the list of interviews.

Common sense suggests that the interview list must be cleared. Don't attempt to get two hours of someone's time without the approval of his or her manager. A short explanation of the project and the interview process can be sent out to the interviewees. Invite them to bring any reports they use that are relevant to the subject area, but stress that preparation is not necessary.

After an initial list of interviewees is compiled, each interview must be scheduled. It is useful to plan the schedules of the interviewers so that the two types of interviews are staggered to some extent. By alternating between learning about the business and learning about available data, reasonable expectations develop about what solutions can be delivered. Team members must also be given time between interviews to review their notes and summarize them for others on the team.

Interviews may be conducted with individuals or with groups. While interviewing small groups together saves time, some of the participants will volunteer less information, particularly if they are in the presence of higher-level colleagues. Speaking to people one at a time ensures due consideration of each relevant perspective on the business process. We prefer to meet with groups only when seeking feedback on a design or prototype.

Equally important to consider is the number of people doing the interviewing. While nothing can substitute for hearing what the vice president of Marketing has to say about the sales process, it is not practical to bring the entire design team to the meeting. Even if the team agrees to limit the talking to one individual, a bevy of developers marching into the vice president's office can be intimidating, humorous, or distracting. Ideally, the team of interviewers is limited to two: one to conduct the interview, and the other to take notes. When increasing this number, be sure that all participants are clear on what their respective roles are.

Preparing for the Interview

It's not necessary to plan a detailed agenda for each interview, but it is wise to do a little bit of preparation in three areas: First, review the project scope. Second, identify the roles of team members conducting the interview. And third, review the open issues, if any, and prepare some questions.

As we have said, the primary objective of the interview is to learn about the business, however, this is not the only objective. Interviews are one of several stages in the project where the project is visible to businesspeople. The interviewer must be careful to manage the expectations of the person being interviewed. We'll talk about how to do this when we discuss the interview process itself. A prerequisite to the management of expectations is a clear understanding of the project scope. What is the business process to be supported? If the project plan states specific functional objectives, what are they? If certain areas are to be saved for a future revision, which ones? The interviewer must possess a clear understanding of these parameters.

TIP

Review project scope prior to the interview. This will allow you to manage expectations and stay on subject.

If more than one person will be conducting the interview, assign roles and set ground rules. Only one person should be doing the interviewing. Identify this primary interviewer. Anyone else who will be present during the interview must be clear on the fact that he or she is not to interrupt, unless on cue from the primary interviewer; instead, he or she should jot down questions that arise. Save a few minutes toward the end of the interview during which the others present can pose additional questions. It is also helpful to identify a note taker. The note taker can interrupt the interview if he or she misses a point or doesn't understand what is being said. Other questions should be saved for the end.

TIP

Identify who will conduct the interview. Anyone else present must save any questions until the end. Designate a note taker if possible.

Last, the interviewer should prepare some questions. In the best interviews, the conversation will naturally take its own direction. By all means, the interviewer should go with the flow, as long as the discussion doesn't stray from the project scope. But a few initial questions will be required to get the conversation started. Think of your questions more as "openers" than as an agenda.

If you are planning the enterprise data warehouse as described in Chapter 14, "Building an Enterprise Data Warehouse," your questions should uncover the various business processes, how they work, and how they are measured. If an enterprise data warehouse has been planned and you are working on the implementation of a data mart, then you already have an idea of the grain, measures, and dimensions. Bring this information with you, and use what you hear to test the design. You may want to share it with the subject toward the end of the interview.

In either situation, after interviews are complete, you must be able to state the objectives of the data warehouse in a series of bullets, much as we have done in many of the chapters in this book. You will also need to make specific design decisions, which are the same whether you are planning an enterprise data warehouse or implementing a data mart. Outlined in Chapter 1, "The Business-Driven Data Warehouse," these decisions include:

- Identification of relevant business process(es)
- Determination of the grain at which the process is measured
- Identification of the measures
- Enumeration of the dimensions by which the measures are evaluated
- An understanding of how this information will be used

Traditional software engineering analysis questions will advance you toward all these ends. "What kinds of decisions do you make? What kind of information do you need to make these decisions intelligently?" These questions help fill in the business process and may lead to the discovery of measures. They will often uncover business needs the data warehouse can address. Because they are open-ended, they are likely to provoke an interesting discussion. Avoid "yes or no" questions.

Successful questions also inquire about self-measurement. "How do you know you are doing well?" or, "How are you measured by your superiors?" Inquiring into reports currently used helps uncover how a process is measured. Ask to have them explained to you. They often reveal a rich set of measures and dimensions. The interviewees will likely launch into a discussion of the shortcomings of existing reports. If they don't, ask them to envision the ideal report that would help them make a particular decision. Ask for copies of reports that are shown to you, and never turn down any that are offered to you.

There are a variety of other things you'll need to know. Find out who else might benefit from the data warehouse, and if there is someone else who might be worth talking to. You'll also need to ask questions that will help you determine the required frequency of the load process. Find out if it is necessary to have the information available 24 hours a day, or if there are possible windows for data loads and maintenance.

At any given time, there are usually specific questions that the data warehouse team wants to address. They may have arisen during previous interviews, or as part of the design process. Compile these questions, and bring them to the interview on a separate list. We call this the list of "open issues," and will save time at the end of the interview to review it.

TIP

Prepare some questions that can be used to stimulate the conversation. Also compile a list of any open issues that you want to address.

Once you've reviewed the scope, identified the roles of the participants, and prepared some questions, you're ready for the interview. Now is the time to clear your mind of any preconceptions about the business, and get ready to learn.

How to Interview

A typical interview can be divided into three parts. During short segments at the beginning and end of the interview, the interviewer will do most of the talking. These parts of the meeting give the interviewee a chance to learn about the data warehouse project. At the beginning of the meeting, the interviewer provides some insight into the data warehouse project and identifies objectives for the interview. At the end of the interview, the interviewer summarizes what has been covered, provides information about next steps in the project, and keeps the door open for future inquiries.

In between these short phases lies the bulk of the interview, during which the interviewer focuses on the key objective: to learn as much about the business process as possible. A technique called *active listening* helps to maximize what can be learned, both in terms of quantity and quality.

Setting Up the Interview

When you sit down at an interview, chances are the person you are meeting has no idea what the interview is all about. Begin by setting the stage. Explain what the project aims to achieve, distinguishing the data warehouse from the other systems the person probably uses. Don't get technical here; the point is to let the interviewee know what's going on and explain why you're there. Mention the scope of the current project, and reference any planning meetings that may have included the business community.

Here's an example in which an interviewer begins a session with a marketing manager:

> *We're in the process of building a database that will allow analysis of the sales process. The steering committee selected it as the first part of a system we call a data warehouse. We'll be taking invoice data directly out of the sales system and structuring it to serve your analytic needs. You will still use the sales system to look at particular orders or invoices, or to check what a particular customer owes. The data warehouse will allow you to ask more general questions that might involve large numbers of orders, like "What is the quarterly trend by customer for a particular product?"*

We're talking to people who are a part of the sales process to understand how you look at it. We're going to use this information to design a prototype system, which we hope to be able to show you within about six weeks. After that, we'll work on the process of loading the sales data into the data warehouse, which is usually the longest part of the project.

Right now, however, we're still learning about how you look at the sales process, which is why we're here. We want to learn what kinds of questions you have about sales, how you evaluate the process, and the ways you look at sales information. Maybe you could start by explaining what you do.

This interviewer has done a nice job in explaining what's going on. He has identified the scope of the project, differentiated the data warehouse from OLTP systems, provided a brief overview of the project, and given a hint at the kind of information he is looking for. There is no need to get technical. As the interview progresses, careful questioning can focus the interviewee as needed.

It is helpful to mention that you have cleared it with the appropriate parties to conduct the interview. Share the interview list so they know who else you will be talking to. If the person you are meeting with is involved in other business processes, be sure you are clear about the current focus. Mention when the other processes are scheduled to be addressed, if you know. Finally, make it clear that there is no structured agenda to the meeting. You intend to let the conversation go wherever it takes you.

Conducting the Interview

Now comes the core of the interview. You must shift from providing information to collecting it. Remember: *You don't know anything.* You need to keep the conversation within bounds, ensuring that you stay within your scope. As long as it stays within bounds, let the conversation go where it will. Listen to what this person has to say, and make sure that you have understood it. To accomplish these goals, we like to use a technique commonly referred to as *active listening*.

Managing the Flow

Do not conduct the interview by going down your list of questions. Working with an agenda is counterproductive, because agendas are based on assumptions about content. You don't know what you are going to be told; an agenda may prevent the interviewee from sharing something important.

Instead, treat the interview as a conversation. Use your planned questions to get the ball rolling, but let the interviewee's responses trigger new questions. You've saved a period at the end of the interview to ensure that you have addressed open issues, so relax and let the conversation take you where it goes. Refer back to your prepared questions only if you can't think of something to ask. You will be surprised to find this isn't often necessary.

As you ask questions and listen to the interviewee, you do need to be sure the conversation stays within the scope of the project. If you sense a divergence, ask a question that refocuses the discussion. Interviews are most likely to digress when you speak with someone whose job places him or her at the crossroads of two or more business processes. These people naturally have a wide variety of concerns, some of which are not relevant.

When the conversation strays, keep listening. Stay with the flow, and give it a chance to come back around to what you consider relevant. If it doesn't, steer it back gently, not abruptly. Suppose you are modeling the shipping process, and have come to talk to an inventory manager. In addition to shipments, the inventory manager is neck deep in orders, inventory, and purchasing. If conversation strays too far off course, you might say something like, "So keeping inventory levels is critical to optimizing your shipping process. What are some of the ways you monitor the shipping process?"

Don't jump too quickly to steer away from another subject area. The person may be introducing a business issue that crosses process boundaries, and those issues can only be answered when both subject areas are addressed. You need to take note of these requirements, even if they won't be fulfilled during the current project. For example, the inventory manager might stress that he pays close attention to a fulfillment rate: the percentage of orders that are shipped within one month. This measurement combines order data with shipment data. The shipments data mart won't address fulfillment rate initially. However, knowing that fulfillment rate is important will impact your design; you need to be ready to integrate with orders in the future. After discussing the fulfillment rate, remember to reset expectations. "I'll have to make a note of this. We'll want to be sure that our sales data mart integrates with the orders data when it is brought on line next year."

TIP

Don't work too hard to manage the flow of the interview. As long as you are on scope, allow the conversation to evolve. Use your list of questions only to start things off, or if you run out of topics to discuss.

Don't worry about how the conversation unfolds. As long as you are learning something, the time is being well spent. How much you learn will depend on how well you can listen.

Active Listening

Active listening is a technique developed by psychologists to help people communicate with one another. We're going to reduce it to three basic components. We've already introduced the first: You must be ready to learn something from this person. We refer to this as the *readiness component*. When the interviewee begins talking, do not attempt to fit his or her comments into a frame of reference you have already developed. If you do, you are not ready to learn. This is why we encourage you to admit that you don't know anything. Recognize that this person is likely to tell you things you don't know, and be ready to try to understand them.

Second, listen—*really listen*. Don't just write down what the interviewees say. Don't take anything in a context that hasn't been set up. Look at the subject matter from their perspective, not yours. You want to understand their point of view. The listening component is the hardest part of conducting an interview. Preparing yourself to learn helps, but it is often hard to abandon your own frame of reference. This is where the third part of active listening comes in: After listening, you will test your understanding of what has been said.

Despite our best efforts, it is unlikely that we will ever be able to completely abandon our frame of reference on a subject. To combat this natural tendency, repeat back to the interviewees the things they are telling you. Put what you think they are saying into your own words. Don't add to what they are saying based on your own frame of reference. Simply repeat back what you have heard. You will make mistakes, and they will correct you. Don't be disappointed when this happens. It is not a failure on your part. To the contrary, it is a success. You've eliminated what otherwise might have been a misunderstanding.

In addition to improving your ability to learn from others, you will find that this technique sets the interviewees at ease. You will no doubt get things wrong as you repeat them back, but they will see that you are working hard to understand them, and will appreciate it. They will also be gratified when you reflect their thoughts accurately, and become more frank in their replies. Contrast this with an interviewer trying to use the meeting to impress the interviewees with his knowledge of the subject. Which approach produces a better rapport?

TIP

Interviewing requires humility. Be ready to be wrong. Listen to what you are told, and repeat it back. This will allow you to make sure you really understand the person you are interviewing.

Let's look at some examples. Our first interviewer is working on a sales data mart. She is talking with a regional sales manager, and the subject of compensation has just come up.

> *Interviewer: How do you track the compensation of the sales reps?*
>
> *Sales manager: There are several components to a compensation package. Each rep starts with a base salary. They also get quarterly sales goals, which we determine annually. The rest of their compensation is tied to these goals through commissions and bonuses. Usually, one commission rate is used for all sales up to their goal. At that point, they earn a bonus. Additional sales are commissioned at a second rate, higher than the first. For most sales reps, there are several tiers at which commission rates further increase.*
>
> *Interviewer: So sales representatives get a base salary. Their sales up to their goal are compensated at one rate. Their sales above the goal are compensated at another rate, and there may be additional levels at which the rate changes again. Oh, and if orders match the goal, they get their bonus as well. Is that right?*
>
> *Sales manager: Yes, except that we don't look at orders. Something is only sold when it actually ships. But the rep is usually compensated under the package that was in effect at the time of the order. So it's possible that someone will earn his or her 1998 bonus when 1998 orders finish shipping sometime in the first quarter of 1999. This requires some acrobatics on the part of our accountants.*

This short exchange is an excellent example of active listening. After hearing a complicated explanation of the compensation plan, the interviewer tried to repeat it back. She mistakenly assumed that sales were orders, but this was corrected. Being wrong actually contributed to the success of the exchange. Had the interviewer not tried to summarize the explanation, an important detail would have been lost. In addition, the slip brought to light some additional detail that helps to understand the process.

The interviewer might follow up by focusing on exceptions to the process. For example, the sales manager said that usually, they get one commission rate for all sales up to their goal. How does it work when this is not the case?

The next interview takes place during construction of an inventory data mart. The interviewer is speaking with a warehouse manager about optimal inventory levels. He starts with a good question:

Interviewer: How do you decide what inventory levels are good, and what inventory levels need to be adjusted?

Warehouse manager: Well, there are a lot of factors, really. Of course, the salespeople like it when orders ship right away, but we can't just stock everything all the time. We need to determine what levels make the most sense based on demand, value, and—

Interviewer: Oh! So you look at the marginal value of inventory. Do you use a LIFO costing approach, or do you have a mechanism to track cost by lot?

Warehouse Manager: . . . Well, we use different costs depending on the situation. When we ship something, we assume we're depleting our oldest stores, and release those costs. But we use a current cost when we're trying to project what it will cost to maintain inventory. Of course, sometimes we are aware of one or more future costs as well.

This interviewer didn't do as well. He made three mistakes. The most serious mistake was to interrupt the warehouse manager in midsentence. He never found out the third component used to determine optimal inventory levels. Allow the conversation to flow where it will; don't try to force it in a particular direction. Never interrupt!

Second, the interviewer excitedly interpreted what he was hearing based on his own experience, jumping to some conclusions about margin. Instead of trying to understand the answer being given, the interviewer forced the manager's comments into a mental framework he had already developed. This might not have been disastrous, were it not for his third mistake: He didn't reflect. Instead, he quickly moved on to some very detailed questions, which the warehouse manager dutifully tried to address. As a result, the interviewer's assumption about the marginal value of inventory remained untested.

Here's part of a third interview. Two members of the team working on a budgeting data mart are talking to an accountant who manages payables.

> *Interviewer: There are a couple of things I am confused about with the budgets. You mentioned that a commitment stays on the books until a payment is issued—but what happens at the end of the year? Suppose the purchase order is written this year, but the payment happens next year? How is the budget impacted?*
>
> *Interviewer 2: I understand this part. A set of transactions offsets the P.O. from last year's budget and adds it to this year's. But how does a cancellation get handled?*
>
> *Payables manager: If the budget has already been carried over, we need to reduce it when the purchase order gets canceled We report those adjustments monthly on a report like this one.*
>
> *(Interviewer 2 makes a note to ask for a copy of the report at the end of the interview.)*
>
> *Interviewer 1: So I order a case of pens in December 1998. Shipment is delayed, and January 1999 rolls along. The office supply budget for 1998 is incremented to account for the unpaid commitment. In essence, I still get to pay for it with last year's budget, since it was already on order. But if I then cancel the order, you roll back the budget. Is that so that people don't place a bunch of orders at the end of the year to hold on to unspent budget?*
>
> *Payables manager: I guess that's the main reason.*
>
> *Interviewer 1: Could you describe exactly how the two budgets are adjusted when the year changes?*

This exchange offers a mix of success and failure. Interviewer 1 is working hard to actively listen. She starts out by admitting confusion, and tries to pinpoint where her understanding breaks down, framing an example around her confusion. Interviewer 2, however, breaks the rule of silence, answering the question himself. This is counter to the objective of learning from the interviewee. If two members of the design team want to discuss the process with each other, there's no reason for the payables manager to be there!

Notice how interpretation of the business according to one's own frame of reference prevents transfer of information. Interviewer 2 does not reflect, instead broadcasting his depth of knowledge. Because his comments about budget carry-over are followed with another question, the interviewee doesn't get a chance to correct it. His interpretation is never tested. We saw this same pattern in our inventory example. Luckily, the situation improves this time.

Interviewer 2 realizes he shouldn't have interrupted. Instead of asking more questions about the report, he does the right thing by making a note to ask for a copy at the end of the meeting. Interviewer 1 takes over and recovers nicely. Although the accountant is not replying to her original question, she goes with the flow. She makes sure she understands what he is saying by repeating it back to him. Once she's sure she understands him, she poses her original question in a new form. If she had jumped straight to the original question as soon as she got the floor back, the value of his comments would have been lost.

Concluding the Interview

The way in which you conclude the interview can be as important as how you conducted it. You must be sure you have collected all the information you came for, but also need to provide the interviewee with some information about what happens next. And of course, you want to leave the door open, should you need to ask additional questions in the future.

You brought a list of open issues to the interview. Take it out toward the end of the interview. Look the list over, and see if there are any questions that have not already been addressed during the conversation. If so, ask them. The longer your list of issues, the more time you should allow for this part of the conversation. Remember that you are getting close to the end of the meeting, so you will need to exercise more control over the direction of the conversation. Usually, you will find that the issues have naturally worked themselves into the conversation.

Next, provide an opportunity for other team members to ask questions. If they have been following the rule of silence, they haven't interrupted with their own questions, instead writing them down. Give everyone a chance to look at their own lists, and pose any questions they have been holding. Usually, they will find that their questions were answered during the course of the interview as well.

Once all the questions are out of the way, sum up the interview. If you can, try to come up with some high-level conclusions about the conversation. "It sounds like the most important thing you need to see is the daily trend in inventory level over time. You also need monthly order and sales volumes by product." If you can't come up with some high-level requirements off the top of your head, ask a simple question like this one: "Of all the information you need, what is the most important?" Or, "If there was just one thing we could do for you, what would it be?"

In concluding the interview, take some time to let the interviewee know what is happening next. You've been given a lot of time and information—extend the simple courtesy of explaining how it will be used. As at the beginning of the interview, it is not necessary to go into detail. Explain the next steps, and give a simple overview of the rest of the project. Offer the interviewee a chance to ask you questions, and answer them. Collect any reports offered to you. Thank the person for his or her time, and find out if he or she would be willing to answer a brief question once in a while.

> *This has been extremely enlightening! Thank you for your time. We're going to be talking to several more people over the next two weeks, and developing an initial design. Would it be all right if I call you with a question occasionally if necessary?*
>
> *After we finish our design, we're going to build a prototype and load it with data, so that we can see how well it addresses your needs. We'll want to show you the prototype and get your feedback. We'll try to produce some of the reports you mentioned, to see how useful it is. We'll be doing this with small groups, probably in three or four weeks. After that, we'll probably refine it a bit, and then spend some time automating the load process. We're hoping to be ready to go into production during third quarter, and there will be some training.*
>
> *Thanks again. You've got my number if you think of anything else I should know. Please send those fulfillment reports down to me when you get them.*

You are not finished when you walk out of the interview. As soon as possible, you need to review and summarize your notes. They don't contain all the detail, and the longer you wait, the less you will remember about the conversation. This will be as useful to you as it is to others on the team who were not present. Format your summary in any way you see fit. You might want to describe anything you have learned about how the business process works or is monitored. Outline potential measures and dimensions. Note anything you learned about grain or frequency of load. Record answers to any open issues. Once you've taken care of all this, look at the current design and think about whether it can be used to answer any of the questions you heard.

Summing Up Interviewing

The data warehouse is built to deliver answers, and it is during interviews that you find out what the questions are. The interviews are important events that shape the data warehouse design. They are also a chance to manage expectations within the business community.

Be ready to learn. You will be in the best position to learn if you admit that your knowledge is imperfect and prepare yourself to be wrong.

Prepare for the interview. Be sure you are clear on the project scope, so that you can keep the interview on track, as well as set proper expectations. Prepare some questions to start off the conversation. Make a list of outstanding issues you want to be sure are addressed.

Identify roles. Only one person does the interviewing.

Go with the flow. Don't follow your list of questions. Think of the interview as a conversation.

Actively listen. Try to understand what you are told from the other person's perspective, not your own. Repeat things back in your own words, and allow the interviewee to correct you. When your mistakes are corrected, you are interviewing successfully!

Share information. At the beginning and end of the interview, provide some insight into what is going on with the data warehouse. Explain where the project is, and where it is going. Estimate when the next event that involves the interviewee will take place.

KEY BUSINESS TERMS

Account. An account is a defined entity of financial importance to a business. Transactions are recorded against accounts. Examples of accounts include a corporate checking account, line of credit, salaries, vacation, and taxes. The chart of accounts for any business is the current set of valid accounts against which transactions may be recorded. Accounts are categorized as either balance sheet accounts or income statement accounts.

Anonymous Transaction. An anonymous transaction is a sale that cannot be associated with an individual, named customer. Despite the efforts of many businesses to improve the collection of customer information, a majority of retail transactions are still anonymous.

The anonymous transaction has important implications in any business attempting to measure customer activity. For example, a grocery store may be able to identify buying habits for customers using credit/debit cards. Should the store make decisions about marketing, pricing, or promotions based on this information? What if these customers only represent 20 percent of register tickets and 25 percent of total sales?

Basic Product. The lowest commonly shared instance of a product offered by a company, with an agreed identifier and a common set of attributes. For a book publisher, the basic product is a book by an author in a specific form, like hardcover, paperback, tape, or CD-ROM. This is a different concept than the combination of author and title. For the Editorial department, author and title may serve to identify the product adequately, but for sales and production, the form of the work is equally important. The basic product is lowest-level definition.

Capacity. The amount of customer demand that can be serviced at a given point in time. Capacity has a maximum limit, beyond which significant capital investment is required.

Commitment. A formal agreement between two parties to exchange goods, services, or money under specific terms. An organization commits funds out of its budget when it issues purchase orders, signs work orders, or awards contracts. Commitments can be made to an organization outside the business, or to another organization within the business. Commitments are sometimes referred to as *obligations*, but not within the U.S. Government, where the term *obligation* has special meaning.

Continuous Process Manufacturing. A manufacturing process that combines constituents into a bulk-quantity product through a continuous process. Process manufacturing includes the production of gasoline, motor oil, and other byproducts from crude oil. Other examples include chemical manufacturing, paint manufacturing, and food additive production.

Cost of Sale. Costs incurred selling and delivering the product to customers.

Cross-selling. The technique of selling additional services to existing customers.

Customer Acquisition Costs. Expenses associated with the procurement of new customers, or with selling additional products or services to existing customers.

Direct Sales. Transactions that are, from the perspective of the producer of the goods, sold directly to the end consumer. For example, health club memberships are normally sold directly to a consumer by health club representatives. Household services, such as plumbing or electrical repairs, are normally sold directly by the company providing the service.

Discrete Manufacturing. A manufacturing process that produces discrete end-item products from various components. Discrete manufacturing examples include automobiles, computers, televisions, and compact discs.

Discriminators. Descriptive characteristics of a product that further describe it and are relevant to purchasing decisions. Discriminators for men's suits would include cloth, color, style/cut, weight, and size. Discriminators can be used in business analysis to better understand what moves merchandise. Automobiles have a different set of discriminators than clothing. Tracking discriminators allows the business analyst to monitor performance of various product styles, influencing production and marketing plans.

Discriminators in service industries are equally important. A bank offering a variety of checking account plans should track the characteristics of each plan in the product dimension. An insurer will carry attributes describing variations of coverage within specific lines of business. In fact, service industries are adept at creating and altering product lines in response to markets. Without the constraints of a typical manufacturer, the service business can assess the marketplace and fill gaps with new product lines. The availability of rich, descriptive product performance data is crucial.

Enterprise Data Warehouse. A planned, integrated, managed store of relevant corporate data optimized for analysis, query, and reporting functions. The optimal design for an enterprise data warehouse is an integrated series of conformed dimension tables and transaction-grained fact tables that provide the business with a comprehensive analytical repository. Building an enterprise data warehouse does not require that dimension and fact tables be populated from an intermediate 3NF operational data store. While some staging of data may be necessary, directly populating fact and dimension tables is the least complex and costly solution.

Execution Cost. The cost of providing goods or services to the customer.

Extended Price. The total price for a group of items. When items are bought, sold, ordered or shipped, they are often done in quantity. For example, each line on an order shows an item, how much it costs, how many are being purchased, and what the total charge is. The total charge is referred to as *extended price*, while the single item price shown is referred to as the *unit price*.

The *unit* and *extended* descriptors are also applied to various other elements of an order. *Unit cost* represents the cost of a single item to the vendor, while *extended cost* multiplies this by the total number of items purchased. Similarly, a business might deal with *extended margin*, *extended discounts*, and so on.

Most of the time, the extended amounts will be recorded in fact tables. They are fully additive, and therefore easier to work with. We can freely aggregate them over a number of dimensions, for useful analysis. Unit amounts are provided as dimensions, when useful for price point analysis.

Financial Accounting. Accounting for external consumption, used in reporting financial results on a periodic basis to shareholders, creditors, and government entities. The source for financial accounting is a company's approved, audited accounting system. This system is protected by well-defined procedures to ensure data is entered correctly. These procedures and the design of the accounting system are carefully designed to prevent irregularities and thwart fraud. The financial accounting system is the scorecard a company shows to the world, especially shareholders and creditors. Those with an equity position in a company use the information to monitor the performance of their investment. Creditors use financial reports to monitor the security of their debt.

Fixed Cost. Costs that remain constant within a broad range of operational activity. Both product and period costs can be classified as fixed or variable. Fixed product costs include factory rent or depreciation, utilities, administrative labor, and property taxes. Variable product costs include direct materials, direct labor, and indirect materials. Some fixed costs are called *committed* fixed costs because they represent the cost of actually continuing in business and are unavoidable. Business licenses and executive salaries are examples of committed fixed costs. Other fixed costs are discretionary and planned in each budgetary cycle. Discretionary fixed costs are usually not product costs. These costs include employee training, company parties, and some administrative salaries.

Fulfillment. Goods provided and actions taken by the vendor to satisfy the value proposition underlying the sale of a product or service. Fulfillment actions vary by industry. Catalog retailers fulfill orders by shipping product. The grocery store fulfills the value proposition of a sale by providing the item to the consumer. Both extend the proposition to include the acceptance of returns in the event the product is of poor quality.

When an item is sold at retail, a portion of the fulfillment responsibility lies with the manufacturer. The item is assumed to have a standard degree of quality and serviceability. The terms of the sale may include a warranty or guarantee. Fulfilling the terms of such promises is a part of fulfillment for the manufacturer.

General Ledger. A ledger in which the financial accounts of a business are formally summarized. Often referred to as *G/L*. The heart of double-entry accounting, the general ledger remains balanced through offsetting transactions to debit and credit accounts. The list of accounts is often referred to as *the chart of accounts.*

Hybrid Process Manufacturing. A manufacturing process that includes elements of continuous and discrete manufacturing. One example of hybrid processes is tire manufacturing, where a discrete item is produced from byproducts of continuing processes. Another example is beer or spirits production, which includes mixing, brewing, aging, and discrete packaging in a single facility.

Indirect Sales. Transactions that are, from the perspective of the producer of the goods, sold through a channel other than the producer's internal staff. For example, manufacturer's often use independent sales representatives to sell products. Movie production companies sell their products through theaters, video stores, and pay-per-view systems.

Intellectual Capital. Intellectual assets, including corporate knowledge, patents, databases, and process structures that can be used to increase the value of an organization.

Intellectual capital is a term popularized by John Stewart, a well-known proponent of knowledge management. Intellectual capital, unlike other capital assets, is tucked away inside of companies, more difficult to find and measure than a computer or office space. For example, the information technology industry suffers today from a severe labor crunch. Replacing an IT worker is costly. Recognizing this reality is easy; measuring a company's ability to deal with it is not. It requires careful monitoring of employee retention and the impact of different employment stewardship actions by the company.

Inventory. The quantity of goods or materials on hand or available for use.

Lift. The difference between the response rate of a marketing effort and the overall sales rate. The lift percentage represents the direct impact of the marketing activity. The overall sales rate may be replaced by the rate for a control group, to refine the calculation.

Managerial Accounting. Accounting intended for internal consumption, used in planning and operating the organization by managers and employees. Managerial accounting is timely, and some degree of imprecision is often accepted. Managerial accounting has countless uses and the data may come from many sources, not just the approved, audited financial accounting system. Many companies use sales force automation software to forecast and record sales for the sales subject area. These forecasts and results, recorded by the sales team, are not the official expectations and results for external consumption, but instead are used internally to manage the sales force.

Nonconformance Costs. Expenses incurred when a customer returns or exchanges a product for any reason.

Occupancy Rate. Percentage of available rooms that are booked. This term can be generalized to *utilization rate*, defined as the percentage of available capacity that is sold or obligated. Applicable across service industries, utilization rate is expressed as *capacity utilized/total capacity*.

Payment. A transaction in which funds are distributed from one party to another. Payments may be made to external organizations, or to an organization within the business. Sometimes referred to as *cash outlay* or *disbursement*.

Product Costs. Costs incurred in producing or acquiring items in finished goods or merchandise inventory. Product costs, sometimes called *manufacturing costs*, are recognized as expenses only when the product is sold. At that time, they are itemized as *cost of goods sold*.

Production Unit. The unit of measure in which production outputs are measured. For a discrete manufacturer it is normally "each," while for process manufacturers it may be liters, gallons, barrels, grams, or some other standard unit.

Quality. Conformance of a product or service to customer expectations. Quality is always defined by the customer, either internal or external. This is an adaptation of the classic "conformance to requirements" definition. For production processes, quality is conformance to requirements. But those requirements are determined by internal customers, like product design engineers who interpret customer needs. Our definition is intended to measure quality relative to the customer's expectations.

Response Rate. The percentage of individuals contacted by a marketing effort that accepted the offer.

Retention Costs. Costs incurred in the process of ensuring that desirable customers remain customers.

Retention Effort. A marketing activity aimed at preventing loss of existing customers.

Service Industry. A business whose primary product is not tangible. Some service industries bill based on time, like doctors, lawyers, plumbers and electricians. Others charge for the specific service rendered. For example, an Internet Access Provider sells access to the Internet, a travel agent receives a commission to arrange your travel itinerary.

Unit Price. The price of a single item

Velocity. A measure of the rate at which inventory moves in and out of the warehouse. Velocity is measured differently from business to business. Often referred to as *turns*, it is usually computed as the ratio of quantity *shipped* during a *period* of time to the quantity *on hand* at a *point* in time.

USING THE CD-ROM

The CD-ROM that accompanies this book contains supplemental materials, which may aid you in understanding the models and reports.

All reports from the book have been included on the CD-ROM in HTML format. Reports are the end result of all the work involved in building a data warehouse. They hold the answers to business questions. As such, they are well worth reviewing. Whether you study the versions printed in the book or the electronic versions on the CD-ROM, an understanding of the reports will deepen your understanding of the business questions they answer.

The CD-ROM also includes models of the databases in this book. These working samples can help deepen your understanding of the dimensional models. We have populated each dimension table with sample data. A review of the information in each column can be very helpful if you are confused about the design. We've also populated the fact tables with enough data to illustrate key concepts. The index to the databases found on the CD suggests what to look for in each fact table. For example, you can study the fact table entries in the banking database from Chapter 3 to understand how a household relates to an account, what happens when an individual leaves a household, and how a Type 2 change happens.

System Requirements

The CD-ROM contains HTML reports and Microsoft Access97 databases. To access the HTML reports, you must have a computer equipped with a CD-ROM drive and a web browser. Refer to the *Using the CD-ROM* section for instructions on accessing the reports. To use the databases, you must have a computer running Microsoft Windows 95 or Windows NT. You will also need software capable of reading databases in Microsoft Access97 format.

Using the CD-ROM

Using your web browser, access the file *default.html* found in the root directory of the CD-ROM. A web page will open that contains links to the databases and reports on the CD-ROM. Just follow the links to the reports or databases that interest you.

The procedure for opening *default.html* is dependent on your browser. Using Microsoft's Internet Explorer, simply choose *Open* from the *File* menu, change to the drive containing the CD-ROM, and select *default.html*. Using Netscape Navigator, select *Open Page* from the *File* menu, click on the *Choose File* button, change to the drive containing the CD-ROM, and select *default.html*. If you are using another browser, check its documentation or on-line help.

Reports

Select the *Reports* link from the main page. You will be presented with an index of reports by chapter. Click on the name of a report and it will be displayed in your browser's window. To return to the index of reports, use your browser's *Back* button.

Databases

To use the databases, you must copy them to your PC. This can be done from the web page on the CD-ROM. Select the *Databases* link from the main page. You will be presented with an index of databases by chapter. When you select a database, the result will depend on the configuration of your computer and browser.

- *Your browser may prompt you to save the database to your hard drive.* Specify an appropriate location on your hard drive. The database will be copied to the location you specified. You can open it with MicrosoftAccess and study it.

- *The database may simply open in Microsoft Access.* Because the CD-ROM is read only, Access will fail to open the database. If this happens when you select a link to a database, then you must *save* the link rather than *select* it. The procedure depends on your browser. Using Internet Explorer, right-click on the link and choose *Save Target As...* Using Netscape Navigator, right click on the link and select *Save Link As...* In both cases, your browser will prompt you to select a file location, then copy the database to the specified location. If you are using a different browser, check its documentation or on-line help.

If you prefer, you can simply copy the databases from the *dbs* folder on the CD-ROM to your computer.

User Assistance and Information

The software accompanying this book is being provided as is without warranty or support of any kind. Should you require basic installation assistance, or if your media is defective, please call our product support number at (212) 850-6194 weekdays between 9 A.M. and 4 P.M. Eastern Standard Time. Or, we can be reached via e-mail at: wprtusw@wiley.com.

To place additional orders or to request information about other Wiley products, please call (800) 879-4539.

INDEX